RAF BOMBER COMMAND
Reflections of War

RAF BOMBER COMMAND
Reflections of War

Volume 3
Battleground Berlin
(July 1943–March 1944)

Martin W Bowman

Pen & Sword
AVIATION

First Published in Great Britain in 2012 by
Pen & Sword Aviation
an imprint of
Pen & Sword Books Ltd
47 Church Street, Barnsley, South Yorkshire S70 2AS

Copyright © Martin W Bowman, 2012

ISBN 978-1-84884-494-0

Typeset in 10/12pt Palatino by
Concept, Huddersfield

Printed and bound in England by
CPI Group (UK) Ltd, Croydon, CRO 4YY

Pen & Sword Books Ltd incorporates the Imprints of Pen & Sword
Aviation, Pen & Sword Family History, Pen & Sword Maritime, Pen & Sword
Military, Pen & Sword Discovery, Wharncliffe Local History, Wharncliffe
True Crime, Wharncliffe Transport, Pen & Sword Select, Pen & Sword
Military Classics, Leo Cooper, The Praetorian Press, Remember When,
Seaforth Publishing and Frontline Publishing.

For a complete list of Pen & Sword titles please contact
PEN & SWORD BOOKS LIMITED
47 Church Street, Barnsley, South Yorkshire, S70 2AS, England
E-mail: enquiries@pen-and-sword.co.uk
Website: www.pen-and-sword.co.uk

Contents

Acknowledgements

Gebhard Aders; Harry Andrews DFC; Frau Anneliese Autenrieth; Mrs Dorothy Bain; Günther Bahr; Charlie 'Jock' Baird; Harry Barker; Irene Barrett-Locke; Raymond V Base; Don Bateman; Steve Beale; A D 'Don' Beatty; Jack Bennett; Andrew Bird; Peter Bone; Alfons Borgmeier; Jack Bosomworth; Len Browning; Don Bruce; George Burton; Jim Burtt-Smith; Maurice Butt; Philip J Camp DFM; City of Norwich Aviation Museum (CONAM); Bob Collis; Jim Coman; B G Cook; John Cook DFM; Rupert 'Tiny' Cooling; Dennis Cooper; Ray Corbett; Coen Cornelissen; Leslie Cromarty DFM; Tom Cushing; Hans-Peter Dabrowski; Rob de Visser; Dr. Karl Dörscheln; J Alan Edwards; Wolfgang Falck; David G Fellowes; Elwyn D Fieldson DFC; Karl Fischer; Søren C Flensted; Vitek Formanek; Stanley Freestone; Ian Frimston; Prof. Dr Ing. Otto H Fries; Air Vice Marshal D J Furner CBE DFC AFC; Ken Gaulton; Jim George; Margery Griffiths, Chairman, 218 Gold Coast Squadron Association; Group Captain J R 'Benny' Goodman DFC* AFC AE; Alex H Gould DFC; Hans Grohmann; Charles Hall; Steve Hall; Jack F Hamilton; Eric Hammel; Erich Handke; James Harding; Frank Harper; Leslie Hay; Gerhard Heilig; Bob Hilliard; Peter C Hinchliffe; Neville Hockaday RNZAF; Werner 'Red' Hoffmann; Ted Howes DFC; Air Commodore Peter Hughes DFC; John Anderson Hurst; Zdenek Hurt; Ab A Jansen; Karl-Ludwig Johanssen; Wilhelm 'Wim' Johnen; Arthur 'Johnnie' Johnson; John B Johnson; Graham B Jones; Hans-Jürgen Jürgens; Erich Kayser; George Kelsey DFC; Les King; Christian Kirsch; Hans Krause; Reg Lawton; J R Lisgo; Chas Lockyer; Günther Lomberg; Peter Loncke; George Luke; Ian McLachlan; Nigel McTeer; B L Eric Mallett RCAF; Len Manning; The Honourable Terence Mansfield; Eric Masters; Bernard 'Max' Meyer DFC; Cyril Miles; Colin Moir; Frank Mouritz; Friedrich Ostheimer; Maurice S Paff; Simon Parry; Path Finder Association; Wing Commander David Penman DSO OBE DFC; Richard Perkins; Peter Petrick; Karl-Georg Pfeiffer; Eric Phillips; Vic Poppa; John Price; Stan Reed; Ernie Reynolds; Peter Richard; Albert E Robinson; Heinz Rökker; Squadron Leader Geoff Rothwell DFC; Fritz Rumpelhardt;

David M Russell; Kees Rijken; Eric Sanderson; Klaus J Scheer; Dr. Dieter Schmidt-Barbo; Karl-Heinz Schoenemann; Jerry Scutts; Johan Schuurman; Group Captain Jack Short; Leslie R Sidwell; Don L Simpkin; SAAF Assn; Albert Spelthahn; Dr Ing. Klaus Th. Spies; Dick Starkey; Squadron Leader Hughie Stiles; Mike 'Taff' Stimson; Ted Strange DFC; Maurice Stoneman; Ken Sweatman; Paul Todd; Fred Tunstall DFC; Hille van Dieren; George Vantilt; Bob Van Wick; Andreas Wachtel; Georg Walser; David Waters; H Wilde; John Williams; H J Wilson; Henk Wilson; Geoffrey and Nick Willatt; Dennis Wiltshire; Louis Patrick Wooldridge DFC; Fred Young DFM; Cal Younger.

I am particularly grateful to my friend and colleague Theo Boiten, with whom I have collaborated on several books, for all of the information on the *Nachtjagd* or German night fighter forces contained herein. And, aviation historians everywhere owe a deep sense of gratitude to his and all the other valuable sources of reference listed in the end notes; in particular, those by the incomparable W R 'Bill' Chorley, Martin Middlebrook and Chris Everitt and Oliver Clutton-Brock. Finally, all of the late authors' books, as listed, who are beyond compare. This book and its companion volumes are dedicated to their memory.

CHAPTER 1

The Way to the Stars

It was some time before we realised the importance of Peenemünde. It was engaged in the development of the V-1 and V-2 rockets. At least, on the night of 17 August 1943, we must have delayed their programme somewhat and ensured that London did not receive as many of them as Hitler would have liked. As an afterthought to the raid, I suppose it was useful to the US space programme that we missed Werner von Braun.

Pilot Officer (later AVM) D J Furner CBE DFC AFC

In Jack Furner's log book his total number of Stirling flights on 214 Squadron is 120, of which 25 were operational. Jack Dixon and his crew and John Verrall's were the only two crews to survive the whole period March to September of 1943.[1] In between Furner's first op on 4/5 April 1943 and the final one, the last on Berlin on 31 August, came most of the targets in the Ruhr, some repeatedly – names like Duisburg, Dortmund, Düsseldorf and Wuppertal; and Hamburg (several); Turin; Krefeld; Mülheim and Nurnberg. There were also mining sorties in the Baltic, off the Friesians and in the mouth of the Gironde River. If pressed to describe specific raids, Furner's highlights would be: Wuppertal on a brilliant night seemingly going up in one awful pillar of smoke ('come and look at this, nav!'); all the other Ruhr towns confused in one's mind; the chaos below of Hamburg's 'firestorm' and the extraordinary beauty of the Alps in moonlight *en route* to Turin on 12 August. But the one that stands out above all others would be Peenemünde 'and for a number of reasons' as will be seen.

It is well nigh impossible to describe in detail each one of the nightly battles – and battles they were. It happens inevitably that so many things are blurred, except for a few really dramatic moments. I can more easily picture in my mind and try to describe in writing, a typical – or average – operation, rather than any one specific instance.

1

The average or typical begins with the briefing. Navigators always had a lot more preparatory work to do than other crewmembers and would have to assemble for their detailed planning of log and chart a good hour before the remainder of the crew came in. By the time complete crews were sitting to hear target details, outline of route markings, weather, defences, bomb load, fuel, signals, encouragement from Commanders and any visiting brass, the navigators would have log flight plan and chart ready. Always at the specific request of my Skipper I would have the fighter-belt pencilled in: he would wish to corkscrew all the way through it, regardless of whether there had been any sightings. Assemble all kit – parachute, Mae West (what fame!), sextant and navigation bag with log, charts, maps, star data, protractor, Dalton 'computer'(!) – simply a graphic representation of the triangle of velocities – dividers, parallel rule. Out to the aircraft at dispersal a good hour before take-off. Run engines. Thorough checks all round each member. I check all navigation equipment – compasses, *Gee*, *H2S*, air position indicator, astrograph (a star map), sextant. Shut down. Last smoke and symbolic pee on the tail wheel. Back into that storeys'-high cabin of the Stirling. Smells of petrol and oil and hot metals. Engines – pilot and bomb aimer go meticulously through take off checks. Line up – await green Aldis. Go. Down the runway, all four engines roaring and spitting flame, rotate. Climb at planned rate, with flight plan indicated airspeed and on planned course adjusted for magnetic variation and compass deviation.

Cross UK coast at planned exit point and at planned height. Change course. Continue climbing across North Sea. Test guns. Passing through 10,000 feet, oxygen masks on. Keep continuous log on pro forma, monitor airspeed and course, get fixes on *Gee*, check wind. Announce enemy coast ahead. Get fix from bomb aimer crossing coast if cloud and visibility allow, check wind. Prepare Skipper for fighter belt: corkscrew: accept that accurate recording of navigational path is now more difficult, as well as stomach more queasy. Other crewmembers report searchlights ahead or off route, or flak, or fighter activity, or ours going down. If somebody were to have switched daylight on at this stage, Heaven knows what we would have seen! Better this individual navigation, though, than the American way all in enforced formation. Too soon the *Gee* goes – jammed by Jerry. *H2S* remains but very difficult to decipher inland whilst corkscrewing. Trust to Dead Reckoning and Path Finder markers at points along the route and at the target. Change course as demanded by flight plan. Reckon to be two minutes early over target? Make a triangle – 60° left for two minutes, 120° right for two minutes, resume track. (The rest of the crew hated that – understandably.) Fighter! – call from rear gunner – much more violent evasive action to throw him off. Target approaches, markers, fires if visible; well lit cloud with markers above if not. Pilot responds to Bomb aimer: left – left or right or steady – interminable steady – come on, come on! – Bombs gone. Course home. Caught in searchlight – brilliantly lit up, we're vulnerable, frightening – violent manoeuvres – hold breath until darkness again. John's got us out of it. Try to assess average airspeed and course during manoeuvres. Lots of flak but we're lucky, not a hit. Same thing all the way out back to the coast – only even more vigilant, fighters more evident. Comparative calm of North Sea, course for home base, descending, oxygen mask off, dirty mark around face, familiar red pundit light flashing, turn to land, breathe wonderful East Anglian summer air – 'Another one tucked away, skip' shouts the rear gunner. Cigarette, debrief, meal, try to sleep, the sun comes up.

The new recruits to the Squadron were able at briefings to judge the difficulties to be faced by the reaction of the more experienced crews. The groans would be loudest in the briefing room for those demanding a long and deep track over occupied territory – e.g. Berlin and Nurnberg. The next worse would be all the Ruhr targets – much shallower penetration but fiendishly defended. And I suppose the lightest reaction would be for a peripheral target, like Kiel (our first) and Hamburg. This all makes sense when you consider that the chance of survival is least with a long defended track. (I'm not counting the low-level mining trips to the Baltic and the Gironde estuary – but they often had some pretty tracer stuff defending them and there were losses even from those sorties.)

In between operations there would be a lot of local flying – air tests, circuits and bumps, practice bombing, simulated sorties, fighter affiliation, familiarization with new aids and so on. The most significant was *H2S* airborne radar with a rotating parabolic dish inside a bulge under the fuselage, which interpreted the ground beneath on a cathode ray tube at the navigator's station, differentiating between dark (no response) for sea, some bright response for land and brighter response still for built up areas. It was a marvel to see but it was crude and because it was transmitting, it drew attention to itself. This airborne radar came onto the Squadron at the beginning of July and Furner was chosen to train other navigators on it.

Summer 1943 was hectic. There were frequent losses: faces would come and go only too quickly but there was little point in dwelling on that. We young men wouldn't wonder until we were some years older what the resulting sad administration was doing to our kindly 'uncle', the Squadron Adjutant George Wright. It was he who would be charged with informing relatives, dealing with personal effects and clearing rooms ready for later arrivals.

But life was not all flying and operations. Crews were granted a week's leave every six weeks, which Furner believes was unique amongst all the Services. 'Harris insisted on it.' While on operations crews took advantage of the Nuffield Leave Scheme. The Foundation paid for accommodation at many hotels in England. On base in the Mess on evenings without flying, an extremely casual and happy-go-lucky atmosphere pervaded, particularly since Chedburgh was a temporary, wartime only station with semi-circular corrugated iron Nissen huts for all offices and accommodation.

There were favourite pubs in Bury St. Edmunds, to which one or other of our broken-down jalopies would carry us; one of the pubs looked exactly like the studio version in *The Way to the Stars*.

On 8/9 July it was Cologne again. At Syerston 1st Lieutenant Gene Rosner's crew were on the Battle Order for their 19th operation and they were told that they would be taking *R-Robert* and a 'second dickey'. The met forecast was that there would be cumulonimbus clouds up to 20,000 feet over the target. Their trip over the North Sea was uneventful and sure enough, over the Belgian coast they were over the clouds as forecast. Six Mosquitoes on 109 Squadron accurately marked with *Oboe* sky-marking and another successful raid followed. Warrant Officer Fred Smooker, Rosner's bomb aimer recalls:

The white flare was dropped at some point north of Cologne where we turned south of the target. Then things began to happen. Search-lights turned the clouds into a dazzling white sea of snow. We began to see that we were not alone on our journey of destruction; in front and to either side could be seen the black silhouettes of our accompanying Lancasters, from whom no help was possible in the event of a disaster. The sea of dazzling white was now beginning to be splashed with jagged cherry-red flashes which disintegrated into red-hot coals. The green flare appeared directly ahead. We were right on track and so was the flak. The jagged flashes were now all around us and I could feel my inside begin its usual churning and my flesh and skin began to tighten, whilst all my instincts told me to cringe and curl up into a ball. The red flare appeared ahead; the pilot told me our airspeed and altitude over the intercom, while I busied myself setting the special adjustments to the bombsight. By now we had ceased our continuous climbing and diving, weaving to port and starboard and were flying straight and level over a white shiny carpet mottled with an angry red glow. One felt that one could get out and walk on it.

Over 280 Lancasters of 1 and 5 Groups devastated the north western and south western sections of the city and a further 48,000 people were bombed out, making a total of 350,000 people losing their homes during the series of three raids in a week. Twenty-four II./NJG1 crews manned the *Himmelbett* boxes in eastern Belgium and despite being hampered by thick layers of cloud destroyed three Lancasters and claimed another seven *Feindberührungen* ('encounters with the enemy'). Seven Lancasters were lost, worst hit being 106 Squadron at Syerston, which accounted for three of the missing aircraft. Fred Smooker got *R-Robert*'s five tons of HE bombs and incendiaries away and they left the holocaust behind as they headed south. They turned onto a westerly heading and were at 22,000 feet when the starboard outer began heating up. Near Cambrai (Nord) at about 03.30 a fighter attacked and set their starboard inner on fire. On intercom Rosner said 'Hey you guys, we gotta bail out. Somebody get me my parachute. Bail out, bail out, bail out ...' The two screaming port engines suddenly stopped dead and the aircraft went down. Only Fred Smooker got out. Rosner and the six others died in the aircraft. They were laid to rest on 11 July. Smooker was not caught by the Germans until after mid-September and did not arrive in PoW camp until about 15 November. For 56 days he was held in solitary confinement in a Paris prison.[2]

R5573, better known as *Admiral-Foo-Banc V* and flown by 20-year-old Sergeant Kenneth Hector 'Wally' McLean RCAF was shot down by a night fighter NNE of Liège. Because the Squadron often dropped sea mines on *Gardening* operations and at the time naval officers were attached to the unit, several of the aircraft displayed Admiral-prefixed characters. McLean, from Vulcan, Alberta was on his first trip with his crew, who all died on the Lancaster, one of several specially fitted with bulged bomb doors for the carriage of 8,000lb bombs. Funerals were held on 10 July. The third Lancaster on the squadron that was lost crashed on fenland near Wisbech in Cambridgeshire with the loss of five of the seven-man crew.

It was on 9/10 July that the next Main Force raid was directed to Gelsenkirchen. Thirteen 'Musical Mosquitoes' again marked with *Oboe* sky-marking but the equipment failed to operate in five of the Mosquitoes. A sixth Mosquito dropped sky-markers in error ten miles north of the target and the raid was not successful. Seven Halifaxes and five Lancasters went missing from a force of 418 aircraft.

Even at 5,000 feet in the spruce forests and meadows on the slopes of the Rhône River valley in the Swiss Alps, 12 July was a very warm day. It was the summer holiday season and many families with children like 14-year-old Frédéric Haldimann were enjoying the stimulating mountain air in villages perched in the valleys running south along the Rhône. Sion, the capital of the canton of Valais with its population of about 10,000 and the adjoining airfield occasionally used by the Swiss Air Force lay amongst the vineyards shimmering in the July heat. On more than one occasion during that spring and summer, the deep quiet of the nights had reverberated from the deep and regular drone of aircraft engines, a constant reminder of Switzerland's close proximity to Germany and Italy. Dusk that evening brought the usual marked drop in temperature as the western horizon was invaded by menacing clouds. The air was sultry and it was more difficult than usual to marshal into bed the children in the Haldimann's small summer house, but finally the candle had been snuffed and a deep quiet had once again descended on the mountains. A few hours later Frédéric was awakened by the distant rumbling of an approaching storm. Gradually the humming drone of hundreds of aircraft engines could be heard in between the thunder. After a short sojourn in Main Force operations, 295 Lancasters of 1, 5 and 8 Groups were heading for Turin again. Their outward route was directly across occupied France to a turning point marked by PFF over Lake Annecy south-west of Geneva in France and from there on an easterly heading across the French/Italian Alps to the target in the Po Valley. Adverse conditions forced 16 Lancasters to abort the operation rather than trying to climb over the Alps. The rest continued on, but at Lancaster operating altitudes, the upper winds had shifted from north-westerly tailwinds to south-west and picked up speed, so a number of aircraft drifted over Switzerland across the Jura Mountains towards the foothills of the Swiss Alps and into more developing thunderstorms. Suddenly, the night was rent by a flash of intense light followed by a sound, which seemed sharper than the previous thunderclaps. With eyes wide open but heavy with sleep, Frédéric Haldimann saw behind curtains of heavy rain as the thunderstorm broke overhead, a deep purple glow near the ridge of the next mountain and he heard the faint crackling of exploding ammunition.

Betty, a 20-year-old WAAF driver, had always been single-minded. When she had signed up with the WAAF in 1940 it had caused trouble as her father thought that she should help with the war effort from home. Her family ran three quarries in and around Sheffield producing Ganister, a clay-like material used to line the high-tensile crucibles that were used for making steel. But her new life was a major shock after a sheltered life in a small village attending the local school and on to Art College in Sheffield. Eventually she found herself in a Nissen hut housing 16 girls from very mixed backgrounds. It was a great leveller and soon they were all queuing for terrible food and hobnobbing with the drinkers at the NAAFI. She was the first WAAF at Castle Donnington. There were 600 airmen building an aerodrome and she was the only qualified driver to start with. A few days later two more girls arrived and they became her best friends. At the dinner dances around Xmas and New Year the men were queuing up for a dance as the females were in such short supply. Betty was spoiled rotten!

By now she was driving a 'crew bus' taking the lads out to the 'kites'. The planes were the mighty Lancasters. 'They flew to Berlin every night and returned in full what the German bombers had done to us at home!' she recalled. Betty had also got engaged to her first love – Pilot Officer Eric Hawkins, a Lancaster navigator, and they were due to be married. On the night of 12/13 July, two days before their wedding, Eric was navigator on *U-Uncle* on 103 Squadron that took off from Elsham Wolds at 22.15 for Turin.

The main weight of the raid fell just north of the centre of the city. Over the target, conditions were excellent with no cloud and very good visibility; so much so that one crew commented on the novel experience of being able to clearly identify features of the town lay-out. The crews were unanimous in praising the PFF technique, the only criticism being that it was slightly late in starting. Visual identification of the two rivers and the town confirmed the accuracy of the attack which seems to have gone very well right from the commencement when marking and bombing was particularly described as both accurate and concentrated. As the attack developed numerous fires were observed and although in the later stages some scatter had developed, large areas in the north of the town and in the triangle formed by the Rivers Po and Dora were reported as being a mass of fire with much black smoke up to very great heights. Large explosions were reported and the two biggest of these accompanied by bursts of flame were at 01.57 and 02.00 hours. Defences in the target area were not very troublesome and one crew in 1 Group described them as 'puerile'. The heavy flak was stated to have ceased about half-way through the attack. There was a moderate amount of light flak and also 50 searchlights whose operation seemed to have been particularly haphazard.

Thirteen Lancasters, including *Z-Zebra* flown by Squadron Leader John Dering Nettleton VC, were lost. After a brief spell instructing with 1661 HCU and being promoted to Wing Commander, the South African had returned to command 44 Squadron at Dunholme Lodge in January 1943. Nettleton's Lancaster was shot down by a German night fighter over the English Channel on his return. All seven on the crew were lost without trace; their names added to those on the Runnymede Memorial. Nettleton's was one of thirteen Lancasters that failed to return from the raid on Turin.

At Bottesford all except three Lancasters on 467 Squadron RAAF were home safe. There was no word from Flight Lieutenant Bob Gibbs and the crew on *B-Baker* or Flying Officer Graham Douglas Mitchell RAAF and the crew on *T-Tommy*, which had taken off from Bottesford at 22.49. The aircraft had hit high-tension wires and crashed on a Swiss mountainside. All the crew were buried with full military honours at Vevy on the shores of Lake Geneva. *L-Lucy* too was overdue but after a long delay Pilot Officer Cedric Arthur Chapman RAAF called in. He was flying with no elevator, had only 15 minutes of fuel remaining and wanted to land immediately. He said that he had practiced landing on cloud on the way back and thought that there was no other fault that would stop him using his limited control to land. He had no choice but to try to land at Bottesford, as he did not have enough fuel to reach an airfield with a longer 'crash' runway or to climb and let his crew bail out. At 22.48 hours Chapman brought *Lucy* in perfectly but suddenly the complete tail plane broke off and the rest of the aircraft crashed and instantly burst into flames. All the crew perished.

At Elsham Wolds no word was received from *U-Uncle* flown by Flying Officer Harold Richmond Graham RCAF. He and all his crew were lost without trace. Eric Hawkins' was one of the seven names added to those on the Runnymede Memorial. The Pope asked for a search for the aircraft and it was found 18 months later complete with the skeletons of the crew. Betty later received a letter from the Papal Office confirming the aeroplane number.[3]

A few days after the Turin raid, Frédéric Haldimann set off on a hike to find the site of the aircraft that had crashed on the mountain near his home. The Swiss Army removed twelve truckloads of wreckage including a fuel tank with two holes caused by AA fire. A Swiss flak battery near the Col du Marchairuz on the Jura Mountains had reported firing on unidentified aircraft and hits had been observed. Some explosive bombs were jettisoned near the hamlet of Surpierre in the canton of Vaud without causing much damage or victims. It is assumed that Flying Officer Mitchell decided to press on to the marked turning point in spite of the adverse weather conditions. Still on the original heading, they overflew south western Switzerland while drifting to the northeast. They penetrated over the Rhône Valley, trying to identify the turning point at Lake Annecy but may have mistaken Lake Léman for the waypoint. Having lost altitude in the process and finding themselves trapped between rising ground and lit-up Cumulonimbus thunderclouds, they flew a race-track course, dropped a flare and jettisoned their bomb load including a 4,000lb cookie in an attempt to lighten their aircraft. Moments later *T-Tommy* brushed its port wing against the side of a north-south mountain ridge at approximately 6,000 feet, swung violently to port and slammed onto the ground, losing its No. 4 engine in the process, which was flung 700 metres away and caught fire. Only the body of Flight Sergeant Hugh Bolger the Australian tail-gunner had escaped the fury of the blaze. He was taken to a permanent resting-place in the municipal cemetery at Vevey.[4]

On 13/14 July over 370 aircraft – mainly Halifaxes – took off for Aachen. At Holme-on-Spalding Moor Lieutenant Leif Erik Hulthin on 76 Squadron, one of several Norwegian pilots on the squadron, revved up the engines on *T-Tommy* and headed down the runway, but the Halifax crashed and blocked the runway, preventing eleven Halifaxes behind him from taking off. A strong tail wind brought the first waves of the Main Force into the target area before Zero Hour with the result that, when the first Path Finder markers were released, an unusually large number of aircraft bombed in the first minutes of the raid. The visibility was good and large areas of Aachen appeared to burst into flame at once and about 3,000 individual buildings containing almost 17,000 flats and apartments were reduced to rubble. Over 1,000 people were killed or injured. Aachen reported that that raid was 'a *Terrorangriff* of the most severe scale ...'

Fifteen Halifaxes, two Lancasters, two Wellingtons and a Stirling were lost. Three of the missing Halifax Vs were from 428 'Ghost' Squadron RCAF at Middleton St. George where *R-Robert* on 419 'Moose' Squadron RCAF was also lost. 2nd Lieutenant B J J Furey USAAF and five crew men survived and were taken into captivity.

Bomber Command turned its attention to a French target on the night of 15/16 July when 165 Halifaxes from 4 and 8 Groups attacked the Peugeot motor factory in the Montbéliard suburb of Sochaux near the French border with Switzerland. The night was clear and only lightly defended and the attack was carried out between 6,000 and 10,000 feet but the centre of the group of markers dropped by the Path Finder crews on 35 Squadron was 700 yards beyond. Only 30 bombs fell in the factory but 600 fell in the town and 132 civilians were killed and 336 injured. Five Halifaxes were lost. Production at the factory, which was only slightly damaged, soon returned to normal.

At the start of the Battle of the Ruhr 'Bomber' Harris had been able to call upon almost 600 heavies for Main Force operations and at the pinnacle of the Battle, near the end of May, more than 800 aircraft took part. Innovations such as Path Finders to find and mark targets with their TIs, and wizardry such as *Oboe*, which enabled crews to find them, were instrumental in the mounting levels of death and destruction. Little it seemed could be done to assuage the bomber losses, which by the end of the campaign had reached high proportions. There was however, a simple but brilliant device, which at a stroke could render German radar defences almost ineffective. On 24/25 July when Harris launched the first of four raids, code-named *Gomorrah,* on the port of Hamburg, each Station Commander was authorised to tell the crews that, 'Tonight you are going to use a new and simple counter-measure called *Window* to protect yourselves against the German defence system. *Window* consists of packets of metal strips, which when dropped in bundles of a thousand at a time at one-minute intervals produce almost the same reactions on

RDF equipment as do aircraft and you should stand a good chance of getting through unscathed.' Strips of black paper with aluminium foil stuck to one side and cut to a length (30cm by 1.5cm) were equivalent to half the wavelength of the *Würzburg* ground and *Lichtenstein* airborne interception, radar. Although *Window* had been devised in 1942 its use had been forbidden until now for fear that the *Luftwaffe* would use it in a new *Blitz* on Great Britain.[5] It was carried on the 791 aircraft[6] which set out for Hamburg.[7]

Gomorrah was carefully chosen and had great significance. In biblical times it was one of the two most powerful and wealthy cities in the southern Jordan valley, the other being Sodom. These two cities warred against Abraham and God's chosen people. After the people of Sodom insulted two visiting Angels, God decided to destroy both cities. The Lord rained upon Sodom and Gomorrah brimstone and fire out of heaven and lo the smoke of the country went up as the smoke of a furnace. In his message of good luck to his crews Harris said that 'The Battle of Hamburg cannot be won in a single night. It is estimated that at least 10,000 tons of bombs will have to be dropped to complete the process of elimination. To achieve the maximum effect of air bombardment this city should be subjected to sustained attack. On the first attack a large number of incendiaries are to be carried in order to saturate the Fire Services.'

Led by *H2S* PFF aircraft, 740 out of 791 bombers dispatched rained down 2,284 tons of high explosive and incendiary bombs in two and a half hours upon the suburb of Barmbeck, on both banks of the Alster, on the suburbs of Hoheluft, Eirnsbiittel and Altona and on the inner city. The advantages enjoyed by Kammhuber's *Himmelbett* system, dependent as it was on radar, had been removed at a stroke by the use of *Window*. The German fighter pilots and their *Bordfunkers* were blind.

Oberleutnant Wilhelm 'Wim' Johnen, *Staffelkapitän* 3./NJG1 who was flying his Bf 110 in the direction of Amsterdam was one who was totally confused. Though the ground stations were giving the night fighters the positions of the bombers Johnen felt that the reports were hasty and nervous. No one knew exactly where the enemy was or what his objective would be. Radio reports contradicted themselves saying that the enemy was over Amsterdam and then suddenly west of Brussels and a moment later they were reported far out to sea. In desperation Johnen flew straight to Amsterdam but he found nothing. At 1,000 feet his *Bordfunker* Facius reported the first enemy bomber on his *Li* set. Johnen swung the Bf 110 round on to the bearing in the direction of the Ruhr, thinking he was bound to approach the stream. Facius continued to read out bearings of 'bombers' but they were travelling at very high speed and Johnen thought that they must be German fighters. Johnen lost his patience but the tense atmosphere was suddenly interrupted by a ground station calling, '*Hamburg, Hamburg. A thousand enemy bombers over Hamburg. Calling all night fighters, calling all night fighters. Full speed for Hamburg.*'

Johnen was speechless with rage. For half an hour he had been chasing an imaginary bomber stream while bombs were falling on Hamburg. It was a long way to the port and by the time Johnen got there Hamburg was blazing like a furnace – 'a horrifying sight'. Incredulously Johnen turned for home.

Twelve bombers were lost in action; four Halifaxes and four Lancasters, a Wellington and three Stirlings. *P-Peter*, a Halifax on 35 Squadron crashed shortly after take-off from Graveley when both outer engines failed and *S-Sugar*, a Polish Wimpy short of fuel, crash landed at Trusthorpe, Lincolnshire returning from the raid. At Holme-on-Spalding Moor there was no word of *M-Mother* on 76 Squadron flown by Flying Officer George Such. All eight crew lay dead in their Halifax V in Germany. One of the Stirlings that failed to return was *P-Peter* flown by the Australian CO on 218 'Gold Coast' Squadron, 39-year-old Wing Commander Don Saville DSO DFC. *P-Peter* was shot down eight kilometres NNW of Neumünster by 23-year-old *Feldwebel* Hans Meissner, a Bf 110 pilot in 2./NJG3. Saville and six crew were killed. One man survived and was taken prisoner. Meissner, whose third victory this was, recalled after the war that:

> My duty was done when the attacked aircraft went down. The object was not to kill the crew but to destroy engines and tanks. Thus I can say that with the exception of my first kills, when I was rather nervous, large numbers of the bombers' crews always succeeded in descending by parachute. I do not mention this in order to extenuate or glorify. It was a bare fact. Our conversations prior to an action and afterwards were sober, without boasting. All of us, friends and adversaries, had at least one thing in common – death, which might have taken any of us at any time.[8]

Harry Fisher, a wireless operator on a 218 Squadron Stirling recalled:

> It was an onerous task tossing out *Window* aluminium although we had been well warned at briefing. I was hampered by my oxygen tube, intercom connections, the darkness and the general difficulties of physical effort at high altitudes but I knew that it was essential to keep to the rate of one bundle per minute and over 90 million strips of *Window* were dropped. Our approach to the target was from well out to sea having left the English coast over Cromer. We were in the third wave, consisting of all Stirling aircraft to attack Hamburg. Visibility was good with light winds, little or no cloud but considerable black smoke over the target. TI markers were considered to be well placed. There was fairly intense heavy flak and moderate light

flak. The heavy flak appeared to burst into 4 or 5 portions which again disintegrated with yellowish flak covering an area of about 100 cubic yards. We bombed from 16,000 feet, aiming point on concentrations of green TIs. Many large fires were seen and defences appeared relatively poor. In the words of 'Bomber' Harris, 'They sowed the wind, now they are reaping the whirlwind.'

Sergeant Harry Barker on 218 Squadron, adds: 'The raid was a horrendous event with vast areas set on fire. No doubt this was a clear signal that as a terror factor the Germans did not have it all their own way in bombing. If we had known the result of our effort I think we would have said that they started it ... But we did not know.'

Less than half of the force had bombed within three miles of the centre of Hamburg and a creep-back six miles long developed, but because Hamburg was such a large city, severe damage was caused in the central and north-western districts, particularly in Altona, Eimsbüttel and Hoheluft. The smoke of Hamburg did indeed 'go up as the smoke of a furnace'. When dawn came on 25 July, a heavy cloud of dust and smoke hung over Hamburg and remained above it throughout the hot summer day which followed, obscuring the sun and seeming to the wretched inhabitants of the city to portend yet more devastation. It did. Over 120 American bombers of VIIIth Bomber Command made a precision attack on the docks and port facilities and the district of Wilhelmsburg, but because of the smoke rising from Hamburg only 68 aircraft were able to bomb. Severe damage was caused to port establishments and wharves, as well as to sea-going ships and docks. It was over in an hour but was repeated next morning when 54 American aircraft appeared once more and they hit the large Neuhoff power works. It appeared to 1st Lieutenant John W McClane Jr., a B-24 Liberator navigator, 'that every section of this huge city was on fire. An ugly pall of smoke was blowing to the southwest. It looked the way that one might imagine Hell to be.'

Brigadier General Fred L Anderson commanding VIIIth Bomber Command flew as an observer on the next raid, on the night of 25/26 July, when bad weather over north Germany prevented all but a handful of Mosquitoes bombing Hamburg. *Window* was still effective so 705 heavies were dispatched to Essen. Canadian Flight Lieutenant 'Rick' Garvey's crew on 83 Squadron had the honour of flying the American general on *Q-Queenie*. The Group Navigation Officer, Squadron Leader Price, also went along on the veteran Lancaster with over 60 bomb symbols painted below the cockpit. A nude female kneeling in front of a bomb, just aft of the front turret had been painted out and replaced by a red devil (Mephistopheles – to whom Faust sold his soul in German legend), thumbing its nose, dancing in the flames with the motto: 'Devils of the Air' underneath.

Eric Phillips, a Stirling rear-gunner on XV Squadron at Mildenhall, Suffolk recalls:

There was full cloud over the target so Path Finders dropped a flare outside the target and the navigator gave the pilot a course on a timed run from the flare and dropped the bombs through cloud. The navigator asked me to watch out for the flare. Within seconds the flare was dropped and just as I reported this, a Ju 88 came in from the port quarter firing two cannons. My rear turret and the starboard outer engine were hit and set on fire. The pilot, thinking the starboard wing was also on fire, ordered bail out. Then the engine fell away from the aircraft and the order to bail out was cancelled. The Stirling lost height from 18,000 down to 8,000. The bombs were dropped at this height in the Essen area and the aircraft then made a safe journey home with me keeping watch from the astrodome, as the rear turret was unserviceable.

On approach to Essen *Johnnie the Wolf*, a 76 Squadron Halifax piloted by Flight Lieutenant Colin McTaggart 'Mick' Shannon DFC RAAF was hit by flak. The port inner engine appeared to have been damaged by shrapnel as vibration set in. Shortly after bombing, at 17,000 feet, the propeller on the port inner became uncontrollable, eventually separating from the engine and smashing into the fuselage. The impact caused a loss of control and when Shannon brought *Johnnie the Wolf* back to level flight it was discovered that Sergeant E W Waterman, the mid-upper gunner had bailed out. Waterman, a professional poacher in civilian life, who normally flew with the 'A' Flight commander but who was filling in for a sick man, was taken prisoner. Shannon made it back to Holme and bellied *Johnnie the Wolf* in without injury to the crew.[9] Twenty-six bombers (or 3.7 per cent of the force) failed to return, of which, 19 were destroyed by night fighters.[10] *Q-Queenie* returned safely to Wyton with General Anderson who also went to Hamburg two nights later with Garvey's crew in the same aircraft.[11]

In all, 627 aircraft out of 705 despatched dropped 2,032 tons of bombs upon Essen. Harris was not exaggerating when he said that 'they inflicted as much damage on the Krupps works as in all previous attacks put together'. Fifty-one other industrial buildings were damaged with another 83 heavily damaged. 'The raid' recorded Goebbels in his diary 'caused a complete stoppage of production in the Krupps works. Speer is much concerned and worried.' The areas particularly damaged included, in addition to the Krupps works, Altenessen, Segeroth, Borbeck, Holsterhausen, Rüttenscheid, Frohnhausen, Delbig and Vogelheim. The fire services of the city had to deal with 270 large and 250 small fires; 340 people lost their lives, 1,128 were wounded and 35,144 rendered homeless while 1,508 houses were destroyed and 1,083 badly damaged.

On the morning after the raid, Doktor Gustav Krupp von Bohlen und Halbach came down to his office from the Villa Hügel, where he lived, cast one look upon the blazing remnants of his works and fell down in a fit. This, since he had not recovered from it, saved him in 1947 from being put on trial as a war criminal.

Harris was intent on sending his bombers back to Hamburg for another major strike, as Eric Phillips, recalls. 'The governor, Bomber Harris, addressed us. He said, 'I feel sure that a further two or three raids on Hamburg, then probably a further six raids on Berlin and the war will finish.'

On the night of 27/28 July 787 aircraft followed a longer route out to Hamburg and back to include a longer flight over the North Sea with the intention of confusing the German *JLOs* as to the intended target. This meant that each aircraft had to carry a smaller bomb load than normal and so it was decided to include a higher proportion of incendiaries than usual. A carpet of bombs of unimaginable density caused the almost complete destruction of six districts of the city and of parts of two others. A total of 2,417 tons of bombs was dropped on the districts to the east of the Alster, which included Hammerbrook, Hohenfelde, Borgfelde and others by 739 bombers and a firestorm was started by a combination of the high temperature prevailing (about 30°C at 6 o'clock in the evening). Fires started in the densely built up working class districts of Hammerbrook and those at Hamm and Borgfelde joined together and then became one gigantic area of fire with air being brought into it with the force of a storm. The firestorm raged for about three hours in an area measuring only two miles by one mile, which received between 550–600 bomb loads and only died down when there was nothing left to burn. About 16,000 multi-storeyed apartments were destroyed and 40,000 people died; most of them by carbon monoxide poisoning.

The damage was 'gigantic', reported *Generalleutnant* Kehrl, the Police President and Air Protection Leader of the city:

Before half an hour had passed, the districts upon which the weight of the attack fell, and which formed part of the crowded dock and port area, where narrow streets and courts abounded, were transformed into a lake of fire covering an area of 22 square kilometres. The effect of this was to heat the air to a temperature which at times was estimated to approach 1,000° centigrade. A vast suction was in this way created so that the air stormed through the streets with immense force, bearing upon it sparks, timber and roof beams and thus spreading the fire still further and further till it became a typhoon such as had never before been witnessed and against which all human resistance was powerless. Trees three feet thick were broken off or uprooted, human beings were thrown to the ground or flung alive into the flames by winds which exceeded 150mph.

[The trunks of strong trees split and broke, younger trees were bent to the ground like willow rods. Seventy thousand of Hamburg's 100,000 trees were lost to this storm.] The panic-stricken citizens knew not where to turn. Flames drove them from the shelters but high-explosive bombs sent them scurrying back again. Once inside, they were suffocated by carbon-monoxide poisoning and their bodies reduced to ashes as though they had been placed in a crematorium, which was indeed what each shelter proved to be.

The only people who escaped death were those who had risked flight at the right moment, or who were near enough to the edge of the sea of flame so that there was some possibility of saving them ... The overall destruction is so radical that literally nothing is left of many people. The force of the gale tore children out of the hands of their parents and whirled them into the fire. People who thought they had gotten out safely, collapsed in the overwhelming heat and died in seconds. Fleeing people had to work their way over the dead and dying. Seventy per cent of the victims died of suffocation, mostly in poisonous carbon dioxide gas, which turned their corpses bright blue, orange and green. So many people died of this poisoning that initially it was thought that the RAF had raided us for the first time with poison gas bombs. Fifteen per cent had died more violent deaths. The rest were charred to a cinder and could not be identified.

Seventeen aircraft failed to return. One pilot reported after returning to base: 'The clouds looked like a blood-soaked cotton swab'. Immediately after the raid about 1,200,000 people fled the city in fear of further raids.

The next raid on Hamburg was on 29/30 July when the objectives for the 777 aircraft that were detailed were the northern and north-eastern districts, which had so far escaped the bombing. Flight Sergeant Fred White, a navigator on 97 Path Finder Squadron at Bourn listened intently to the briefing. He would fly 68 operations in all and had the same pilot and flight engineer almost throughout his two tours. His pilot was Flying Officer (later Squadron Leader) Charles Peter Crauford de Wesselow, a surgeon's son of White Russian origins who had re-mustered from the Brigade of Guards and spoke several languages fluently. In November 1942 de Wesselow and his crew on 614 Squadron force-landed in Portugal in a Blenheim and were interned until January 1943. The precise, immaculate de Wesselow collected antique glass and could call on a rower's physique for throwing a Lancaster around the sky. Fred White was working in the shoe trade in Kettering before he volunteered for the RAF as flight crew in December 1940 at the age of 20. He recalls:

To be honest, that first raid especially was terrifying, what you might call a 'bit dicey'. We were caught in a searchlight cone over Hamburg and it took us about eight minutes to get out. It might not sound long, but when you are caught in the searchlights over the target, it feels a very long time indeed. Our Lancaster was designated 'U' on the squadron. The squadron had lost the last four 'U' planes in successive raids. We made it back, but with very heavy shrapnel damage.

A Lancaster and a Stirling crashed on take-off and took no further part in the operation. The Main Force was detailed to approach Hamburg from almost due north but the Path Finders arrived two miles too far to the east and marked an area south of the devastated firestorm area. Creep-back stretched about four miles along the devastated area and heavy bombing was reported in the residential districts of Wandsbek and Barmbek and parts of the Uhelnhorst and Winterhude. In all, 726 aircraft dropped 2,382 tons on the city and caused a widespread fire area but there was no firestorm. Danish workers arriving at their own frontier from Hamburg's bombed war factories said, according to the Copenhagen correspondent of the Stockholm *Aftonbladet* that 'Hamburg had ceased to exist as an organised city.' Twenty-eight aircraft were shot down and a Stirling crash landed at RAF Coltishall on the return.

One of two Stirlings lost on 218 Squadron was *A-Apple* flown by Sergeant Raymond Stuart Pickard. Bert 'Andy' Anderson, the mid-upper gunner recalled:

We were hit by flak and caught in the searchlights. Our bomb bay was hit and as we were carrying incendiary bombs the aircraft caught fire. Pickard and Earl Bray RCAF our rear gunner were killed. I was wounded by a 20mm shell just as I left my turret to get my chest pack. The rest of us were taken prisoner. Me and twelve other wounded airmen that were shot down on the raid were under the *SS* supervisory orders from the *Gestapo* chief in Hamburg. Two Serbian PoW doctors were allowed to treat our wounds at 10 am each day. They were searched on arrival in our hut as they were not allowed to issue any sedatives. One of the American airmen died during the three months that we were held captive by the *SS*. A Polish PoW took our names and our service numbers and made his escape to Sweden. All this information was passed on to the *Luftwaffe* as well as the Allies and we were rescued by the Luftwaffe who sent us to a *Luftwaffe* hospital in Wismar near Lübeck. After *Dulag Luft* I was sent to *Stalag IVB* where I shared the same hut as our engineer, WOp and bomb aimer.[12]

One of the missing was the 460 Squadron RAAF Lancaster at Binbrook flown by Flying Officer Alan Johnson, which was destroyed by *Hauptmann* Prinz zur Lippe-Weissenfeld on detachment with NJG3. *Oberleutnant*

Joachim Wendtland a *Jägerleitoffizier* (*JLO,* or GCI-controller) who flew with Weissenfeld as an observer recalled:

> The dark shape of the *Viermot* was clearly visible against the night sky above us. It was a Lancaster. The pilot hit his left wing with his first attack and burning pieces flew off. The pilot was a little disappointed that the bomber was not shot down by this first attack. He had wanted to show me how to hit it between the two engines and finish it off quickly. The Lancaster kept straight and level all the time, without any evasive action. For the second attack Prinz zur Lippe used his special method. He slid under the bomber, pulled up the nose suddenly, fired a burst and dropped away quickly in case the bomber blew up. It didn't although pieces were still falling off it. We attacked again. The bomber still did not explode. In the fourth attack his wing started burning after half a second, we saw the Lancaster go down into a wood near a railway.

Cliff O'Riordan, who had celebrated his return from La Spezia in April with a 'pub crawl' in London, was killed. The 33-year-old Australian gunner, his pilot and the four other members of the crew were all lost without trace. Their names were added to the memorial at Runnymede.

On the night of 30/31 July 273 aircraft were dispatched to bomb Remscheid on the southern edge of the Ruhr, which had not previously been bombed. The *Oboe* ground-marking and the bombing were exceptionally accurate and 83 per cent of the town was devastated although only 871 tons of bombs were dropped. German defences were quickly overcoming the effects of *Window* and fifteen aircraft were shot down. Two more bombers were lost when a Lancaster crashed at Downham Market and a Stirling crashed at King's Cliffe in Northamptonshire. On 218 'Gold Coast' Squadron, 21-year-old Acting Flight Sergeant Arthur Louis Aaron, a former Air Training Corps cadet from Leeds whose mother was of Swiss extraction, was nearly one of these losses. Only coolness under pressure by the whole crew enabled their safe return. Sergeant Malcolm Mitchem the flight engineer recalled:

> We were late on our timing. We were delayed due to being coned in searchlights near Amsterdam, entailing losing height and direction to evade them then regaining height whilst still loaded. We were cutting off corners to get round Düsseldorf to get to the target and back into our bomb slot time for our wave and height. We never did catch up and going in to the target with gunners were told to keep our eyes peeled watching above for higher waves of aircraft going in.

Despite this they were hit by three incendiaries dropped from above. Two 4 pounders penetrated the starboard wing between No. 2 and No. 4

main tanks. Fortunately, they remained unignited and were discovered there when the crew landed back at Downham Market, their home airfield. A 30-pounder penetrated the fuselage roof. It drove the hydraulic lines, which would have powered the mid-under turret (not fitted) through the floor of the fuselage into the well where the turret would otherwise have been. The incendiary caught fire and set light to the hydraulic fluid gushing from the fractured pipes. Having nearly been struck as it penetrated the aircraft, 'Jimmie' Guy the wireless operator, who had been by the flare chute pushing out wads of *Window*, called up on the intercom to report that the aircraft was on fire. The aircraft filled with thick black smoke and fumes and flames roared up through the fuselage floor and out of the gashed roof as a great flare of flame. Whilst Arthur Aaron and Flight Sergeant Alan Larden RCAF, the bomb aimer, pressed on with the task of reaching and bombing the target, Mitchem came off intercom, grabbed some portable fire extinguishers and went back to fight the fire. The flare of flame and the fire-glow in the fuselage attracted the searchlights, which again coned the aircraft. Having dropped their bombs, Aaron started a diving, twisting descent to forestall the flak and escape the searchlights.

Alan Larden said:

Arthur had opened his side window to force the smoke to the back of the aircraft and by then 'Jimmie' Guy the wireless operator and I were able to work our way back along the aircraft to Jim Richmond in the mid-upper turret. Jim had been trapped there above the fire. With the aid of portable oxygen cylinders we were able to help him to the front of the aircraft to recover.

With all the smoke and the eerie glow cast by the searchlights and the flames Malcolm Mitchem, who was off intercom, was confused about the state of the aircraft.

With all the diving and turning I thought that the aircraft was out of control and that maybe all the others had bailed out. I began to return up front to reach my own parachute when I met Alan and 'Jimmie' Guy coming back with more extinguishers after they had moved Jim Richmond forward. The incendiary had burnt its way through the floor and fallen out. We were able then to extinguish what remained of the fire around the hole left in the floor.

By now, Arthur Aaron had descended towards the Cologne/Düsseldorf gap in the searchlight belt and eventually escaped the glare of the lights. They had lost a lot of height and were streaking for home on an even keel at low level across Holland. When they had crossed the Dutch coast and were out over the North Sea they could relax a little. Flasks were opened and coffee was pressed upon Malcolm who was coughing and retching from all the smoke and extinguisher fumes. They landed back at Downham Market at 03.05 hours after a very eventful 4 ½ hour flight. The *London Gazette* of 19 October 1943 announced the award of the DFM to Arthur Aaron who had proved to be 'an exceptional captain and leader'.[13]

On 2 August after a day of heavy thunderstorms, 740 bomber crews were briefed for the fourth raid on Hamburg. They were told that the weather was extremely bad and that cumulonimbus clouds covered the route up to 20,000 feet. Above that height the sky was reported to be clear but the bombing force encountered a large thunderstorm area over Germany and no Path Finder marking was possible. Flight Lieutenant Robert Burr on 44 (Rhodesia) Squadron was one of those who succeeded in dropping his bombs that night but many crews turned back early or bombed alternative targets. Burr said:

> We took off one by one in a flurry of pounding rain and found our-selves immediately in a huge cu-nim cloud. The airspeed indicator fluctuated by 30 mph or more and the rate of climb indicator wobbled crazily up and down. The aircraft was tossed and buffeted by the swirling currents of air and we could only climb very slowly as we edged painfully higher. Fifty hard-won feet would be lost in an instant as we hit a powerful down draught and then just as suddenly we would gain fifty feet like a fast moving lift, as we were carried upwards by a stream of rising air.

With great difficulty Burr forced his Lancaster to 16,000 feet and then set course over the North Sea feeling glad that:

> ... my wrists and arms were strong, for it was only with the utmost difficulty that this aircraft could be kept on an even keel. At 17,000 feet the Lancaster was still in heavy cloud and would climb no higher. Presently lightning began to play around it and 'all the metal parts of the aircraft shone with the blue spikes of St. Elmo's fire ... About a quarter of a mile to port was another aircraft flying on a parallel course ... It seemed to be a mass of flame and I realised that it, too, must be covered with St. Elmo's fire ... I stared at this flying beacon and suddenly, as I watched a streak of lightning split the heavens. There was a huge flash and burning fragments broke away. What remained of the aircraft plunged to earth.

Thirty aircraft failed to return as a result of enemy action (a Stirling collided with a Dornier Do 217 and all were killed) and icing (one crew abandoning their Halifax over Sweden), taking total losses on the four raids to 79. Three more aircraft including Halifax *O-Oboe* flown by Flying Officer J G Jenkins on 10 Squadron, crashed on their return. Before reaching the target *O-Oboe* was attacked by a Ju 88 and Jenkins was compelled to jettison his bombs and take evasive action. The rear gunner eventually shot the night fighter down in flames but not before both of *Oboe*'s elevators had been shot away, the wings and fuel tanks damaged and the port tyre punctured. Incredibly, none of the crew was injured and Jenkins, despite the difficulty of controlling the aircraft, returned to base at Melbourne and made a safe landing. 'Bring-em-back-alive Jenkins' as he became known, brought *N-Nuts* home from Hannover a month later when on 22/23 September an attacking night fighter shot away his windscreen and extensively damaged both sides of the fuselage and the hydraulic system. The bombs refused to jettison and so Jenkins headed the Halifax out over the North Sea and all the crew bailed out safely near Patrington, Yorkshire.

At Hamburg, dawn on 3 August broke upon a city sunk 'in a great silence' after the 'howling and raging of the fire storms' and bathed in the unreal light of rays filtered through a canopy of smoke. Everywhere lay dust, soot and ashes ... The streets were covered with hundreds of bodies. 'No worthwhile concentration over the target' had been achieved. (Only scattered bombing took place and 1,426 tons struck the city). But then it was hardly necessary. More than 6,000 acres of Hamburg smouldered in ruins. Over four nights, 3,095 bombers were dispatched, 2,500 attacked and 8,621 tons of bombs were dropped, 4,309 tons of them being incendiary bombs. In these raids, including the small daylight American attacks, it was computed by the Police President that 40,385 dwelling-houses and 275,000 flats, representing 61 per cent of the living accommodation of the city, had been destroyed or rendered uninhabitable. Some 580 industrial and armament establishments were in a similar condition and so were 2,632 shops, 76 public offices, 24 hospitals, 277 schools, 58 churches, 83 banks, 12 bridges and one menagerie, the famous Hagenbeck Zoo, which was wiped out in the first raid. Half the city had been totally devastated. The total population had been reduced by about 30 per cent and the working population by 25 per cent. The number of persons known to have lost their lives was 41,800; the injured, many of whom died, numbered 37,439. To these must be added some thousands more missing.

ACM Sir Arthur Harris said 'In spite of all that happened at Hamburg, bombing proved a comparatively humane method. For one thing, it saved the flower of the youth of this country and of our allies from being mown down by the military in the field, as it was in Flanders in the war of 1914–1918.' *Gauleiter* Kaufmann, in his first report to Josef Goebbels spoke of a catastrophe, the extent of which simply staggers the imagination. He spoke of about 800,000 homeless people wandering up and down the streets not knowing what to do.' Goebbels wrote 'A city of a million inhabitants has been destroyed in a manner unparalleled in history. We are faced with problems that are almost impossible of solution. Food must be found for this population of a million. Shelter must be secured. The people must be evacuated as far as possible. They must be given clothing.' *Generalfeldmarschall* Erhard Milch State Secretary of the *Reichsluftfahrtministerium* (RLM or *Reich* Air Ministry), went further. 'It's much blacker than [Albert] Speer [the German Armaments Minister] paints it. If we get just five or six more attacks like these on Hamburg, the German people will just lay down their tools, however great their willpower ...' (In his speech to a conference of *Gauleiters* on 6 October Milch said that in Hamburg particularly the production of variable pitch propellers had suffered very severely because of the loss to these factories of 3,000 skilled workers who were still missing.) Up to the time of these attacks, the production of 500-ton *U-boats* had been between eight and nine a month. After, it fell to between two and three, partly owing to the direct damage inflicted on the yards and workshops and partly because of absenteeism. Speer admitted that 'Hamburg put the fear of God in me – *Gauleiter* Kaufmann teletyped Hitler repeatedly, begging him to visit the stricken city. When these pleas proved fruitless, he asked Hitler at least to receive a delegation of some of the more heroic rescue crews. But Hitler refused even that.'[14]

Paralyzed by *Window, Nachtjagd* and the *Flakwaffe* were unable to offer any significant resistance. Adolph Galland added:

A wave of terror radiated from the suffering city and spread throughout Germany. Appalling details of the great fires were recounted and their glow could be seen for days from a distance of 120 miles. A stream of haggard, terrified refugees flowed into the neighbouring provinces. In every large town people said: 'What happened to Hamburg yesterday can happen to us tomorrow.' Berlin was evacuated with signs of panic. In spite of the strictest reticence in the official communiqués, the Terror of Hamburg spread rapidly to the remotest villages of the Reich. Psychologically the war at that moment had perhaps reached its most critical point. Stalingrad had been worse but Hamburg was not hundreds of miles away on the Volga but on the Elbe, right in the heart of Germany. After Hamburg in the wide circle of the political and military command could be heard the words: 'The war is lost.'

The Bomber Command ORS, which analysed the Hamburg raids said:

The very low casualties incurred on the first two raids were largely due to the temporary disorganisation of the German fighter defences by a new countermeasure which precluded the vectoring of controlled night fighters. The final attack was ruined by unexpected deterioration of weather conditions over the target. Eighty-seven aircraft is a high price in itself but in comparison with the loss suffered by Germany in the almost complete annihilation of her second city, it can only be regarded as minute. The 'Hafen' with its imposing array of shipbuilding yards, docks, warehouses and administrative buildings was the basis of Hamburg's contribution to German economic life ... The destruction of Hamburg by bombing was thus far the stiffest task yet undertaken in air warfare. It was not until 1 August that smoke from the conflagrations cleared sufficiently to make reconnaissance possible. The heavily damaged areas covered 6,200 acres out of the 8,380 acres which comprise Hamburg's closely built-up residential area. All parts of the city and dock were shattered – all four main shipbuilding yards were hit, five floating docks were sunk or badly damaged, 150 industrial plants were destroyed or badly damaged, plus massive disruption of communications and power.

On average, British losses during the Hamburg raids were no more than 2.8 per cent, whereas in the previous 12 months, losses had risen from 3.7 to 4.3 per cent. *Window* neutralized the *Würzburg* GCI and GL radars and short range AI and completely destroyed the basis of GCI interception. Controlled anti-aircraft fire was almost completely disrupted at night and only fixed box barrages remained possible. The new British tactics also combined the use of PFF, the massed bomber stream and new target finding equipment (*H2S*). This combination resulted in total chaos to the German night fighter defence system, which was unable to obtain a true picture of the air situation or control the night fighters in the air. Until they received better equipment, the only method German fighter pilots could use to overcome the crisis caused by *Window* was the *Wilde Sau* tactic.[15]

On the night of Friday 30/31 July nine of 105 and 109 Squadron's Mosquitoes each carrying four red TIs, marked Remscheid, a centre of the German machine-tool industry on the southern edge of the Ruhr, which was the target for over 270 aircraft. This was the first raid on the town. Weather over the target was clear and the raid was well concentrated on a town with a population of 107,000 that manufactured machine precision tools from high-grade steel. The largest factory, Alexanderwerk AG, employed nearly 3,000 workers and covered 75 acres. It produced special machinery for the chemical industry, motor components and small arms. There were 25 smaller factories in the town, as well as railway workshops that specialised in the repair of goods wagons. The *Oboe* ground-marking and the bombing by the comparatively small Main Force were exceptionally accurate and 83 per cent of the town was destroyed. Remscheid was still blazing on Saturday at midday with smoke to a height of 14,000 feet over the town. This brought the Battle of the Ruhr to an end after 18,506 sorties in which 57,034 tons of bombs had been dropped for a loss of 1,038 aircraft.[16]

In the spring of 1943 Sergeant James W Boynton was a Lancaster rear gunner on 156 Squadron and flew a Path Finder tour of ops with Flight Lieutenant R E Young and crew at RAF Warboys near Huntingdon. Boynton recalls:

For ten of those operations during the battle of the Ruhr and Hamburg we flew *N for Nan*. In early August the Squadron started to receive aircraft fitted with the new blind bombing equipment *H2S* and so *Nan* was transferred to 61 Squadron after surviving 25 hazardous Path Finder operations. Little did we know that she was a lucky aircraft and would go on to complete a further 105 ops over the following year. [17]

At Warboys it was usually about 11 o'clock in the morning that word got around the station that ops were on for the following night. Aircrew looked for their names on the Ops Battle Order that was posted in the Squadron office. Some names appeared on the list despite having been on ops the previous night and not landing back at base until six or seven that morning. These crews had to be awakened by the billet orderlies at mid-day in order for them to prepare for the coming operation. After a mid-day lunch our crew would meet in the aircrew locker room, draw our chutes and then board the crew bus which took us out to our aircraft dispersal. Once the ground crew had completed the aircraft's daily inspections and dealt with any problems reported from the previous operation, we took her up on a night flying test (NFT). This usually lasted about an hour and consisted of each crew member checking over all his operational equipment and making sure everything was working correctly. The Skipper would fly out over the north Norfolk coast to the coastal inlet called the Wash. After checking the area for shipping, we would drop a flame float target into the sea and fire off a few hundred rounds to make sure the eight Browning .303 machine guns were working properly. It also provided good gunnery practice.

After returning to base and taxiing the aircraft to its dispersal, the petrol bowser would arrive and the ground crew would begin to fill the aircraft's petrol tanks and the armourers set about loading the correct TIs and bomb load aboard the aircraft for the coming operation. If we had had a rough week doing a few ops on the trot, the Medical Officer (MO) would issue us with Wakey-Wakey pills to keep us awake and alert during the long flight. However, we never took them until the very last moment because sometimes the op was scrubbed just before take-off due to dodgy weather *en-route*, which meant another sleepless night if we had taken a pill too early.

During the early months of 1943 operational briefings were usually held at 16.00 hours. The actual take-off times depended upon the distance to the target, weather and the rise and setting of the moon.

After specialist briefings all the aircrews came together in the Squadron briefing room. At the far end of the room a large map of Western Europe displayed, with thick red tapes, the route to and from the target. When everyone was settled, the station commander arrived and various officers gave us the gen on the night's operation. The Flying Control officer gave us times of take-off in aircraft order. Next the Intelligence officer described the route out and home, the time to open the attack with our marker flares and where they were to be placed in the target area. Sometimes we would be briefed to drop markers *en-route* to keep the main force on the correct path away from heavy flak. Bitter experience had shown that anyone wandering off track 15 or 20 miles would almost certainly become a sitting duck for both fighters and flak. The Squadron Commander then briefed us on where the most flak and fighters were likely to be encountered. Lastly, the Met man would give us his weather forecast *en route*, over the target and for our return in the early hours. Unfortunately he usually got it wrong somewhere along the way, resulting in some of the experienced crews taking the Mickey out of him by shouting out, 'Was your seaweed wet or dry today?' Such banter helped to relieve the tension. All the pilots and navigators would set their watches on the time check; the station commander would wish us luck and the briefing was over.

This was followed by a pre-op meal and then we would all try and relax until about an hour and half before take-off when the whole crew would meet up again in the locker room. There we collected all our flying gear including our chutes, Mae West, helmets, flying boots, silk under gloves and gauntlets. In addition, because of the intense cold experienced in Lancaster rear turrets, gunners were issued with special electrically heated clothing, which included an overall, gloves and slippers that fitted inside flying boots. All of which offered some welcome comfort and protection against the extremely low temperatures encountered above 10,000 feet. However, on hot summer nights I never got fully dressed in my flying gear until the aircraft had climbed to a cooler altitude. If I had dressed in my full flying kit on the ground my perspiration would have frozen on me once airborne. After kitting-out we went by crew bus out to the aircraft which was by then bombed up and ready to go.

On take-off there was always a small crowd of officers, WAAFs and airmen to wave us off. While on the take-off run I always turned the rear turret facing the port beam with the turret back doors open just in case of a ground loop crash. In many such accidents the rear gunner often came off the best as the aircraft's main beam area took most of the impact. At around 6,000 feet I left the turret, got fully dressed and then climbed back in to settle down to concentrate on the task ahead. Later, when I started to feel cold I'd plug my electrically heated suit into the aircraft's power supply. We had climbed to our operational height of 20,000 feet by the time we reached the coast and, sometimes on a clear starlit night, I would watch the Norfolk shore line rapidly fade into the distance and wondered if we would ever see it again.

Over the North Sea our Skipper always flew straight and level until the enemy coast was sighted by the bomb aimer. After that it was weaving all the way to the target. In our opinion to fly straight and level over enemy territory was just plain suicide for a slow heavily laden bomber. At our first crew meeting the Skipper said he believed the only way to survive a tour of forty Path Finder operations was to have a well disciplined and highly trained crew and a big slice of all the luck going. After completing a few operations we realised that we would encounter more heavy flak areas the deeper we penetrated German air space. So the procedure we adopted to counter the German predicted flak batteries, was to fly in an irregular pattern by descending 500–600 feet and then climbing slowly back and also weaving from left to right of the set course. The whole crew, apart from the navigator, were on fighter and friendly aircraft collision watch. The gun turrets on our aircraft never stopped moving from side to side for the duration of the operation. This constant movement and scanning the sky made our aircraft a hard target for both German night fighters and ground defences. Once over enemy territory many aircraft would be seen going down in flames on the way to the target. Those I actually saw crash on the ground I reported to the navigator giving him their approximate position, he then plotted them on his chart. On some deep penetration operations over Germany, I saw a dozen or more aircraft go down behind us and many more burning on the ground.

One of the most hated anti-bomber defences employed by the Germans was parachute flares dropped by high flying Ju 88 night fighters. These flares would burst just below the bomber stream and illuminate the whole area thus presenting many bombers as silhouetted targets for the night fighters waiting above. These flares burned so brightly that it was like driving down a well lit road at night and temporarily blinded anyone who was close by. In such circumstances there was nothing the Skipper could do apart from weave more violently than usual and try to fly out of range. The same applied when we got ourselves coned in searchlights. Most large city targets such as Berlin had a radar controlled master beam, which was blue in colour. If it locked onto an aircraft, another ten to fifteen searchlight beams quickly latched onto the victim who became a sitting duck for the heavy flak batteries. Experienced bomber crews found the only way to escape the master beam was to dive away from the expected flak barrage coming up from below. The last 20 miles to the target had to be flown straight and level in order to make sure target indicators and bombs were placed accurately on the target aiming point. This was a really dodgy period and we were lucky if we were not hit by something or other. Many aircraft were lost at this point, some in collisions and others hit by bombs from above. Stirling and Halifax bombers could only reach about 17,000 feet so they got the lot, the small flak: as well as the heavy, plus more attention from the night fighters.

Whilst over the target area, I would often see the fighters attacking bombers silhouetted against the fires on the ground. However, once away from the brightly lit area identifying a fighter was not easy against a black sky. The German night fighter always had the advantage over the bombers and very few were shot down by bomber crews. It was always a great relief when the bomb aimer said, 'Bombs gone'. The aircraft would rear up and wobble as the weight of the bombs left the aircraft, then we knew all we had to do was go home but that could be nearly as bad as getting there. The route home would be more or less straight apart from trying to avoid any known well defended areas. On some nights if conditions were right the Skipper would climb to 27,000 feet then put the nose down and really belt for home. The only snag being that by flying so high the temperature outside was sometimes as low as 60 below freezing. This froze the anti-freeze in the pipes that fired the guns in the rear turret making them useless until they thawed out at a lower altitude. However, the mid-upper guns were electrically fired so were not affected.

Once we had crossed the enemy coast and were well out over the North Sea the Skipper would bring us down to 10,000 feet, below oxygen-using height. Everything would then start to warm up and we could relax a little more. Tommy Evans the bomb aimer would come to the rear turret and bring me a flask of coffee and although smoking was banned while flying, many of us broke that rule. After all the operational stress we had suffered over the past few hours that mug of coffee and a Woodbine went down really well. I personally always carried a good supply of baccy and well-filled petrol lighter, just in case we were shot down and managed to get on the run for a while.

On odd occasions a message would come from base that Bandits (enemy fighters) were suspected of being in the area. That meant no relaxation until we were actually back over base. We would then be given a height at which to circle the airfield and a landing number. When our turn came Air Traffic Control radioed permission to land and once down the Skipper taxied the aircraft around the perimeter track to our dispersal and we were welcomed back by our ground crew before being picked up by the crew bus and taken to the locker room. After handing in our flying gear we then went along to the debriefing room where a WAAF officer served us with a mug of coffee well laced with rum and the Padre would hand sandwiches around. Then we would sit around a table with an intelligence officer and debriefing would begin. 'Did you have any difficulty finding the target? At what time were the TIs placed on the aiming point? How heavy was the flak? Did you encounter any fighters? Did you see any aircraft shot down? How far from the target could the fires be seen?' and many other such questions until he had all the information we could give. Next we collected our personal belongings, including a brown envelope containing our wills and last letters home. These had been deposited and locked away in the Squadron office for safe keeping before take-off. After that we went to the Mess for an aircrew breakfast before seeking out our billet in a state of utter exhaustion. Hopefully we could get a good morning's sleep before being called once again to go to war.[18]

On 7/8 August 197 Lancasters of 1, 5 and 8 Groups attacked targets in Genoa, Milan and Turin. One of the Path Finders who led the way for the Main Force was Wing Commander John Searby of 83 Squadron who was the Master Bomber or the 'Master of Ceremonies' at Turin. Before joining the Path Finders, Searby had commanded 106 Squadron at Syerston where he had succeeded Wing Commander Guy Gibson when he left to raise 617 Squadron. Searby's first meeting with Gibson in the autumn of 1942 was on posting to 106 as a flight commander and his interview was not the happiest. Searby recalled that Gibson had lost three 'good crews' the previous night over Cologne and he was short of sleep and a 'bit on edge'. In reply to his question about his past history Searby said that he had recently come off the Atlantic Ferry, following which he had done a few Wellington sorties 'but nothing of any consequence'. Gibson heard Searby out, obviously not interested and 'impatient for him to finish'. Gibson walked over to the window with his back to Searby and then spat out: 'Atlantic Ferry! You can forget all that. This is the real thing. And anyone who doesn't like it can get out.' Searby had said nothing. He began to dislike Gibson but he saw the letters to the next-of-kin lying on his CO's desk awaiting signature and made allowance for his mood. Later Searby learned that writing letters was always his first priority. 'Gibson was truthful if somewhat blunt' recalled Searby. They became good friends and few months later Searby succeeded him. Later, in the Path Finder Force under Don Bennett 'where the task was the more demanding', Searby's technical skill, combined with his leadership (and humanity) was learned from Gibson.[19]

The Master Bomber arrived over Turin first to take charge of the dropping of marker flares by the Path Finders and he then continued to circle over the target area to orchestrate the bombing more effectively.

When he noticed that creep-back was taking place he instructed the later bombers to aim forward of the fires so that bombing was more concentrated in the target area. This achieved only limited success but this was a trial in preparation for the role Searby would fulfil in the successful raid on Peenemünde later that same month.

Geoffrey Willatt, bomb aimer in Pilot Officer Robbie Robertson's crew in 106 Squadron, which were part of the force attacking Milan, recalls:

Milan was a quite different trip involving a long haul over German-occupied France to Lake Geneva, where Switzerland was lit up like a Christmas tree. The Swiss had obviously decided that Allied aircraft must not mistake their towns for the blacked-out French ones. Now we were going over the Alps to Italy. We were gazing at the snow-covered mountains not far below, when a little stream of tracer bullets popped up towards us like a string of luminous sausages – quite impossible from the top of a mountain but we all saw it. Robbie said, 'Do you think this was Hannibal's route over the Alps with his elephants?' I had been supplied with maps of North Africa, because the loss of one engine would restrict the height of the flight home, preventing a return over the Alps. I couldn't help half-wishing this might happen. In fact, one crew did have to do this and landed in the desert, being immediately surrounded by fearsome Bedouins on camels, with primitive rifles. They fired a green flare, scaring them off and then found they were, in fact, friendly and took the crew to the nearest Allied base, where the desert war was in progress. A new engine was fitted after a few days and they were able to fly home. I bombed Milan from much lower than usual – about 10,000 feet. The resulting photo showed Milan Cathedral – what desecration!

Then to Mannheim, on 9/10 August, attacked all the time by very intense flak, some of which hit us with a noise like rattling gravel thrown up at a window – very loud really, to be heard above the roar of the engines. One piece of shrapnel made a hole in the Perspex nose through which I was looking and a small piece hit me in the eye and made my eyes water but didn't cause much harm. They found holes under the fuselage when we got back.

A total of 457 aircraft raided Mannheim. Bomber Command lost six Halifaxes and three Lancasters. Two of the aircraft were shot down by *Leutnant* Norbert Pietrek of 2./NJG4 at Florennes airfield in southern Belgium. Pietrek, who had claimed two bombers destroyed on the night of the last Mannheim raid in April, was again piloting a Bf 110F-4. His crew consisted of *Unteroffizier* Paul Gärtig, his *Bordfunker* whom he called *Paulchen* (little Paul), and his *Bordschütze* was Otto Scherer, who was a replacement for Bauchens who had hepatitis and was in hospital. Pietrek's first victim of the night was *K-King*, a Halifax on 405 'Vancouver' Squadron RCAF at Gransden Lodge piloted by Flight Lieutenant Kenneth MacGregor Gray RCAF who was from Medicine Hat, Alberta, as was one his crew, five of whom were Canadians. Pietrek slid under the bomber and from twenty metres below, intending to fire his four machine guns and two 2cm cannon into its starboard wing. Only the four machine guns fired and one of these failed and could not be cocked, but it was enough. The Halifax burst into flames and plunged burning over his port wing to crash at Awenne in Belgium. All seven crewmembers were killed.

With only three machine guns working Pietrek stalked his second victim, *K-King of the Air*, a Lancaster piloted by John Whitley on 61 Squadron at Syerston. The all-sergeant crew were on their fifth operation. Again Pietrek positioned his Bf 110 twenty metres beneath his quarry and then he pulled up and fired a full burst into the two starboard engines. He must have hit him he thought, but the Lancaster, which jettisoned its bombs, flew on apparently undamaged. Another of Pietrek's guns had failed and he was now down to two 'little squirters'. This left only the fuselage as the aiming point and if possible the four 1,000 rounds of ammunition in the rear turret so Pietrek tried for the ammunition. Sergeant John Topham Kendall RCAF the rear gunner saw the Bf 110 and bailed out immediately but his head hit Pietrek's port wing. Next Pietrek took out Sergeant Nevil Temple Holmes the mid-upper gunner, and finally, at ten metres' range the *Leutnant* fired into the bottom right of the rear turret where two of the four ammunition boxes were located and then he did the same to the bottom left. After about ten seconds there were flames. The Lancaster caught fire at the back 'like a cigar' and a few minutes later went down. Sergeant George Spriggs the flight engineer was killed. In the bright glare of the crash the Bf 110 crew saw four open parachutes descending. As the inferno spread 'Fred' Gardiner the WOp had wasted no time in bailing out. Completely disorientated he pulled the ripcord. He and John Whitley, 'Whiz' Walker and Peter Smith the navigator all evaded. Pietrek landed back at Florennes where his crew found a scrap of skin with a bunch of red hair on the port wing of their Bf 110.[20]

Geoffrey Willatt continues:

Nürnburg came next. It was strange to think we'd damaged this lovely medieval city, which I'd visited only a few years before. We were now the most experienced aircrew on our station and were sent to a bomb-sight factory on a morale-boosting tour, being fussed over by a lot of factory girls. We weren't allowed in one part of the factory which was top secret. In fact they were making a bomb sight, which we were currently using and was almost out of date! The bomb-sights, in any case, at this stage in the war, were really very primitive and indeed, after the war, it was found that our bombing was not very efficient and depended on each individual crew's navigation to find the target and the bomb-aimer, me for instance, pressing the 'tit' at the right time. I wonder if the American method of formation flying to the target, relying on one master navigator and one master bomb-aimer was better? There was a radiogram in the Officers' Mess and a pile of records, one of which had been a favourite – the Inkspots singing *I like coffee, I like tea*. Dickie knew that there was a superstition in the Mess that anyone putting this record on would be shot down that night but he played it with a large grin saying, 'What nonsense' and of course, we came back safely from Nürnburg that night.

Eighteen aircraft did not return. One was ditched in the English Channel and the crew taken into captivity. Five more crashed in England; a Stirling dived into Pevensey Bay and a Halifax was abandoned near Selsey Bill. Others returned with dead and wounded on board their aircraft. Reg Fayers the navigator on Halifax *H-Honkytonk* on 76 Squadron at Holme-on-Spalding Moor said in a letter to his wife Phyllis at Ploughlane Dairy in Sudbury, Suffolk that they were on their way back from Nuremburg when he visited the Elsan toilet just as they ran into flak. A large chunk of shrapnel hit the port outer engine, which promptly caught fire:

At the same minute Sergeant Herbert Thomas Whittlesea – a nice kid with bags of enthusiasm – who was flying second dickey, said, 'I think I've been hit skip. I think I'm going to pass out.' By the time we were out of the flak, Lew [Sergeant Lew Barnes] found Whitt to be unconscious – no more than five minutes at the most. It took several more minutes for Lew and Phil to get Whitt back to the rest position and find the wound and treat him. Anyway I think that Whitt was already dead. He died very soon anyway and there was so much blood about that he must have died from the loss of it and the shock of course.

They eventually landed at Ford. Fayers wrote in his log: 'second dickey died.' It was simply nothing more than that. Next day they examined *Honkytonk* and discovered that the flak fragment that killed Whittlesea was no more than an inch and a half across. It had come through the nose of the Halifax, up through two pieces of metal, right through Fayers' seat while he was at the Elsan, hitting Whittlesea in an important artery in his thigh and he bled to death. Fayers added, 'I don't think there's more than a breath of wind or a feather's weight between life and death.'[21]

But life had to go on. 'Dirty footmarks on the Officers' Mess ceiling could be seen one morning' says Geoffrey Willatt. At a party the night before, a WAAF officer had been turned upside down after dipping her shoes in paint and held to walk upside down. I wasn't there. The CO was very cross and made the culprits clean it off and redecorate the ceiling.'

The night of Thursday 12th/Friday 13th of August was a long one for 321 Lancasters and 183 Halifaxes to Milan, while 152 aircraft of 3 and 8 Groups were detailed to bomb Turin.

Flight Sergeant Alan Larden RCAF the bomb aimer on Flight Sergeant Arthur Louis Aaron's Stirling crew on 218 Squadron, recalls:

On 12th August we set out in *O-Oboe* on our first Italian raid. The 'we' were Art Aaron, Cornelius 'Bill' Brennan RCAF, Thomas 'Jimmy' Guy, Malcolm 'Mitch' Mitchem, Thomas 'Mac' McCabe, Jimmy Richmond and me. Two Canucks and five Limeys. It was a lovely, warm evening as we left and it was just getting dusk. The red and green lights and powerful throb of 80-odd aircraft engines and the host of well-wishing Norfolk villagers filled us with buoyant, adventurous spirit, which was a welcome change to our nightly quota of 30 and 40 per cent losses in the first days of the 'Battle of the Ruhr'. We got the green and our trundle changed to a run and just as we settled into the old charging gallop down the runway we left the deck to the waves and cries of the good folk of Downham Market, who lined our perimeter fence and adjacent roads. The old routine started. A bit of brake to stop the wheels turning; wheels up, 2,450 revs; flaps in, etc and our climb until 'set course' time.

Malcolm Mitchem continues:

The late take-off gave a chance for darkness to settle in on the southerly course towards the Channel and the French coast, so power was soon reduced for economical cruise setting to allow *Oboe* to climb on its long journey as fuel burned off. The route outbound took us across London and the stream of over 200 heavy bombers halted traffic in the streets as occupants looked up and waved; Londoners coming out into their streets and gardens waved as they surmised that retribution for their miseries of enemy night-bombing was passing overhead.

They had been well briefed and were quite pleased with the target; Turin for the Stirlings and Milan for 6 Group. One of those heading for Milan was Sergeant William Thomas Kent, a Halifax tail gunner who was born in New York and brought up all over America. He looked out and thought that the little villages 'sure looked pretty'. Kent, whose father was an actor, lived with his stepfather, a night-club owner, for nine years in Hollywood, California, joined the RCAF and put in for flying. But after he 'washed out' he had put in for air gunnery. He was in Coastal Command for a while, on Sunderlands, before being sent to a bomber squadron. All the rest of the crew were English. 'The pilot got married on a 48-hour pass and we all had a big party. His wife was a WAAF and so was his sister and so was his mother. Wonderful family they made.' Kent had flown his first op to Dortmund on 4/5 May and had been on the second one and the three to Hamburg in July:

> On the second Dortmund 'job' we got hit hard. Our port engine blew up. We went into a dive from 20,000 feet and didn't pull out until 2,000. If I could have picked up my parachute that night I would have bailed out but the force of the pullout was too much. I couldn't get out of my seat, so I stuck there. Had a lot of fun shooting out the searchlights when we got down on the deck ...

Hitting Italian targets was fun and such pretty scenery. On the run to Milan he kept looking at the Alps and saying to his pilot on intercom, 'Hell those mountains don't look so big. We've got bigger ones out in California.' And then the pilot said to him, 'Well just look to your left, right now'. Kent did: 'And there was a big damn peak sticking up in the moonlight with snow all over it. Mont Blanc.'[22]

Milan was considered a successful raid and two Halifaxes and one Lancaster were lost to enemy action. Two others collided and crashed at Plaidstow, Sussex and a 101 Squadron Lancaster collided with a Beaufighter at Ford on landing. Sergeant Graham 'Mick' Cullen, a New Zealander, was the wireless operator on Flight Lieutenant Robert Megginson's Stirling crew on XV Squadron at Mildenhall. Megginson was a second tour man who had completed a period of instructing in Canada. Cullen recalls:

> Trips to Northern Italy were regarded as the best of the lot, very little flak and not too much interference from fighters. These raids were usually carried out during the full moon period and the magnificent sight of the snow covered Alps had to be seen to be believed. On one occasion, as the Stirling droned its way towards the target flying about 1,000 feet above the mountains, the crew marvelled at the brilliance of the moonlight reflecting its silver rays on the snow covered backcloth. Suddenly, a pyrotechnic scene erupted ahead of us as the green and red marker flares cascaded down marking the death of a pathfinder aircraft. As we watched in awe we clearly saw the mushrooming canopies of the parachutes as some of the crew floated down. I must admit that even our sorrow and concern for the crew could not override the beauty of the scene.[23]

Alan Larden and the rest of the crew on *O-Oboe* meanwhile, headed for Turin:

Being the first time for us on an Italian target all had a busy after-noon preparing new data and now, all these dots in the sky swung at the same instant and joined the stream of Halis coming down from the North. Up where we were it was still daylight and our armada of some 600-odd ships were visible right to the South Coast. The clouds below looked like a verminous white blanket with those black dots crawling on the surface. The French coast at Caen was crossed at 10,000 feet and we continued on enjoying a pleasant ride in brilliant August moonlight, the gunners with their 'dark side' to worry about and myself cursing the multitudinous rivers of rolling France and the equally numerous pieces of topographical map from which I was supposed to find out which was which. As Bill's *Gee* was not too bad, I didn't care much and kept a weather eye peeled for Ju 88s. It seemed no time till the fields and farms changed to the rugged parts of Le Creusot and then the Alps were upon us. We tried getting old *Oboe* up to 18,000 feet but had to settle for about 15,000 as the starboard inner's heat gauge went practically off the clock. Pilot Art, with me in the co-pilot's seat, were all eyes. Mitch had his head over my shoulder and the intercom was full of the excited comments of all at the grandeur or the Alps in the moonlight and then Lake Constance and the bright lights of Geneva and finally tremendous, towering, castle-like Mont Blanc with its crown of clouds and snow.

Boy', said Art. 'Would I like to climb that.'

Suddenly before us, there was the target. The mountains had stopped like the edge of the table and up front a few miles, a black smudge in the moonlight was Turin. Four or five waving search-lights, the odd gun flash on the ground and its subsequent deadly twinkle in the puffy sky above. It didn't take me long to slither down to the bombsight and get cracking nor for Mitch to climb into my seat and get his fingers on the bomb bay door releases. Amidst these pleasant thoughts of 'Ha piece of cake' and 'Ha lovely prang' came Rich's voice over the intercom.

'Watch the bloke up front, Art.'

'OK Rich. Christ, he's firing at us. Fire back at him, Rich.'

'I can't; the wing tip is in the way.'[24]

All this chatter came to me on my knees over the bombsight head. All thought passed from my mind. It was a complete blank and as I turned my head to starboard half a dozen little finger holes were punched in the fuselage, two feet from my face, in seemingly deliberate procession. I was awakened from my shock by Mitch's horror-filled voice, sounding as if he had a mouthful of his stomach, gasping out.

'My God, fellows, look at Art. Oh, poor Art. Give me a hand, Alan.'

As I emerged from the nose, in front of me Bill lay crumpled on the floor of the rear of the nav station, his pencil dividers and instruments scattered over his torn and bloodied Mercators. His face was up, his chewing gum still between his lips and his eyes were open. He had been standing to confirm a *Gee* fix for the course out of the target area. One of the bullets which had passed under Mitchem's seat hit the armpit of his raised right arm and into his heart; he did not live long enough to close his eyes. Jimmy reported 'Bill's had it'. As I swung up into the cockpit I could see Art hunched to the port side, his face covered with blood and a gaping wound, his right arm dangling limp and useless. The instrument panel was a mess of broken, bloodstained glass, as was the pilot's side of the windscreen. Mitch was really fighting the controls and every couple of seconds throwing agonised glances in Art's direction. I could see we were right down amongst the mountain peaks and for some unknown reason, Mitch just slid out of the seat and I into it. I guess it was our lengthy training and respect for each other's jobs, coupled with the fact that our engines weren't in the healthiest shape that prompted the involuntary action. While I kept us in the air, flying down the valleys, picking the lowest peaks to scrape over and trying to keep track of our general direction on the compass, Mitch gathered the rest of the crew and had two of them give Art morphine injections and bundle him up amidships between the main spar (but not until after he had tried to tell us to head for England, finally scratching the message shakily in the back of Bill's log with his left hand). After I gave him the old 'OK' sign and pointed over the mountains in the general direction of north-west he submitted to the rough first aid of Mac and Jimmy. As the starboard inner engine was again dangerously warm, I decided we just couldn't make it over the higher mountains to the West. We couldn't jettison and the thought of bailing out in those cold, snowy, wind-driven peaks invited as much danger as sticking with the ship. I took the only alternative and headed over the lower mountains towards Austria. As more air got between us and the ground I decided to try and get to the nearest British occupied part, which was Sicily. Accordingly, from heading eastward we turned through south gradually to head westward. The rest of the crew as well as me had had plenty of the mountains and the gentler hills of Italy, compared with the Alps, helped them to agree on our destination.

Considerable time had elapsed by the time we crossed the Italian coast at Spezia. After Mitch had checked his engines and fuel he came and took over again for a while, whilst I induced the crew not to be backward about moving Bill's body from the gangway and told the gunners to check the dinghies and parachutes for damage and get them in readiness. To manage the aircraft was considerable work for we had no trimming tabs (the cables had been shot away and were dangling from the roof). With the one engine cut back, one's left leg felt as if it was going to be shoved into one's stomach. The rear gunner was given a post facing the engineer's panel and was to yell when the first warning light came in the fuel indicators. Mitch and I were in the pilot and co-pilot's seats respectively (we had let the mid-upper gunner try his hand at flying but now that we were clear of the most dangerous long-range fighter areas, we thought we could dispense with his 'evasive tactics' – he sure chased the needle of the automatic horizon up and down) when the rear gunner's first shout came over the phones. As there was a five minute warning on the indicators Mitch's reaction wasn't immediate but poor Mac's was. Mitch gave me instructions on how to get the last drop out of the tanks. When one engine was heard to cough and start to gulp for lack of fuel I would cut the throttle right off and then he would switch on another tank and I would shove the throttle right ahead to the gate and gradually throttle back 'till the engines sounded synchronised (two of our rev counters were u/s) and we would proceed on our merry way 'till the next little red light startled us all over again.

About this time Jimmy Guy informed us that Group had just faded out on the wireless. They had received our message all right but we couldn't receive them strongly enough to understand their instructions. The sky was clear now and the moon made that romantic, silvery path on the dappled waters of the Mediterranean. However, we failed to see much beauty in the scenery and embarked on another 'round table conference' about how we would behave when we got to Sicily. To be, or not to be, land on the earth or the seas; wheels up or down; land or bail out. The discussion was quite lively, sensible and at times with a range of humour and all the time little Jimmy kept his distress signals pounding out. I wondered, about now, why I was perspiring so much and put my hand in my hip pocket for a handkerchief and then in my side pocket. I couldn't find a hanky but my hand did feel sticky. When I looked, it was covered in blood and my right leg was pretty well soaked, I showed it to Mitch and he looked me over and pointed to my hip pocket and removed my escape kit, which had been ripped by a couple of bullets. I wasn't suffering and was quite busy so I paid no attention.

Mitch showed me his right flying boot, which had been cut in two at the ankle by three bullets. We had nearly four hours of this highly precarious state of existence and of late had been getting loop bearings to home from Jimmy. Finally, on the horizon, a couple of searchlights came in view, joined by a third, occasionally, to form an aerodrome's tripod. Now the excitement ran high. Friend or foe? We sure didn't know but we did want to change our mode of living. I homed right over the beams and let Jimmy get a reciprocal and a couple of miles out to sea turned around and came back over the 'drome. All the time, I had been trying to get in touch by R/T for instructions but no joy. The first turn around was a right hand one as there were mountains back of the field it was kind of steep for such a novice. The lights below were on and our discussion at the moment was if Art would find a crash landing harder to take than if we dropped him by a static cord. Fate stepped in again, though. Art's morphine had worn off as we approached the aerodrome and in his exuberance, McCabe had imparted the good news to Art that we were safe. Arthur, his valiant spirit supporting his death-cheated body, motioned to occupy the pilot's seat. His face, practically shot in two, was black with caked blood and his right forearm was held on by a few pieces of tendon. [At that time it was not known that a bullet had penetrated his chest. His lower face was a gaping hole where his jaw had been and of course he could not speak.] Who could deny such an indomitable spirit?

As Mitch held the co-pilot's controls I slid out of the seat to help Art into it. I then took over the co-pilot's position as Mitch resumed his watch at the engineer's panel. Art had only the one hand to handle the control column and only by shaking his head could he communicate. Three times, with the crew in crash positions, did he make a let-down to approach land. Twice he shook his head 'No' and had me advance the throttles and roar round again. On the third approach Mitch, highly perturbed, said that he was bailing out if we attempted another circuit as we did not have enough petrol to complete it. Art began to pull back on the controls to go round again. I yelled to go down, that there wasn't enough fuel for another half circuit but he shook his head in the negative and continued to pull back. Quicker than it takes to tell I gave him a thump on the chest to make him let go of the control column and he collapsed completely when I did so. Mitch helped ease him out of the seat and I resumed it again. I'll never erase the look on his face from my memory. By the time I got hold of the controls we were at the point of stalling and only a few hundred feet off the ground. As we were falling off the left wingtip I shoved the controls hard forward and held on as we gained speed towards the desert sands. Just lucky, I guess because as I pulled back the nose came up and we tobogganed in for a wheels-up landing. The aircraft was full of sand dust and cries of joy and congratulations from the two Jimmies and Mac, who had been lying down in their crash positions not knowing of the drama up front for about 15 tense minutes. Needless to say no time was wasted in vacating the premises. Aside from bent propeller tips no damage was visible.

A small Bedford truck full of uniformed men had been bouncing over the sand to meet us and it was with some relief that we noted the shape of the helmets, which confirmed our hopes that we had landed in 'occupied territory'. As the airmen ran towards us, who should I see in the forefront but Sergeant Lapointe who was on my course at Air Observers course at Quebec city. I was quite impressed by the coincidence of this. On reflection I think Art's thinking was impaired by the awful pain he must have been in for he just seemed to ignore the fact that the fuel was not there to keep flying. A subsequent check showed all cross-balancing cocks had been opened and 15 gallons had drained to the starboard wing tip tank. I'm not an expert but I hardly think Mitch was in error in his threat to bail out. Maybe Art was hoping that the faulty undercarriage would correct itself in another circuit – no one knows. We certainly were the object of God's providence though; for if we had landed on the runway we would have been wrapped up like sardines in a can for we found out from the CO that the runway was made of PSP (pierced steel planking). He was quite grateful in fact for his airfield would have been out of use for some days. It was 06.00 hours on Friday the 13th and we had landed at Bone, North Africa, after six hours of hopeful wandering about the sky.

Malcolm Mitcham adds:

We were of course exhilarated at our close escape. Rich helped relieve the tensions in his rich Yorkshire accent: 'Eeh, we've had worse rides on a double-decker bus.'

Art was quickly rushed to the hospital at the base where they had to operate to remove a bullet from his right chest cavity. Likely it was the one which shattered his elbow. We were all checked through by the MO. Mitch and I were the only ones who had been touched and we were sure lucky. Two chips of aluminium were taken from the tip of my nose. A bullet had creased the front of my collarbone and they removed two bullets from my right buttock. An airman later in the day presented me with the safety buckle from my Sutton harness. Two bullets had made direct hits upon it and jammed it in the release position. If I had bailed out I would have fallen completely out of my parachute harness as soon as the 'chute opened. All morning we silently prayed for good news about Art and, at first, he seemed to be holding his own and we were all so thankful. However, I think it was at early evening, word came that he had succumbed. His valiant heart could stand no more and had finally stopped.

Whilst inspecting Arthur Aaron's Stirling Sergeant Doug Smith, on a detachment from 155 MU serving at Bone recovered five or six bullets from the cooling fins of the starboard inner engine and these, on checking over, appeared to be British bullets. This led him to immediately think that the Stirling had not been shot up by an enemy fighter. These bullets were handed over to the Armaments Officer of the station and nothing more was heard of the matter for 40 years. Two days after their crash landing, inspection of the damage to *Oboe* disclosed that a 1,000lb special delay bomb had failed to jettison with the others and remained in its cradle in the bomb bay. If the bomb had torn away from its cradle during the belly landing and exploded no would have known any details of *Oboe*'s last flight, giving rise to the award of the highest decoration for valour.[25]

On 3 November 1943 the *London Gazette* announced that Acting Flight Sergeant Arthur Louis Aaron DFM had been awarded a posthumous VC for action on 13 August 1943. The citation said, 'Had he been content, when grievously wounded, to lie still and conserve his failing strength, he would probably have recovered but he saw it as his duty to exert himself to the utmost, if necessary with his last breath, to ensure that his aircraft and crew did not fall into enemy hands. In appalling conditions he showed the greatest qualities of courage, determination and leadership and, though wounded and dying, he set an example of devotion to duty which has seldom been equalled and never surpassed.' Flight Sergeant Allan W Larden received the Conspicuous Gallantry Medal and the DFM was awarded to Sergeants Malcolm Mitchem and 'Jimmie' Guy.

Turin was hit by 112 Stirlings, 34 Halifaxes and six Lancasters and two Stirlings failed to return.

On 14/15 August one Lancaster was shot down on the raid on Milan and seven were lost on the raid on the same city the night following, mostly to German fighters, which were waiting for the bombers' return over France. Two Lancasters on 467 Squadron at Bottesford were shot down near Chartres. *Y-Yorker* was flown by Wing Commander Cosme Gomm DSO DFC the CO, who was killed. The only member of his crew to survive was Sergeant James Lee, the 20-year-old flight engineer and youngest on the crew. His parachute had been damaged but luckily he landed on a hayrick. He suffered burns and spent the rest of the war in captivity. *F-Freddie* flown by Flight Lieutenant Jack Sullivan was attacked from below by a night fighter 'that came from nowhere'. A magnesium flare was hit and the back of the Lancaster erupted into an inferno. Only Sergeant Ken Harvey the flight engineer, who was virtually blinded by the glare and Flying Officer T H F Entract, the bomb aimer, got out. An eighth Lancaster crashed on return to Scampton, killing five and injuring two on the crew.

On 16/17 August 154 aircraft of 3 and 8 Groups set off for the Fiat works in Turin once more. At Gransden Lodge Flight Lieutenant 'Tony'

Weber on 405 'Vancouver' Squadron RCAF was detailed to act as primary Pathfinder:[26]

It was to be a long trip – eight hours of flying with no second pilot – in my faithful old Lancaster LQ-X, which my ground crew had modified with great enthusiasm in several ways to suit my type of flying. A downward viewing hole had been cut aft of the bomb bay, a modification subsequently adopted by the whole of 405 Squadron. The mid-upper turret had been removed in order to reduce drag. (I was at that time using my mid upper gunner to man the lower viewing hole.) The Perspex panels from the rear turret had been removed – bit draughty but it considerably improved visibility. Many hours had been spent at the factory, hand polishing this Perspex but my gunner just had to see the fighter, which could be homing in on us, before the fighter saw us. Then I had all the tracer bullets removed from the ammo belts. They only showed the enemy how inadequate the range of our 0.303 inch guns was compared to their cannons.

We took-off from Gransden Lodge as the sun was setting, with a full moon rising. Our route took us directly over the City of London, something never risked before. It must have been a grand sight for the battered Londoners, as there were more than 300 of us that night. The display was intended as a morale booster for those on the ground who had suffered so much in the *Blitz*. London had received its first hammering from the *Luftwaffe* on 7 September 1940. We crossed the English coast at Beachy Head and the French coast at Dieppe. Twenty miles east of Paris we set course directly for the Alps, which we crossed near Albertville at 15,000 feet, then on to Lac du Bourget which was clearly visible in the moonlight. This was the point where we were to make a time and direction run into the target. This technique was used in order to avoid being confused by dummy targets at which, the Germans were past masters. On this leg we were dead on time and somewhat surprised to find that Turin was a blaze of activity. Searchlights were scanning the skies and guns were firing away at least five minutes before we were due to be on target. So who was the fool who had got to the target too early? We questioned our timing but there were over four minutes to go to zero hour. We found out later that this was just a show of force to frighten us off. No one had got there ahead of us. It was so different from targets in Germany, which always lay dark and menacing until the first marker went down, then all hell broke loose.

The bulk of the Turin force was made up of just over 100 Stirlings. Flight Lieutenant Robert Megginson's crew on XV Squadron, accompanied by Air Commodore H Kirkpatrick from 3 Group HQ, who had decided to go along for experience, were in one of them, as Sergeant Graham 'Mick' Cullen the wireless operator recalls:

Crossing the South of France, we began to experience trouble with the engines which had started to heat up. Climbing to gain more height to cross the Alps, one of the engines deteriorated to the extent that it seized up completely. It was impossible to maintain height so we meandered our way through the mountains, watching carefully in the light of the full moon for the peaks that towered above us. Having safely negotiated the Alps we finally arrived over the target area, which in our case was a small factory. However, due to low cloud we could not locate the building and so attacked the main target. Owing to our engine problems we bombed at a lower level than the other crews. We unloaded our cargo and left the area as quickly as possible.

Flight Lieutenant Tony Weber continues:

The Fiat factory was duly marked and our return was uneventful until we reached Bayeaux at 13,000 feet. Here we were hit by predicted flak from a large battery of guns. A shell hit our port inner motor, shattering the propeller boss. A prop blade came crashing through the fuselage, taking with it the engineer's panel. We still had an hour's run to base and now with no knowledge of our fuel load in the event of the fuel tanks having been holed, we made for our nearest airfield which was Beaulieu, where we requested an emergency landing. Poor old LQ-X was not handling well. Unknown to us our port tyre was punctured and as we landed we slewed off the runway, folding up the undercarriage which, in turn, caused the 'drome to be closed until our wreck had been dragged away. We were not at all popular at Beaulieu.

Sergeant 'Mick' Cullen on Flight Lieutenant Megginson's crew continues:

The Skipper debated with the rest of the crew as to whether we should carry on and land in North Africa for repairs but it was decided to try and get our VIP passenger back to Mildenhall. Once again we successfully negotiated the valleys through the Alps but this caused a strain on the already overheated engines. As we crossed out over France, a second engine had to be stopped. We were now in an emergency situation. We decided to forget Mildenhall and land at the first available airfield which turned out to be Tangmere on the south coast. Unfortunately, fog had closed our bomber bases in East Anglia and all aircraft were diverted to fighter airfields along the same coastline. As we were preparing to land an aircraft with a strange call sign came on the air requesting priority for an emergency landing, saying he had only two motors going. The runway was cleared and a rather old and battered Stirling bomber with, of course, only two engines going, touched down. Our situation was now critical and as Megginson put *O-Orange* on the runway another engine seized completely. An inspection the following day revealed that two of the engines had completely melted the pistons to the block. We had a couple of days' unexpected holiday while Mildenhall flew down two new engines together with our ground crew to fit them. We then all returned to base aboard BK818.

Mick Cullen was looking forward to getting back to Mildenhall but his welcome was a cold one. Being young and not very thoughtful he had, in the excitement of the situation, neglected to notify his fiancée Brenda that he was all right. Brenda Jaggard, a local girl from Beck Row, was originally a waitress at the 'Bird In The Hand' at Mildenhall. Later she became a barmaid. A friendship grew between Brenda and her New Zealand sergeant, which came to the attention of George Ashley, the landlord of the 'Bird'. In due time he began to allow Mick Cullen and the crew a little credit when they were short of funds.

By early August Warrant Officer Warren 'Pluto' Wilson's crew on 467 Squadron RAAF had completed 24 operational sorties since arriving at Bottesford on 10 March and the crew were known as one of the old sweats on the Squadron. Together with other experienced crews, they were taken off routine bombing trips and became engaged in special low level time and distance bombing practice over the Wainfleet bombing range near Skegness. At first they thought it strange that it was the most experienced crews who were degraded in this way but as the results were being scrutinised by senior staff from Group Headquarters, headed by the Air Officer Commanding (AOC) AVM the Honourable Sir Ralph Cochrane KBE CB AFC, they soon realised that there was some hidden purpose behind this special training.

Born in 1895 as the youngest son of the 1st Baron Cochrane of Cults, Cochrane had joined the Royal Navy in 1912 before transferring to the RAF in 1918. He had served extensively in the Middle East during the early 1920s, being mentioned in despatches for operations in Kurdistan in 1923. His CO was Squadron Leader Arthur T Harris AFC, while his fellow flight commander was Robert Saundby. A few days later Cochrane visited Bottesford and told the selected aircrews that they must do better and reduce the number of bombing errors. At this stage they had no idea what was going on but there were rumours circulating around the camp that they might be going to attack the German dams again[27] or maybe the Dortmund-Ems Canal.

At Wyton on 16 August, together with his crew, Group Captain John Searby studied a model of the target together with Don Bennett and his staff. 'This model, beautifully constructed,' recalls the CO of 83 Squadron, 'was the result of taking photographs from our reconnaissance aircraft some time earlier. We endeavoured to memorize certain features, which lay near the three aiming points and discussed with Bennett the essential features. We did not know any more than that this was an experimental station.'

In fact the Allies had been acquiring evidence that Peenemünde was the site of advanced weapon research, especially rocket technology and by late June 1943 the War Cabinet had scheduled Peenemünde as a high priority target for Bomber Command. 'Bomber' Harris had requested a delay until the longer nights of late summer would make his aircraft less vulnerable. A force of 596 heavies, including for the first time, Lancasters of 6 (Canadian) Group, would be dispatched. Fifty-four Stirlings of 3 Group would also make the trip. One of these was *Z-Zebra* on 214 Squadron at Chedburgh flown by John Verrall. His navigator, Pilot Officer Jack Furner recalls:

> Peenemünde was to be our last but two, although we didn't know that at the time. We were certainly reaching the slightly twitchy stage in the 20s. The briefing was highly unusual. Not a major city with an aiming point somewhere in the centre designed to take out as much industry as possible but a strange place on the Baltic coast which none of us had ever heard of. 'It's a secret place where new experimental equipments are being developed', the briefers said. There were a number of discrete aiming points (another unusual feature): ours was a particular part of the Experimental Establishment and other Group(s) would be targeting the actual living quarters of the scientists involved. We were to go in over the target at a much lower level than usual – at about 8,000 feet. And there was moonlight. 'But there are only light flak defences' the briefers said. The route looked nice – a quick dash across Denmark, through the Baltic and turn on to the target from a headland to the north of it, just a few miles from coast. A snip, we thought.

At the briefing at Wyton the Pathfinder crews were told that if they did not knock out this important target that night it would be laid on again the next night and every night until the job was done. John Searby recalled:

> To return to a target on successive nights might mean stiffer defences and heavier casualties. Once the element of surprise was gone no one could say how much effort and how many lives might be required to take out Peenemünde ... Having shown our hands with a first abortive attempt, the *Nazis* would take steps to move out much vital

equipment together with the scientists and technicians. In short, the moment would have passed and might never occur again.

From the low dais in front of the large map of Europe with its coloured tapes and pins, which marked the heavily defended areas of occupied territory, I watched the faces of my crews. They were impressed by the urgency but not worried, for the job would be done to the best of their ability. I caught the eye of Brian Slade, veteran Pathfinder captain at 21 years of age and he grinned; he was all for it. Against the background of Essen, Berlin, Hamburg, Munich, Cologne and similar bloodbaths Peenemünde did not, at this stage, make much impression. In fact, the reactions of the crews were one of relief at the prospect of a sortie to northern Germany. The only real hazard lay in the long penetration under conditions of full moonlight with the possible increased fighter activity. No one had heard of this insignificant pimple sticking out of Pomerania and there was nothing humdrum about the operation; hence Brian's smile. Alas, he would be lost over the 'Big City' in five short days.[28]

The plan for the night's operations was well-conceived and in the course of the briefing I acquainted the crews with the fact that Mosquitoes of 139 Squadron would make a 'spoof' attack on Berlin with the object of holding the German night fighters in that region, or at least a proportion of them. By the time the ruse was discovered many fighters would require refuelling before proceeding to the scene of the actual attack. Clearly we could not hope for this plan to do more than delay the opposition but if it worked long enough to enable the Pathfinders and following waves of heavy bombers to make an effective start on the destruction of the target much would have been accomplished. The full moon was at once a friend and an enemy. It would help the bombers initially but on balance it would serve the cause of the German night fighters even more: with so much light there would be scope for the freelance or 'catseye' fighter and this would greatly increase the strength of the opposition.

Flight Lieutenant Tony Weber's crew had just returned to Gransden Lodge after putting down at Beaulieu following the exhausting raid over the Alps to the Fiat Works on 16/17 August when to their dismay they were confronted with the news that they were on ops again that night:

It was after lunch before a lift was arranged to get us back to base. We were dead tired, not having seen a bed for 36 hours. My crew and I were able to snatch a couple of hours' sleep before the briefing. Little did we know that we were in for another eight hour trip again that very night. The mood of the crews at briefing that afternoon was far from good. Had they all gone mad at Air Ministry? Didn't they know how tired we all were, especially our crew who had been shot up and crash-landed away from base? The MO's solution was to dish out extra doses of caffeine tablets for those who needed them. The briefing was given by our AOC, Don Bennett. He explained the urgency and importance of the mission. How Hitler's men were developing a sinister weapon at Peenemünde and production details would be ready for delivery to the contractors soon. Group Captain Searby was to be the Master Bomber of the raid and would be in contact with all of us over our radio telephones.

After briefing, my crew had hot baths and a good meal, after which, we were feeling better again and ready for take-off. *D-Donald* was to be our replacement aircraft. On their own initiative our faithful ground crew had cut out a downward viewing hole for the mid upper gunner and had fitted this new station with intercom, oxygen and hold down straps and a plug for his heated suit. They well knew that I would be at a loss without our blind spot being covered. They had even found time to fit the navigator and wireless operator with lap straps. These straps were necessary since my defence against a fighter taking aim at us from below (which was where all attacks came from at this stage) involved negative gravity, by diving straight down at him and praying that he would take the necessary evasive action in time to avoid a collision. This was the only defence I had from such an attack and it gave the fighter pilot no time to fire his cannons if he was to avoid a collision. I had used this method of defence on several occasions and had never known a Jerry to come back for a second dose. However, the first time I used it, it was a disaster for my navigator who finished up on the roof with all his charts, etc, lost.

Flying Officer Bill Day's Stirling crew on 90 Squadron at Tuddenham had also flown on the operation to the Fiat Works and they too were ready for a few days' rest but their Flight Commander, Squadron Leader Freeman told them, 'Sorry to tell you lads but you are ON tonight; it's another maximum effort. Grab a bite to eat and report for briefing in just over an hour's time – you will see all the details on the notice board.'

Sergeant William Alexander Wilkie Wanless RCAF, a Halifax rear gunner on 76 Squadron at Holme-on-Spalding Moor, recalls:

This was the only briefing I ever went to when the briefing hut was surrounded by Service Police. We had to go to the door with the crew and show our identification with our pilot. We were told that if a word leaked out about the target we wouldn't go that night and the source would be summarily executed. So we paid attention; we said that this had got to be a 'biggie'. We were also told that if we didn't get it that night we would be going back every night; tonight they didn't expect you but from then on they will expect you but you will still have to go back.

Sergeant Ron James, Bill Day's mid-upper gunner, adds:

From all the activity that was going on around us we knew that this was something out of the ordinary: an Air Commodore from 3 Group HQ, SPs guarding the approaches to the Briefing Room and the 'erks' [ground crew] scurrying around like blue-arsed flies – what had they cooked up for us this time? As the wall map was exposed a gasp went up – Berlin? No, someplace on the Baltic – but there is no town there! The Group Captain got to his feet and began. 'I realize after yesterday how tired you must be but tonight's target must be totally destroyed. The Germans have a factory here,' pointing to the map, 'that is producing night fighter equipment, which is so sophisticated that if it is put into general use we could lose the air war. It is so important that not only we are going to bomb it to extinction but we are going to get the scientists too. And that will be your job. Our Group will go in first, flying much lower than usual and carrying armour piercing bombs. You bomb aimers will be given detailed maps of the living quarters that have to be attacked. PFF will mark the target as normal but in this case a master bomber is to be used on a German target for the first time. He will talk you through the raid on an open frequency so there should be no slip ups. If any crew does not feel up to the task after a sleepless night I quite understand and they can see me after briefing but I have to warn you that if this target is not obliterated tonight, you will have to go again tomorrow and every succeeding night until the job is done – I know that I can rely on you and that you will not let me down. Good luck to you all!'

Of course no crew bothered to see the Groupie afterwards. The briefing continued, with the Intelligence Officer telling us that only twelve light calibre AA guns protected the site and, as we would be operating in full moonlight, the target would be easily discernible. Someone asked. 'What is the name of this place we are going to?' He replied – 'Peenemünde'.[29]

Sergeant Charles Cawthorne on Warren 'Pluto' Wilson's crew on 467 Squadron RAAF at Bottesford, wrote:

On 17 August, all speculation ended when we were detailed to attend the pre-operation briefing and it immediately became apparent that something very special had been planned. Security around the operations block was unusually severe with RAF Police in far greater numbers than usual. There was a great buzz of speculation amongst the crews as we entered the large briefing room. The assembled crews were brought to attention as the station's senior officers entered the room accompanied by a very senior officer from Group Headquarters. The curtain over the map of western Europe was pulled back to reveal red route marker tapes leading to a small target called Peenemünde on the German Baltic coast sited between Rostock and Stettin. I wondered what all the fuss was about because we had never heard of this little place called Peenemünde and the Squadron had attacked both Rostock and Stettin quite recently.

Pilot Officer Frank Dixon RAAF was the only Australian on the otherwise all-sergeant crew on JA901 *N-Nuts*, better known on the Squadron as *Nuts To The Nazis*. Many Aussies, and Dixon was no exception, did not like the way promotion was decided. As Dixon saw it, the system did not favour 'the son of a labouring man from the bush ... but again later in the war we might have confounded them on that one.' Dixon's navigator was E W Dickson, an Englishman. Both men had had 'a good look at each other' on parade at Litchfield when Dixon thought that he heard his name called, but it was the navigator with the same name and different spelling. They later introduced themselves and 'crewed up'. Dixon would often go either to Dickson's home or the navigator's aunt's 'little country pub' in Oxfordshire where they could 'kick up their heels'. Now Peenemünde beckoned. When Dixon had flown his 'second dickey trip' on another Baltic target, at Stettin, he 'had just thought that there was no way you could possibly fly an aeroplane through all that stuff that you could see bursting out there.' And it had seemed that 'there was no way in all the darkness that the best navigator in the world was ever going to find the target.'[30]

Charles Cawthorne continues:

The briefing was opened with a statement from the visiting officer from Group. He said. 'Peenemünde is a German military research establishment whose scientists are working on new Radio Detection Finding (RDF) equipment as a countermeasure against our night bombers and therefore is a very important target that has to be destroyed at all costs. That is why the operation has been planned to take place in full moon flying conditions and must be carried out at low level. It is imperative that this target is destroyed and I must warn you that if you are unsuccessful tonight, then the Squadron will have to return tomorrow night and on successive nights until complete destruction is achieved'. It was only later when the V-2 rockets started to fall on London in September 1944 that we in Bomber Command and the general public learned the true purpose of this raid i.e. the destruction of the secret V-2 rocket research and production facility.

The Squadron Commander then said it was to be a precision attack on three main target areas. The first and second waves would attack on Path Finder TIs but 5 Group squadrons were to bomb last in the third wave and would use the new time and distance bombing method as the target would probably be obscured by smoke from the first and second wave attacks.[31] The objective for the third wave aircraft was the Experimental Works, which consisted of over 70 small buildings. This complex contained vital development data and equipment and the accommodation block, which housed General Dornberger the V-2 Project Director and his Deputy, Wernher von Braun. We did not learn this until much later. The crews were then informed that a Master Bomber, Group Captain John Searby commanding 83 Path Finder Squadron would control all phases of the raid by circling the target area and if necessary give instructions over the VHF radio to the Path Finders should the TIs need re-positioning or to stop main force creep-back developing. As we listened to the briefing it became clear that this operation was a formidable task but we were determined to succeed as none of us fancied our chances of survival if we had to return again the next night.[32]

Squadron Leader Alfred Sydney 'Ray' Raphael DFC, a 27-year-old Londoner who was 'holding the fort' as 467 Squadron Commander after the loss of Wing Commander Gomm only two nights before, had a premonition that he would not return. During the briefing he became extremely agitated about fighter concentrations along the chosen route and found it impossible to hide his discomfort. Intelligence Officer Marie Cooper recalled that: 'He emerged from briefing with his usual calm gone, muttering "Too many fighters on that route!" When the rest came out they all looked a bit ruffled and one chap said; "He got more than a bit worked up about the fighters." '[33]

At Wyton John Searby saw his crews away and then he and his crew went out to W-William standing waiting on the far side of 'B' Flight dispersal area. 'It was a fine evening, warm and pleasant, the sun about to set,' recalled Searby 'and the long twilight beginning a time for the river pub down at the 'Ferry' where 83 Squadron foregathered.' Searby supposed that 'there would never again be gatherings quite like that and to recapture the atmosphere was impossible. All was warmth and friendliness with much laughter ...' W-William was ready. They were ready. Their part was to control the bombing over the full 45 minutes of the Bomber Command attack and 'stay with it'. At the prearranged hour Frank Forster pressed the starter buttons and the four Merlins came to life. 'We would set out five minutes ahead of the others in order to have time to make a run across the targets and verify the landmarks we had noted the day previously.'

At Gransden Lodge Tony Weber took off as the sun was setting:

We had not been given time for the usual pre-op test flight. We were glad for the twilight take-off. With our full all-up weight and as there was no wind that night we would need every inch of the runway. I do believe that it was only due to the curvature of the earth that *D-Donald* got off the ground at all. As usual there was to be total radio silence and we were mustered for take-off by means of lights.

On 106 Squadron at Syerston as senior crew, Pilot Officer Robbie Robertson's special task was, after dropping bombs from low level, to fly over the target several times, taking a film by a camera fastened beneath their Lancaster. But their sortie did not go according to plan, as Geoffrey Willatt recalls:

As we taxied out to the end of the runway and started to surge forward, the green light signal turned to red, prompted by a bystander bravely rushing into our path and waving his arms, because one of our engines was pouring out oil and about to catch fire. That night there was no replacement aircraft available, so we didn't take part in a trip, which caused many losses to aircraft and crew in our squadron but was a raid of vital importance at that time in the war. By this time our crew and indeed everyone, was getting nervous and edgy with mental strain and the fatigue of doing many dangerous raids in quick succession and the constant thought that probably the next trip would be our last. I am sure this feeling is also felt by soldiers and sailors but our strange life was very disturbing, because we were, for several hours, in extreme danger, followed by several hours in perfect safety and comfort, or even at home. However, here we were and it had to be done.

Charles Cawthorne recalls:

At 21.30 hours our Aussie Skipper turned our heavily laden Lanc onto the main runway and once the aircraft was lined up he slowly opened the throttles while I watched the needles swing round in the boost and rev gauges. At the same time my left hand followed the Skipper's right as he pushed forward the throttle levers. As the aircraft gained speed the navigator called out the indicated air speed (IAS) over the intercom. With full rudder control and all four engines pulling, the Skipper called for me to take over the throttle levers and push them through the gate for maximum power. Moments later with gauges showing 3,000 rpm with +14lb/square inch boost, the aircraft reached a speed of 100 knots IAS and took off into a cloud-less summer evening sky. With a positive rate of climb established the Skipper called for the undercarriage to be raised and engines set to a climbing power of 2,850 rpm with +9lb/square inch boost. This was quickly followed by a series of flap adjustments and once the airframe was clean our Lancaster PO-F *Freddie* climbed away at 155 knots to join the third wave of the bomber stream off the north Lincolnshire coast. To see scores of heavy bombers assembling in bright moonlight over the North Sea was quite an exhilarating experience. Usually we carried out ops on dark moon-less nights and the only indication other aircraft were around was when we ran through prop wash turbulence or occasionally we saw the red glow from aircraft engine exhausts.

At 23.35 hours we crossed the Danish coast twelve miles north of the island of Sylt and from our operational height of 18,000 feet I could clearly see small villages and farm houses in the brightly lit countryside. Forty minutes later we were flying over the Baltic and the moonlight presented an eerie picture as numerous islands were clearly outlined against the sea. At this juncture we were flying south-east at 8,000 feet some twenty miles off shore, midway between Rostock and Stettin. In the nose of the aircraft our Aussie bomb aimer, Swill Campbell, was busy map reading and called over the intercom that we were approaching the headland of Arkona on the north-eastern tip of the island of Rügen. We were now only 40 miles from the target and the Skipper turned south to follow the coastline that led directly to Peenemünde.

Flight Lieutenant Tony Weber continues:

We crossed the Dutch coast at Alkmaar at 15,000 feet still on full climb power. How I missed our own LQ-X, which would have been at 17,000 feet by now with the power setting reduced to fast cruise, 2,400 rpm at 4lbs boost. As it was we were still at 2,600 rpm at 6lbs boost, giving a rich mixture and a high rate of fuel consumption. All went well, there was no cloud cover and the moon was full. We set the Sky Marker just north of Osnabrück. This type of marker floated in the air on a parachute for several minutes and was set in place to serve as a route marker for the main force. This was necessary to avoid stragglers and to try to saturate the defences. A few minutes later, when we were between Bremen and Hannover, Clair Nutting our rear gunner (*Arse-end Charlie*) called the warning 'Fighter! Fighter!' Thanks to the ground crew having removed the Perspex from this aircraft, Clair had spotted the fighter while he was still homing in on us. I throttled back, set the revs to the maximum 3,000 rpm and lowered 10° of flap. This rapidly reduced our speed and gave better manoeuvrability. Clair gave a non-stop commentary on the position of the fighter, which was soon picked up as a Messerschmitt. Cradock took up the commentary before our assailant, who was attempting to fly about 200 feet directly below us, was lost to view by the rear gunner. Cradock reported, 'Enemy firing!' but Nutting corrected this to be only '*Back* firing!' which meant that the enemy fighter had seen us and slammed his throttles closed in an attempt to match our speed. In so doing he had caused a weak mixture backfiring. As yet we had given no indication that we had seen the fighter which was rapidly closing in to firing position. We had no guns to bring to bear; now was the time for stick full forward. At negative gravity the motors cut out, the exhaust flames extinguished and we all fervently prayed that Jerry would use all his skills to avoid us as we came straight down onto him. We do not know by how much we missed him but we never saw him again. He no doubt had a tale to tell when he got back to the mess.

Ian Hewitt, our navigator (who was with Don Bennett on the ill-fated raid on the *Tirpitz* in Norway in April 1942, when they were shot down and escaped on foot through the freezing snow via Sweden) was rather upset at the disturbance as the tools of his trade were scattered all over the place. On getting his act together again he informed us that we were running three minutes late. Due to the poor performance of the aircraft we had used up precious spare time and would have to cut corners and head straight for the target. By then we were close to Stendal. We only hoped that this diversion would not reveal the true target but if we were to get there on time, which was the name of the game, we had no alternative. Oh, how I missed our old Lanc! The main force was to open the attack on each marked position with concrete piercing bombs, followed by anti-personnel bombs. The route chosen was to make it look as if Berlin would again be the target for the night. We were to fly straight for Berlin, where Mosquitoes would go in ahead and drop target indicators. On reaching the outskirts of the city we were to turn north and head for Peenemünde. It was hoped that this would get the German fighters off the ground too soon, in defence of the wrong target. Fortunately for us this ruse worked, as some of us were to spend more than 20 minutes over the real target area, which had to be moved three times during the raid. Now we were on our own again and ran the risk of being singled out for special treatment.

In the moonlight John Searby could see the whitewashed cottages on the southern tip of Langeland. The exhaust stubs of the Merlins glowed red and his crew felt 'pretty well naked'. Many eyes were watching them and he realised that his aircraft must stick out like a sore thumb since they were ahead of the main body by several minutes. On approach to the research station, Scrivener, John Searby's navigator informed his Skipper to prepare for a course change:

Five minutes to Rügen Island when we alter course to one-seven-oh degrees. To my disappointment I observed a sheet of cloud ahead but on closer inspection it proved to be higher than at first estimated and I could fly beneath it easily, keeping the island in sight. Shortly after this we were over the tip of Usedom on which, Peenemünde was located. In the bright moonlight we flew close to the objective and Ross, Forster, Scrivener and I took a close look at that which so far we had only seen as a model. It was all there – the airfield at the tip and the development station spreading along the coast on the east side. We ran directly down the line of the buildings and checked off one by one the important features. Hundreds of smoke canisters were commencing to belch out fumes and the wind from off the sea is carrying the smoke across the target area. That could be serious. In succession we passed over the three aiming points: the development factory, the rocket assembly plant and the large living site where the German workers and technical staffs were housed. 'Light flak opening up Skipper,' from Ross my bomb aimer. The green and red shells shot past the aircraft and we turned out to sea where in the moonlight I observed two ships anchored. As we neared them they opened up with both light and heavy flak but the shooting was poor and the aircraft was in no danger at present. We pulled away to the north and stood off a short distance from the coast. Within two minutes to go before 'H' hour, when the heavy bombing would commence, we waited for the preliminary marking of the target to begin.

Tony Weber arrived over the target on time and he heard *Toffee One* calling up and telling them to make their first run in:

How relieved I was to hear Group Captain Searby the Master Bomber call up. In the event of *Toffee One* not turning up, I was third in line, with the call sign *Candy*. (I cannot remember who *Toffee Two* was). There was no enemy action to be seen. They had not defended the place as it would have given away its real importance. A smoke screen was soon set off but as we were to use the lighthouse to the northwest of the target as the aiming point with the bomb sight set to give a known overshoot, it did not bother us. We were to use this as a datum point for a bombing run at a precise heading and speed, with a false height set on the bomb sight. This would result in an anticipated overshoot, hopefully placing the markers on the target. It was our duty to mark the three aiming points at set times but because Peenemünde from the air was just another airfield, this was not to be an ordinary marking exercise. We flew over the lighthouse on a reciprocal course and then made a hairclip turn back over the lighthouse to drop the first marker. For the first time we were using the much improved marker bomb known as the 'Red Spot Fire', which burst at 3,000 feet and burnt on the ground as a vivid crimson fire for about ten minutes. Its appearance was easy to recognise and difficult to simulate. It cascaded to the ground in an unmistakable manner and became known as the *Christmas Tree Marker*. The procedure was repeated three times at different settings, all of which proved most accurate.

John Searby continues:

Suddenly, the area was lit up by brilliant light from the flares as the first wave of Pathfinders passed over and red target indicators dropped in dazzling cascade to the ground. Ross had his eyes glued to the aiming point and startled us all with a shout that their first markers had fallen to the south by more than a mile but in the same instant another clutch of red markers fell almost an equal distance to the north and a yellow marker, most important of all, fell between the two, virtually on the mark … backed up at once by the green target indicators. Immediately, I broadcast to the bombers approaching the target and instructed them to bomb the green markers which we judged to be accurate. We made another turn out to sea and the flak ships had another go at us but it was not their night and we passed round in a circle for another run across the aiming point.

By now the area was beginning to assume the familiar spectacle of a target under massive attack: bursting bombs, masses of billowing smoke through which the sliding beams of the searchlights crossed and re-crossed. The red bursts from heavy anti-aircraft mingled with it all and yet we could not say that the defences were anything but light in character. This happy situation continued for 20 minutes until the second aiming point, the actual rocket factory, was under heavy bombardment. Because the target area was rapidly becoming a veritable inferno in which it became increasingly difficult to identify the various features, we flew lower on our next orbit and to my horror the gunners informed me that they had seen large 4,000lb bombs falling past our aircraft. This was most alarming but was to be expected since many bombers were flying well above the height at which we were orbiting. Curiously enough, this simple fact had quite escaped notice when considering how best to do our job and yet it was the most obvious one. The possibility of our being walloped by a passing 'blockbuster' was more frightening than anything the enemy could do.

Sergeant Ron James continues:

It was water nearly all the way: across the North Sea, then south of Esbjerg in Denmark and along the shores of the Baltic. Surprisingly even flying in perfect conditions some of our crews managed to stray over the defended areas of Lübeck and Rostock and were given a hot reception at both places. We arrived early at Rügen Island north of Usedom, a designated turning point for the run-in to the target and although PFF had not yet put down their markers, it was rapidly approaching H-Hour. Bill decided to press on, expecting the markers to be released before we came into bombing range. What happened was that we overshot Peenemünde and the TIs went down behind us. Apart from circling to get back into the 'stream', a dangerous manoeuvre in this situation, it also meant that we would be late in arriving. Bill informed us that he was going back on a reciprocal course and would fly below the incoming bombers to avoid a head on collision. Down we went to about 2,500 feet and back into the fray. That run-in was perilous in the extreme. There was a mass of machines concentrated above over a very small target and despite the bombs whistling down – a situation which we were quickly coming to terms with – the explosions from the ground tossed us around like a cork. Meanwhile, the Germans had found a few score guns to supplement those twelve we had been led to expect. They didn't have to aim; just hosepipe straight up. One Halifax, which must have overshot too, was keeping us company barely thirty yards away. He received a direct hit and dived into the ground; but our luck held and we came through without a scratch.

Flight Lieutenant Tony Weber again:

Bombing on the marker by the main force was more accurate than usual, no doubt due to the absence of heavy flak. The second and third marker runs went as planned and we had not as yet been molested by fighters. It was another very long trip as we were routed out of the target north around Denmark and back over the North Sea in an attempt to avoid the night fighters. However, this ruse did not work. By the time the raid was over the fighters had refuelled and gave chase. I wonder how many of our gunners were asleep when they were attacked on the return journey. Many of them had not slept for over two days.

Sergeant Ron James adds:

The Mosquitoes over Berlin did a grand job, by drawing off the enemy fighters. We in the first wave made good our escape but, once they [the night fighters] realized that Peenemünde was the target;

they arrived in time to intercept the following groups. They pursued us along the Baltic and combats occurred right up to the North Sea. Due to the moonlight conditions they had a field day and forty-four bombers were lost, twelve of which I saw shot down.

Wilkie Wanless and the crew of their Halifax were in the first wave:

Before we had been bombing at 16,000 feet with the Halifax but Peenemünde was 4,000 feet. If you were shot down at 4,000 or 5,000 feet your chances of getting out were slim. It was the only low level I would ever be on and we were there before there were any markers. Our navigator had a movie camera to take pictures for the RAF Film unit. We kept flying back and forth over the target and the navigator kept saying, 'I think the damn thing's working now; do another run.' This was just terribly nerve-wracking. The fighters had all been decoyed to Berlin, which was fine for the first wave or two but then the Germans caught on that it wasn't Berlin and the fighters refuelled. The ones that had the range headed for Peenemünde. They shot down a lot of aircraft from the Canadian Group in the last wave.

Charles Cawthorne continues:

Approaching the target we could see the raid ahead progressing as the first and second wave aircraft bombed the red and green TIs laid down by the Path Finders and from our position at the rear of the bomber stream there appeared to be little enemy opposition with only moderate light flak and few searchlights. Over our VHF radio set we heard the calm voice of Group Captain Searby assuring the third wave crews that the raid was progressing in a satisfactory way and to standby for further orders. A few minutes later at 00.42 hours the Master Bomber ordered the Lancasters of 5 Group to commence their timed bombing runs from the designated starting point at the southern tip of the island. At this point during every bombing raid, aircraft became particularly vulnerable to flak or night fighter attack and on this occasion the seven mile bombing run seemed endless as we frantically searched the crowded sky for the enemy and to avoid a collision with a friendly aircraft. At last, our bomb aimer announced 'Bombs gone' and the aircraft wobbled as it was relieved of its heavy load. The Skipper held the same course until the aiming point photograph had been taken and then much to the relief of everyone on board turned back over the sea to start our journey home.

As we left the immediate target area we felt elated that our outward flight had been uneventful and we had made a successful bombing run but as we commenced our return journey we became

aware of increased enemy activity in our vicinity as burning aircraft began to fallout of the sky at an alarming rate. It seemed as if
the third wave of the bomber stream was being attacked by a huge
armada of enemy night fighters who were taking full advantage of
the bright moonlight conditions. Later, we found out that the German
night fighters had been successfully lured away from the Peenemünde
area by a diversionary raid on Berlin. However, once the German
fighter controllers realised that this was not the main target, the night
fighters were ordered to pursue the bombers over Peenemünde.

The German ground controllers were fooled into thinking the bombers
were headed for Stettin and the 'spoof' by eight Mosquitoes of 139
Squadron led by Group Captain 'Slosher' Slee aiming for Berlin drew
more fighters away from the Peenemünde force. However, 40 Lancasters,
Halifaxes and Stirlings[34] were shot down. In the wild mêlée over the
target, *Nachtjagd* claimed 33 aircraft with total claims from the Peenemünde
force amounting to 38 victories. One of the victors was *Hauptmann* Peter
Spoden of 5./NJG5 who would become one of Germany's leading *Tame
Boar* pilots. He had trained for 27 months to be a fighter pilot and in
his first attack on the night of the Hamburg raid, 27/28 July, he could
not find anyone in his Bf 110 because of *Window*. Now it seemed that
he might be frustrated again by the enemy's clever spoofing tactics, as he
recalls:

> The British tricked us. There were 200 fighters over Berlin being held
> by six Mosquitoes. I was there. Then we saw that it was on fire in the
> north but it wasn't Berlin. They had ordered us to stay in Berlin and
> it had started to burn in Peenemünde. We flew there very fast. I shot
> one down.[35] At that particular moment you do not think about the
> other crew. You have to shoot between the two engines and we had
> been trained to do that. It was said, 'Shoot between the two engines,
> it will go on fire and they will have a chance to bail out.' So I shot
> between the two engines to give them a chance to bail out. When
> I shot somebody down I was so excited. I landed and went to the
> crash site and spoke to the only survivor [Sergeant W Sparks, bomb
> aimer]. I felt free, as if I had achieved what I had been trained to do.
> How can I explain how I felt? Like an avenger for Essen.[36]

A deadly new weapons system was introduced on this night. Two crews
flying Bf 110s fitted with *Schräge Musik* ('Oblique Music')[37]found the
bomber stream and destroyed six bombers.

This device, invented by an armourer, Paul Mahle of II./NJG5, comprised two 20mm MG FF cannon mounted behind the rear cockpit
bulkhead of the Bf 110 and Ju 88 night fighters and was arranged to fire
forwards and upwards at an angle of between 70 and 80°. *Unteroffizier*

Walter Hölker of 5./NJG5 shot down two bombers before his aircraft was hit by return fire from a Lancaster rear gunner who exploded some portable oxygen bottles. The German pilot was hit by three pieces of metal in the back of his head and about forty in the rest of his body. *Leutnant* Peter Erhardt destroyed four bombers. Towards midnight thirteen II./NJG1 crews took off from St-Trond for the *Gruppe's* first *Wild Boar* operation of the war. They returned with claims for thirteen victories, mainly over Peenemünde, nine of which were consequently confirmed by the *Reichsluftfahrtministerium* (RLM or *Reich* Air Ministry). These included five *Schräge Musik* kills by *Leutnant* Dieter Musset and his *Bordfunker Obergefreiter* Helmut Hafner of the 5th *Staffel*, flying a Bf 110G-4,[38], and which were their first (and last) victories of the war. Musset recalled:

From the Berlin area I observed enemy activity to the north. I promptly flew in that direction and positioned myself at a height of 14,000 feet over the enemy's target. Against the glow of the burning target I saw from above numerous enemy aircraft flying over it in close formations of seven or eight. I went down and placed myself at 11,000 feet behind one enemy formation. I attacked one enemy with two bursts of fire from direct astern, registering good strikes on the port inner engine, which at once caught fire. The E/A tipped over to port and went down. Enemy counter-fire from rear gunner was ineffective. Owing to an immediate second engagement, I could only follow E/A's descent on fire as far as a layer of mist. I then attacked a four-engined E/A at 8,500 feet from astern, range 30–40 yards. E/A at once burned brightly in both wings and fuselage. I observed it till it crashed in flames. At 01.50 I was already in position to attack another E/A from slightly above, starboard astern and range 60–70 yards. Strikes were seen in the starboard wing and E/A blew up. I observed burning fragments hit the ground at 01.52. Five minutes later I attacked another four-engined E/A at 6,000 feet from 100 yards astern. Heavy counter-fire from rear gunner scored hits in both wings of own aircraft. Burning brightly in both wings and fuselage E/A went into a vertical dive. After its crash I saw the wreckage burning. At 01.59 I was ready to attack again. E/A took strong evasive action by weaving. Enemy counter-fire was ineffective. While E/A was in a turn to port, I got in a burst from port astern and range 40–50 yards that set the port wing on fire. E/A plunged to the ground burning brightly and I observed the crash at 02.01.

A few minutes later I attacked another E/A that took violent evasive action by weaving. On the first attack my cannon went out of action owing to burst barrels. I then made three further attacks with machine guns and observed good strikes on starboard wing without setting it on fire. Owing to heavy counter-fire from rear gunner, I suffered hits in port engine. At the same time I came under attack from enemy aircraft on the starboard beam, which wounded my wireless operator in the left shoulder and set my port engine on fire. I broke off the action, cut my port engine and flew westwards away from target area. No radio contact with the ground could be established. As I was constantly losing height, at 6,000 feet I gave the order to bail out. As I did so, I struck the tail unit with both legs, thereby breaking my right thigh and left shin-bone. After normal landings by parachute my *Bordfunker* and I were taken to the reserve military hospital at Güstrow.[39]

Sam Hall, a Path Finder navigator on 83 Squadron, recalled:

After we had bombed the mid-upper gunner said, 'There's a fighter coming in – it's got a Lanc; it's got another; it's got another.' Three Lancasters were going down in flames. You didn't waste too much time thinking about it. So many things were going on – all sorts of lights in the sky and flashes on the ground. I knew the first Master Bomber on the raid. When he got back to Wyton he was still bathed in perspiration. He'd had to fly above the target for the whole extent of the raid.

One of the German pilots ordered off to intercept bombers on the return flight was *Oberleutnant* Hans Meissner, flying a Messerschmitt 110 of II./NJG3 at Schleswig. Shortly after 02.00 hours on the morning of the 18th he was directed to the area of radar station *Ameise* in south-eastern Denmark. Meissner recalled:

Unfortunately the R/T was so badly jammed that we could make no contact with *Ameise* and could get no information. Meanwhile we were at 2,500 metres as we approached the Apenrader Bight. My *Bordschutze* picked up several contacts on the *Lichtenstein*, which passed across the tubes very quickly, so at first we took it to be *Window*. As the contacts were below I went into a descent and picked up speed. At 02.54 hours I saw the first Lancaster at about 2,000 metres, flying directly in front of me on a westerly heading.' [Meissner's quarry was the 49 Squadron Lancaster at Fiskerton flown by Pilot Officer Thomas Edwin Tomlin DFC]. I closed in and opened fire from about 150 metres, somewhat to the right and 50 metres below. The No. 3 engine caught fire. As I broke away below him, return fire from the rear gunner passed to my left. From the beginning of the engagement both aircraft were illuminated from time to time by our own searchlights. The Lancaster pilot attempted to escape in a diving turn to the left, but as he did so he came into my sights and I was able to give him a short burst. He went down at 02.56 hours, crashing a few hundred yards from Ufer. [All seven crew were killed].

I immediately set off eastwards, obtained another contact from my radar operator, descended and saw a Lancaster [another 49 Squadron aircraft, which was piloted by Flying Officer Harry John Randall] flying directly above me on a westerly heading. I fired from more or less the same position, again at No. 3 engine. He went into a dive and crashed at 03.01 hours, on the shore of the Apenrader Bight. [All of the Lancaster crew were killed.] After that I headed north and my radar operator soon picked up yet another contact. I was able to make out the aircraft about 1,200 metres away. My first attack was the same as the others, from 150 metres range, a little to the right and 50 metres below. As the No. 3 engine caught fire we were held by a searchlight and in spite of the moonlight the effect was dazzling. The Lancaster pilot pulled his aircraft up (perhaps he was also dazzled, or maybe he wanted to reduce speed quickly so that I would over-shoot or they could abandon). The enemy aircraft now filled my horizon; I pulled up to within 20 metres and with a few rounds set the No. 2 engine and the fuselage on fire. The aircraft broke up and crashed at 03.11 hours, two kilometres to the west of Ustrup. [Oil from the exploding bomber spattered the Messerschmitt's canopy and Meissner was forced to break off the action.]

Leaving the target area John Searby's Lancaster was at the tail end of the bomber stream heading back over the Baltic:

Our best chance of survival lay in losing our identity amongst them. After our last pass across the target we turned starboard instead of port and said farewell to the persevering gunners on the flak ships off the coast. We did not feel cocky, only thankful and if we could survive the attentions of the night fighters during the next hour or so all would be well. Alas, our hopes were short-lived for within a matter of minutes of leaving Peenemünde the battle was on again. 'Rear gunner to captain; fighter attacking from astern and below,' and I heard the rattle of the four machine guns in the same instant. Heaving on the controls violently, I brought the Lancaster in a sharp turn to starboard 'nose down', a manoeuvre which strained every rivet in her frame and red tracers streamed past without finding us. The fighter was attacking in a climb and the nose down attitude proved more effective than the turn, though the combination made the evasive action complete. 'Captain to gunners; watch for him returning,' and there was complete silence amongst the crew. Every man took a point of vantage from which he could observe the night sky. Classically, I expected the enemy to attack from the dark side, with the Lancaster silhouetted against the moon and the rear turret was watching this flank, the dorsal gunner taking the starboard side.

Suddenly, 'Mid-upper gunner to captain; fighter coming in starboard quarter down' and the Lancaster heaved over in a smart turn towards the attacking fighter. Both turrets opened fire and I saw the enemy's tracer bullets pass a little behind our tail. An excited shout from Flight Lieutenant Coley our mid-upper informed me that he had got in a burst and hit the fighter and we claimed this German as damaged since we did not see him crash. Certainly, this was no time in which to stay and look for him. We sped on into the night. The fires of Peenemünde made an impressive glow behind us as we left Stralsund on our right and lost height over the Baltic Sea. Any elation we may have felt over the apparent success of the operation was tempered by the knowledge that the German night fighters were taking a fearful toll of our returning bomber stream.

My crew were tired but for the next hour and a half unremitting vigilance would be needed. Fighter aircraft from all over northern Germany were concentrating on the Lancasters and Halifaxes and in the bright moonlight, conditions were perfect for interception. By flying at a low altitude over the sea we might hope to escape attention for a while, since the majority of the combats we witnessed were taking place around 8,000 to 10,000 feet. The chief danger for us lay in the distribution of light flak guns along the coast and on the many small islands in the Little Belt.

'Mid-upper to captain ... Lancaster on fire to port.' I looked to the left of the aircraft and watched a small point of bright light grow rapidly until the aircraft was entirely visible – illuminated by its own burning fuselage. The fighter struck again and his tracer bullets ploughed through the flaming mass, which quickly broke apart and plunged into the sea below. In a moment or two we observed another bomber shot down a few miles ahead of us and this one exploded in mid-air. Combats took place the whole way across the sea to the Danish mainland, where the leading wave of the bomber stream was now located.

'Crossing the coast Skipper,' from the bomb aimer and immediately one felt relieved. How many times had one heard this simple but significant phrase; the feeling of escape from danger and things which go bang in the night? Ahead of us the bomber stream wound its way home; we were certainly the last. Sharp eyes continued to search the sky and the surface below. A convoy of German ships making its way down the coast could strike us down in a moment at the low height we were flying. The full moon cast cloud shadows on the sea below – our faithful Rolls Merlins drummed on a fine even note as we continued our course to the west. I eased my straps a little to take some of the ache away. I felt grubby and the rubber lining of my face mask was sticky against my cheeks, the familiar stench of the aircraft – oil, body odours and the strange indefinable smell given off by the heated radar and electrical equipment – all combined to make one think of getting clean again. I thought about the gunners, Coley and Preece, cramped in their turrets, staring into the dark hour after hour, hands always on the gun controls, flung madly against their straps when the aircraft took evasive action. 'Captain to mid-upper, can you see anything?'

'Mid-upper to captain; all quiet.'

'Rear gunner to captain: nothing to report.'

Nothing to report and the likelihood of interception was decreasing every second as we flew towards England.

Flight Lieutenant Tony Weber again:

Between the engineer and the navigator a calculation was made of our fuel needs and it was soon realised that with our reserves we were not going to make it back if we did follow the briefed route over the North Sea. It was to risk a straight line run home on our own, or not being able to make it at all. We were to be on our own again from deep in Germany, in an aircraft which seemed to be fitted with a built-in headwind. It was essential to fly at our most economical speed and motor setting in case we were to be intercepted again. I reduced the revs to the lowest setting, which was 1,800 rpm and set the supercharger into low gear and used whatever boost was available at the altitude. Trading altitude for distance flown and holding our speed at 180 knots, we were losing height rapidly and passed between Hamburg and Bremen at 1,000 feet. Taking advantage of the moonlight we relied on George Sweeney, our bomb aimer, to map read for us at low level to avoid built-up areas. We looked on George as an old man – he was 31 years old. We were able to fly below the range of the German radar and fortunately, had not been detected on our descent.

One big danger lay ahead of us and that was the heavily fortified Dutch coast. We made a run for it just north of the Isle of Texel at almost zero feet. Not a shot was fired at us on this return journey. Gransden Lodge, our home base, was reached with all fuel tank indicators in the red. Don Bennett was back at our station for the debriefing. As usual we were the first back but this time not because of a faster aircraft; rather from having taken a short cut home. Bennett was keen to hear at first hand our report of the raid. I was annoyed that he questioned me about my trimming of the aircraft and he was annoyed about the high fuel consumption and ordered an enquiry. Had I perhaps left some flap down? D-Donald was tested and found to be way out of trim, hence the heavy going. I was exonerated.

Our heavy losses took place on the return flight over the North Sea, as the German fighters, now refuelled, were ordered to chase us over the sea beyond their point of no return, being assured of being picked up by their very efficient air sea rescue. It is strange how fate plays such a hand. Had my replacement aircraft been in good trim, or had I not lost my old LQ-X, I would have flown back on the route which turned out to be a killing field for the German Fighter Command. As soon as we were under the impression that we were out of range of the fighters we would have certainly relaxed and may have been just another of the casualties.

After debriefing, we were given our usual generous tot of Navy rum, which would have been better appreciated at the other end of the operation before we left; and then a good breakfast of eggs and bacon, which was traditional and an unheard of luxury in those days of strict rationing; then to bed to sleep the clock round. On leave in London when the first of the expected V-1s went off, I couldn't help wondering whether it had all been worth the effort. But then war is cruel and by today's standards we were only children.

After seven and a half hours in the air John Searby's crew had picked up the Wyton flashing beacon and landed, to be driven immediately to the interrogation room where Duncan Sandys was waiting:[40]

He had already gathered much information from the crew reports but wanted final confirmation from me. I could only say that from what I had seen this had been a successful operation but I could not confirm the destruction of Peenemünde. We must await the photo reconnaissance aircraft with its detailed survey of the area. Mr. Sandys was very pressing and this was understandable but he appreciated the necessity for caution and in any event he had heard enough to convince him that the job was well done. Even had we known what lay behind it all I don't think it would have made the slightest difference; the determination and 'press on' spirit of the bomber crews never varied regardless of the character of defences of the target.

Dr R V Jones, the famous British scientist, recalled:

I was not consulted about the aiming points in the raid, nor would I have expected this to be necessary; but in retrospect I wish that I had. Bomber Command had originally intended to make its main attack on the development works and installation at Peenemünde but Sandys convinced the Command that it was even more important to attack the housing estate, which contained the homes of the scientists

and engineers associated with the rocket project. I would probably
not have agreed with this emphasis because much of their essential
work had probably been done and the main object should be to smash
the research and manufacturing facilities. But with the emphasis
on the housing estate and with the unfortunate miscarriage of two
important path finding 'markers', a substantial proportion of our
bombs fell to the south of the establishment itself and particularly in
the camp, which the used the foreign labourers, including these who
had risked so much to get information through to us. We never had
another report from them and 600 of them were killed as compared
with 130 or so German scientists, engineers and other staff ...[41]

The initial marking over the residential area went awry and the TIs fell
around the forced workers camp at Trassenheide more than a mile to
the south, where 500–600 foreign workers, mostly Polish, were trapped
inside the wooden barracks. (The daylight reconnaissance twelve hours
after the attack revealed 27 buildings in the northern manufacturing area
destroyed and 40 huts in the living and sleeping quarters completely
flattened.) Once rectified Operation *Hydra* went more or less according
to plan and a number of important members of the technical team were
killed. They included Dr Walther Thiel, the engineer heading the V-2
liquid oxygen propulsion department and second in importance only to
Wernher von Braun, the chief scientist. 1 Group's attack on the assembly
buildings was hampered by a strong cross wind but substantial damage
was inflicted and this left only 5 and 6 Groups to complete the operation
by bombing the experimental site.

Sergeant W L Miller, a flight engineer on 460 Squadron said, 'Over
the target, we were being kicked about in front and underneath, mostly
by exploding 'cookies'. My God, I now knew what a fly feels like being
dangled over a coal fire on which chestnuts are roasting. Below was a
jumble of fire and wreckage.'[42]

Another flight engineer, Bill Griffiths, on 115 Squadron recalled. 'It
gave me a lot of pleasure to hit those fucking buildings. It really did.
"Bombs Gone: Right, we got the bastards" I thought.'

'After we got back,' says Wilkie Wanless 'the results came in and there
was a message from 'Bomber' Harris saying, "Congratulations boys on a
job well done." I don't think it was as successful as they said it was.'

The trip had not been 'the snip' that Jack Furner had thought it
would be:

The intensive flak over the target was far worse than briefed –
we were bouncing around on a dense carpet of it; and on the way
home, flak ships accurately placed all the way along our track, or so
it seemed to us. It proved all very tiring for Skipper John Verrall. He

lined up the aircraft for the final approach to Chedburgh exactly eight hours after take-off and ever so slightly misjudged his touch-down point on the runway. Proud old EF404 ran off the end of the runway and into a ditch. We were shaken but unhurt.

On the 434 'Bluenose' Squadron RCAF ops board at Tholthorpe 13 miles North West of York were three blank spaces. Flight Lieutenant Ian Lorne Colquhoun and his crew of Halifax *M-Mother* had gone down to a night fighter near Wolgast. The pilot and three of his crew died in the aircraft; the three others who survived were taken prisoner. Flight Sergeant Fred Piper MID and four of the crew of *T-Tommy*, including 27-year-old bomb aimer Sergeant Robert Carson Jordan of Glen Rose, Texas were dead; the Hallybag being hit by flak and abandoned over Westerland. Two men survived and were taken prisoner. *G–George* flown by Sergeant Gregg McIntyre Johnston RCAF was missing too. Johnston was killed but he stayed at the controls long enough for all six of his crew to bail out safely.

At Middleton St. George there was no word from three Halifax V crews on 428 'Ghost' Squadron RCAF. *V-Victor* and *F-Freddie* had gone down in the Baltic with the loss of all fourteen crew and *I-Ink* had come down on land near Barth-Velgast where the pilot and one of his crew lay dead. Five men were lucky to escape and they were taken prisoner. Hearts were in mouths at the 467 Squadron RAAF base at Bottesford in Leicestershire too. Squadron Leader 'Ray' Raphael DFC and crew would not be coming home; the Lancaster having crashed in a lake while approaching the target. All eight crew were dead. *N-Nuts To The Nazis* flown by Frank Dixon was also missing. *Leutnant* Peter Erhardt of II./NJG5 flying a Bf 110 night fighter shot the Lancaster down near Greifswald. The two gunners lay dead in the Lancaster. Dixon, E W Dickson, R Garnett the rear gunner and two other crew members were taken prisoner. Garnett recalls:

We were hit, just a very gently judder, but the speed of the aircraft was affected. The sensation was though the aircraft had hit a very big cloud of cotton wool. We saw no tracer. That was a complete mystery to us gunners. We couldn't see how an aircraft could be hit by invisible fire like that. Then immediately a real stream of fire and sparks came back past my turret from the port wing. It was just like a real gunpowder plot night, just like a bonfire being lit. Dixon told us to get out at once. I heard him asking for someone to pass his parachute.

After leaving the target Warrant Officer 'Pluto' Wilson piloting *F–Freddie* called over the intercom for everyone to be extra vigilant. But without warning the crew felt their Lancaster judder, as it was riddled with both

machine gun and 20mm cannon fire from a Bf 109G *Wilde Sau* fighter.
Sergeant 'Paddy' Barry the rear gunner, recalled:

It was an explosive and confused situation. It happened so quickly
and dramatically. Cannon fire ripped in from the 109. There was
an explosion inside the bomber. The fighter came up, exposing his
belly and I got a burst in before my hydraulics were destroyed and
the turret immobilised. Everything went haywire. The ammunition
started exploding in the ducts; the damned aircraft was on fire and
in a mad screaming dive at a sharp angle. It was, I thought, a death
dive. I sat there completely relaxed, waiting to die.

Standing beside the pilot, Charles Cawthorne clearly recalled seeing
tracer bullet trails looping high over their port wing and hearing the
terrifying noise of the enemy's ammunition hitting the aircraft.

George Oliver our mid-upper gunner made an immediate response
to the attack and our rugged Australian Skipper put the aircraft into
a violent dive to port in the hope of escaping further attention from
the fighter. However, after losing several thousand feet of altitude
he announced he was having great difficulty in getting the aircraft
out of the dive. Without further ado I leaned over to assist by grasping the control column with both hands and together we pulled it
back until the aircraft responded and we were flying straight and
level again. On recovery, I checked the engine gauges and fuel control
panel and looking aft saw what looked like the whole of the rear
fuselage on fire with thick black acrid smoke billowing forward. Out
of the smoke climbing over the main spar came George the mid-upper
gunner and he was soon joined by David the wireless operator. Both
had their chutes clipped on ready to jump out of the front emergency
exit. I reported the fire to the Skipper and expected him to give the
order to abandon aircraft but to my amazement he coolly said, 'Well
go and put the bloody thing out then'. If it had not been for those
cool calculated words, we would have all finished our ops tour there
and then.

Armed with fire extinguishers, George and I went aft over the
main spar to tackle the blaze and there we were quickly joined by
David. We found the ammunition lines to the rear turret ablaze with
one round setting fire to the next with alarming speed. The fuselage
was full of thick smoke which made our progress difficult and soon
it was realised the dead man's handle, a device for rotating the rear
turret in the event of hydraulic failure, had received a direct hit.
The turret's hydraulic oil supply had been sprayed around the floor
not only adding fuel to the fire but making it difficult to stand in
our rubber flying boots. When all extinguishers had been emptied,

we resorted to smothering the blaze with our gloved hands and eventually we succeeded in putting the fire out.

It was then that we realised that 'Paddy' Barry was wounded and trapped in his turret. With the aid of the aircraft axe, George, the mid-upper gunner managed to open the back doors of the rear turret and I assisted in manoeuvring 'Paddy' over the tail plane and up to the rest bed near the main spar. Despite Paddy's precarious state [his face was lacerated by shards of Perspex and blood was pouring from a wound in his leg] we had to leave him and return to our crew positions to report on the fire damage sustained from the night fighter attack and take stock of the battle that was taking place all around us in the bomber stream. From the flight engineer's panel I calculated that we were losing a considerable amount of fuel and after reporting this to the Skipper and navigator it was decided we would divert to an airfield in neutral Sweden. At this juncture Swill, the bomb aimer and I were told by the Skipper to make Paddy as comfortable as possible. By the light of a masked torch, we realised he had sustained a serious injury to his left foot from an exploding cannon shell. I attempted to inject morphine to ease his pain but could not get through his protective clothing. In desperation, I started to cut away his flying boot, which was torn and saturated with blood. In the semi-darkness of the fuselage it was difficult to see any detail and what I thought to be a large piece of boot was in fact a piece of skin, which I immediately replaced and bound the wound with a shell bandage. I then returned to my seat in the cockpit and after rechecking the fuel gauges I realised the self sealing fuel tanks had been effective and the loss of fuel had been stemmed. Following a hurried crew conference, it was decided we had sufficient fuel to attempt the return journey over the North Sea to England.

The Skipper then announced he was still having trouble controlling the aircraft which continuously wanted to climb and it was necessary for him to stand on the rudder pedals and wedge his back against the seat with fully extended arms to prevent the aircraft climbing. In an endeavour to relieve the physical effort of the situation the Skipper and I removed our Mae Wests and after inflating, jammed them both between the control column and the pilot's seat. We did not realise that the problem was caused by the loss of our elevator trim tabs, which had been shot away during the night fighter attack.

By the time we crossed the enemy coast the Skipper was completely exhausted and it became necessary for me to fly the aircraft over the relatively safe area of the North Sea. With great difficulty we changed seats and by the grace of God, nothing untoward happened during the sea crossing. Approaching the Lincolnshire coast the Skipper took over again and David Booth, the wireless operator, called our base for a priority landing due to our seriously wounded gunner and the precarious state of the aircraft. Bottesford responded to our request and the Skipper ordered all crew members to their crash positions for an emergency landing. I had to remain in my normal crew position to assist the Skipper with the handling of the aircraft. On final approach, I was fully prepared to select full flap which was the normal procedure but the Skipper quickly reminded me that only a couple of weeks before an Aussie pilot on the Squadron called Tillotson had suffered a complete fracture of the rear fuselage on his aircraft following full flap selection after suffering serious battle damage to the rear fuselage. His aircraft's tail fell off with disastrous results. I didn't require any further warning and my hand kept a respectful distance away from the flap lever.

In the early morning light after nearly seven hours in the air we glided over the threshold of the runway and touched down at 04.20 hours. With engines spluttering we taxied off the runway and came to a stop on the grass, where we were immediately attended by the fire and ambulance staff who carefully extricated Paddy, our injured gunner. It was now quite light and on evacuating the aircraft through the rear door, I was amazed to see the extent of the damage we had sustained. Internally the skin of the rear fuselage was charred and black from the intense fire and shafts of light pointed to where machine gun bullets and cannon shells had entered and exited the aircraft. Externally, the wings, rear fuselage, tail plane and both rudders were all severely perforated by machine gun and cannon fire. Overall PO-F *Freddie* was in an appalling state but miraculously all four engines were undamaged and had functioned perfectly throughout the flight to bring us home.

After debriefing, we went for our post-op egg and bacon breakfast. Before retiring to our billets for a well earned rest we visited sick quarters to see Paddy [who at one point had been given the last rites by a Catholic chaplain] before he was transferred to the local hospital. He later became one of plastic surgeon Archibald McKindoe's war-time guinea pigs and was ultimately fully restored to health despite a much damaged ankle. Two days later we were all delighted to hear that our Skipper had gained the immediate award of the DFC and George Oliver the mid-upper gunner, who was confirmed as having shot down the attacking Me 109 before vacating his turret was awarded the Conspicuous Gallantry Medal. All the remaining crew members received the appropriate DFC or DFM decoration at the end of the tour. Within days of this episode, we were on operations again and following two raids on Berlin our crew were awarded Tour Complete status by the Squadron Commander on 9 September 1943. We were in fact the first crew to survive a tour of bombing operations with 467 Squadron RAAF since it was formed at RAF Scampton in November 1942.

Ron James concludes:

> It had been a costly day for the Allied air forces: the Americans losing sixty bombers on the Schweinfurt raid and the RAF's total bringing it over the one hundred mark. The Americans were taught a valuable lesson that day: that long range penetration over Germany without fighter cover all the way, was not a viable proposition. Unfortunately, it took the British longer to realize that by sending out a large bomber force during a full moon period was a recipe for disaster. Later raids on Berlin and Nuremburg would hammer home this point. Only the spoof raid on Berlin, which drew off the enemy fighters whilst we bombed Peenemünde, saved us from being massacred. Not until much later did we learn that the pre-emptive strike was to destroy Hitler's V-weapons, the V-1 and V-2. At the time all we lads could think of was, 'Thank God it's over, now maybe we can get some sleep'. Forty-eight hours without shut-eye is a long time and when we eventually did get our heads down we slept through until evening.

Not being detailed for ops on the night of 22 August, 'Mick' Cullen the wireless operator on Flight Lieutenant Robert Megginson's crew on XV Squadron at Mildenhall took Brenda Jaggard to 'The Bird' at Beck Row for a drink to celebrate her birthday. The rest of the crew decided to go with him and they all spent the evening together. After closing time, Brenda invited them all back to her parents' home, where they were always made welcome. The rest of the evening was spent with Pilot Officer Desmond 'Mitch' Mitchell the rear gunner, seated at the piano playing the popular songs of the day, with Mick, Brenda and the others happily singing along. The evening came to an end with much laughter and happiness.

The following evening Megginson's crew were detailed to take part in the first raid for many months on Berlin. *O-Orange* left the runway at Mildenhall at 20.40 hours and struggled into the air, crossing the Norfolk coast at Cromer and heading east. The weather was clear and visibility excellent; it was obvious that the enemy night fighters would be active.

Notes

1. Later statistics would show that 600 Stirling bombers were lost out of 1,750 built; 62 were lost in August 1943 alone.
2. Rosner had been awarded a Purple Heart.
3. Betty married W/O (later Squadron Leader) Stan Haywood DFC* in the last year of the war. He was a Flying Instructor when she met him. He had flown 'ops' whilst at White Waltham, Lincolnshire, flying on 10 raids to Berlin in Wellingtons and then he flew another 30 on Lancasters.

4. The others who died were Flying Officer Graham Mitchell RAAF; Sergeant Benjamin Kenneth Hall Evans, P/O Harold Raymond St. George RAAF, F/O Walter Henry Morgan, F/S John Martin Maher RAAF and F/S Anthony David Terry RAAF. Another Lancaster participating in the Turin raid crashed into a mountainside overlooking the southern shore of Lake Léman at 00.55, local time. ED412 EM-Q on 207 Squadron was flown by P/O Horace Badge and crew and had taken off at 22.35 from Langar. While Swiss flak may be implied in this crash, the difficult weather conditions prevailing at this time and place with widespread thunderstorms with icing as well as shifting upper winds were most probably a contributing factor. Here again, there were no survivors.

5. The London firm Vane Ltd had delivered the first parcel of *Window*, which Bomber Command planned to use in the first 'Thousand-Bomber Raid' on Cologne on 30/31 May 1942 but at the last minute William Sholto Douglas, head of Fighter Command, had halted deployment of *Window* because he was afraid the Germans might learn to use *Window* against his own British night fighters. In August 1942 the Japanese were dropping *giman-shi* ('tricking paper') virtually every night in their bombing raids on Guadalcanal, to paralyze US radar-guided antiaircraft guns. The idea of gluing thin electrical wires between paper strips approximately 1-inch wide and 30 inches long – equal to half the wave length of the US gun-laying radar – came from Corvette Captain Hajime Sudo, chief of radar defence for the Imperial Japanese Navy. The strips, dropped in packets of 20 strips each, cut down substantially on Japanese losses in night bombing raids. At last, at a staff conference on Thursday 15 July 1943 Churchill stated that he would accept responsibility for initiating *Window* operations. *The Air War: 1939–1945* by Janusz Piekalkiewicz. (Sudwest Verlag GmbH 1978)

6. 347 Lancasters, 246 Halifaxes, 125 Stirlings and 73 Wellingtons.

7. During the Battle of Hamburg 24/25 July–2/3 August 1943 *Window* prevented about 100–130 potential Bomber Command losses.

8. *The Bombing of Nuremburg* by James Campbell (Futura 1973).

9. F/L 'Mick' Shannon DFC and crew FTR from the operation to Mannheim on 9/10 August when *C-Charlie* crashed at Wimeraux-Aubengue with the loss of all seven crew.

10. At Graveley a 35 Squadron Halifax piloted by Flight Sergeant N J Matich RNZAF crashed at Paxton, Huntingdonshire. (P/O Matich DFM and his crew FTR from the operation on Hannover on 27/28 September 1943. Matich evaded, 4 PoW, 2 KIA). *C-Charlie*, a 77 Squadron Halifax II crashed at Elvington on return with no injuries to Sergeant D A R King RNZAF and crew. *H-Harry* a 158 Squadron Halifax II crashed at Lowthorpe, Yorkshire killing all the crew. *K-King*, a 432 'Leaside' Squadron Wimpy ditched off Cromer and all the crew were rescued. Lancaster AR-G^2 on 460 Squadron RAAF flown by Flight Sergeant L J 'Mick' Christensen RAAF crashed on return to Binbrook. Again everyone escaped injury.

11. *Claims To Fame: The Lancaster* by Norman Franks (Arms & Armour 1994)

12. 218 Gold Coast Squadron Assoc Newsletter No. 37 November 2005.

13. Martin Cocker, writing in 218 Gold Coast Squadron Newsletter No. 26.

14. *Inside the Third Reich*.

15. During July 1943 to early March 1944 *Wild Boar Geschwader* claimed 330 bombers destroyed at night and the force was expanded to three *Geschwadern* with JG 300 stationed around Berlin, JG 301 defending the Frankfurt/Main area and JG 302 based in the Munich/Vienna area. A record 290 victories were achieved by German night fighter pilots in August 1943 and 80% were credited to the *Wild Boar* units and to twin-engined crews operating in *Wild Boar* fashion.

16. (4.3 per cent). The Battle of the Ruhr was fought over 99 nights and 55 days and 24,355 heavy bomber sorties were flown. The main Battle of the Ruhr lasted for four months, during which, 43 major raids were carried out. Two thirds of these were against the Ruhr and the rest were to other areas including Stettin on the Baltic, Munich in Bavaria and Pilzen in Czechoslovakia and Turin in Italy.

17. ED860 swung off the runway on take-off at Skellingthorpe on 28/29 October 1944. It dug in and the undercarriage collapsed. The starboard outer engine was ripped off, all the nose and lower part of the fuselage, including the bomb bay, were crushed. Fortunately the bomb load did not explode but the aircraft was a write-off.

18. *Thundering Through The Clear Air; No. 61 (Lincoln Imp) Squadron At War* by Derek Brammer (Tucann Books, 1997)

19. *Out of the Blue: The Role of Luck in Air Warfare 1917–1966* edited by Laddie Lucas (Hutchinson 1985) and *Peenemünde: Great Raids. No. 1* by Air Commodore John Searby (The Nutshell Press, Chippenham)

20. See *Night Airwar; Personal recollections of the conflict over Europe, 1939–45* by Theo Boiten. (Crowood Press 1999) and *RAF Evaders: The Comprehensive Story of Thousands of Escapers and their Escape Lines, Western Europe, 1940–1945* by Oliver Clutton-Brock (Grub Street 2009). Fred Gardiner and a fellow evadee were flown home in a Lysander on 13 September. Peter Smith eventually crossed the Pyrenees into Spain on 13 October. John Whitley and 'Whiz' Walker reached Switzerland on the night of 20/21 December. Two weeks after shooting down Whitley's Stirling Norbert Pietreck returned from a night sortie on one engine. He crashed and received severe head injuries. Barely recovered he was involved in another crash-landing in October and again he suffered head injuries. He never flew operationally again. In October 1945 he was arrested by the Soviets and spent the next 10 years in captivity.

21. IWM Sound Archive. 653 aircraft were dispatched. 8 Halifaxes, 6 Lancasters and 4 Stirlings – were lost.

22. He flew 29 operational trips in all before joining the 8th Air Force. Adapted from *First of the Many* by Captain John R 'Tex' McCrary and David E Scherman (1944).

23. See *Bomber Squadron: Men Who Flew with XV* by Martyn R Ford-Jones (William Kimber 1987).

24. Obviously, during the approach to the target, *O-Oboe* had begun to catch up with another aircraft in the stream. One thing Jim Richmond did mention was that the mid-upper turret of some aircraft was fitted with an external rail against which the guns could depress no lower. The idea of this was to prevent the guns depressing into the area of the wings, tail-plane and rudder and in effect, shooting one's self down. The Stirling was fitted with electronic sensors, which cut out the fire from the guns when they passed into these

same areas. It was as a consequence of this that Jim could not open warning fire on the other Stirling that was firing at them because it had passed into the area shielded by Aaron's Stirling's own wingtips. This fire which raked them from wingtip to wingtip came so suddenly and hit Arthur so quickly that he did not have time to take any avoiding action to permit Jim a shot in the direction of the other Stirling.

25. 218 Gold Coast Squadron Assoc Newsletter, No. 36.

26. 'As it required about 15 sorties to learn the ropes and so become efficient at the game, it became obvious that the Path Finder Force could not accept the limit of 30 trips before standing down, as was the rule in the main force of Bomber Command. In order to take advantage of the experience gained and to keep abreast of changing tactics on both sides, it was decided to extend our first tour of ops to 45. It was necessary to have eight aiming point pictures to your credit if you were to be trusted to mark a target. To get a good photograph of the target necessitated flying straight and level for a minute after the bombs were released. (I am sure that minute had well over 100 seconds in it.) So, to become a Master Bomber required about 40 trips. When one brought back eight such aiming point photographs, one received the Permanent award of the Path Finder Force Badge and a parchment signed by AVM D C D Bennett. My award was signed on 13 October 1943. Pilots treasured this document more than a *gong*, as it was the result of many trips requiring great accuracy.'

27. The dams had been bombed by 617 Squadron on the night of 16/17 May 1943.

28. F/L Ivor Charles Brian Slade DFC who had set himself the target of flying the 'double' Path Finder tour of 60 ops was killed flying the 59th operation when his Lancaster was hit at the start of the bomb run. Five of his crew were KIA, only one crewmember survived and he was taken prisoner.

29. *Nachtjagd: The Night Fighter versus Bomber War over the Third Reich 1939–45* by Theo Boiten (Crowood 1997).

30. See *Chased By The Sun*.

31. Their aiming points were the housing estate where the scientists and technical staff lived and the assembly buildings. After a last minute change of plan 3 and 4 Groups were assigned to the first aiming point (the workers accommodation area); 1 Group the second (the factory building the missiles) and 5 and 6 Groups the third (the experimental site).

32. *Thundering Through The Clear Air; No. 61 (Lincoln Imp) Squadron At War* by Derek Brammer. (Toucann Books, 1997)

33. *Flying For Freedom; Life and Death in Bomber Command* by Tony Redding (Cerberus 2005).

34. 6.7% of the force.

35. Lancaster III JA897 on 44 Squadron flown by Sergeant William John Drew.

36. On the night of 23/24 August 1943 during the RAF raid on Berlin Spoden was hit in the leg when his Bf 110 was hit by return fire from a Stirling and he and his crew had to bail out. Spoden bailed out but he hit the tailplane and the speed of the aircraft pinned him for some time before he eventually broke free and pulled the ripcord. He lost consciousness and came too in a garden of a house in Berlin. His *Bordfunker* survived but his flight mechanic was killed. Spoden was hospitalized and only returned to action again in early

November 1943. Late that same month he claimed his fourth *Abschuss* when he shot down a Lancaster. Spoden finished the war as *Gruppenkommandeur* of I./NJG6 with 24 night and 1 day (the latter probably unconfirmed) victories (a USAAF B-17 on 6 March 1944) in NJG5 and NJG6. He was awarded the *Deutsches Kreuz*. Post war Spoden was a senior *Lufthansa* pilot.

37. *Schrage Musik* was in fact a modernized version of a combat technique used in 1916 by Gerhard Fieseler, then a front-line pilot in Macedonia. His friends used to call it 'fieseling'. With this tactic Fieseler was able to stand up to overwhelming odds and won 21 air kills without receiving a single machine-gun hit. In spring 1918 when Fieseler was a pilot in 38 Fighter Squadron on the Balkans Front, he took a round-turreted Lewis machine-gun from a Breguet he had shot down and mounted it in the upper wing indentation of his Fokker D VII, in front of the pilot's seat, so that he could fire it upward at an angle. Each time he attacked he would fly underneath the enemy aircraft and his slanted MG rarely missed its target.

38. G9+JN.

39. Musset's Bf 110 crashed north of Güstrow at 0250 hours. When he had recovered from his injuries he joined *Stab.* II./NJG1. Musset died in a flying accident at Harderode on 9/10 February 1945.

40. Sandys was Joint Parliamentary Secretary at the Ministry of Supply and Chairman of the 'Crossbow' Committee which Winston Churchill had formed in 1943 to examine evidence from all sources on the secret German developments of flying bombs and rockets and which was now charged with responsibility for reporting on the effects of these rockets and bombs and upon the progress of counter-measures and future precautions to meet them. See *Bomber Harris* by Dudley Saward.

41. Extract from *Most Secret War* by R V Jones *Sunday Telegraph* 26 February 1978.

42. Miller would be shot down over Berlin on 2/3 December flying on the crew of P/O James Herbert John English DFC RAAF. Miller was taken prisoner.

CHAPTER 2

The Road to Berlin

We approached Berlin through a vast number of searchlights, with flak bursts all around. There were dark silhouettes of other bombers and night fighters passing and re-passing in front and around. We saw one bomber in front being hit and bursting into flames. One parachute was seen to open but the rest of the crew 'bought it'. We successfully ran the gauntlet and dropped our bombs over the biggest and widest conflagration of fires, flashes and columns of smoke.

Geoffrey Willatt, bomb aimer, 106 Squadron,
Berlin raid 23/24 August 1943

At airfields throughout Bomber Command on 23 August 1943 a rumour spread that the bombing of Berlin was on the cards. Geoffrey Willatt on Robbie Robertson's crew on 106 Squadron at Syerston recalls: 'Sure enough, on entering the briefing room, there was the large map plainly showing that Berlin was the target for 710 Lancasters, Halifaxes and Stirlings.'[1]

James Campbell, a Scot born in Inverness, who flew 38 operations on Halifax bombers on 158 Squadron at Lissett, which flew the most Halifax sorties in Bomber Command, describes the scene at briefing time:[2]

Eye catching Air Ministry contents bills with bold headlines scream-ing, *'Have You Done This?'* *'This is Important'*. *'Remember That?'* plastered the green painted walls of the main briefing room. Air-crews sprawled over the rough wooden forms and leaned inertly across the ink-stained tables. Others, who could not find seats, lounged along the walls in attitudes of complete and utter boredom. Through the blue-white haze of tobacco smoke a hundred-and-sixty voices rose in a noisy babble. The older crews made pungent remarks, bitterly resenting that the early transport into town had been cancelled until the briefing was over. A shuffling of massed feet, punctuated by a few wooden forms crashing to the floor, greeted the

72

Wing Commander [C C 'Jock' Calder] as he entered. He leapt lightly on the raised dais in front of the huge wall map constructed from sections of Mercator charts. He searched the rows of white faces in front of him, contemplating for a full half minute the assortment of brevets and uniforms. 'Sit down, gentlemen! Smoke, if you wish,' he said crisply. The clamour of conversation had died down and the aircrews were seated quietly on the wooden forms in front of the plain tables. The Wing Commander toyed with a bright red pin. Attached to the pin was a long narrow red cord. He surveyed the room for a few moments ... 'Tonight – it's Berlin again!' He waited until the low murmur of whispered comments died. He handed the red cord to the Squadron navigation officer and watched him plunge the pin into the black square that was Lissett. Deftly the navigation officer placed another pin in a minute triangle over a DR position in the North Sea. Swiftly, from there, he laid off the legs to the enemy coast, then across Germany to Berlin.

'I don't put a great deal on what they think about you at Group. If you have had higher losses than other squadrons, then you're obviously not as efficient as they are ... And if you go out thinking you won't come back' thundered the Wing Commander, 'you give the Hun that psychological advantage which comes from your own inferiority.' A cathedral silence stifled the room. Someone at the back coughed. The sound reverberated sharply. 'For the benefit of the new crews, I must remind you that you do not divulge the target or anything which may identify it – not even to the rest of your crew. They will know soon enough at the main briefing at 17.00 hours.'

When the wing commander completed his briefing of the pilots, the navigation officer took over. Then came the bombing officer. Slowly and clearly they gave their instructions, repeating some points, stressing others. Two hours later, the main briefing hall was packed. This time the gunners, wireless operators and flight engineers were in the big room. The wing commander, a billiard cue in his right hand, traced on the map the course and heights they were to fly at, the estimated time of arrival at their turning points. He told them – and there was a sigh of relief at his words – that twenty minutes before they crossed the enemy coast 22 aircraft from the OTUs would make a dummy feint a hundred miles from their landfall.

The Bombing Leader said his piece, thankful he himself was not going out; he had an unpleasant memory of the last time he had gone to Berlin. He revealed that the Pathfinders would take as their aiming point the Unter-den-Linden. They would mark it with red indicators. The backers-up would aim at the reds with green markers in as tight a circle as the Mark 14 bombsight would allow.

'So your primary aiming points are the reds. If they are bombed out or otherwise obscured, bomb the greens.' He moved over to allow the Met Officer to be seen. Suddenly he hesitated; 'Remember,' he added sternly. 'Check your bombing stations for hang-ups.'

The Met Officer, a mild soft-spoken man with large horn-rimmed glasses, nervously unrolled his chart. He might as well keep it rolled, he thought. It was always the sign for a ripple of laughter to go round the room. He resented deeply this enforced role of briefing jester, for there were only two questions they ever wanted to know. The rest were phrased either to raise a laugh or make him look foolish. Glancing apprehensively at his weather chart, he was about to amplify a point he was making when a long-haired bomb aimer with a Cockney accent rose to his feet. 'Say, what's it like over the target? Is it likely to be clear?'

He waited for a moment. He half turned to the Wing Commander and the Group Captain. They were smiling faintly but still, they were smiling. The Met Officer spun round quickly, flushed and icily retorted; 'I was coming to that. Obviously, since you are to bomb visually, we expect fairly clear conditions.' A loud cheer burst from the centre of the hall as they applauded his retort … Finally, the wing commander stepped briskly forward. 'That's all then, except – Good Luck Gentlemen and Good Bombing.'

Seventeen Mosquitoes were being used to mark various points on the route to Berlin in order to help keep the Main Force on the correct track and Wing Commander 'Johnny' Fauquier DSO** DFC the Canadian Commanding Officer on 405 'Vancouver' Squadron RCAF was the Master Bomber. Fauquier 'had been a bush pilot in the 1930s, a splendid flyer who had flown in all sorts of aeroplanes in the northern territories. He was really experienced and was regarded as a real warrior.'[3] He had made a name for himself as a tough individual of few words; his curt manner meant that he did not have to say a great deal. Later, he would step down from the prized rank of Air Commodore to take command of 617 Squadron from Wing Commander James 'Willie' Tait DSO* DFC.[4]

'Mick' Cullen the wireless operator on Flight Lieutenant Robert Megginson's crew on XV Squadron recalls:

Having reached the turning point 30 miles south of Berlin, our navigator, Pilot Officer Burrows, gave Megginson the new course. We carried out our bomb run without any problems and when Andy Haydon called 'bombs gone' Megginson turned onto the course for home. It was at this point we were attacked by a night fighter, which fired aggressively before losing us. The Skipper called for a damage report and one by one the crew responded from their respective stations that all was well. That is except for 'Mitch'. There being no reply, Megginson instructed me to investigate. I made my way down the fuselage towards the rear turret, feeling slightly apprehensive.

The turret was jammed but with the aid of an axe I managed to break open the doors. The night fighter had turned the turret into a twisted mass of tangled steel and shattered perspex and there, slumped over the gun butts, lay Mitch. I gently eased him back and found he had been killed by a solitary bullet through his left eye. I informed the Skipper of the situation and then proceeded to remove Mitch's body from the turret. I struggled for a few minutes and then called Andy Haydon on the intercom to come down and assist me and between us we managed to extricate 'Mitch' from the wreckage. Although the guns were useless, Megginson requested me to occupy the shattered turret to watch for night fighters on the homeward Journey. With no heating it was a cold, uncomfortable and unenviable trip. On return to Mildenhall the rest of the crew were given a few days' leave. We all travelled to Rugby to attend Mitch's funeral.'[5]

Sergeant Ron James had decided that he was going with his crew on the operation – their 13th – even though he had seen the MO about a rash that had appeared on his body and which was diagnosed as shingles:

It was not an entirely brave decision, for I realized, that if at the end of our tour I still had ops to make up, it would mean I would have to fly with another crew to finish my quota – rather a daunting prospect if that crew was fresh out of Conversion Unit. Berlin or the 'Big City' was never easy; in fact it was bloody hard and here I was a willing volunteer! 'At least,' I thought to myself, 'here we are flying through 7/10th cloud cover; only sixty miles from the target and no sign of trouble.' Then it happened! We hit a real bad storm and started to ice up. The only way through was under it, so down we went and by the time we had fought a way out, there was Berlin stretched out before us. Hundreds of searchlights were sweeping the sky, a sky now completely clear of cloud. It is perhaps perverse to say that there was no sign of flak but this could only mean that night fighters were up in force. By the time we had dropped our bombs we had barely reached our normal ceiling and thus far we had been lucky but now that luck changed. A Master Searchlight caught us spot on and within seconds we were held by at least thirty others and were well and truly 'coned'. If AA guns had been used I think our chances of survival would have been minimal but on this particular night it was the turn of their fighters. 'Gunners watch out – a *Boozer* warning.' Even as Bill Day was throwing *Roger* into a series of turns and dives, he still managed to keep us informed – not that we needed it.
   'Fighter astern and below – corkscrew – Go!' from Mitch [Sergeant Colin Mitchinson the Australian rear gunner] as a FW 190 came into attack. The fighter closed and raked our aircraft with his cannons but

Mitch caught it with a well aimed burst from his Brownings and we saw him break up and fall away. All this action was happening within seconds. Even whilst the combat was taking place, I reported two other 190s coming in to attack: one on the port side, the other on the starboard. It was unfortunate that our port inner engine, the one which powered my turret, was knocked out by the first burst of cannon fire – so, apart from giving evasive action commands, I was unable to help Mitch in any way.

Once again we were hit; and now in a vertical dive. Someone screamed: there was a smell of burning and petrol fumes. This, I thought, was the time to get out; convinced that the aircraft was out of control. Even as I struggled from my seat, it was obvious from the G-force that no way I was going to make it. I relaxed and a great calm came over me as I sat waiting for the inevitable. What happened next I can only describe as miraculous – my mind floated clear of my body and I could see myself sitting in the turret – 'If this is death,' I thought 'what is there to be afraid of? It is wonderful but what the folks will think back home – I am too young to die.' Suddenly, I became aware that the aircraft was levelling out. How we survived that dive I shall never know, the wings would have dropped off on a less sturdy plane. Our attackers had disappeared and now flying low over Berlin's suburbs we could see houses and gardens quite clearly. It was time for taking stock of the damage and our chances of returning home. Jimmy Fenn the WOp had 20mm shell fragments in his legs but nothing serious: the port inner engine was out of action and a fuel pipe cut; the pilot's control panel damaged and many instruments u/s with general damage in the fuselage and bomb aimer's compartment. Our worst fear was that the escaping high octane fuel was awash right down the length of the fuselage and one spark would have finished us off.

James Campbell on 158 Squadron wrote:

The fighter flares floated down when eight minutes from the city. They burst in brilliant pools of light on each side of the bomber stream. And they burned lazily as they lit up the broad avenue to Berlin. As first they drifted in strings of twos and threes. Then rapidly they fell, wiping away the cover of darkness shielding the bombers. The first combats were on. An orange glow splashed the darkness below and I caught the fiery outline of a Lancaster plunging earth-wards, tracer streaming from her rear turret.

Campbell pulled off his leather gauntlets and dragged a pair of newly washed white silk gloves from his pocket. He thrust his hands into them and screwed and twisted the silk until his fingers fitted smoothly into the sockets. The heavy flying gloves were too bulky for him to feel sensitively in the blacked-out nose for the delicate switches on the bomb panel. Campbell later wrote:

White gloves brought to his mind the executioners of old, masked men in hooded headgear, bending slightly as they leaned on their axes. He smiled into his oxygen mask and looked out of the transparent nose. The smile died on his lips. A searchlight flashed on, dead, straight and blinding. As rapidly as it appeared it went out. Suddenly, it was there again, slowly toppling backwards as if pointing their course to the fighters hurtling through the night to the defence of Berlin. Within seconds the darkness was pierced by hundreds of other groping beams. Must have been one of the master searchlights.

Another batch of flares burst above and ahead. Specially converted Ju 88s were, beyond any doubt, flying along the bomber's track, releasing them at timed intervals, making it easier for the fighters to select their 'kills'. The flares threw the black floating puffs left by the spent AA shells into sharp terrifying relief.

Campbell was grateful that he could not hear the mass thunder of the barrage below, above the roar of the bomber's four engines. The spine-tingling crump of the shells as they burst uncomfortably close spewing out their shrapnel jarred his tensed nerves.

'The petrified sky was getting brighter'. Campbell looked up sharply and saw the dim silhouette of a Halifax, below his port quarter, 'suck in long lines of tracer and burst into a rich deep glow'.

The exploding bomber cart-wheeled slowly and illuminated a Lancaster on its starboard bow. The Lancaster pilot corkscrewed violently away from the stricken bomber, to be caught relentlessly by a searchlight. Bombers were exploding ahead, below and on each side, sky-writing their death trails in spirals of black smoke. The red target indicators sailed down, plump in the middle of the forest of searchlights, trailing through the flak in a leisurely fall of fiery bells of colour. They splashed lazily over the ground, beckoning impatiently to the armada above, gurgling voraciously as they waited to receive the bombs. After them came the secondary markers, equally vivid clusters of bewitching greens. The bomb aimer pressed the bomb release button as the red TIs crawled over the cross hilt in the graticule sight. 'Bombs Gone!' At the same time his right hand flicked down the four switches controlling the bomb stations he had purposely left unselected. Then he shot across the jettison bars. That lot should fall clear of the markers to burst, he hoped, in the suburbs.[6]

The Path Finders were unable to identify the centre of the city by *H2S* and had marked an area in the southern outskirts of the city. The Main Force arrived late and many bombers cut a corner and approached from the south-west instead of using the planned south-south-east approach. This resulted in more bombs falling in the sparsely populated southern suburbs of Berlin and in open country than would otherwise have been the case, and 25 villages reported bombs. Even so, it was the Big City's most serious bombing raid of the war so far with a wide range of industrial, housing and public properties being hit and over 2,600 individual buildings destroyed or seriously damaged.[7]

Flight Sergeant Gil Marsh's Stirling on 622 Squadron at Mildenhall was coned in searchlights over Berlin and a *Wild Boar* night fighter homed in. A cannon shell exploded in the cockpit, tearing a hole in Marsh's thigh and cutting his sciatic nerve. He managed to evade the fighter by diving steeply but the hydraulics to the rear gun turret was cut and one engine was on fire. Pain, loss of blood and bouts of unconsciousness affected the pilot but the aircraft was kept under control by the navigator and the bomb aimer. Eventually, Marsh had to be removed from his seat and the Canadian bomb aimer, Sergeant John Bailey, flew the Stirling back to Mildenhall where he landed it safely. He was helped by the fact that he had nearly completed pilot training before being transferred to bomb aiming duties. He was awarded the Conspicuous Gallantry Medal and immediate commission for his actions.[8]

Sergeant Ron James continues:

The homeward course took us once more over the Baltic Sea and on our starboard side we could see the Swedish coast. 'This is the pilot to crew – we have a problem' (an understatement if ever there was one). 'There is no way we can tell how much fuel we have left and it seems unlikely that we are going to make it all the way home. We have two alternatives: bail out over Sweden or go as far as we can; send out a "Mayday" and take to the dinghy.' Bill asked us for our opinion on which course to take, and I said, 'With all the damage to the wings, I think that it is probable that the dinghy will be u/s. Frankly, I'm for Sweden, it's a neutral country and as we know, it is easy to get back to the UK from there.' Two other members agreed with me but three others were willing to take a chance. Then Bill with the casting vote said, 'Let's press on.' I do not think we had any choice. I am sure Bill had already decided his course of action; he was just sounding us out. Somehow we limped – I think that would be the right word – across the North Sea; very lucky indeed not to have received the attentions of the enemy. By waiting until the engines cut and then quickly switching from one wing tank to another, we had almost made it! A 'Mayday' call was sent out and an answering message told us to return to base. We replied that our fuel was almost exhausted and we would not make it. We tried again but still the same answer. It was now up to us. Why we had not been given another 'drome near the coast to make a diversion was a mystery to us.

Bill was now convinced that at any moment we would drop out of the sky. All fuel tanks had been drained dry and there was no telling of how much was left in the last tank. 'Crew – stand by! We have just crossed the coast and in a few minutes I am going to head *Roger* back out to sea but I will give you time to make your jump.' As if on cue, a row of lights appeared below us illuminating a runway. 'Hold tight lads – take crash positions – I'm going in.' Almost before we had time to reach our stations we were landing. We touched a small hill on the way in and slithered to a stop at the end of the airfield. A second miracle happened that night; despite all the fuel loose inside the aircraft we did not blow up. Our Guardian Angel must have been looking after us, for even one spark in the right place would have seen our early demise. The next thing we knew was that many helping hands were assisting us to vacate the aircraft. Mitch was unconscious and I was very dazed and in no position to help him or myself for that matter. We had landed at Bodney, Norfolk; only taken over that day by a Thunderbolt squadron of the 352nd Fighter Group USAAF. It was only through the initiative of a private first-class that we had been able to put down at all. At the time he had been in the control tower looking around when he had heard our distress call. Not knowing the lighting system, he had started throwing switches and succeeded in illuminating the runway with one line of lights. For our Skipper Bill there was another surprise in store for the first man he saw was one of his best friends from back home in Canada. This friend was now a fighter pilot serving with the American forces.[9]

The raid on Berlin was only partially successful but casualties were heavy considering the relatively inaccurate bombing: 854 people were killed and 83 more civilians were listed as missing. Many deaths were caused by an unusually high proportion of people not having sought shelter in their allocated air-raid shelters as they were ordered to do. When Doktor Goebbels, who as well as being Minister of Propaganda was also Berlin's Gauleiter, received the report on the number of killed outside the shelters, he 'nearly went nuts'. Over 2,600 buildings, most of them houses, were destroyed or seriously damaged. Bomber Command too had suffered its greatest loss of aircraft in one night in the war so far. The flak and night fighter defences were extremely fierce and 63 aircraft, 27 of them Halifaxes, were lost or written off. Seventeen Lancasters and 16 Stirlings made up the rest of the losses. At Downham Market three Stirlings were lost. Squadron Leader Waldo Harry Bentley Hiles DSO DFC on 623 Squadron and two others on 218 Squadron failed to return. Hiles had completed two tours on 218 Squadron before being posted as a staff officer to 3 Group HQ. All the crew including the rear gunner, Flight Sergeant Desmond Michael De Silva DFM who was from British Guiana and who had volunteered to join his former Skipper, were killed. Chedburgh lost two Stirlings. One was *X-X-Ray* on 620 Squadron flown by Sergeant George MacDonald, a former Glasgow policeman, which was shot down by a Ju 88. The regular rear gunner was sick with flu and was replaced by a gunner straight from training school who froze when the night fighter attacked. He was killed by a cannon shell. MacDonald told the crew, 'For Christsakes get out!' Flying Officer E Walker the bomb aimer and Flying Officer J D Sutton the navigator got out just as the port wing dropped off. Squadron Leader A P Philipsen who was on an acclimatisation flight with the crew was the only other survivor.

M-Mother, the Stirling flown by Pilot Officer Ray Hartwell on 214 Squadron went down after attacks by a night fighter and all seven crew were taken prisoner. At Lakenheath no word was received from four Stirlings on 149 and 199 Squadrons. At Mepal, 75 Squadron were missing three Stirlings. At Wratting Common two Stirlings on 90 Squadron were lost and at Mildenhall two Stirlings were lost, with all the crew dead. The loss of the 16 Stirlings was a 12.9 per cent loss rate, which compared to 5.1 per cent for the Lancasters and 9.2 per cent for the Halifaxes.

Halifax *Q-Queenie* on 76 Squadron crashed at Holme on Spalding Moor on the return. Pilot Officer W E Elder RNZAF and one crew member was injured. Wilkie Wanless, who was now a pilot officer, and the four others on the crew, walked away unharmed. It was the second time that Elder and Wanless had survived a crash landing. Elder was uninjured on the night of 27/28 July when he crashed at Shipdham in Norfolk returning from the raid on Hamburg. When *W-William* had crashed at Manston on the night of 14/15 April returning from Stuttgart, Wilkie Wanless' pilot, Sergeant Michael Frederick Weir, had died of his injuries later. Four Halifax IIs on 35 Squadron that were lost included *R-Robert* piloted by Flight Lieutenant Harry Webster DFC, which carried Group Captain Basil Vernon Robinson DSO DFC* AFC who was now the Graveley Station Commander All eight men were killed. Nineteen Lancasters also were lost. Probably the first to go down was *S-Sugar*, a 7 Squadron Blind Marker aircraft flown by Squadron Leader Charles J Lofthouse OBE DFC, which carried the Oakington Station Commander, Group Captain A H Willetts DSO. *Sugar* was shot down by a night fighter near Oranienburg. Lofthouse, one arm broken, came down in a tree near a hut used by a Concentration Camp outside working party. He was taken prisoner immediately. All seven other men on *S-Sugar* were soon captured. *C-Charlie* on 100 Squadron had crashed on take-off from Grimsby and four more of the squadron's Lancasters were lost on the operation. *X-X-Ray* on 97 Squadron at Bourn was shot down near Döberitz. Near

Shouldham on the return over Norfolk, *Q-Queenie*, flown by Sergeant Cliff Chatten was attacked by *Oberleutnant* Wilhelm Schmitter, *Staffelkapitän* of 15./KG2 flying a Me 410A-1 Intruder. Unnoticed by the crew of the Lancaster, Schmitter closed in on his target and his *Bordfunker* opened fire with the twin 13mm remotely controlled MG 131 guns fitted in the fuselage barbettes and controlled from the cockpit. Shells exploded in the Lancaster's fuselage and starboard wing. Flight Sergeant John Robert Kraemer RAAF the mid-upper gunner was killed and Chatten was wounded in his legs and chest. He ordered the rest of the crew to bail out and left it late to get out. As he came down in his parachute he was injured when the Lancaster exploded below him. After this experience three of the crew refused to fly again but Chatten, a confirmed teetotaller, recovered to fly a full tour of operations. Just four minutes after his attack on Chatten's Lancaster, Schmitter dropped eight bombs on an airfield west of Cambridge and headed for base at Soesterberg in Holland. Eight kilometres off Zeebrugge, Belgium Schmitter's Me 410 became the target for a RAF night fighter and was so damaged in its fuselage and one of the engines that he and his *Bordfunker*, *Oberfeldwebel* Heinz Gräber were forced to bail out into the sea. Gräber was unlucky and hit the 410's tail as he jumped clear, breaking both his legs. Exhausted and unable to climb into their dinghies, the two men fired flares into the sky and they were fortunate that a flak post at Zeebrugge spotted them. Schmitter and Gräber were picked up by a rescue boat from the *Marine Untergruppe* Zeebrugge one and a half hours later.[10]

Sixteen Stirlings failed to return from Berlin. *L-Leather*, a 90 Squadron Stirling III piloted by Sergeant Frank W Mulvey, a big Canadian, crashed in the North Sea north-west of Cuxhaven and went down 'like a steamroller' with four of the crew. The wireless operator continued to send out distress signals and was probably killed when he was thrown against his set as they hit the sea. The mid-upper gunner was thrown through the door of the wooden bulkhead and right up the fuselage. The bomb aimer was stood behind the pilot's seat trying to help and he died also. Mulvey, who was concussed had managed to scramble out while the cockpit was under water and had come up from below. Sergeant J Burland the flight engineer and Sergeant J A Pighills the tail gunner got him into the dinghy. Mulvey recovered from his concussion and when the dinghy got toppled over during a storm he turned it over again by brute strength. They were rescued after precisely 7 days, 16 hours and 10 minutes adrift after being spotted by Ju 52s with degaussing rings for clearing minefields. A boat took them to Cuxhaven where they recovered fast on 'a copious provision of lemon barley water' and spent the rest of the war in a prison camp.[11]

Five Halifax IIs on 78 Squadron failed to make it back to Breighton. *C-Charlie* piloted by Flying Officer John Austin was very badly shot about by night fighters and he tried gallantly to reach Breighton but the Halifax crashed into the North Sea. Austin and two of the crew were killed. As the Halifax sank, an empty fuel tank broke free, onto which Sergeant G E Russell the rear gunner helped his three injured colleagues. In the sixteen hours before help arrived one of the men fell into the sea and drowned, and the two others died from their injuries soon after being taken aboard the ASR launch. Russell was awarded a DFM for his brave attempt to save his fellow crew members.

K-King and *E-Easy* were instructed to divert to Leconfield. While circling this aerodrome in readiness for landing a collision occurred and both aircraft were destroyed. Sergeant John Greet the mid-upper gunner on *E-Easy* was the only man to survive the collision. He woke up two weeks later in Beverley Hospital, suffering from fractures to the base of his skull and right femur. So serious were these injuries that almost five years were to elapse before he was fully recovered.[12]

Another five missing Halifaxes were on 158 Squadron at Lissett. Pilot Officer H B Frisby RAAF, the pilot of *C-Charlie*, bailed out safely and he and five other members of his crew who also survived, were taken prisoner. (Later, in *Stalag Luft III* at Sagan, Frisby earned a reputation as a very skilful forger and map maker and his efforts were rewarded when, in March 1944, his fake identity cards and maps were used by the escapers after the Great Escape). Following the loss of *K-King* Flying Officer F A Unwin and five of his crew survived and they were captured.

A-Apple flown by Sergeant Tom Edwards crashed near Döberitz where the pilot's body and two of his crew were recovered from the wreckage. Four other men who had bailed out were rounded up and taken into captivity. A fourth Halifax was lost when *E-Easy* piloted by Flight Sergeant William Arnold 'Bill' Burgum RAAF was attacked just north of Berlin by *Oberleutnant* Rudolf 'Rudi' Altendorf of 2./NJG4. Burgum, whose crew had flown their first op on the Peenemünde raid, turned and flew south to what looked like an open field but it was a swamp and the Halifax crashed into it after part of the wing broke off on the approach. All seven crew were killed in the crash.

For six operations 21-year-old Flight Lieutenant Harold Kevin Hornibrook RAAF, who was from Brisbane and a pilot on 158 Squadron, had managed to evade enemy night fighters and escape the searchlights, but over Berlin he was a sitting duck. Despite his repeated corkscrewing the searchlights held *L-Leather* in their grip and then a night fighter pounced, firing a fusillade of incendiary shells into the Halifax until ten fires were burning fiercely. Flight Sergeant Graham Albert George McLeod RAAF the rear gunner was killed and Sergeant L G Chesson the mid-upper gunner was gravely injured. Three crew members bailed out in quick order leaving just Hornibrook and Pilot Officer Alan E Bryett, the 21-year-old bomb aimer, alone in the aircraft, which was now rapidly spiralling down from 20,000 feet. Bryett had taken the precaution of putting his parachute on and he got to the escape hatch but he could not get it open. It was jammed. Hornibrook came down from his controls, got the escape hatch opened and pushed Bryett out saying, 'I'm coming.' Once out of the burning Halifax Bryett pulled his D-ring and his parachute opened and he landed in something soft, which seemed like bushes. He was still blinded by the searchlights. When his sight returned after about twenty minutes, to his horror he discovered that he was in a forest about 80 feet up a tree and the Halifax had crashed nearby. Eventually, Bryett, who was badly covered in blood, got down to the ground with some difficulty. Kevin Hornibrook had saved the bomb aimer's life, probably at the cost of his own.

> The pilot couldn't get out, he couldn't pull his parachute and he couldn't save his life and he gave his life for me. It's something I think about every day. The whole of the last sixty years is through him, in that one moment of time, when he did what all captains of aircraft would do. He saved his crew but he lost his own life.[13]

Pilot Officer Robbie Robertson's crew returned safely, as Geoffrey Willatt recalls:

> On the way home and well clear of the target, Robbie was taken short. He put the plane on automatic pilot and went back to the Elsan closet in the rear. Just as he'd lowered his trousers and sat down, there was a sudden fault in the automatic pilot, causing the nose to lift in an alarming way and bringing the 'plane near to stalling. The flight engineer disconnected it and the pilot ran forward, pulling up his trousers to take manual charge again. I was supposed to be the emergency pilot but he arrived back, thank goodness, before I had time to climb up from my position in the nose.

On the night of 27/28 August when 674 heavy bombers[14] took off for Nürnburg they were routed over London, as Geoffrey Willatt recalls:

> When civilian morale was low, we were routed on our raid directly over London, flying very low, presumably so that Londoners could say, 'There go our brave boys to bomb hell out of Germany, in revenge for the carnage the Germans have caused to us.' The London searchlights were switched on, blindingly lighting us up and at the same time destroying our night vision. The result was a completely blind crossing of the Channel and beyond, during which, we could see neither landmarks nor night fighters, so we could not take avoiding action. We were well into France before our night vision was restored.[15]

Nürnburg was found to be free of cloud but it was very dark. The marking was to be mainly by 47 PFF *H2S* aircraft that were to check their equipment beforehand by the dropping of a 1,000lb bomb on Heilbronn. At the target the initial PFF markers were accurate but a creep-back quickly developed, which could not be stopped as only 28 aircraft were able to mark because so many Path Finder aircraft were having difficulties with their *H2S* sets. The Master Bomber could do little to persuade the Main Force to move their bombing forward as only a quarter of the crews could hear his broadcasts and it was estimated that most of the bombing fell in open country south-south-west of the city but bombs were scattered across the south-eastern and eastern suburbs. Thirty-six aircraft including eleven Stirlings, which represented a loss rate of 10.6 per cent, failed to return.

On 30/31 August 660 heavies targeted the twin towns of Mönchengladbach and Rheydt; the first major attack on these cities since 11/12 August 1941. Unlike the two-phase operations of 1944–45, which would allow a two or three hour gap between waves, this was a two minute pause while the Path Finders transferred the marking from the former to the latter. The main force crews exploited accurate marking in what was the first major raid on these targets and over 2,300 buildings were destroyed. About half of the built-up area in each town was devastated. Twenty-five aircraft failed to return; 22 of which were shot down by *Tame Boars*. Six of the missing aircraft were Stirlings, over 100 of which made up the force. At Holme-on-Spalding Moor 76 Squadron lost three aircraft. One crashed on take-off, *P-Peter* crash-landed at Bradwell Bay in Essex and a third was shot down and crashed at Roermond. A 78 Squadron Halifax crashed near Wisbech and all the crew were killed. Pilot Officer James Bowman, who had ditched in the sea returning from Dortmund at the beginning of May, crash-landed at Pocklington on return to base. Two Wellingtons on 466 Squadron RAAF collided and crashed at Howden and Goole in Yorkshire killing everyone on board the two aircraft. *V-Victor* on 51 Squadron had a lucky escape when the pilot began his let down for landing at Snaith and at 4,000 feet, ten miles south-east of Ossington another aircraft on the port bow closing head-on and very fast hit their port wing. The collision swung the Halifax 60° off its previous heading and a violent vibration started in that wing. The collision also set off the destruction charges in the IFF and *Gee* sets, which caught fire and filled the interior with smoke. The top of the rear turret had been pushed in, momentarily stunning the gunner. The fuselage had gashes in it and the flight engineer reported that the port tail assembled appeared to be missing. When the pilot tried to reduce speed further the rudder suddenly locked to starboard, stalled and the starboard wing dropped, the Halifax going into a spiral. Incredibly, the pilot managed to regain control and returned the Halifax to its normal heading and landing back at base. The

Halifax was repaired and put back into service only to be lost on the raid on Leipzig in December.[16]

On the last night of August the Main Force assembled in a giant stream and headed for the 'Big City' once more.[17] Of the 622 bombers detailed for the raid, over 100 aircraft were again Stirlings. One of the 3 Group stations at this time was Chedburgh, home to 620 Squadron's Stirlings. John Martin, a flight engineer, had flown about 25 bombing operations and he was an old sweat by now:

> Everyone else had gone. Sergeant William Whitfield, the fellow who slept in the next bed to me, arrived. He was the flight engineer on another crew [captained by Pilot Officer Macquarie James Campbell RAAF]. They went to get briefed for their operation that night and when they came out we went in for ours. I asked 'Taffy' 'What do you think of the operation tonight?' He said to me, 'With this crew, I have got no hope, no hope in this wide world getting through with this! They're hopeless.'

Nine Mosquitoes of 105 and 109 Squadrons route-marked for the heavies by dropping red TIs near Damvillers in north-east France and Green TIs near Luxembourg. The enemy used 'fighter flares' to decoy the bombers away from the target and there was some cloud in the target area. This, together with difficulties with H2S equipment and enemy action, all combined to cause the Path Finder markers to be dropped well south of the centre of the target area and the Main Force bombing to be even further back; bombs fell up to thirty miles back along the line of approach. The intensely bright white flares dropped in clusters of a dozen or more from about 20,000 feet at the corners of the target area and a double strip apparently dropped by rapidly moving aircraft around the perimeter of the area and igniting at about 17,000 feet lasted for several minutes and served to illuminate the bomber stream. About two-thirds of the fifty aircraft that were lost were shot down over Berlin by night fighters.

Geoffrey Willatt on 106 Squadron recalls:

> Having released our bombs, we were told to come north out of the target towards Norway. We were climbing to a safe corridor above clouds which contained very severe icing – a very dangerous hazard. Many planes had been lost in such conditions, when all controls sometimes became frozen solid. Robbie, from time to time, called up each member of the crew on the intercom to find out whether all were fit and functioning properly. We wore oxygen masks through-out the entire trip, oxygen being switched on always at 10,000 feet. The devastating effects of oxygen loss had been demonstrated to us when in a practice chamber we sat playing cards, all wearing masks. Oxygen supply was switched off one person's mask, unknown to

him. He began to behave as if drunk, laughing and falling about and finally collapsing unconscious.

To return to our flight out of Berlin: Robbie called us all up in turn but there was no answer from the rear gunner. Being the person least occupied at that time, I volunteered to go back to investigate. There were, apart from the main supply, small bottles of oxygen at various emergency points, which could be temporarily fixed to our masks. This supply would only last a few minutes, i.e. until the main supply could be reached for re-connection. I hooked up my mask with one of these bottles and stumbled back along the length of the plane to find the rear gunner lying unconscious over his guns with his mask off his face. Obviously, I had to drag him to connect up with the nearest connecting point. In trying to do this I tripped over something and accidentally ripped off my own mask and bottle. I remember standing there losing my senses and falling over backwards. Apparently, Robbie then sent the flight engineer back, who found us both lying side by side. Robbie then decided to dive down through the dangerous icy clouds to oxygen level, where masks were not needed. I regained consciousness, to hear the alarming crackling of ice on the wings just before we came out of cloud over the North Sea. We arrived safely back at Syerston.

Twenty Halifaxes, ten Lancasters and 17 Stirlings were missing and one Stirling crash landed at RAF Coltishall on return. The loss of 17 Stirlings was a staggering 16 per cent of the total losses! John Martin on 620 Squadron was in the astrodome of his Stirling when they got to Berlin and he had a very good view:

I was able to read the registration on the side of *P-Peter*, Taff's Stirling, going over ahead of me. It was like flying down Royal Avenue in Belfast; all the lights were on, everything was as clear as a bell. Once you started into Berlin, you never thought you were going to get to the other end of the city. It was so long. A fighter came up and right in front of me shot *P-Peter* down and that was the end of Big Taff Whitfield and four others on the crew. Two men survived and were captured.

A Lancaster on 61 Squadron at Syerston piloted by Squadron Leader Dennis Crosby Wellburn DFC crashed near Bleasby, Notts after a collision with a 1654 CU Lancaster. The Canadian pilot from Vancouver in British Columbia and his crew were killed.

Halifax *P-Peter* on 419 'Moose' Squadron at Middleton St. George and an all-sergeant crew who were on their 16th operation was also involved in a collision, with a night fighter. Victor J A 'Windy' Wintzer RCAF the bomb aimer had just released the bombs and Bill Cameron RCAF the pilot was preparing to turn for home when it happened. The outer tip of the port wing had been sliced away and the port outer engine caught fire, which J T 'Paddy' Mullany the flight engineer extinguished but the propeller refused to feather. Finally, with the Halifax down to 5,000 feet, Cameron, who was from Sarnia, Ontario, gave the order to evacuate the aircraft. He and fellow Ontarian, George Ernest Percy 'Ernie' Birtch the diminutive navigator on the crew never made it and they died in the aircraft, so too 'Windy' Wintzer and 'Paddy' Mullany. Beverly Scharf the six foot mid-upper gunner, who also hailed from Sarnia, bailed out safely, as did Bert Boos the rear-gunner from Calgary. Les Duggan the WOp/AG and former roundsman for the Co-op who had turned 21 on the night of the Peenemünde raid also made it out but he not only lost over five of his 13 stones in PoW camp; his nerves too were shot to pieces.[18] Two other Halifaxes on 419 also failed to return.

A Lancaster on 106 Squadron crashed in Romney Marshes in Kent on return. One of the ten Lancasters that was missing was *L-London* on 97 Squadron at Bourn flown by Wing Commander Kenneth Holstead 'Bobby' Burns DFC* which exploded and crashed in the target area killing two of the crew. The American wing commander lost a hand and he and the four other members of his crew survived and they were taken into captivity. Burns was repatriated but after being fitted with a false hand, resumed his flying career.[19] Next day, the MO examined Robbie Robinson's crew and said that they would suffer no ill effects. Geoffrey Willatt recalls:

Apart from a bump on my head and a headache, I was feeling normal. Apparently, one can be 'out' from oxygen loss for quite a long time before finally expiring. After getting some sleep, we went to Nottingham for an evening's drinking to celebrate the completion of Dickie Fairweather's tour of operations but we lost him for the rest of the evening. On our return to Syerston, he told us a barman had refused to serve him because he was black. With his usual sense of humour, he joked about it but we promised we'd beat up the pub in question the next time we were in town.

Meanwhile, after this raid Goebbels ordered the evacuation from Berlin of all children and all adults not engaged in war work to country areas or to towns in Eastern Germany where air raids were not anticipated. Jack Furner recalls:

On 1 September John Verrall's crew was told by George Wright that we had finished our tour. I was still 21 years old and the other five were about the same. John Verrall got drunk for the very first time since I had met him back at Westcott. He touched not one drop of alcohol through the tour: when our tour-end was announced he made up for it all in one night. If he hadn't been as prudent as he was, we might well have joined the dismal statistics. Crew discipline and meticulous planning were his watchwords. Regardless of expected fighter strength, he would always insist that I announce the crossing of the fighter belt: he would corkscrew vigorously throughout the width of the belt, regardless of sightings. I am quite convinced that this tactic, more than any other, got us through the Stirling tour. He was adamant about chit-chat on the intercom, immediately stifling any trivialities. He did the most remarkable things with the Stirling when caught in searchlights – I once looked out from my curtains and saw the source of a light ABOVE us. (The navigator had an important advantage over many of the other members of the crew. The pilot, the bomb aimer and the gunners were all peering into the dark and from time to time seeing our own people go down. The navigator was busy most of the time, thrashing figures around, writing up a log, his constant concern being 'where am I, where am I going next and when am I going to get there? Not for him, for instance, the stark loneliness of squatting in a freezing turret searching the darkness for God knows what.)

We said farewell to our comrades and to a newly arrived CO, Canadian Wing Commander Desmond McGlinn. Then we all went our different ways. I was posted to HQ 3 Group to carry out analysis of operational logs and charts with a view to recommending how best to achieve maximum concentration of effort. It was always the stragglers – the ones who had been using inaccurate winds – who bought it from fighter attack. Generally speaking, the more concentrated the bomber stream the less the losses. During the course of 1943 it became normal practice to signal back calculated wind speeds and directions in order to harmonise that all-important factor. In November that year, I learnt that both Johnny Verrall and I had been awarded DFCs. They were sent through the post with a nice little note from George VI: *Buckingham Palace. I greatly regret that I am unable to give you personally the award, which you have so well earned. I now send it to you with my congratulations and my best wishes for your future happiness. George RI.*

On the night of 2/3 September 30 OTU Wellingtons and six *Oboe* Mosquitoes and five Lancasters of the Path Finders were dispatched to ammunition dumps in the Forêt de Mormal near Englefontaine in France, about 40 kilometres southeast of Valenciennes. *Oboe* Mosquitoes marked successfully and bomber crews dropped their bombs squarely on the dumps. The following evening six *Oboe* Mosquitoes carried out a similar operation in the Forêt de Raismes ten kilometres northwest of Valenciennes for thirty OTU Wellingtons and six Halifaxes.[20] At Langar on 3 September Wynford Vaughan Thomas, a BBC Home Service commentator, and Reginald Pidsley, a sound engineer who would record his

lot Officer W H Eager's crew on 'P' Flight, 61 Squadron at Syerston on 15 July 1943 with Lancaster
V4236 QR-K *K-Kitty* and the ground crew. Standing L-R: Flight Lieutenant Hewish, radio operator
m Heston; 23-year-old Pilot Officer Eager, who was from Winnipeg; Sergeant Stone, WOp from
ntypridd; Sergeant Vanner, rear gunner from Romford; Sergeant Petts, navigator from Ripley;
rgeant Sharrard, mid-upper gunner from Toronto; and Sergeant Lawrence, flight engineer from
rnsley. Seated L-R: Leading Aircraftman W Long; Corporal C Bowyer and Leading Aircraftman
3lackwood. On 9/10 August 1943 this Lancaster (and a Halifax II) were shot down on the trip to
annheim by *Leutnant* Norbert Pietrek of II./NJG 4. Three of Sergeant J C Whitley's crew on the
ncaster, which crashed at Marbehan, Luxembourg, were KIA. Whitley and three others evaded
pture.

Pilot Officer R Brown's Stirling crew at interrogation at Mildenha[ll] after their return from operation [on] Berlin on 22/23 November 1943. Seated left to right: Pilot Officer R Brown; Sergeant W Brodie, flig[ht] engineer; Sergeant F Forde, wireless operator; Flight Sergeant P Harwood, bomb aimer and Sergeant F Tidmas, navigator. Th[is] was the last bombing raid on Germany in which Stirlings took part. (*IWM*)

WAAF sparking plug testers at Snaith, home base for Halifaxes [of] 51 Squadron. (*IWM*)

Lancaster III ED664 AR-A^2 *A-Aussie* on 460 Squadron RAAF at Binbrook in 1943. This aircraft was lost on the operation on Berlin on 23/24 November 1943. There were no survivors on Flight Sergeant Maurice Joseph Freeman RAAF's crew.

Flight Lieutenant John Alfred 'Red' Wakeford DFC entering Lancaster III ED689/WS-K on 9 Squadron for his 50th operation at Bardney on 20 June 1943. The target was Friedrichshafen and after bombing, the Lancasters landed at Blida in North Africa, returning two nights later and attacking Spezia en route. On 3/4 July 1943 luck ran out for the Wakeford crew and the same Lancaster when they were the only loss on the squadron in a raid on Cologne. All eight crew including Wakeford and Flying Officer Jonah B Reeves RCAF, an American from New York State, were killed. (*IWM*)

Lancaster III EE190 QR-M on 61 Squadron which was wrecked in landing at Blida, Algeria following the attack by twelve Lancasters on 617 Squadron and twelve more in 5 Group on targets in Northern Italy, one near Bologna and the other near Genoa, on 15/16 July 1943. There were no injuries to Flight Lieutenant T A Stewart RNZAF and crew. (*IWM*)

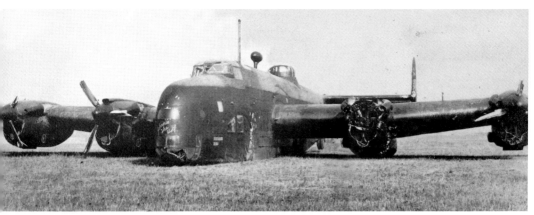

At 04.26 hours on 26 July 1943, Flight Lieutenant Colin McTaggart 'Mick' Shannon DFC RAAF on
76 Squadron crash-landed Halifax V Series I (Special) DK148/MP-G at Holme-on-Spalding Moor.
On approach to Essen the port inner engine appeared to have been damaged by shrapnel as
vibration set in. Shortly after bombing, at 17,000 feet, the propeller on the port inner became
uncontrollable, eventually separating from the engine and slashing into the aircraft's nose. The
impact caused a loss of control and when Shannon brought *Johnnie the Wolf* back to level flight it
was discovered that Sergeant G W Waterman, the mid-upper gunner had bailed out. The broken
wooden propeller blades lessened engine damage but in this case the damage sustained in flight,
plus that of the crash-landing, rendered the Halifax a write-off. Two weeks later, on the night of
9/10 August, Shannon and crew failed to return from the raid on Mannheim. All were killed.

Late hay is taken beside 77 Squadron's Halifax II DT807/KN having its port engine checked at
dispersal at Elvington in mid-July 1943. DT807 was lost on its 32nd sortie on 3/4 October 1943 on
the Kassel raid. Sergeant Harold Edward Cracknell and four crew were killed. Two sergeants who
survived were taken into captivity. (*IWM*)

(*Left*) Wing Commander 'Johnny' Fauquier DSO** DFC, the Canadian Commanding Officer on 405 'Vancouver' Squadron RCAF was the Master Bomber on the Berlin raid 23/24 August 1943.

(*Right*) Wing Commander Kenneth Holstead 'Bobby' Burns DSO DFC*, who resumed his flying career after he was repatriated from a German PoW camp in 1944. He had been shot down on the Berlin raid on 31 August 1943 when he lost a hand and he and four crew were taken prisoner. Two men were killed. Burns later served on the PFF Headquarters' staff. (*IWM*)

Halifax JD379/KN-M on 77 Squadron at Elvington, flown by Flight Sergeant Alexander Massie and crew was one of the 56 RAF Bomber Command aircraft that FTR from Berlin on 23/24 August 1943. Hit by flak, the bomber came down at Quelch, north of Celle. Massie and two crew were killed, the rest were taken prisoner.

Halifax II HR782/MH-V on 51 Squadron with Flying Officer R Burchett and crew successfully carried out an attack on Mönchengladbach during the night of 29/30 August 1943. At 04.03 hours, while at 4,000 feet, ten miles south-east of their base at Ossington, there was a collision with a Lancaster from an HCU, thought to be on a reciprocal course. The top of the port fin was knocked off and both port propellers were damaged. Burchett could only keep control by increasing speed, but he successfully brought the aircraft down at 180mph. HR782 was finally lost on the Leipzig raid of 3/4 December 1943. The pilot, Flight Sergeant Stanley Ainsworth, and one of his crew were KIA. The five other crew members were taken prisoner.

Standing in front of Wellington HE984/HD:H *Snifter* with its insignia of Hitler, Mussolini, Goring and Goebbels confronted by a canine puddle are Flight Sergeant J P Hetherington, bomb-aimer; Pilot Officer J H Cameron, pilot; Pilot Officer J J Allen, navigator; Flight Sergeant J Samuels, Wop/AG; and Pilot Officer A C Winston, rear gunner. This crew was an Australian 'Gen' crew on 66 Squadron RAAF and completed their tour on 30/31 August 1943, the penultimate operation before the squadron was stood down to convert from Wellingtons to Halifaxes. The last of five Royal Australian Air Force heavy bomber squadrons to become operational with Bomber Command, 466 served as part of 4 Group.

Flight Sergeant S Mason and his crew on Stirling EH906/WP-T on 90 Squadron at interrogation at Wratting Common following the 23/24 August 1943 operation on Berlin. A few minutes after midnight the crew sang 'Happy Birthday' on the intercom as Mason turned 21. EH906 FTR on its 39th sortie on 5 March 1944, a SOE operation dropping equipment to the French Resistance. Flight Lieutenant Cyril Vincent French, who crash-landed at Ste-Hilaire-de-Gondilly, was killed. Three men were taken prisoner and three evaded capture. *(IWM)*

Halifax crews on 78 Squadron at Breighton eat breakfast after returning from Berlin in the early hours of 1 September 1943. *(IWM)*

The crew of the first Canadian-built Lancaster X to arrive in Britain, KB700, which was delivered to 5 'Vancouver' Squadron RCAF and christened the *Ruhr Express*, on arrival at Northolt, Middlesex 15 September 1943. Left to right: Squadron Leader Reg Lane DSO DFC, pilot; Pilot Officer Johnny Ferrere, navigator; Sergeant Ross Webb, WOp/AG; Flight Sergeant Reg Burgar, mid-upper gunner with 'Bambi'; Pilot Officer Steve Boczar, second pilot; Flight Sergeant R Wright DFM, bomb aimer and Sergeant Mike Baczinski, flight engineer. Reg Lane had arrived in England in August 1941 to join in as a bomber pilot and he flew a tour of thirty 'ops' on Halifaxes on 35 Squadron. He flew a second tour on path finders and in July 1943 was awarded the DSO after completing fifty-one operations over an eighteen-month period. When he returned to Canada to fly the *Ruhr Express* to England the press claimed that he had been selected 'as much for his photogenic appearance as his brilliant piloting skills'. In October 1943 he took over 405 Squadron and on 17 November flew the first trip of his third tour. At the age of 24 Reg Lane was promoted to Group Captain and he flew his last op as Master Bomber against Caen just before the invasion. Later in the year he was awarded a bar to his DFC. He returned to Canada in June 1946. The *Ruhr Express* later joined 419 'Moose' Squadron RCAF at Middleton St George where it was destroyed when it ran off the end of the runway on the return from Nuremberg on its 49th operational sortie, on 3 January 1945. (*IWM*)

Bristol Hercules air-cooled radial engined Lancaster II DS689 *S-Sugar* on 426 Squadron at Linton on Ouse, which was lost on the operation on Stuttgart on 7/8 October 1943 when it crashed at Rachecourt-sur-Blaise. Pilot Officer Malcolm Barnes Summers RCAF and five of his crew were killed. Two men evaded capture.

Debriefing a 1660 HCU crew at Swinderby on 23 November 1943 following the raid on Berlin. Twenty-six aircraft, eleven of them Lancasters, were lost. 1660 HCU had been formed from the Conversion Flights on 61, 97 and 106 Squadrons in October 1942. Twenty-four OTUs (Operational Training Units) and eight HCUs (twelve of them equipped or partly equipped with Lancasters at one time or another) contributed mixed crews of pupils and instructors for operations. Additionally there were four Lancaster Finishing Schools. *(IWM)*

Station personnel at Fiskerton look at the night flash photographs following the 22/23 November Berlin raid. (*IWM*)

1 the Leipzig operation on 4 December 1943, Lancaster III, ED470 *O-Orange* on 50 Squadron was ked by fire from a night fighter, which shot part of the tail-plane away, destroyed the flaps and maged both gun turrets. Flying Officer J Lees RCAF (standing, left) bombed the target before ing the battle-scarred aircraft home to Skellingthorpe, Lincolnshire. The holes in the fuselage re made by the night-fighter's 20mm cannon shells. ED470 went MIA on 61 Squadron on /24 September 1944 when it crashed into the Waal on the raid on Münster. Flying Officer Albert ith Hornibrook RCAF and crew were killed. (*IWM*)

Lancaster II DS704 EQ-W on 408 'Goose' Squadron at Linton-on-Ouse, which was lost with Pilot Officer L C Morrison RAAF's crew on the operation on Frankfurt on 20/21 December 1943. Morrison and three of his crew evaded, two were killed and one was taken into captivity.

On the night of 20/21 December 1943, Halifax II HR868/MH-B on 51 Squadron at Snaith was attacked by a night fighter en route to Frankfurt. The bomb aimer was killed and a fire started in the bomb bay, which blew itself out, but it was not possible to jettison the bombs. HR868 was repaired and later served on 1656 HCU. (*IWM*)

ncaster III ED713 *Nulli Secundus* on 576 Squadron at Elsham Wolds which FTR with Flying Officer
hard Lloyd Hughes and crew on 23/24 December 1943 on the raid on Berlin when it crashed
ar Hannover. Hughes and three of his crew were killed; three crewmembers survived and were
:en prisoner.

ncaster I R5729/KM-A on 44 'Rhodesia' Squadron at Dunholme Lodge, Lincolnshire just prior to
: Berlin operation on the night of 2/3 January 1944. R5729 and Pilot Officer Louis Curatolo RCAF
d crew FTR from the operation on Brunswick on 14/15 January 1944. This aircraft had completed
re than seventy operations, the first being to Duisburg in July 1942. (*IWM*)

A crew on 44 'Rhodesia' Squadron are debriefed at Dunholme Lodge following the raid on Berlin 3 January 1944. (*IWM*)

Pilot Officer V A Reed DFM, a gunnery instructor and a veteran of one tour of 'ops', points out the recognition characteristics of the Short Stirling to air gunners on a refresher course at a gunnery school in January 1944.

(...)ncaster JO-P on 467 Squadron RAAF snowed-in at Waddington in January 1944.

(...)eft) Pilot Officer Cyril Arthur Wakley on 97 Squadron at his wedding. He and three of his (...)ncaster crew were killed on the operation on Berlin on the night of 20/21 January 1944. The dead (...)cluded his rear gunner, Technical Sergeant Ben H Stedman USAAF. The other three members of (...)e crew were taken into captivity.

(...)ight) Maurice Chick and his crew on 83 Squadron beside Lancaster III JA967 *The Saint He Will Be* (...)ck. This aircraft and Flight Lieutenant Horace Robert Hyde's crew were lost on 29 January 1944 (...)hen they were involved in an outbound collision with a 463 Squadron RAAF Lancaster and (...)ashed on the Danish Island of Als. There were no survivors from either crew. Hyde had (...)eviously had a miraculous escape when his Lancaster (JA686) exploded at dispersal at Wyton on (...)e night of 26/27 November 1943 after an electrical fault ignited the photo flash. One of his crew (...)ed and two others, who were injured, died a few hours later. A WAAF and four airmen were (...)led on the ground.

Sergeant R Shorter, formerly with the Metropolitan Police, sews the aircrew brevet and stripes onto his tunic after passing out as a flight engineer at 4 School of Technical Training at St Athan in South Wales in February 1944. (*IWM*)

Pilot Officer C Calton on 619 Squadron in February 1944.

impressions on a one sided wax '78' disc four miles high over Berlin, stood by to fly with Ken Letchford and his crew on 207 Squadron. Because of the high casualty rates among Halifax and Stirling aircraft in recent raids on the 'Big City', the raid would be made up entirely of 316 Lancasters. Earlier in the day crews carried out their usual NFTs (Night Flying Test) while for others it was an opportunity for an air firing exercise.

On 156 Squadron at Warboys in Huntingdonshire 22-year-old Flying Officer Clifford Foderingham DFC RCAF an ex-Spitfire pilot, born in Toronto, lifted off in Lancaster *U-Uncle* and headed towards south Norfolk. He and his crew had flown on nine ops in the past six weeks. Foderingham's father was from Georgetown, British Guyana and his mother was from Hartlepool. While on 101 Squadron at Stradishall he had ditched his Wellington III in the North Sea returning from the raid on Osnabrück on 17/18 August 1942 and he was awarded the DFC in November. Flying Officer Angus Stewart DFM the wireless operator, who was from Ontario, received his award for helping two of the injured in the ditching. Navigator Flying Officer William Gordon DFC suffered a leg injury in the ditching but he returned to action in January 1943. Before joining the RAF in 1938 Flight Lieutenant Kenneth Watkins the 28-year-old rear gunner from Westcliff-on-Sea had a varied peacetime career as a salesman and an actor. The 30-year-old bomb aimer Flight Sergeant Horace Ross was from Saskatchewan. Flying Officer Robert Hood DFM the 23-year-old Australian flight engineer from Sydney had been commissioned in December 1942. In April 1943 he had been awarded the DFC after completing 27 ops.

At midday in the vicinity of Kenninghall *U-Uncle* could be seen circling around over the village church. To 14-year-old Brian Womack it seemed that the aircraft was trying to miss the village. It was on fire and when it crashed at Green Farm nearby there was 'just a big bang'. Young Brian wanted to see what was 'up' but his father would not let him. Young Jim Gooderham who lived at the family home at Dairy Farm, North Lopham, was doing some work for his father in the barn when he heard the explosion. He rushed out and saw a thick pall of smoke. His father was not there at the time so Jim hopped on his bicycle and set off towards the smoke. At the crash scene the devastated aircraft was spread over two fields; it was so unrecognizable that for many years he thought that it was a Blenheim. 'There was nothing we could do for the crew' he recalled. They had carried no parachutes aboard the aircraft for the exercise.

That night four Mosquitoes dropped 'spoof' flares well away from the route to Berlin to decoy night fighters away from the bomber stream, which approached the city from the north-east. The real marking was mostly short of the target and the bombing that did reach the built up area fell in residential parts of Charlottenburg and Moabit and in the industrial area called Siemenstadt.[21] Twenty-three Lancasters failed to return. *S-Sugar* on 97 Squadron piloted by Flying Officer Peter de Wesselow returned to Bourn without making an attack and jettisoned its bombs, but a TI exploded causing severe structural damage that resulted in *Sugar* being declared beyond repair. He cursed his luck, but at least no one was injured.[22]

After a night of minor operations, on 5/6 September just over 600 crews were alerted for a double attack on Mannheim and Ludwigshafen. The aiming point was in the eastern half of Mannheim with an approach from the west. At Elvington Pilot Officer Frank Mathers CGM RAAF and crew on 77 Squadron were on the Battle Order and were set to fly Halifax *K-King*. Mathers' CGM had been for his 'exceptional skill, courage and fortitude in most harassing circumstances' on the Mülheim raid two months' earlier when Sergeant Ted French the wireless operator and Flight Sergeant Bill Speedie the rear gunner, who had displayed 'conduct worthy of the highest praise' had each received the DFM. They would fly the same positions on *K-King*. Flying Officer William Rhymer Simpson the air gunnery instructor would be doing the navigation on the trip while 18-year-old Guy Anthony Muffett would occupy the mid-upper turret.

At Syerston the Station Commander, Group Captain Francis Samuel Hodder decided to fly on the raid on the 106 Squadron Lancaster flown by Pilot Officer Robbie Robertson. Sergeant James Cunliffe was also a last minute addition to the crew as a replacement for Moseley, the English flight engineer. The rest of the usual crew consisted of Sergeant Frank Stanford Green RCAF, navigator, Sergeants Arthur Taylor the wireless operator and Freddy Tysall the mid-upper gunner and Flying Officer Shadbolt the rear gunner. Geoffrey Willatt the bomb aimer had no unusual feelings before the trip – 'definitely no premonitions' – but he felt the usual 'hot, excited sensation, usually identified with an important interview, or an innings at cricket'. He had left wife Audrey in bed with a bit of a headache and quite expected to slip off home and see her again at midday on Monday:

> We were briefed for what was at least an easier trip than the last two to the 'Big City' and had eaten rather indigestibly greasy Spam and fried egg. There was the familiar sitting round in the mess, half hoping the trip would be 'scrubbed' for bad weather but at the same time wishing to do one more trip towards finishing a tour of 'ops' – probably two more only. We dressed at the flight hut, checked everything in the aircraft and then taxied to the take-off point. There were groups of people at the watch-office and at the end of the runway holding their thumbs up – the farmer and family sitting on a gate giving the good luck sign. Engines wide open just after Robbie said, 'OK boys, here we go,' followed by that nerve-shattering roar, which would last throughout the trip. It was a perfect take-off but gave me my usual breath-holding feeling till we were safely off

the deck and up to 1,000 feet. Up to this height, a failure in any of the engines, or a small mistake by the pilot, if you're loaded with explosives and it's *kaput*.

At last we'd gained sufficient height and left the neighbourhood of our base for the coast, with a last look from me where Audrey would be waiting for me the next day. Oxygen turned on and as darkness finally closed in protectively we crossed the English coast. No pinpoint on the enemy coast, as the ground was obscured by the cloud but there were a few ineffective fingers of searchlights and a few half-hearted flashes from coastal batteries. We were now seemingly floating on the upper fringe of a grey cloud, which sent sparks of static lightning off my guns and bomb sight – not a dangerous kind of cloud and protective in a way but making things bumpy. I had no special worries about Mannheim as a target and didn't expect an undue amount of opposition – the usual bunches of searchlights, flak and hovering fighters but not to compare with the Ruhr ('Happy Valley') or Berlin.

Pilot Officer Reg Lawton the navigator on Stirling *U-Uncle* on 196 Squadron at Witchford piloted by Squadron Leader D M Edmondson was making his first trip to Germany:

It was Edmondson's second trip, as he had done one as observer and he came back and thoroughly alarmed us. Anyway this trip went well until we reached the target. As we approached, the pilot told me to leave the navigating in my curtained cabin and come and sit in the right-hand seat and open the bomb-doors. This was a big mistake. It was not my job. I didn't even know how to do it. I was horrified at the sight of what was going on outside. With enemy flares lighting up the sky many of our planes looked like they were in daylight and I lost my night vision. We were risking our lives for nothing because the target seemed to be one vast fire, without our load. We were hit repeatedly by flak [over Spayer] and I hurriedly got back to my navigation as the bombs were going. The bomb-aimer and rear gunner both called out 'enemy fighters attacking' and we went into violent evasive action for some minutes. I should never have left my work as I was now called on for a course for home, with all my timing lost as well as courses flown during the evasive action. The pilot was exhausted. He had operated the fire extinguishers in both inboard engines, which was successful and he then restarted both these engines. And they worked! Bristol radials – marvellous. The starboard outer engine, which gave all the power to our instruments, was just a mass of tangled struts in a huge hole in the wing. I gave a course for our next turning point (which was halfway between Paris and the coast).

Having bombed at 17,500 feet, which was the maximum a Stirling could get too, we started back at 12,000 feet. We were very slow and steadily losing height. After a bit I took an astro-fix but the plane was vibrating so much I took no notice of it. It put us well south of track and actually I was dead right. I was just going to give the pilot the change of course north for the coast when we were plastered by flak again. We had flown straight and alone into the defences of Paris. We survived this and after some minutes the pilot called me up and told me to go forward and see if I could pinpoint our position as we crossed the coast. I gingerly went down the steps into the nose, because some of the extreme front had been shot away and the bomb-aimer was injured in the eyes, so there was quite a wind blowing and cold too. I saw the coast pass under us but could not locate the area and I didn't know in the dark where to plug in my intercom. When I climbed back the pilot was very relieved as he thought I had fallen out of the wreckage. We were now down to 1,000 feet and the engines were on fire again. The flight engineer had been telling us long ago we were out of petrol and at this height we flew right through the London balloon barrage. I don't know why we didn't make for one of the 'crash' aerodromes but I got us back to our own station. As we were burning we came in to crash-land, without any preliminaries, such as doing a circuit. We had no flaps and came in much too fast. As we touched down the fuselage broke in two at the trailing edge of the wings. The front part we were in skidded a long way off the runway and headed straight for the control tower, which gave them a fright. We all scrambled out and were OK except for the bomb aimer who soon recovered. No one commiserated with us. No one praised us. No medals were offered. We were shaken and worried that all trips were like this but I was not frightened at any stage (6 hours 50 minutes flying time) nor did the rest of the crew seem to be.[23]

The raid was successful but 34 aircraft were missing.[24]

At Elvington there was no word from two Halifax IIs on 77 Squadron that were overdue. While in the target area Flight Sergeant Douglas Charles William Hamblyn RNZAF, the pilot of U-Uncle, was obliged to dive steeply in order to avoid a mid-air collision. Level flight was resumed at 11,000 feet but soon afterwards the Halifax was raked by fire from a night fighter. The New Zealand pilot was mortally wounded, and flames quickly spread along the entire length of the fuselage. Out of control, U-Uncle crashed in the target area. Only three men bailed out and they were rounded up and taken into captivity. Elsewhere K-King and Pilot Officer Mathers' crew lay dead in their crumpled and smashed Halifax awaiting burial in Durnbach War Cemetery.

On 9 Squadron EE136 WS-R better known as *Spirit of Russia*, with Pilot Officer Jimmy McCubbin in command, was attacked by a night fighter near the target. Cannon fire destroyed the port fin, damaged the R/T and mid-upper turret and wounded Rhodesian Flight Sergeant 'Charlie' Houbert in the head and shoulder. Houbert had fired 20 rounds before being hit and he took no further part in the combat. During five attacks on the Lancaster Flight Sergeant Jim 'Geordie' Elliott the rear gunner poured 3,000 rounds into the fighter. In the final attack Elliott's fire scored hits and the fighter burst into flames and dived under the starboard wing leaving a trail of fire behind it, seen by both the flight engineer and Ken Pagnell the bomb-aimer. Elliott was awarded an enemy fighter 'destroyed' and he also received the DFM. Though badly damaged *Spirit of Russia* made it back to Bardney where there were 'too many hits even to start to count'. The damage put the Lancaster out of action until November. In the meantime McCubbin received the DFC and became tour-expired.[25]

At Syerston the 106 Squadron Lancaster III flown by 'Robbie' Robertson was overdue. Geoffrey Willatt recalls:

We came clear of the cloud a few minutes before TOT (Time On Target) and there it was – the family party. A ring of weaving searchlights, the air filled with flashes from flak, cascades of red, yellow and green markers, dull red fires where buildings were alight and winking bright white patches where incendiaries had missed a mark. And above all, a thick black pall of smoke, rising to at least 15,000 feet, glowing red on one side where the fires were reflected. I was too busy during the next few minutes to be frightened – nonsense, I was always scared stiff – but these few minutes when we drifted slowly and evenly through all flak and danger (we must be clearly silhouetted against the fires for the fighters to see) must seem hours to the rest of the crew. The great danger is that the gunner will be fascinated by the amazing scene and forget to look for the enemy. At last I said, 'Bombs gone' and the aircraft bounced up as the 'cookie' went. A further period straight and level while the photo was taken; and then we turned off. The air seemed full of aircraft and quite near, a squirt of cannon fire streamed through the air like a string of red sausages and we drifted through puffs of smoke from nearby bursts of flak. A Halifax with one wing on fire charged past our nose, losing height in a shallow dive. Robbie said, 'Better get out of this' and down went the nose, leaving me with that 'lift' feeling and for a second I literally left the floor. Then the navigator gave the next course to turn on to; we turned, levelled up and Robbie said, 'On course.' Then it happened. The most startling thing about it was the noise. Normally, you can hear nothing above the roar of the engines – not even flak (unless splinters hit the aircraft – a frequent occurrence) or bombs dropping. This then was a metallic, ripping, shattering, clicking sound, repeated three or four times at split second intervals. The nearest simile I can think of is the noise made by two billiard balls cracked together but magnified a thousand times and loud enough to make my head sing. I involuntarily ducked down and back and saw that my position for my particular job had, for the moment, saved my life. There was a wide hole in the instrument panel behind and above my head and another in the side of the nose, a few inches above my head as I'd crouched down.

From this time it all seemed to take hours but I suppose it was only a few seconds before I really did things. The engines still roared but the nose seemed to be dropping. I knelt on the step and poked my head into the pilot's compartment. All three seats were empty. This was shock enough in itself but then I could see a chaotic mess of people lying in a static heap at the side of the pilot's seat and inextricably entangled with the controls. They were all hit and probably dead, Robbie definitely so, hit in the head. We were now diving steeply, with the port inner engine and port wing on fire and a long streamer of flame streaking back. Obviously this was the moment of crisis so common to movies, where one is ice-cold and efficient. Anyway, I'd always said that if anything happened, I'd be through the hole in a few seconds. I tried to call up on the intercom – it was dead – and it was impossible to climb back over the bodies to speak to anyone. No alternative but to go through the hole. 'Chute clipped on, helmet off, hatch pulled open and through the hole feet first, lowering myself on my elbows and hanging onto the rip-cord handle with my right hand. Whoosh! And there I was in mid-air, immediately followed by a sickening jerk on my groin as the 'chute opened. I don't remember pulling the cord: I was probably unconscious from lack of oxygen; anyway, I was fighting for breath. There was a horrible tearing and burning feeling between my legs where the harness pulled and my fur collar was clapped tightly over my face and ears. Both my boots were tugged off by the wind and my feet were freezing cold. I drifted slowly down recovering my breath and trying to ease the pain in my groin. The target was still burning nicely, bombs thumping, flak cracking and searchlights waving about. What a good thing I wasn't dangling in the air in the middle of it! Then my 'chute started to rock and rotate and behave like something at Nottingham Goose Fair. I tried to remember instructions, pulling alternative ropes but my groin hurt me too much to think clearly. The great thing was that I was so far safe but might hit a house or something equally hard on 'arriving'.

I suppose I descended for about a quarter of an hour and tried to make out ground detail; strips of alternate light and dark – long and narrow and probably factory workshops. The parachute drill kept running through my mind – twist if necessary by crossing straps so as to face downwind with knees slightly bent but braced and arm across the face to protect it. Land slightly on the toes and bend the knees. Thump! I landed on my heels, sideways, straight legs and leaning backwards – not per textbook and five minutes earlier than I'd expected. A few minutes to recover my breath and to think that at least I was still alive and on the ground and then I found that the total damage was bruised heels, a piece bitten out of my tongue, a pain in the chest (afterwards found to be two cracked ribs) and a splitting headache; all this in addition to the throbbing pain in my groin, which I took to be a rupture. A horrid period followed while I lay on the damp grass and wondered what I could've done to save the rest of the crew – obviously nothing, since the 'kite' probably blew up within minutes and a blazing aircraft would be attacked again and again by fighters, being perfectly visible. The next illogical thought was that perhaps someone had managed to fly it, the fire had gone out and they were on their way back to England without me. Above all, I felt so far away from home and everyone there. I had to move every few minutes to ease the pain and eventually it improved a bit. My eyes grew accustomed to the dark and I saw I was in a narrow field near a railway and a signal box. At last I rolled up in my 'chute and went to sleep, waking at dawn feeling very cold and miserable.

I buried everything that would identify me as RAF, sorted out my compass and map and crawled into some bushes, dragging my 'chute with me just as a farm cart slowly creaked by a few yards away, driven by a sleepy old farmer – my first German. I lay in a narrow strip of four-foot grape vines next to a railway, with no house in sight. Last night's glow of fire from the target and the rising sun, together with the destination boards on passing trains, gave me my exact position on the silk handkerchief map, which we all carried, together with a button compass. My next Germans came in hundreds – crowded in the compartments of trains, perched on observation platforms between coaches, jammed in corridors – civilians, soldiers, sailors, all kinds. I lay under the vines thinking of home and worrying a lot about how long it would be before all at home were notified. I must try and walk to a neutral country and get sent home – service instructions. Sleep in the daytime and walk at night, conserving carefully my scanty rations. But there was the problem of shoes, which I solved by making sandals from my parachute with a tiny penknife with scissors attached which I always carried. I kept sucking sour grapes, thirst being a big problem and crawled round my grape patch spying out the land. The trains all passed too fast to jump on at night – therefore I must walk. I finally went to sleep after having buried everything except the few things I should carry and put your photo in the back of my watch.

I was woken by a persistent tearing sound but luckily didn't move because this was caused by a farm girl picking peas a few feet from my head and at the end of my grape patch. She was in a most indelicate position with her back turned to me in a wide skirt, bending forward to pluck the peas. I wonder what she'd have done if I'd popped up suddenly from my bushes? I lay still until she, an old man and others beyond the railway went home. My bitten tongue was swollen but my groin and chest felt much better. I put my fisherman's jersey over my battle-dress and stood up for a good look round, miraculously missing being seen by the signalman going off duty. I was seen by the driver of a passing engine. The railway track led roughly in the right direction – the Swiss frontier – and I set off down it; I was prepared to duck down at the side of the track if a train came. My sandals were not a success and slipped off every few yards until I was almost barefoot after only half an hour. I narrowly escaped a signalman in his box and nearly walked straight into a station! I therefore left the line and struck across country, which included a bewildering alternation of breast-high grape vines, plough land, stubble, vegetables and streams. Skirting a farmhouse, where a dog barked every time I moved, I fell into a stream, which just about finished my sandals. After about three hours' stumbling, I crouched for a long time wondering how to cross a wide stream. It turned out to be a road with the newly risen moon shining on it. I was finally convinced by a man riding along it on a bicycle. I was obviously tired and a bit 'dopey'. I struck a main crossroads and thought what fun it would be to 'thumb' a lift to Strasbourg but I finally set off down the minor road. I'd had enough cross-country stumbling. I had to nip smartly behind a tree about every five minutes whilst cyclists came by – must be a night-shift somewhere near here. At one point there were no trees, so I lay flat on the ground at the side of the road.

A village and town had to be avoided and I fell down a steep bank when leaving the road. At last, when I thought I was too tired to go any further and was sitting under a tree chewing a sour pear (they seemed as nice as peaches as by now I was *very* thirsty), the sky started to get grey. I wandered round trying to find a lair to hide in during the day and after trying a cabbage patch and a patch of vines, came across the 'escapers' friend' – a haystack. But it was not a proper one and consisted of bean-straw (pyramid-shaped) and raised a foot off the ground on a framework; it was prickly and draughty and full of bugs. I chewed another Horlicks tablet, slept for a bit and woke to find my legs sticking out and a farmer ploughing a hundred yards away. I was now feeling cramped, cold, depressed and bug-ridden but above all, thirsty. The RAF says quite glibly, 'Walk to a neutral country,' but without shoes this seemed pretty hopeless, particularly as the nearest route went across some mountains. Supposing I was almost certainly caught eventually, further walking would only prolong the time till you were notified that I was safe. This was an awful, depressed and useless state of mind to be in but I suppose my condition accounted for it. Anyway, the whole thing was quickly decided for me. A scratching sound began on the other side of my haystack. I lay still for about half an hour after it stopped, hoping it had only been a rabbit or mouse but just in case it was human. I resisted the impulse to look for a long time and then poked my head out, to see nothing. The ploughing farmer was now some distance away so I crawled out and cautiously looked round the stack. I was face to face with an old peasant with a pitchfork who must have been patiently waiting for me to emerge, for he didn't seem in the least surprised, although he looked very frightened. There were farm people dotted round the fields in all directions; I was definitely caught. I didn't like men with pitchforks even if they did look scared, so I said timidly 'RAF' and tried not to look like a terror-bomber. He looked rather vague but pointed to the village nearby and said, '*Sechs kamerad tod da*' (six friends dead there) and just stood gazing at me. It was a long walk to the village and all the way the groups of workers just stood and watched me from all sides. An odd feeling, slopping slowly along (I was tired) in the remains of my sandals with everyone looking but nobody making a movement. I tried *Guten morgen* in my best school German to one who looked a bit hostile but he didn't answer.

A hundred yards beyond reaching the road a postman and three other men were talking to some women. They immediately surrounded me and grabbed my arm, which made me think of tales (true) of lynching but I think they were all rather scared until a soldier appeared with a rifle. He was quite friendly after searching me and muttering '*pistolen*'. They all seemed to think I ought to have a revolver and seemed quite worried that they couldn't find it. He led me to the wreckage of an aircraft in a field while we talked quite happily in a mixture of French and German and signs. To my complete astonishment he suddenly said, 'Robertson, Shadbolt, Taylor, Green' and pointed to an irregular lump under a tarpaulin. This was very shaking – an extraordinary coincidence that I should have wandered all this way and arrived at the bodies and wreckage of my own aircraft! He started to lead me towards the remains but changed his mind and wouldn't let me go any further; perhaps I was looking upset. I suppose I should have argued and tried to identify but I was, in my present state, very thankful that he'd stopped me. I was sat on a blanket and given black bread, grapes (ripe this time) and his water bottle to drink from (wine tasting like nectar – my first drink for two nights and a day) while he searched me again. Quite a crowd had now gathered but they all seemed sorry for me and had great fun with my utility lighter and my packet of escape food but didn't try to steal anything. The local bobby – fat, elderly and self-important – arrived on a bicycle and led me through staring throngs to the police station in the village and sat me on a chair in his office. I'd tried to look dignified on the walk but it was difficult in nearly bare feet and two days' beard and dirt. I was questioned by the bobby, a local civilian and the French-speaking soldier and conveniently didn't understand any leading questions except my name, number and names of the crew. They said there were six bodies and they gave four names; 'Pilot Officer Robertson – hit in the head; Flying Officer Shadbolt, hit in the arms; Sergeant Green, navigator and Sergeant Taylor, wireless operator. They then produced an unopened 'chute, covered with blood, presumably the engineer's; or maybe a wrong 'chute.[26]

Cunliffe, Group Captain Hodder and Sergeant Freddy Tysall the chirpy Cockney mid-upper gunner were dead too. Geoffrey Willatt was the only one on the crew to survive. He would spend the next two years in *Stalag Luft III* at Sagan as a prisoner of war. It was a fate shared by thousands of others.

A monotonous existence behind the wire was surely preferable to death or serious injury in the air. One of the worst fates that could befall a bomber crewman was fire. On 14 September Flight Sergeant 'Bert' Bradford RNZAF on 115 Squadron at Little Snoring was piloting a Lancaster II on an air test over Norfolk and he feathered two engines at 1,200 feet. In the next instant the Lancaster was hurtling towards the ground and it crashed at Magdalen Fen about four miles north of RAF Downham Market, killing six of the eight men on board. Flight Sergeant Ivan Williamson DFC RNZAF the W/T operator recalled:

The aircraft hit with a hell of a crash. The props flew off, engines ran away and quickly caught fire. We bounced on some high ground, became airborne again. The next contact with the ground was a rail embankment, into which we nose-dived. We had 1,500 gallons of high-octane fuel aboard. The fuel tanks exploded on impact and, lit by the engines, became a wall of flaming petrol. The aircraft broke its back just behind the second spar, flipped over the embankment and Sergeant Michael Read the bomb aimer and I were airborne for about 70 yards. We passed through the wall of petrol and became flaming torches, landing in a foot of mud, water and lots of bull-rushes where we burned quite furiously. Fortunately an old carpenter working nearby ran to the crash as fast as his 72 years would allow. He looked at the carnage, decided there was no hope of survivors and came over to investigate the two columns of smoke some distance away. He found us and rolled us into the mud to put out our fires. Apparently my uniform by now was almost completely burnt off. Read was in slightly better shape, although his arm was broken in two places. I had lost my helmet and was fairly well singed about my face and hands. My shoulder blade was broken and about six ribs were broken. A sizeable lump of flesh was grounched out of my groin and a perfect print of a Lancaster spar, including two bolt heads, was imprinted on my back.

There seems no doubt that we would have burned to death if the carpenter had not been there. He had picked me by my 'Kiwi' accent. I insisted I was out cold but he said: 'Oh no boy, your language, it were real thick. It were real bad.' Most of it was directed at a nurse. It seems incredible that a Red Cross nurse should be waiting for a train half a mile away with her emergency kit. She was soon on the spot and administered injections. I was apparently quite violent, insisting she shouldn't waste her bloody time on me but concentrate her efforts on the rest of the crew, who were much worse off. I hung my head, a little ashamed but I had no idea about all this. We were taken to Ely hospital and I was an in-patient for two months. Officers of the investigating committee questioned me. Apparently the only part of the aircraft completely whole was the engineer's panel. I became one of Archibald McIndoe's (a fellow New Zealander and father of skin grafts) 'guinea pigs' at East Grinstead hospital. I was photographed every morning and got a copy of my early grafts. I healed like a healthy animal and it wasn't long before I was disgracing myself, getting a hard-on in my saline bath.

I went back to the squadron as a lost soul and crewed up twice with new crews but was taken off the battle order by Wing Commander Anmaud, a great airman, both times. Neither crew survived their first op. I later crewed up with a crew who had seven trips in Stirlings but the pilot and bomb aimer went LMF. They were stripped of all rank and the crew were finally broken up after six trips, four of which were to Berlin. I went on with 75 (New Zealand) Squadron later and in all did 44 operations. I had incredible luck all the way through. It would be no exaggeration to say I missed death at least ten times during war and since. Life was cheap those pretty hard days.

Notes

1. 335 Lancasters, 251 Halifaxes, 124 Stirlings.
2. *Maximum Effort* (Futura 1957).
3. *Lancaster The Biography* by S/L Tony Iveson DFC and Brian Milton (André Deutsch, 2009).
4. *Barnes Wallis' Bombs: Tallboy, Dambuster & Grand Slam* by Stephen Flower. Tempus 2002)

5. Crews claimed a concentrated attack on Turin. The raid concluded the Bomber Command attacks on Italian cities, which begun in June 1940. Mick Cullen and Brenda Jaggard married on 7 August 1944 at St. John's Church, Beck Row. The Air Force padre officiated at the wedding, which was attended by over 100 guests. After the war ended they settled down in New Zealand. See *Bomber Squadron: Men Who Flew with XV* by Martyn R Ford-Jones (William Kimber 1987).

6. Adapted from *Maximum Effort* (Futura 1957)

7. The worst damage was in the residential areas of Lankwitz and Lichterfelde and the worst industrial damage was in Mariendorf and Marienfelde districts well south of the city centre. More industrial damage was caused in the Tempelhof area, nearer the centre and some of those bombs, which actually hit the centre of the city fell by chance in the 'government quarter' where the Wilhelmstrasse was recorded as having not a building undamaged. Twenty ships on Berlin's canals were sunk. *The Bomber Command War Diaries: An Operational Reference Book 1939–1945*. Martin Middlebrook and Chris Everitt. (Midland Publishing 1985).

8. Flight Sergeant O H White DFM* a New Zealand pilot on 75 Squadron also received a commission and the CGM for getting his Stirling back after the tail gunner was killed in a fighter attack and three other crewmembers had bailed out in error. White, a pre-war yachtsman, flew home navigating by the stars and crash-landed at Mepal. *The Berlin Raids* by Martin Middlebrook.

9. 'The crew' adds Ron James 'told us later that they had been entertained like Royalty by the Americans but Jimmy and I were soon away to hospital; Jimmy to Ely and myself to Stradishall. Apart from suffering from severe concussion, the Shingles were now a mass of blisters encircling my body (It took years for the scars to disappear). Bill Day received an immediate DFC, Sergeant Colin Mitchinson the DFM. Stirling EH908 *R-Roger* was repaired and finally written off on 12 November 1943 when the control column jammed and it crashed at Hundon near Stradishall. *Nachtjagd: The Night Fighter versus Bomber War over the Third Reich 1939–45* by Theo Boiten (Crowood 1997).

10. *Intruders over Britain: The Luftwaffe Night Fighter Offensive 1940 to 1945* by Simon W Parry (ARP 2003). On 8 November 1943, Schmitter and his *Bordfunker*, *Uffz* Felix Hainzinger, were killed when their Me 410 was shot down near Eastbourne by Squadron Leader W H Maguire DFC and Flying Officer W D Jones on 85 Squadron flying a Mosquito XII. Schmitter was posthumously promoted to *Major* and awarded the Oak leaves to his *Ritterkreuz*.

11. *The Berlin Raids* by Martin Middlebrook. A second Stirling on 90 Squadron crashed in the Ijsselmeer with the loss of all the crew.

12. Chorley. When John Greet's wife have birth to a daughter, she was christened Beverley.

13. On 23/24 September 1944 Kevin Hornibrook's 20-year-old brother F/O Albert Keith Hornibrook on 61 Squadron was KIA piloting a Lancaster on the operation to Münster.

14. 349 Lancasters, 221 Halifaxes, 104 Stirlings.

15. *The Bomber Command War Diaries: An Operational Reference Book 1939–1945* by Martin Middlebrook and Chris Everitt. (Midland 1985).

16. See *Handley Page Halifax: From Hell to Victory and Beyond* by K A Merrick (Chevron Publishing 2009)

17. In a separate operation 30 OTU Wellingtons and 6 *Oboe* Mosquitoes and five Halifaxes of the Path Finders bombed an ammunition dump in the Forêt de Hesdin in northern France.

18. *Bomber Boys* by Mel Rolfe (Grub Street 2004, Bounty Books 2007).

19. *Into the Silk* by Ian Mackersey (Robert Hale 1956). Four other members of his crew survived and were taken into captivity. Pilot Officer Earle George Dolby DFC RCAF and Warrant Officer Oliver Lambert DFM the rear gunner were killed.

20. On 8/9 September when 257 bombers, including five American B-17 Flying Fortresses, attacked the German long-range gun batteries near Boulogne the *Oboe* Mosquitoes marked the target with green LB TIs and red TIs. The marking and bombing was poor and the gun batteries were largely untouched.

21. Middlebrook.

22. *Bomber Command* by Max Hastings (Pan 1979).

23. Stirling EE973 was written off after the crash landing at Witchford. 'Our next trip' adds Lawton, 'the bombing of the entrance to the Mont Cenis tunnel in France, was uneventful and that made us a lot happier. Then Stirlings were taken off bombing as they were outclassed by Lancasters and were death-traps, 5,000 feet below the Lancs' where they were just right for all the flak and bombs from above.' Late in November 1943 Bill Day's crew finished their tour. 'We were loath to leave,' says James. After losing a total of 43 aircraft in six months, or to put it another way, two complete squadrons, to say that we enjoyed our stay seems rather paradoxical but it was true.' Five of the crew went on to complete a second tour; Ron James on B-17 Fortresses on 214 Squadron in 100 Group (Bomber Support).

24. 13 Halifaxes, 13 Lancasters and 8 Stirlings, or 5.6% of the force.

25. *Spirit of Russia* had flown 93 sorties when it was re-assigned to 189 Squadron in October 1944. By the time it was taken off ops, the last on 2/3 February 1945, EE136 had 109 bombs painted below the cockpit.

26. *Bombs And Barbed Wire: My War in the RAF and Stalag Luft III*, Geoffrey Willatt. (Parapress Ltd, 1995).

CHAPTER 3

Silver Wings in the Moonlight

I dreamed that my lover had gone for a moonlight walk.
I spoke to the moon but the moon wouldn't talk.

Hubert C 'Nick' Knilans had left Delavan High School in Wisconsin in 1935 and in the summer months he milked cows and worked the horses on the family farm in Walworth County. Delavan was a thriving manufacturing town about half way between Milwaukee and Chicago where Knilans looked for jobs when winter came. But Knilans' ambitions lay elsewhere. In October 1941 when his call-up papers had run out, the 24-year-old had driven up to Canada to join the RCAF with the intention to become a 'Yank' in Canadian clothing in Bomber Command. At that time the United States was still neutral but many adventurous young Americans were not prepared to wait for the call to arms. They 'defected' to Canada and 'signed on' to join the RAF with the intention of becoming a fully fledged pilot on fighter or bomber aircraft; men like Pilot Officer Hubert Clarence 'Nick' Knilans, who became a Lancaster pilot on 619 Squadron at Woodhall Spa, one and a half miles from the Victorian spa town. At the time most Americans wished to remain neutral, millions choosing to follow the progress of the *Blitz* and the war in Europe by tuning in to Edward R Murrow, head of CBS European Bureau in London for his penetrating radio broadcasts, *This Is London*. Millions more digested the column inches graphically written by reporters who were syndicated in many hundreds of newspapers throughout the USA, but not all columnists were as enthusiastic as Murrow when it came to championing the British cause. Boake Carter, who was syndicated in 83 newspapers with a combined circulation of more than seven million readers asked, 'Where does the Roosevelt Administration derive the idea that Americans want to go gallivanting forth to play Sir Galahad again?' Walter Winchell, syndicated in 150 newspapers, 8.5 million-circulation,

102

struck home; saying, 'The future of American youth is on top of American soil not underneath European dirt.'[1]

American observers in Germany and career officers such as General Raymond Lee, the US Military Attaché in London, also remained sceptical about Britain's massive industrial commitment to heavy bombers. During a lunch at the Dorchester, Lee told the assembled British officials and four Air Marshals that 'the British had no proof yet that their bombing had been any more effective than the German bombing of England'. He added, 'I thought they were asking the United States for a good deal when they wanted it to divest itself of all its bombers and devote a lot of production capacity to the construction of more bombers, thereby committing the US to the policy of reducing Germany by bombing, without affording sufficient proof that this was possible.' Attitudes had changed little after America entered the war. In April 1942 the American air attaché in London reported to Washington that, 'The British public have an erroneous belief, which has been fostered by effective RAF publicity, that the German war machine can be destroyed and the nation defeated by intensive bombing.' While General Lee never flew an 'op' in a Lancaster as Murrow would, he did at least venture northeast to see what Bomber Command was capable of and he observed RAF bomber crews at a station somewhere in England.

They were a queer conglomeration, these men – some educated and sensitive, some rough-haired and burly and drawn from all parts the Empire, Great Britain, Canada, New Zealand and Australia ... Some, of them were humming, some were singing, some were laughing and others were standing serious and thoughtful. It looked like the dressing room where the jockeys sit waiting before a great steeplechase ... [At take-off] the control officer flashed a green ray for a split second, which was the signal that this plane was designated for take-off. Its roaring grew louder and louder as it dragged its heavy tail towards the starting point like a slow, nearly helpless monster. About twenty yards away we could just discern a vast dinosaurish shape; after a moment, as if stopping to make up its mind; it lumbered forward, raising its tail just as it passed us and turning from something very heavy and clumsy into a lightly poised shape, rushing through the night like a pterodactyl. At this instant, a white light was flashed upon it and a Canadian boy from Vancouver who was standing beside me, put down its number and the moment of departure. It vanished from sight at once and we stood, staring down the field, where in a few seconds a flashing green light announced that it had left the ground ... A great calm settled over the place as the last droning motors faded out in the distance and we all drove back to the control room where a staff hang onto the instruments on a long night vigil ... I went to sleep thinking of the youngsters I had seen, all now 150 miles away; straining their eyes through a black-ness relieved only by the star-spangled vault above them.[2]

One of the growing band of 'star-spangled' pilots who flew a Lancaster on the night of 23/24 September 1943 when 627 bombers set out for Mannheim, was Pilot Officer 'Nick' Knilans. He already knew the odds. Bomber Command was in the midst of an offensive against German cities with four raids on Hannover in September–October. Hannover had been the target for 711 bombers the night before. The Main Force had arrived over the city in good weather but there was a stronger wind than forecast and most of the attack fell up to five miles from the aiming point and at the end as far as nine miles from the AP. It did not help when the backers up aimed their TI greens at reds instead of yellows. Some 2,500 tons of bombs were dropped mainly in suburban areas and open country. At least 20 out of the 26 bombers lost were shot down over the target by both single-engined and twin-engined night fighters that engaged the bomber stream *en masse* and in *Wild Boar* fashion over the burning city. Flak too was 'intense'. There was no reason to think that Mannheim's defences would be any different.

On the outward flight Knilans experienced divine intervention:

The upper sky before me was still somewhat lighted. A figure of a woman, several thousand feet above slowly emerged into my startled view. I recognized this vision as that of a girl I had loved very much. She had died six years before at the age of 19. I had kissed her good-bye one evening and a short while later her father had telephoned me to say that she was dead from pneumonia, unsuspected until it was too late. I had been one of the pall bearers. Now, she had a slight smile on her lips as I flew towards her ... The vision soon vanished into the darkening sky. I said nothing to the crew then or later. I did not know whether she had appeared to reassure me that she would keep me from harm, or that she was welcoming me into her world of the hereafter. I certainly hoped it wouldn't be the latter ... Maybe, I thought, someone was trying to point, for me, a way ...[3]

Knilans would remain at Woodhall Spa for eighteen months of operations on 619 Squadron and in that time 42 Lancasters with 294 men aboard were lost and most of the men killed. In the first six months, no crew was able to complete its first tour. One Canadian pilot's hair turned from brown to grey before he was shot down. The strain of continuous operations began to affect Knilans' 22-year-old rear gunner, Sergeant Gordon Hunter 'Jerry' Jackson, a Scot from Dumfries. When he received a telegram from his wife, Phoebe, in Scotland that he had a new-born son, Jackson rushed over to see Acting Wing Commander William 'Jock' Abercromby and he asked to be taken off flying duties. Abercromby was thirty-three years old and from Inverness-shire. The 'Wingco' told Jackson that he was due for leave in a week's time and that he could see the baby then. In the meantime the rear gunner had to remain on flying status.

On Friday 24 September Harold Wakefield a flight engineer on Halifaxes on 51 Squadron wrote lyrically and confidently to his parents describing his first two operations, to Hannover and to Mannheim:

The first trip on Wednesday night to Hannover we weren't nervous, more excited. The only time we were scared, was when we arrived a little way off the target. When we saw the fires, searchlights and ack-ack, we did feel nervous for a second but it passed over. Johnny said, 'OK blokes, I'm not stopping here long, it ain't healthy, let's get back for the eggs and bacon'. (We have egg and bacon before we go and again as soon as we get back. It's worth it to get two lots of egg and bacon.) So he turned in, opened up the engines, put the nose down for extra speed and we dived over Hannover at about 250, dropped the goods and were out again, all in about two minutes. One of the lads said over the intercom, 'Coo, ain't it pretty.' Another said, 'Blimey, it's just like Blackpool illuminations.' Some of the things they say are really funny. Last night I wasn't the slightest bit nervous or excited, honestly. It's rather boring.

Two in two nights, it's not often that happens. We do on average two or three a week. I enjoyed every minute of it and believe me there's not much of those two cities left. Jerry's certainly going through it. One minute the place is peaceful and then in about 30 minutes it's a mass of blazing ruins, on fire from end to end. Flames and smoke thousands of feet high. They're just swamped. I could still see the fires burning, the glow in the sky, when we were 200 miles away and that's not exaggerating. Plane after plane, one after the other, just shoving 'em down. Poor Jerry, It's terrible what they're going through. But we enjoy doing it just the same. Their defences aren't bad, but just bewildered. We're all in and out so quickly that they don't have time to get going. Their flak doesn't seem to be able to reach us. But it explodes underneath us and shakes us a bit; it's quite a pleasant sensation though. They rely chiefly on their night fighters. But they're not so hot. Nothing we can't deal with and if we see them coming first they don't stand an earthly because there are eight belching machine guns waiting for 'em and I've seen more than one Jerry fighter going down in flames, bless 'em. Yes I'd much sooner be up where we are than down below at Jerry's end. He knows what bombing is now alright, believe me. It's mass slaughter, with Jerry at the receiving end and he won't be able to stand it much longer. Hannover and Mannheim are heaps of rubble now and I'll bet those fires will burn for days. I think the Jerry firemen are the hardest worked blokes of the war.

It's nice on the way back home, when we get well away from the target and get the coffee out and the chocolates. It makes me hungry. We've had no trouble at all yet and I've done my job to the satisfaction of everyone. Johnny our pilot is wonderful. He can throw our kite about like an Austin Seven. A searchlight picked us up over Hannover but Johnny was out of that in about two seconds. A fighter got on our tail but Jock had him spotted and told Johnny, a couple of twists and turns and that fighter was soon disposed of, he lost us altogether. Poor old Jock was mad though because he didn't have a burst at it. There's no need for guns on our kite because Johnny can lose 'em in two shakes. It's a piece of cake.

We've got a rest for two or three nights now, to catch up on our sleep. I don't feel any different. My nerves are better, if anything.

Well, I thought you'd want to know, because you've always liked to know what I'm doing and I thought you'd be getting suspicious if I didn't tell you soon. But there's no reason at all for you to worry, because I know I'm going to be OK and I've always got my parachute handy ...

At Downham Market on 27 September Pilot Officer William Francis Cecil Knight DFC's crew on 218 Squadron was one of 678 crews detailed to bomb Hannover that night. After briefing they went through their usual rituals and various idiosyncrasies designed to bring them good luck. In the early hours of the morning on return from ops Sergeant Alfred Charles Petre, a Londoner and the WOp/AG on the crew, would always enter the Sergeants Mess and play the same record on the gramophone: Flanagan and Allen singing *Underneath the Arches*. That night the Pathfinders were misled by strong winds. Just four visual markers identified the aiming point, although some crews made as many as four runs over the city trying to identify it. Only 612 aircraft dropped their bombs and mostly fell on an area five miles north of the city. RAF crews were not yet expert with the new *H2S* navigational radar, which showed up an expanse of water very well, but the Steinhuder See, a large lake which was used as a way point, had been almost completely covered with boards and nets. Millions of strips of *Window* were dropped and a diversion raid on Brunswick by 21 Lancasters and six Mosquitoes was successful in drawing off some of the night fighters, but no fewer than 39 bombers were shot down.[4] Eighteen of the missing were Halifaxes and three of them were on 10 Squadron. *L-Leather* piloted by Pilot Officer Harry Cockrem RAAF was attacked by a Focke-Wulf 190 who came up through his own flak and fired at the Halifax from below, while a Junkers Ju 88 flew behind the bomber acting as a decoy. The Halifax began to burn and the calm voice of the Australian pilot said, 'Prepare to abandon.' The intercom then cut out as the small fire ate through the electrical wires. Pilot Officer Harold Nash, the navigator, had a feeling of unease in his stomach the whole time he was on ops. He liked Dickens and just before putting his flying suit on he was reading *Pickwick Papers* and he kept reading the same page over and over again:

Nothing was absorbed, nothing went in. There was a confusion in my mind; a kind of inner alienation from my usual calm. But we were good actors. We all pretended that everything was well. There was a flight lieutenant whom I liked a lot. He'd done about 18 operations but one day he got into the cockpit and he couldn't fly it off. He was trembling. He was reduced to the ranks and on his documents was written the words 'LMF.' He was a fantastic chap and there were several like that. I think that if I hadn't been shot down – it was I think my 13th operation – I might have gone that way myself eventually.

I was off the intercom. The Skipper was swaying the aircraft from one side to the other. I didn't take a great deal of notice because we often did that over Germany to avoid fighters. But suddenly there was this huge rat-a-tat and the whole plane shuddered and shattered. Soon it was on fire. Fear is a strange experience: To begin with the plane was going down slowly and we must have been at about 19,000 or 20,000 feet. We couldn't get the trapdoor open and I thought 'God, I'm going to die.' Now I was a coward and I sat down on the step and I went very calm. It was a kind of peace. I was certain that one member was praying. I gave the pilot his parachute; that was an agreement between us. Suddenly the door opened and I helped a very badly wounded man out. It was the bomb aimer. He said he thought he would die before he hit the ground. The bomb aimer's chute was all over the nose of the aircraft. Somehow in his haste he pulled the cord and the thing had opened. Then I sprang and counted to 10 slowly like a good boy. I must have been going head-over-heels because every now and again the fire of the plane appeared only to disappear again. I counted 10 and then pulled the cord. My left-boot shot off. I wanted to see clouds but there were trees. I'd almost pulled the cord too late and I landed straightaway in the corner of a field. I hid the parachute under bushes as instructed. As soon as I realised I was safe I began to tremble again. All the fear came back. My first thought was to get to Holland. I knew that in September there was a triangle of stars, the base of which is roughly east/west and I thought of going west. I'd only gone a few yards and there was what I thought was a huge German gun pointing to the sky. I went gingerly around it but it wasn't a gun. It was a road barrier that was up. I went on for four nights. I hid and slept in the day. I remember one 6 o'clock looking at my watch and thinking about this girl in York who would be waiting for me that day. We weren't supposed to be on this operation. A crew had gone sick. We were going on a week's leave the next day but we were called to take their place. I had this date with her but she would realise eventually what had happened when I didn't turn up.

It was sheer fear that kept me going. By my final afternoon my socks had worn out I was so tired, even though I tried going to sleep in the day. I can remember being awakened by four boys, German boys from a neighbouring village playing soldiers. One had got a dummy rifle on his shoulder and he saw me lying behind a bush. He didn't come right across. He just stood there and looked and then went on to catch up his companions. He probably thought that I was a forced worker. There were lots of them in Germany. I was tired, demoralised – I'd got a growth of beard, I was dirty, hungry and thirsty, lying in the early October sunshine. I went to sleep and was awakened by three women sitting talking. I was in a copse over-hanging a road. On the other side of the road was a river. I decided to remain in the copse. They were talking for two hours without realising that there was a British airman within a few yards of them. I finally came out of my hiding place and arrived at three cottages. The door opened and a man came out. I said slowly, in bits of schoolboy German, 'English airman'. He was going to walk past me as I was giving myself up. I pulled back my brown inner suit and he saw the wings and the penny dropped. He took me into the house. It was barely furnished and there was a baby in the corner in a wooden box. He left me with his wife and went off into the village to get the village policeman. He must have realised I was harmless even then. The policeman came and put handcuffs on me. He had a Hitler haircut and moustache.

Nash and Sergeant P D Craven the flight engineer were the only two crew members to survive.

As well as the 18 Halifaxes that were lost there were ten missing Stirlings, a Wellington and ten Lancasters. One of the missing Lancasters was flown by Squadron Leader John Herbert Kennard DFC on 103 Squadron at Elsham Wolds who was on his second tour. Don Charlwood recalled that 'besides a DFC he wore two operational adornments – the usual ops cap and a wide moustache, the whistle worn as he alone wore it, on a cord over his shoulder. His eyes were dark and staring as though constant peering into the darkness had left them so. He was, I believe, little more than a boy and it was sometimes said on the squadron that he wore his moustache to disguise his youth.'[5]

One of the Stirlings that was missing and had ditched in the sea was probably the victim of an intruder flown by *Oberleutnant* Rudolf Abrahamczik of 14./KG2 who claimed a *Viermot* off Cromer. Four of the crew were killed; three survived to be taken prisoner.[6] In a separate intruder action Abrahamczik shot down the Lancaster flown by Pilot Officer Desmond Skipper on 101 Squadron in flames near Wickenby after he had been refused permission to land back at Ludford Magna and was told to head for Lindholme. There were no survivors.[7] Seven other aircraft crashed or crash-landed at bases on their return, claiming the lives of 16 crew and injuring five.

At Downham Market no word was received from *A-Apple* and Pilot Officer Knight's crew. They had all been killed. In the early hours of 28 September someone else entered the sergeants' mess and played *Underneath The Arches.*

After a break in operations, over 350 aircraft took off on the night of 29/30 September for Bochum, home of the huge Bochumer Verein steel-works, producing 160,000 tons a month. *Oboe*-assisted Path Finder aircraft marked the target and the bombing was concentrated. Five Halifaxes and four Lancaster IIIs failed to return. Two of the Halifax Vs that were lost were from 434 'Bluenose' Squadron RCAF at Tholthorpe. *L-Leather* piloted by 2nd Lieutenant J T Clary USAAF was shot down by a night fighter and crashed in Holland. Four of his crew, including fellow American, Sergeant R W Stewart the mid-upper gunner, were taken prisoner. Eighteen-year-old Sergeant Bert Scudder and one other were killed; the American pilot managed to evade capture.

A total of 178 victories were credited to German night fighters in September, and during October 149 RAF bombers were destroyed by *Nachtjagd.* On the night of 1/2 October, 243 Lancasters and eight Mosquitoes of 1, 5 and 8 Groups set out for Hagen, one of the many industrial towns in the Ruhr. At Binbrook Pilot Officer Scott RAAF on 460 Squadron RAAF hauled his Lancaster off the runway for what was to be his 24th operation over occupied Europe. Over Holland the Australian's aircraft was hit by anti aircraft fire and the cockpit canopy was shattered, fragments of the Perspex lodged in an eye and, with his face covered in blood and only partial sight, Scott decided to press on to the target and dropped his bombs on the aiming point. The raid was a complete success achieved on a totally cloud-covered target of small size. Two of the town's four industrial areas were severely hit and a third suffered lesser damage. An important factory, which manufactured accumulator batteries for *U-boats,* was among the 46 industrial factories that were destroyed and 166 damaged. Battery output to the *Untersee Boots* was slowed down considerably. Thirty thousand people were bombed out as over 3,400 fires, of which 100 were 'large', ravaged the town. One Lancaster failed to return and a second was lost when it crashed on return in the Bristol Channel with the loss of all seven crew.

Next day was filled with considerable tension on the Lancaster stations of 1, 5 and 8 Groups in the Lincolnshire and East Anglian flat lands. Sir

Arthur Harris was in the midst of a campaign of area bombing German cities at night using Lancasters and Halifaxes, while B-24 Liberators and B-17 Flying Fortresses of the US 8th and 12th Air Forces stoked the fires by day. At a station in Lincolnshire, D W Pye, a WOp/AG on Lancaster *Q-Queenie* – 'a grand job, tuned up to perfection' wrote:

We were on the 'programme' for that night's operation [2/3 October] and the usual rumours were going the rounds in the mess as to where they were going. We knew that we had on board our Lancaster a 2,200 gallon petrol load and so the trip must be in the region of a ten-hour 'Op' – quite a long one. We reported to the Briefing Room at 17.00 hours. This was it. Now we would know the worst. We learned that our target was Munich, a tough one, with about eleven hundred ack-ack guns, 300 searchlights and on top of that a good chance of heavy night fighter defence on the way in and out. We [around 290 Lancasters and two B-17s] were being routed-in over France, across the Alps skirting the Swiss border and down south; a nasty way if one got engine trouble and had to climb the 16,000 feet to clear such peaks as Mont Blanc.

Once in the aircraft we did our last pre-flight checks. All was OK so we climbed out again for a last natter, a cup of tea, a smoke and a joke or two with our ground crew. The Commanding Officer came up in his jeep, asked if all was well and wished us all the best. Then he was on to the next dispersal point and crew. A hard job the CO had; he knew for sure that a number of the boys he was talking to would not come back and tomorrow he would have the task of writing to their mothers, wives and sweethearts. The Skipper checked the time and, seeing that we were the first off, we switched on, revved up and taxied out on to the runway. The 'green' came from the Airfield Controller and we were off, tearing down the runway and up into the night, circling, climbing and eventually setting course on the first leg of our route to Munich.

It was a dark night, with cloud above us and cloud below. One felt very lonely in a world of one's own with a population of only seven, each with a job to do and each dependent upon the other doing his job and doing it right if all were to survive. But one knew that one was with the best and most reliable chaps in the world.

So the trip went on with no real incident. The night was clear and moonlit and the mountains below looked beautiful and even peaceful. Little could we guess what a menace they would be upon our return. My crew, along with three others were to fly over the target five minutes before the main force and find the wind's speed and direction, which I had then to radio back to ensure accurate bombing. This added considerably to the danger of the 'Op' for us, as it meant that the full force of Munich's defence would be thrown at just four aircraft until the main force arrived. Anyhow, on to the target we ran and then all hell burst loose. In the twenty trips I had done before never had I seen such a density of ack-ack fire. It seemed to cover the whole town. We were picked up with searchlights within seconds of entering the target area. Having to find the wind direction necessitated the Skipper keeping our plane on a straight and level course for a while, which meant that if we were to do our duty we could not take evasive action. We were right in the midst of the flak now and still we had not been hit. Then we got it, a direct hit on the outer starboard engine. It packed up like a light gone out and the whole of that side of the aircraft became a mass of holes from shrapnel. But we were lucky: not one of us was wounded. Just before the hit we had completed getting the wind, so I got cracking in sending it back. I repeated it three times to make sure of its reception and then informed the Skipper of what I had done. That was the main part of our job completed. We have only to run out and come in again with the main force to bomb – and then for home. That is going to be a difficult job, though, for I see on looking round again that one engine was finished altogether and another was only working on half power.

The Skipper came on to the intercom to the whole crew and asked if we were still all OK. We were, except for the bomb-aimer's flying-suit that had been cut right across the chest by a piece of flying shrapnel: a lucky miss. The Skipper asked us if we feel that we would be justified in ditching the bombs and getting out as quickly as possible but we are all in full agreement that we have to run in again and finish the bombing. By this time the main force had arrived and we turned towards the target to commence our bombing run. Our height was now down to 8,000 feet and we could not climb any higher, though we could maintain this height with care. The flares had gone down and the target area was bathed in a brilliant white light. The markers were exploding and the Master Bomber had commenced his instructions over the wireless. He told us that the markers were not quite on target and that we must not bomb until he had been down to assess how we must aim in relation to the red marker-bombs.

We could see the Master Bomber's Lancaster far below us and going lower all the time. The light anti-aircraft guns were all after him now but his words came through quite clear and confident: 'Bomb in such and such an area away from the markers.' Then we saw his plane burst into flames. It was going down afire from nose to tail but his instructions still came through. He passed all the information we needed and then: 'Cheerio, lads, this is it,' he called and dived to the ground in a mass of flames.[8]

By this time we had got quite a way over the target and our bomb-aimer informed the Skipper that if we were to bomb accurately we should have to run round again. So we turned round out of the target area and made a half-circle to get back on to a new bombing run. We managed this without further mishap and started on our third run over the target. I thought, 'If we keep this up much longer, old *Queenie* will know Munich pretty well.'

Our bomb-aimer's instructions to the pilot were now coming over the intercom: 'Left, left, right, left, left, steady, steady, on aiming point, steady, bombs, gone.' We felt the plane give its customary jump after being freed of the seven-ton weight of HE and we had started on the long flight home.

Visibility over the target was clear but the initial marking was scattered. A record was established when almost four tons of bombs per minute were dropped on the city in a 25-minute period between 22.30 and 22.55 hours. Heavy bombing developed over the southern and south-eastern districts of Munich but later stages of the raid fell up to 15 miles back along the approach route. Most of this inaccurate bombing was carried out by 5 Group Lancasters, which were again attempting their 'time-and-distance' bombing method independently of the Path Finder marking. The 5 Group crews were unable to pick out the Wurmsee Lake, which was the starting-point for their timed run.

D W Pye continues:

We ran into more flak but a few more holes wouldn't make much difference for the plane was more like a sieve than anything else. There were still no wounded aboard and the rear and mid-upper gunners were getting a bit of their own back with shooting out searchlights. They finished a couple of them and that cheered us up considerably. We knew that we had a very tough job to get back. As we could only just maintain a height of 8,000 feet, it meant we had to work our way through the Alps, flying down the passes and keep a sharp look-out for any unexpected peaks. It was rather nerve-racking to see the mountains towering up above the plane but we got through, thanks to the brilliant flying of our Skipper. We carried on over France and now another big snag appeared. The engineer said that we had barely enough petrol to reach the coast of England. The problem was whether to land in France and try to avoid capture or to carry on and possibly have to ditch in the sea. We decided to keep going and to help us maintain height we threw out all the equipment we could manage without. This helped a little and we went limping on. One good thing about this trip was that so far we had not met up with any German fighter planes.

We were now over the sea, the tanks were very nearly empty and I tried to contact a wireless station to inform them of our plight and position. I got in touch with Manston and they told me we were to try to reach them, when they would have everything ready for a crash landing. We went in a direct line for Manston. We were all tense, praying and hoping for just an extra bit of luck to pull us through. The coast came into sight and then the lights of the 'drome. We got fastened down but when the Skipper checked the flaps and undercarriage he found that the latter would not come down. It must be badly damaged, so we informed Control that we would have to make a belly-landing. The Skipper asked us if we would like to bail out while he brought the aircraft in alone. We all told him that he had brought us all this way back and we would rather take our chance with him than otherwise.

We were now in line with the runway and losing height rapidly when the outer port engine started coughing and spluttering, then cut out altogether. The other engines followed suit in quick succession but now we were nearly on the deck. We went tearing up the runway and what happened next is difficult to describe because the plane did everything but loop-the-loop. There was a dreadful racket of tearing metal, banging and crashing but we eventually came to a stop. The wings had been torn from the fuselage, the tail we had left halfway down the runway and the nose of the plane was crumpled in like a broken egg-shell. But the thing that mattered really was that except for a goodly number of minor cuts, abrasions and bruises, we were quite all right. The fire-tender came up with the ambulance in close attendance and the next thing we knew was that we were in bed in hospital, quite fit but according to the MO, suffering from 'severe strain and operational shock'. We were only 'invalids' for one night and then it was back to base.[9]

'H Squared' on 103 Squadron was also lucky to return after a Me 110 put over 400 bullet holes in the Lancaster just after leaving Munich, as Norman Bolt the mid upper gunner, recalls:

The rear turret caught eight holes, my turret caught twelve, the *H2S* was smashed and the rear gunner was knocked to hell. There was just a great hole, which I nearly fell down when I jumped out of the mid upper to put out a fire in the mid oxygen point. Miraculously not one of the crew was injured, nor was a vital part re controls or petrol tanks hit. We returned to Elsham Woods and the Skipper said 'I am going to put her down hard – I've got two greens (for the undercarriage) but I'm not sure' – to which the rear gunner said 'don't you always put it down hard?' We landed OK but when the tail wheel touched the deck all hell was let loose. When we left the Lanc at dispersal all the rear gunner got from the Skipper was 'that will teach you to criticise my landings'![10]

Seven bombers were shot down by night fighters on the raid and a 467 Squadron Lancaster ditched 25 miles off Beachy Head. All except one of the crew perished.

At Bardney on 3 October Ron Walkup's crew on 9 Squadron sat around their table in the Briefing Room looking anxiously at the black screen which covered the wall map that held the answer to all their thoughts – the target. They had completed 11 operations together, the trips ranging all over Germany including Hamburg, Munich, Mannheim, Hannover and the Ruhr and so it could be said that they were settling down into an experienced team, which included Sergeant Angus Leslie the 23-year-old mid-upper-gunner and M C Wright the navigator. Even so, they still had to come face to face with the enemy. They were not to know at briefing on 3 October that this was to be the night. The Squadron Commander pulled the screen to one side to reveal that the target was the Henschel and Fiesler aircraft factories at Kassel, which made V-1 flying bombs. Just over 200 Lancaster crews were included in the force of 547 aircraft that were detailed and 9 Squadron was putting on 12 aircraft in the first wave. 'The route,' recalls Wright 'would take us in north of the Ruhr and out to the south. There was nothing unusual about the target and as usual we were warned to expect a strong concentration of searchlights and anti-aircraft guns.'

At Woodhall Spa Pilot Officer 'Nick' Knilans' crew on 619 Squadron were also 'on'. Wing Commander 'Jock' Abercromby had told the American Skipper that Jerry Jackson was deeply troubled, but Knilans said nothing to his rear gunner. He did not need to know that his Skipper knew. As they assembled around the Lancaster before take-off they congratulated Jackson on the birth of his son. Knilans recalled:

He was a chain smoker anyway, so no one thought of his nervousness as anything out of the ordinary. He seemed less despondent as we took our stations. At 21.21 hours we were at 19,000 feet over Germany and turning for our target when 'Monica', the fighter-detection device, indicated an aircraft within 300 yards, which we believed to be another Lancaster – until a stream of tracer cannon and machine gun bullets came through the port wing and thudded into the fuselage. I dived to starboard and yelled down the intercom to Jerry; 'Can you see him?' There was no reply. Roy, the mid-upper gunner, noticed tracer entering the rear turret and causing an explosion and he was temporarily blinded by Perspex, which hit him in the eyes. We had to feather the port inner engine but we went on to bomb and stayed with the stream.

M C Wright continues:

> Within a few minutes of time on target, Ron Walkup reported no sign of Path Finder activity, nor anything else for that matter. Suddenly we were lit up like the fairy on a Christmas tree and almost at once both gunners sighted a Focke Wulf 190 at about 700 yards passing from starboard to the port quarter. The rear gunner told the pilot to start the standard corkscrew manoeuvre, but the fighter hung-on and at 600 yards both our gunners opened fire. The FW 190 replied with cannon and his initial burst cleanly shot away the cupola of our mid-upper turret, also severing the electrical and oxygen supplies to both turrets: Angus Leslie was killed by a shell through the head. At 300 yards the fighter and Wally Mullet the rear gunner exchanged fire again and the latter could see his shots hit the fighter's engine. It turned sharply to port, rolled over on its back and when alongside the Lancaster at about 100 yards it exploded. Pieces of fighter thudded against the side of the Lancaster; Wally lost consciousness through lack of oxygen. Ron Walkup decided to lose height until oxygen was no longer needed and in the end Wally suffered nothing more than mild frostbite as a result of the loss of electricity to his heated flying suit.

The *H2S* 'blind marker' aircraft overshot the aiming point at Kassel by some distance and the 'visual markers' were unable to correct the error because of thick haze which restricted visibility. *Nachtjagd* claimed 17 of the 24 heavies shot down for nine *Tame Boar* losses.

Pilot Officer Wilkie Wanless was the rear gunner on the crew of *P-Peter*, the 76 Squadron Halifax flown by Pilot Officer Arthur Thorp, briefed for Kassel where they flew the diversion, flying past Kassel and then turning and going back. Wanless, who was on his 24th operation, recalled:

> After the turn coming back we got hit by a fighter. Nobody saw him. He came up underneath us with his upward firing cannons. He hit the starboard wing and he must have hit the fuselage too because he killed the mid-upper gunner. We were a ball of fire. Everyone got out except the mid-upper gunner [Sergeant John Thomas Zuidmulder] and the pilot. Why the pilot didn't get out I have no idea. I spoke to Thorp from the rear turret. I said, 'this is the rear gunner – I'm going out; everyone else has gone.' I pulled my chute in, buckled it on and flipped out backwards. I was always very apprehensive about getting run into by another aircraft in the stream, so I did a delayed drop, landed in a potato patch, undid my chute, buried it under some potato tops, took off my sheepskin trousers. I'd taken my helmet off in the aircraft; otherwise you would break your neck if

you bailed out with it on. It was about 9 o'clock at night. I walked out to what I thought had been a river but it·was an Autobahn. I walked out on to the highway and trundled along until I became absolutely exhausted when the nervous reaction set in. I crawled into some brush and went to sleep. I thought I'd get to Switzerland. We had escape kits and a beautiful silk map so I knew where I was. I was a mess. I'd fallen in a few ditches. The second night I hid and the third day I was in a ditch by a farmer's field. He came to look at his hay crop and saw me there. I pretended I was French with my schoolboy language. He just shrugged and walked away. Within a short time three men arrived and arrested me, marched me into the town hall. The *Gestapo* called in an old man who had been in England in the First World War to interpret. They phoned Berlin. When they phoned Berlin they said '*Vilhelm Alexander Vilkie Vanless*'. I kept saying, 'No, no, no – William Alexander Wilkie Wanless.' They locked me up in the city jail and during the night a couple of *Luftwaffe* guys arrived in a Black Maria and took me to the air base. They assigned me an armed guard and he took me by train to Frankfurt and the interrogation centre. I was amazed to look up in Frankfurt station and see all the glass. I thought we would have broken it all by then. An elderly German went by and saw 'Canada' on my shoulder. He looked terribly disturbed and started screaming. It was a mob scene in seconds and my escort had to get his *Luger* out. He grabbed me by the arm and said 'run' and we just ran down the platform as the train was coming in. You couldn't hold it against anybody. The RAF had been there a night or two before; the Americans had been there a day or two before. You could feel for them.

On the way to the target Flight Sergeant Gordon G Wright RCAF, bomb aimer on Stirling *G-George* on 15 Squadron at Mildenhall, flown by Flight Sergeant A V Wood, made his way back to relieve the wireless operator of the task of throwing out bundles of *Window*. He began the job there on the floor of the Stirling just in front of the main spar. After only a few minutes of ejecting the *Window* Wright heard Flight Sergeant W T E 'Bill' Highland RAAF the rear gunner tell the pilot, 'Go port.' The gunner had spotted a Bf 110 closing quickly and the pilot immediately began the diving manoeuvre to port. Just as he did so, Highland began firing at the fighter and at almost the same instant *Oberleutnant* Fritz Lau of III./NJG1, who was their attacker, opened fire. The former *Lufthansa* airline pilot raked the Stirling with cannon shells from tail to cockpit. Intercom communication with both Highland and Sergeant Rex Blanchard the mid-upper gunner was then lost, as the intercom system was damaged. The aircraft's hydraulics was also knocked out and in a few moments a large fire broke out in the centre of the fuselage.

Though seriously wounded in the right hip, Sergeant J R Arrowsmith the wireless operator came forward at this point. The navigator, Flight Sergeant J S Curtis RNZAF had left his table to confer with the pilot about their position. He then returned to his table to try and recover his maps which were being blown around in the fuselage due to a large hole that had been blasted just above his position. Had he been sitting there during the fighter attack he would almost certainly have been killed instantly. Now the dazed and injured wireless operator reached the navigator and asked him what they were going to do. Gordon Wright joined them by stepping carefully over the body of Sergeant Leslie Graham the flight engineer, who had been killed in the attack. The pilot, who was struggling to keep the crippled bomber stabilized, then gave the order, 'Abandon aircraft.'

Wright responded quickly, grabbing the pilot's parachute from behind his seat and fastening it onto his skipper. He then followed Arrowsmith to the front escape hatch. When Wright reached the hatch he found it had slammed shut again. Now the Stirling, in its death throes, was entering a slow spiral, pinning the navigator alternately to the floor or the ceiling and frustrating his attempts to leave the plane. Finally, Wright managed to open the hatch again and, after contacting the pilot, he and the wireless operator and the navigator, bailed out. With the Stirling now down to less than 3,000 feet, the pilot was able to switch on the auto-pilot, leave his seat and make his way forward to the escape hatch only to find that once again it had slammed shut. The Stirling continued to spiral downward. The centre section and right wing were now burning furiously and the 6,000lb load of incendiaries remained in the bomb bay. The disabled hydraulic system meant that the bomb doors could not be opened and the crew had been unable to get rid of the bomb load. *G-George* fell through a height of 1,500 feet when Wood at last got to the escape hatch and somehow re-opened it. He left the aircraft with no time to spare. The Stirling crashed at Haste in the northern suburbs of Osnabrück.

Fighter action had caused some bombers to crash on return. A Stirling plummeted into a field at Scottow near RAF Coltishall injuring six and killing one of the crew. At Middleton St. George a 419 'Moose' Squadron Halifax crashed on landing and a 428 'Ghost' Squadron Halifax on the same station was wrecked after landing at Tangmere. Many of the Halifaxes, Lancasters and Stirlings that returned from Kassel carried dead and wounded aboard. Ron Walkup eventually landed at Ford at 04.00 after a lonely return flight at low level. A quick examination by the Squadron engineer soon confirmed that the aircraft was a write-off, riddled from the middle to the tail with bullet holes and the upper turret disappeared altogether. But of greatest interest were pieces of FW 190 embedded in the fuselage. This was one claim that could not be denied. Wally was awarded the DFM and the crew all went to Boston to celebrate.

Heading for home Nick Knilans had dropped to 12,000 feet and he sent the flight engineer aft to check on Jerry Jackson. He found him slumped over his guns. Knilans wrote:

> When we landed I told the crew they need not stay on to see Jerry taken from his turret. The ground crew were unable to open the turret doors, as the force of the cannon shells had driven Jerry against them and I had to use a screwdriver to prise them apart. Then I got hold of Jerry's collar and pulled him backwards, free of the turret. His body was stiff as I lowered it to the ground and took off his goggles, oxygen mask and helmet. His still features were unmarked. I brushed back a fallen lock of hair. His forehead was icy cold. The middle of his flying suit was badly torn and bloodstained. After examining him, one of the ambulance helpers suddenly became ill and had to walk away. The cannon shells had cut Jerry in half.
>
> I stayed behind in the darkness, depressed at losing my friend. When I got to the briefing room the Squadron doctor told me that Jerry must have died instantaneously. He gave me two sleeping pills but I gave them to a WAAF who was overcome with grief. She was a good friend of Jerry's and he had given her his personal effects to send to his parents if he failed to return. Before drifting off to sleep, I prayed that God would see Jerry into heaven.[11]

In his office on the same airfield Abercromby tore up the pass for Jerry Jackson. A telegram would be going out to the gunner's next-of-kin. At Bardney a similarly worded telegram was being sent to Kathleen Leslie in Romford telling her that her husband Angus was dead.

On 4/5 October just over 400 aircraft attacked Frankfurt. Clear weather and good Path Finder resulted in extensive devastation to the eastern half of the city and in the inland docks on the River Main, both areas being described by the Germans, as a 'sea of flames'. *Tame* and *Wild Boars* claimed twelve victories though eleven bombers – five Halifaxes, three Lancasters and one of three American-crewed B-17s – were lost. *Y-Yorker* on 156 Squadron at Warboys, one of the Lancasters that went missing in action, was piloted by Squadron Leader Arthur Sydney Cook DFC DFM RAAF, who at 21 years of age was one of the youngest officers of his rank to be killed on operations. His six crew members also died. *J-Johnny*, a 427 'Lion' Squadron RCAF Halifax and Warrant Officer Ellwin Clair Champion's crew, which included navigator, Flying Officer Tod J Thomas USAAF, failed to return to Leeming when they crashed at Haut-Fays in Luxembourg on the homeward trip. They were buried in Hotton War Cemetery, Thomas later being interred in the US Military Cemetery at Neuville-en-Condroz in Belgium. Sergeant J W Brant USAAF, tail gunner on the crew of Pilot Officer Cecil James Morley Wilkie CGM was also buried there after their Lancaster on 50 Squadron crashed in the southern suburbs of Frankfurt with the loss of all the crew. Brant now rests in his hometown in the state of Illinois.

Two Halifaxes that made it back crashed on their return to England. *G-George* on 35 Squadron at Graveley was very badly damaged by flak over the target and was crash-landed near Biggin Hill airfield. The aircraft caught fire and the four injured crew were treated at the Kent and Sussex Hospital. A 429 'Bison' Squadron RCAF Halifax flown by Flight Lieutenant Pentony that was badly shot about by a night fighter, which destroyed the outer starboard motor and damaged the fuel tanks, ran low on petrol and was abandoned near Crowborough in Sussex. Two crew men were killed. Pentony and the five others including Flight Sergeant George James Byers RCAF who was on his 'second dickey' flight, survived. Byers rejoined his own crew, all of whom were lost without trace in November on the operation to Düsseldorf.

Two Stirlings also failed to return from the raid on Frankfurt. *M-Mike* on 75 Squadron at Mepal six miles west of Ely, crashed at Russelsheim killing all seven crew, and *J-Johnny* on XV Squadron, flown by Flight Sergeant Norman L Thomas RAAF was hit by bombs over the target. At Mildenhall his fiancée Joyce, a WAAF radio operator, was understandably worried. The couple had met on one of the year's lovely days and evenings, for 1943 was a beautiful spring and summer:

At times the war seemed very far away until I looked at the wings on his tunic and my heart would lurch and I'd wonder, 'how long, how long?' He never talked of it; it was always the other crews who'd got 'the chop' or 'bought it'. Funny how most air crews grew a shell around them and accepted (outwardly at any rate) the empty chairs at the table after a raid. But we didn't waste any time talking about it – there were the usual dances and pictures – Vera Lynn singing *Silver Wings in the Moonlight, Yours, You'll Never Know* – all the sentimental songs that made the heart ache when the leave was over and there were just the letters; always the letters ... Every letter had a number in the corner that meant so many ops done. Some days there were 50 or 60 aircraft missing and you thought 'you know' but on this particular Tuesday morning I said to my mother 'Thank goodness only eleven aircraft are missing today; Norman will be safe. I'll see him tomorrow.' In the event the telegram didn't come and I had this feeling that something was wrong, so I decided to ring the Sergeant's Mess. When I asked if Norman was there a young pilot said, 'Oh he's missing from Monday night's raid.'

I just said 'Oh' and he said, 'Oh my God; who are you?' I said that I was his fiancée. He was very embarrassed and said, 'I thought you were the telephone operator. I'm sorry. I shouldn't have said anything.'

I said, 'Oh that's all right; do you know any details?'

He said, 'No, I'm sorry, I don't.'

I said, 'Oh thanks very much,' and just hung up. I thought, 'It might be his "turn" tomorrow.' Then after about four days I could hear Norman's voice in my head, all the time saying, 'I'm all right Joycie, I'm fair dinkum.' I spoke to my father and he said, 'Well look, he's got a 50–50 chance; don't bank too much on it.'

Norman Thomas was one of the lucky ones. He and his crew were prisoners in *Stalag Luft IVB* at Torgau.

Ludford Magna or 'Mudford Magma', as it was known because it was still marshy although built on one of the highest stretches of the Lincolnshire Wolds, was home to special Lancasters on 101 Squadron. It was a three flight squadron, flying up to 24 Lancasters in the bomber stream, armed and loaded with bombs just like the other heavy bombers but with an extra crew member in each squadron aircraft to jam enemy radio transmissions. *ABC* or *Airborne Cigar* night fighter communications was a massive piece of equipment consisting of four VHF wireless sets. One scanned up and down the airwaves, seeking transmissions from enemy fighters. When a blip showed on the operator's CRT scope a German-speaking special operator positioned half way down the fuselage between the main spar and the mid-upper turret, tuned one of the other sets to that frequency and listened in. If the speaker was a *Jägerleitoffizier* (*JLO*, or GCI-controller) the special operator would flood the enemy controller's instructions with interference.

Sergeant Gerhard Heilig, born on 19 April 1925 in Budapest, Hungary of an Austrian journalist and a Hungarian mother, both members of Jewish families, was one of the special operators on 214 Squadron and later 101 Squadron. As a 13-year-old Gerhard had been shipped to Great Britain in December 1938 on a special children's transport, thus escaping the threatening doom. During the early war years, after a spell at a Quaker school in Yorkshire, Gerhard learned the trade of electrician at a school for refugees in Leeds and got a job as a telephone engineer in London. Meanwhile, he had become very interested in aviation, which led to him deciding to volunteer for aircrew duties in the spring of 1943. On reaching the minimum age in the summer of that year, he was trained as a radio operator, to become involved in the highly secret airborne jamming war. Heilig recalls:

We were informed that the sole object of the squadron was to carry special operators like ourselves along in the main bomber stream and it would be our duty to find, identify and jam enemy fighter control transmissions, causing havoc and confusion to their defences.

The whole thing was so secret that not even the Commanding Officer knew what it was all about.[12]

Sergeant Sam Brookes was a special operator who arrived at Ludford after a course, which before the war had been of two years duration and had now been condensed into six months because of the enormous demand for aircrew. Called up that spring the RAF said he could elect to be trained as a pilot but he would have to wait to join up for a year:

Alternatively, they had vacancies for rear gunners – come next Monday. I was keen to get started but ... ummm. There was a third choice, be a wireless operator in three months. That sounded like a reasonable compromise and I took it. August Bank holiday 1943 found me reporting to the ACRC (Air Crew Reception Centre), at Lord's cricket ground for induction and training. I joined a squad of 30 likely lads, all destined to train as wireless operators and we started initial training. Three weeks of inoculations and square bashing to commence. We lived in commandeered luxury flats along Prince Consort Road, marching to be fed in a similarly commandeered cafe at the zoo just across the road in Regents Park. Then to Bridgnorth to 19 ITW (Initial Training Wing), where we started the rudiments of wireless training and began to absorb Morse code. November came and we moved to No. 2 Radio School at Yatesbury in Wiltshire – a huge wooden-hutted camp in the middle of nowhere but with a small grass airfield next door, from which we would be flown to do our training for wireless operating in the air.

I proudly became a sergeant wireless operator and stood by for posting to OTU, the next stage towards operational flying but within a week four of us were told that the remainder of our training would be cut by some months. We would be posted to a familiarisation unit to get used to flying in heavy bombers and would probably be flying on operations within a month! The job we were to do would be to fly in Lancasters as an extra crew member with the specific task of operating special jamming equipment designed to prevent the *Luftwaffe* night fighter pilots from hearing directions from their ground controllers. It was a very exciting time. We were sent to No. 1 LFS (Lancaster Finishing School) at Hemswell, north of Lincoln, to fly for ten hours familiarization on four-engined bombers. After the stately de Havilland Dominie and tiny Percival Proctors the Lancaster was large, loud, fast and fierce.

Upon arrival the first thing was a few days' introduction to the equipment we were to operate. I have no idea why they named it *ABC*. It consisted of three enormous powerful transmitters covering the radio voice bands used by the *Luftwaffe*. To help identify the place to jam there was a panoramic receiver covering the same bands. The receiver scanned up and down the bands at high speed and the result of its travel was shown on a time-base calibrated across a cathode ray tube in front of the operator. If there was any traffic on the band it showed as a blip at the appropriate frequency along the line of light that was the time-base. When a 'blip' appeared, one could immediately spot tune the receiver to it and listen to the transmission. If the language was German then it only took a moment to swing the first of the transmitters to the same frequency, press a switch and leave a powerful jamming warble there to prevent the underlying voice being heard. The other two transmitters could then be brought in on other 'blips'. If 24 aircraft were flying, spread through the Bomber stream, then there were a potential 72 loud jamming transmissions blotting out the night fighters' directions.

The Germans tried all manner of devices to overcome the jamming, including having their instructions sung by Wagnerian sopranos. This was to fool our operators into thinking it was just a civilian channel and not worth jamming. I think *ABC* probably did a useful job, but who can say what difference it made. Anyway, it was an absorbing time for keen, fit, young men who thought only of the challenges and excitements of their task and little of the risks they were about to run. Next step was to get 'crewed up'. The normal seven-man crews for Lancasters had been made up and had been flying together for months before arrival at the Squadron. We Special Duty Operators now had to tag on to established crews and it was left largely to us to find out with which pilot we, in our ignorance, might wish to fly.

The *Airborne Cigar* Lancasters made their operational debut on the moonless night of 7/8 October when over 340 Lancasters raided Stuttgart. The *ABC* aircraft played their part on their debut but any signal transmitted by a bomber could be used by a fighter to locate it and in time losses on 101 Squadron, who flew more operations than most other squadrons, would lose heavily, as the enemy sought to diminish their effectiveness.

What really confused the *Jägerleitoffizier* were the diversions by Mosquitoes to Munich, Emden and Aachen[13] such that only a few night fighters reached the Stuttgart area and only then at the end of the raid. Just three Lancasters were lost and a Lancaster on 408 'Goose' Squadron RCAF was abandoned near Pickering, Yorkshire shortly after take-off from Linton-on-Ouse. Moments later the aircraft crashed into a farm killing George Strickland, a 51-year-old famer who died as the bomb load exploded.[14]

Pilot Officer Donald Wares and crew were flying their first operation on 49 Squadron at Fiskerton. They had been given a brand new Lancaster but during pre-flight checks the Lancaster developed engine trouble and they were instead given *P-Peter*, which had been on the squadron since the previous December. They took off late and by the time they were over Holland the rest of the Main Force was on its way home. Wares pressed on regardless and they were attacked six or seven times by night fighters. Though they managed to drop their bombs on the target it was like being in the 'middle of a firework display' as the flak gunners fired everything they had got at the single bomber daring to cross the target area. Then a night fighter pumped cannon shells into the starboard side of the Lancaster and the outer engine caught fire. Wares feathered it and they carried on at 18,000 feet on three engines. Ten minutes later the fire had spread to the starboard inner engine and that too was feathered. Steadily losing height *P-Peter* finally slammed into high ground near Bézimont in the Fôret-de-Commercy. The flight engineer, bomb aimer and navigator were killed. Sergeant Gilbert Attwood the mid-upper gunner and Flying Officer Archie Fitzgerald RAAF the rear gunner had broken arms and legs and were soon captured. Sergeant Ray Barlow the WOp/AG regained consciousness inside the blazing Lancaster and found Wares unconscious in his seat. Barlow finally managed to open the sliding window beside his seat and they both jumped out into the burning undergrowth. They flew the scene as exploding bullets whizzed about them. Barlow and Wares made it to Switzerland where they were interned.[15]

The two other Lancaster losses were on 9 Squadron at Bardney. Pilot Officer Arthur Mair and his crew were killed, the Lancaster crashing near Böblingen, south-west of Stuttgart. *C-Charlie* piloted by 23-year-old Lieutenant Eric George Roberts USAAF crashed at Kiechlinsbergen near Endingen about 90 miles after the target. Pilot Officer W Chadwick the bomb aimer, who managed to get out through the forward escape hatch, was the only survivor. Roberts, from Merchantville, Camden County, New Jersey had only arrived on the squadron a month earlier.[16]

Bridge Farm, Bradfield, in the heart of rural north Norfolk was the home of William and Matilda Gibbons and their son Jack. Farming was pretty tough in the thirties and forties, with no cars, tractors or combine harvesters; nor a telephone or electricity in the house. The 8th of October had been just another day and as is the habit of the farming community, they retired early. On the many RAF airfields across East Anglia it was a different story. Just over 500 aircraft of the main force, including 26 Wellingtons of 300 (Polish) and ten on 432 'Leaside' Squadron RCAF – the Wimpys flying their last main force bombing operation of the war – would once again visit Hannover. At a certain position the Lancasters, Halifaxes, Wimpys and eight Mosquitoes would turn towards Hannover leaving 119 bombers, 95 of them Stirlings, as decoys still heading for Bremen. Pilot Officer Phil Dyson and his 196 Squadron crew were detailed to fly Stirling III *C-Charlie* from their base at Witchford in Cambridge-shire on what they hoped would be the final op of their first tour. At briefing that night a strong emphasis had been placed on the need for navigational accuracy and perfect timing: lone aircraft would be sitting ducks for the Luftwaffe night fighter crews, so when *C-Charlie*'s take-off was delayed it was an unwelcome complication, as Phil Dyson recalls:

The pre-flight checks which every self-preserving pilot carried out very carefully indeed, revealed that the pilot's escape hatch was unlocked. Combined efforts to move the locking lever over to the 'shut' position failed to secure the hatch but, finally with the assist-ance of a sergeant fitter it was declared well and truly locked and *C-Charlie* roared down the runway three minutes' late. We had gained little more than 50 feet in height after take-off when Jack Parker, the rear gunner, remarked that something had just hit the tail and, simultaneously, I announced the loss of the escape hatch above my head. With commendable imagination my 19-year-old flight engineer, Peter Hooker, commandeered the navigator's green canvas chart case and within a few minutes, with the skill of a surgeon, he had fixed a canopy above my head which reduced the gale to a fairly stiff breeze. The decision was made, perhaps unwisely, to proceed on course to Bremen and increased boost gradually made up for lost time. We approached the Dutch coast and we could see the unseen stream of those in front attracting the attention of the German ack-ack on the Frisian Islands. Trouble rarely comes singly they say. The flight engineer suddenly reported the port inner engine was giving trouble (it was running very hot although that was not an infrequent occurrence), but two minutes later he requested me to cut the offend-ing engine – which I did – and feather the propeller. The spectre of an engine fire constantly haunted aircrews. There was hardly time to consider the prospect of flying over Bremen with three engines when my young engineer somewhat tremulously exclaimed 'Skipper, the port outer, the same bloody thing. We've lost oil pressure and the temperature is way above limit. We've got to feather the port outer.'

There was no argument and *C-Charlie* swung around on to a reciprocal course pointing homewards and we lightened the load by releasing our 6,000lb bomb load. Once the calculations had been made, several hundred gallons of petrol were also jettisoned over the North Sea. *C-Charlie* gave an almost audible sigh of relief and bravely responded to full trim and full rudder to continue on a course to East Anglia.

Unlike the two previous raids on Hannover there was no 20-mile timed run from the Steinhuder Lake to confuse crews and in clear conditions the initial *H2S*-guided blind markers placed their Yellow TIs very accurately around the aiming point in the centre of Hannover, which was brilliantly illuminated. The Main Force, following their usual procedure, bombed the first red TIs that they saw, which in this case were nearest to the AP. About 70 per cent bombed before these TIs were extinguished, with the result that an exceptionally concentrated attack developed with a creep-back of only two miles, all within the built-up area. It was estimated that 54 per cent of the built-up area was destroyed by fire. Unlike the night previously the *JLO* correctly identified the likely target and many night fighters arrived in the Hannover area before the raid was over. *Nachtjagd* destroyed all 27 bombers lost. Flight Sergeant 'Blue' Ellery, an Australian pilot of a crew that arrived on 460 Squadron RAAF at Binbrook earlier in the day was told that he would be flying that night as second dickey with Wing Commander R A Norman DFC RAAF, the Commanding Officer on *K-King*. This Lancaster failed to return. Norman survived and was taken prisoner. So too 'Blue' Ellery, who had yet to unpack his kit.[17]

Nachtjagd claimed ten more aircraft on Bremen although just two bombers, both Stirlings, were shot down (and a third would not make it home). Keith Deyell on 620 Squadron recalls:

We were lucky it was not four. About 20 minutes from the target we were attacked by a fighter. I was sitting by the open rear hatch chucking out leaflets when our rear gunner opened up at the same time as the attacker, which was on the fine port quarter, slightly lower than us. We received damage from end to end and the rear turret was badly damaged as we went into evasive action and I stood up and kicked out the leaflets by the bundle. The engagement was short but in that time through the open hatch I saw two tails of fire from an aircraft below; those were the details that went into our combat report. Perhaps intelligence already knew about German jets but did not want aircrew to get the wind up so kept it under wraps. Although we received a great deal of damage there were no casualties and everything still worked so we pressed on to the target, bombed and returned. The rear gunner had lost most of the Perspex from his turret and the bulkhead doors were splintered. Even his chute in its stowage was riddled and his flying suit had nicks all over it, some of the instruments in the cockpit had lost their glass and in between where I had been, the disused lower turret hydraulic piping had been fractured showering me with fragments and oil. On inspecting the aircraft later we found 96 groups of damage yet nothing had been serious but I did find one neat group of five holes in the back end of the bomb bay step where I had been sitting and that caused me to break out in a cold sweat! They were right between my legs as I had jumped up to kick out the bundles![18]

Y-Yorker, one of seventeen Halifaxes on 35 Squadron that marked Bremen, crashed at Bradfield in Norfolk. Flying Officer Melville 'Max' Muller had taken off from Graveley in Huntingdonshire at 22.46 hours. Derrick Coleman, the 19-year-old air bomber and radar operator recalls:

About 50 miles from the target I had left the *H2S* and moved into the nose in preparation for a visual bombing run using the Mk.XIV bombsight. There was no moon, no cloud and visibility was good in a bright starlight sky. Ross Whitfield had gone to an Australian Squadron and his place as rear-gunner had been taken by a Canadian, Sergeant 'Benny' Bent. 'Benny' saw a Ju 88 at 200 yards on the fine port quarter slightly up and closing in fast; he told his captain to 'corkscrew port; port.' The enemy aircraft opened fire at 200 yards with cannon firing a very dull trace, hitting our Halifax and setting the port outer engine on fire. 'Benny' returned the fire with two short bursts, aiming point blank and hitting the fighter, causing it to pull up sharply. We were now in a spin and the Ju 88 appeared to Sergeant Bent to be hanging on its props on the starboard beam. He gave it another very short burst; observing strikes and saw it fall away, apparently out of control. By now we were falling fast in a spin with flames pouring from the port outer engine. 'Max' Muller regained control after losing 8,000 feet in height but as the port outer engine was u/s and the port inner engine appeared to have been damaged, the aileron and elevator controls also damaged, besides the turret being u/s and other damage to the aircraft, the bombs were jettisoned and course set for base. I was terrified during the spin as I was pinned to the floor of the bomb-aimer's position, could not move and thought this was the end. Max Muller did a magnificent job in getting the aircraft back to England, gradually losing height all the way and using full right rudder to keep the aircraft straight. My brief attempt to help by tying my intercom lead round the rudder bar and pulling was very ineffective.

We crossed the English coast in daylight attempting to reach RAF Coltishall but crashed a few miles short; just not enough power to hedge-hop in. The aircraft passed between two trees, which hit the wings. It was a complete write-off, although the nose and part of the fuselage remained reasonably intact. At least one of the engines had been torn away and was on fire. All the crew escaped injury except for Tommy Ellwood the flight engineer, who had taken up his crash position behind the main spar and sustained a bad cut over one eye which required stitching. Blazing petrol set fire to the back of 'Benny's flying clothing but 'Hoop' Arnott the mid-upper gunner rolled him over and put the flames out. There was no doubt in the minds of all crew that we owed our lives to the amazing ability and strength of the pilot, Max Muller.

Eighty-one year old William and 75-year-old Matilda Gibbons living at Bridge Farm nearby thought at first that their unexpected visitors were Germans but when they realized that they were RAF they were invited inside and given cups of tea until transport arrived. Jack Gibbons cycled to the next village of Antingham and with difficulty managed to arouse the postmistress in order to phone the police. The crew were transported to the hospital at RAF Coltishall and after the necessary care were taken by road back to Graveley. William never really recovered from the trauma of that night. He died 55 days after the crash and Matilda passed away just seven days later. They were buried together in Trunch cemetery nearby.[19]

Phil Dyson piloting *C-Charlie* had decided to land at Woodbridge where so many American aircraft in distress had successfully landed:

But hopes were dashed when 'Bud' Rattigan our Canadian wireless op calmly informed us that the whole of East Anglia was enveloped in a thick ground mist. We were left with the alternative of ditching the aircraft. Coming up to the East Anglian coast we were at 3,000 feet and I made a slow turn to run parallel with the shore. It was very dark but the land was more discernible than I thought it would be and the coast ahead appeared to be long and straight. Ditching was something one could not practise, but learning the ditching procedure was a lesson which each individual crew member took very seriously. The pilot had to be securely strapped into his seat – and was not and could do little for myself for I needed both hands to control the aircraft.

'Norman', I called to the bomb aimer, who occupied the adjacent seat, 'Fasten my seat belt'. There were four stages which met on a central clip-in device. It was dark and Norman groped around. Meanwhile, throttle back and reduce speed one-third flap and to the wireless op, 'Bud', who had already sent out distress signals, 'Let the trailing aerial out.' I needed his instant warning when the aerial touched the water at 20 feet as the signal to cut the engines, pull back on the control column and stall *C-Charlie* in tail-first. We were down to 500 feet and Norman was still fumbling around.

'Norman, strap in quickly and hold the strap across my chest.'

It seemed no more than seconds after I had throttled right back that *C-Charlie* hit the water with an immense thud and the impact threw me forward with an almighty bang as my head struck the window in front and we went down. Momentarily concussed, a flood of cold sea water crashed through the hatch above and instantly revived me and I jumped onto the seat and squeezed my bulky figure through that small aperture. Miraculously, *C-Charlie* was afloat and I could see my friends climbing out of the mid upper gun escape hatch one by one, all except one. We found Norman Luff, the bomb aimer, entangled with the control column and we freed him and dragged him out of the pilot's escape hatch. Down by the port wing the dinghy was there and waiting, fully inflated and we gingerly clambered down, fearful lest we put our feet through the base. Pete cut the lanyard and Jack and 'Bud' inexpertly paddled us towards the shore where we could see a light and hear a voice shouting repeatedly, 'Steer this way, straight towards the light'. In a few minutes we entered the surf and stepped ashore where the voice continued. 'Now one behind the other and follow me' and we crunched our way up a steep shingled beach. At the top we could hear female voices and they led us towards a large house where we took off our soaking uniforms and flying kit and wrapped ourselves in a variety of garments. They tendered first aid to Norman who had a deep gash in his leg. They fed us and eventually provided us with beds for the few hours left before dawn. These angels were members of the Women's Royal Naval Auxiliary and 'manned' a listening post where they had heard our Mayday call, never dreaming we would drop in to visit them at Hemsby, which lies 10 miles north of Great Yarmouth, Norfolk. In the early hours of the morning I slipped out of the house and saw the huge tail of the Stirling standing like a sentinel 300 yards off shore. Later we all lined up with several of our hostesses to have our photographs taken with our staunch friend C-Charlie in the background. We had been very lucky in a number of ways, not least in the fact that we had landed just off a mined beach.

Mr. Winston Churchill in a message of congratulation on 11 October to Air Chief Marshal Sir Arthur Harris said:

Your command, with day-bomber formations of the Eighth Air Force fighting alongside it, is playing a foremost part in the converging attack on Germany now being conducted by the forces of the United Nations on a prodigious scale. Your officers and men will, I know, continue their efforts in spite of the intense resistance offered, until they are rewarded by the final downfall of the enemy. These growing successes have only been achieved by the devotion, endurance and courage for which Bomber Command is renowned. Airmen and air-women of Britain, the Dominions and our allies have worked whole-heartedly together to perfect the mighty offensive weapon which you wield in a battle watched by the world.

Three more large-scale *Tame Boar* operations were mounted during October. On the 18/19th when Bomber Command attacked Hannover with 360 Lancasters, the target area was covered by cloud and the Path Finders were not successful in marking the city. The raid was scattered with most bombs falling in open country north and north-west of

Hannover. The *JLO* directed 190 twin-engined fighters into the stream 51 minutes before the Path Finders arrived over the city and 14 victories were claimed for two own losses. The actual losses were 18 Lancasters, five per cent of those that had set out. Three of the missing aircraft were on 103 Squadron at Elsham Wolds, two of which crashed east of Erichshagen. There were no survivors from all three Lancasters. A 115 Squadron Lancaster crashed on return to Little Snoring in North Norfolk, injuring two of the crew. Another Lancaster ditched east of Aldburgh. Eleven more Lancasters landed with damage inflicted in the fighter attacks.

Bomber Command was stood down the following night. Then, on the 20/21st, 358 Lancasters of 1, 5, 6 and 8 Groups were dispatched on the long trip to Leipzig, 90 miles southwest of Berlin, for the first serious raid on the city. The weather was described as 'appalling'; just 271 aircraft bombed the correct area and the rest of the bombing was very scattered. About 220 night fighters were despatched, returning with claims for 11 Lancasters destroyed for nine own losses. Sixteen Lancasters failed to return. One was *R-Robert*, a Mk.III, the first 625 Squadron crew reported missing since its formation at Kelstern, high on the Lincolnshire Wolds northwest of Louth on 1 October. All seven men on Pilot Officer W P Cameron's crew died on the aircraft which crashed off Oosterend, Holland. Another *R-Robert*, on 405 'Vancouver' Squadron RCAF at Gransden Lodge, was flown by Pilot Officer Kemble Wood RAAF. His crew included three Canadians, which he thought might have been the reason that they had been posted to 405, the first-formed of the RCAF Squadrons in Bomber Command and the only one in the Path Finders. The crew had been together for about six months and Warrant Officer O O Johnson RCAF said that they were all the very best of friends and that the life of a crew like theirs made the strongest friends that anyone could ever have. An inveterate letter writer, Kemble Wood had penned his 99th letter to his wife Ethel on 16 October. She would not receive a hundred. Her husband and all his crew except Johnson were killed when *R-Robert* crashed near Werlte at Harrenstätte. On 24 October funerals for those who died were held there. The next telegram that Ethel received was the one telling her that her husband had been killed in action.[20]

On 22/23 October 28 Lancasters and eight Mosquitoes of 8 Group set out to bomb Frankfurt as a diversion for over 560 Lancasters and Halifaxes heading for Kassel for the second raid on this city that month. Their targets were the Henschel locomotive-engine plant, the largest of its kind in Europe, and the Fieseler aircraft plant. One hundred and twenty-five bombers were forced to return early because of severe icing *en route*. As on the previous raid 19 days earlier, the blind markers overshot the aiming point but, the visual markers following on accurately marked the centre in the light of their flares and Kassel was subjected to an exceptionally accurate and concentrated raid. They created 3,600 fires that were still burning seven days after the raid, the firestorm destroying 63 per cent of all Kassel's living accommodation. A Mosquito reconnaissance pilot reported that:

> Kassel was a single sheet of flame from which violent explosions were continuously erupting. You could see the smoke up to an altitude of 16,000 feet. We approached the city repeatedly from different directions but after the raid we found no opportunity to take aerial photographs due to the dense clouds of smoke. The rising wind caused the sea of flame to spread more and more. Now the extent of the destruction in Kassel must virtually match that in Hamburg.

Over 4,300 apartment blocks were reduced to ruins and more than 150 industrial premises and dozens of public buildings were destroyed or seriously damaged. In the oldest part of town in the main business shopping centre between the river and Konigsplatz no building was left intact. The damage extended to the industrial districts on both sides of the River Fulda as well as to suburbs. The Western suburbs and outlying townships were badly hit and the north-eastern suburb of Wolfshanger was devastated. Between 100,000 and 120,000 people had to leave their homes and over 5,500 people died. The Fieseler factory was so badly damaged that the V-1 assault on Britain was delayed. Enemy action was hampered by strong *Window* jamming of the Fighter R/T Frequency and the diversion to Frankfurt where all the bombers returned safely. It was on this night that broadcasts code-named *Corona* that were intended to interrupt and confuse the *JLOs'* R/T transmissions in the 2.5 to 6 MHz band to their night fighters, began. The enemy transmissions were monitored at an RAF ground radio station at West Kingsdown (later Canterbury) in Kent using captured *FuG 10* receivers. When the communication channel to be disrupted had been identified, a SO (special operator) would begin to feed into it misleading or contradictory information and this would be broadcast from four GPO Transmitters (three at Rugby and one at Leafield) by an executive order telephoned from the monitoring station. At first SOs would not attempt to divert night fighter pilots to the wrong target but would transmit misleading instructions such as false fog warnings or landing instructions.[21] The *JLO* became so agitated that he began swearing but the British *Corona* operator reacted quickly and sharply, saying 'The Englishman is now swearing' only for the German controller to shout: 'It is not the Englishman who is swearing; it is me!' Even so, despite the jamming and spoofing over 190 *Tame Boars* claimed 40 kills, mainly in *Wild Boar* fashion in the target area and to the north of Kassel. The attackers lost only six fighters; one may have been that which collided with a Halifax flown by Lieutenant Leif Hulthin on 76 Squadron, who was on his 26th trip. The Norwegian, who had crashed at the start of the Aachen operation in July, was well-known for his calm readiness to circle a target until he was certain of his aiming point.[22] He and his Halifax went down at Welda five kilometres southwest of Warburg; all his crew including Pilot Officer Alf Barden, just 18 years old, were killed.

P-Peter, a 158 Squadron Halifax, had crashed on take-off from Lissett when a tyre burst and a fire broke out but the crew had escaped serious injury. Two other Halifax IIs on the Squadron failed to return from Kassel, as did two Lancasters on 166 Squadron at Kirmington. The pilot of one survived and was taken into captivity but the rest of his crew were killed. Flight Lieutenant Charles Neville Hammond DFC, the pilot of the other Lancaster, and five of his crew including Master Sergeant John W Walton USAAF were also killed. Another American died on *A-Apple*, a 419 'Moose' Squadron RCAF Halifax II at Middleton St. George flown by Wing Commander Gordon Archibald McMurdy RCAF. The Skipper and four of his crew, including Flight Sergeant Francis Weatherford Peterkin, a 'Yank in Canadian clothing' died. Three men survived. One of them was Sergeant Jack Woods who was flying his 15th operation as the wireless operator:

> Our aircraft was hit by flak a few minutes after we bombed the target. It must have hit something vital because the order to bail out came within seconds. The navigator opened the nose hatch and he and the bomb aimer jumped out. Somebody else went out before me; I think it must have been the second pilot – a new chap on his first trip. I felt the pack hit me in the face when I jumped, as it was bound to with the chest-type chutes and I might have been dazed, because I only seemed to be in the air for a few seconds before I landed, close by a railway line. When I took the chute off I saw blood dripping on the silk – I'd got a few cuts when we were hit. I stuffed the chute in a hedge and started to walk along the line. I ought to have hidden for a while and made a plan but I didn't think it out well enough. I didn't know whether it was Christmas or Easter, actually. I just went on walking until the Germans picked me up – railway workers, they were.[23]

Altogether, the RAF lost 43 aircraft on the operation to Kassel. At Melbourne three Lancasters on 10 Squadron failed to return and it was the same story on 103 Squadron at Elsham Wolds. At Leeming four Halifax Vs on 427 'Lion' Squadron RCAF were missing and at Tholthorpe four Halifax Vs had fallen victim to flak and fighters. Besides those already mentioned, seven other Squadrons including 100 Squadron at Grimsby each lost two bombers. *O-Orange*, the Lancaster flown by Pilot Officer Peter Ronald Andrews, crashed into the side of a hill as the crew were returning to base. Andrews and two crew men died; four were injured. HW-J^2 piloted by Flight Sergeant Hilton George Brownjohn RAAF, which failed to make it home to Grimsby, went down on the east bank of the Weser. The Australian and one of his crew died in the wreckage of the Lancaster. Five men including 1st Lieutenant H A Rainbird USAAF were captured after bailing out and they were taken into captivity.[24]

All manner of German aircraft were employed against the bombers this night and they included Dornier 217s and Ju 88s. Z-*Zebra*, the Lancaster piloted by 28-year-old Flying Officer Albert Edward Manning, who was on his second op on 9 Squadron, was attacked by one of the Dorniers. Manning, who was from Ipswich, had a somewhat cosmopolitan crew that was not unique in Bomber Command: the bomb aimer was from Winnipeg, the WOp was from Melbourne, the flight engineer was from Hornsey and two of the gunners were from Scotland and Chichester while Sergeant John James Zammit came from New York. Manning's 27-year-old mid-upper gunner, Sergeant Gilbert George Provis and the rear gunner both sighted the enemy aircraft 300 yards starboard quarter up. The rear gunner told Manning to corkscrew starboard and both gunners opened fire on their attacker as the Dornier's machine gun fire passed over the Lancaster. Standing in the astrodome, Flying Officer James White Hearn the 30-year-old navigator from Bonnyrigg sighted a second enemy aircraft port quarter up at 400 yards. As Hearn warned the gunners the attacker opened fire and hit the Lancaster all along the port side. Hearn was slightly injured. Provis, who was a Welshman from Ystrad, was killed and the rear gunner was wounded. As the two attackers broke away Hearn saw two Ju 88s closing in, one on either beam down. They fired but missed. Manning continued to corkscrew throughout the attacks, which happened almost simultaneously. The hydraulic pipes below Manning's seat were severed but he managed to get the Lancaster back to Bardney.[25]

At Leconfield on 3 November *J-Johnny*, a Halifax II on 466 Squadron RAAF that was in the process of converting from Wimpys to the radial-engined Halifax III, took off on an air to sea firing practice and exploded and crashed in the sea off Flamborough Head with the loss of the entire crew. All except one were Australian. At Holme-on-Spalding Moor that same morning a thickish haze with several patches of very low cloud persisted. Flying Officer 'Fred' Hall on 76 Squadron was preparing his navigation charts in readiness for that night's operation to Düsseldorf, which, after a lapse of almost five months was earmarked for a raid by just over 570 bombers. The young navigator was therefore unavailable when his pilot, Flight Lieutenant Jimmy Steele and the others took their faithful Halifax *Betty the Heffulump* up for an air test. Miss Dorothy Robson BSc who was from the Royal Aircraft Establishment at Farnborough was invited to fly with the crew. Small and vivacious, she was known affectionately as 'Bomb-Sight Bertha' because the 23-year-old who came from Hartlepool and had studied at Leeds University for her degree was the acknowledged expert in the function of the Mk.XIV bomb-sight, designed by Professor P M S Blackett and Dr. Braddon. She would say that it embarrassed her to lecture bomb aimers but she never showed it. Her manner was conversational and easy and her vast knowledge earned great respect. Dorothy and six airmen boarded the Halifax for the short flight. At 11.55 hours *Betty the Heffulump* crashed 300 yards north-east of Allotment Farm between Goodmanham and Middleton-on-the-Wolds. Three of the crew were killed instantly and one died shortly after being admitted to hospital. Jimmy Steele, Miss Robson and Flight Sergeant Harry Welch RCAF the rear gunner were injured. The English pilot and the Canadian rear gunner died of their injuries the following day; Miss Robson succumbed on 5 November.[26]

Sergeant Harold Church (Harry to all his RAF friends) was the 21-year-old navigator on Norman Carfoot's crew on 49 Squadron at Fiskerton, a few miles east of Lincoln:

We did not know, we could not know, that within two hours some of us would die, violently. Statistically, we were aware that there was at least a 5 per cent chance we would not return that night or any other such night, but we refused to admit it, even to ourselves. A one in twenty chance tonight did not necessarily mean a certainty by twenty such nights. It happened to others, so we persuaded ourselves; we believed, or pretended to believe, we were immune, even though, privately, most of us were scared of what lay ahead. Even if we had known, there was little anyone of us could do except report sick and it was too late for that now. It would be unthinkable to desert comrades with whom work and pleasure had been shared. Besides, any action deliberately taken to avoid participation would result in disgrace. A month earlier, one friend, a flight sergeant, suffering from extreme stress, had asked to be relieved of any more operational flying. The letters 'LMF' had been duly entered in his service book and he had been reduced to the ranks and sent elsewhere and was now probably cleaning lavatories or whitewashing coal. It was harsh treatment for such a person, a volunteer, as we all were, who was genuinely at the end of his tether, but possibly advisable in order to attempt to ensure that expensive training was not wasted. Fortunately such action was necessary only for a few. It is surprising how much value is attached to self-esteem. What was it that Shakespeare wrote, in *Hamlet*? 'This above all: to thine own self be true. And it must follow, as the night the day, Thou canst not then be false to any man.' If we had opted out, we would remember and be ashamed of ourselves for the rest of our lives.

Fourteen colleagues had failed to return one night the previous week. We had raised our glasses and toasted 'Absent Friends' and then those friends had been replaced almost immediately by new crews, who would soon become friends, even if only for a short time. Such was life – and death – in the autumn of 1943 on a Lancaster bomber station. 49 Squadron was one of many in 5 Group, regarded by many and certainly by the crews themselves, as the elite of Bomber Command. Unlike most bomber squadrons, here painted emblems of blondes or bombs on the fuselages were scorned. This squadron was above such fripperies; the Lancasters flew unadorned, their crews proud of their individuality. Only the RAF roundels, the squadron identification letters (EA) and the individual aircraft letters were displayed. Nothing else was necessary. If questioned, though, they would have had to admit that the lack of emblems was based on pure superstition. Earlier in the war a few crews on the squadron had had their aircraft decorated with emblems and it so happened that they were the ones that failed to return. So the commanding officer, or someone else in authority, had decreed that such adornments were not welcome. Many airmen were superstitious and a large number of them carried mascots on their operations.

On the evening of 3 November our crew of seven stood by the huge undercarriage of our Lancaster, *E-Easy*, flies open, ready for the ritual urination before climbing into the aircraft's dark and narrow interior. As well as fulfilling a superstitious need, this was a very practical thing to do, as there would be no other reasonable opportunity for several hours. True, there was the Elsan (the chemical urinal) but there was little time to use that. The stars twinkled brightly in the early November sky; mist lay like a silver carpet on the damp grass; the dope on the wings and fuselage contributed to the unmistakable and evocative smell of a wartime airfield at night, one that cannot be described to those who have not experienced it. The heightened awareness of the senses augmented the sights, sounds and smells to produce a feeling of excitement and adventure. This feeling was a natural one for young men. I was born and bred in Hemsby, Norfolk. I was able to boast, quite modestly of course, that I had never been lost in the air. I neglected to mention that on one occasion I had got lost in Lincoln after drinking a few pints! Some of our crew were still teenagers. Older men (over 30 years of age) were often considered unsuitable for the job and they usually had more sense than to volunteer for flying duties, even though they did get paid an extra shilling or so a day as flying pay. Was it by reason of their youth or their hairstyle that RAF air-crews were nicknamed the 'Brylcreem Boys' by some in the other armed services?

This was the seventeenth 'op' for most of the crew, although the great majority of them had been undertaken with another squadron before being posted to this special one. 'Op', short for operation, sounded more casual, less ostentatious, than the American 'mission'.

We had only thirteen more to do after this one to complete our tour. Completing a tour was not a simple exercise; towards the end of 1943 few crews managed to complete thirty operations over enemy territory. However, they did have the privilege of a week's leave every month or so. If they were lucky and the weather was suitable, the tour could be completed in four to six months. Then they would be entitled to a long rest, probably as instructors, before beginning another tour. Needless to say, the completion of those thirty operations provided a reason for great celebration, both by and for the fortunate crew. Unfortunately many crews did not complete a tour at the same time; some individuals missed operations for one reason or another and then had to function as a replacement with another crew.

E-Easy was an almost new Lancaster, only weeks old. It had been delivered to the squadron by a young female pilot. Many aircraft were flown to the operating squadrons by young women of the Air Transport Auxiliary, who, by reason of their sex, were not allowed to fly on operations. I for one felt envious and quite inadequate when seeing these slips of girls piloting huge aircraft so competently. At Elementary Flying Training School, more than a year before, I had learned to fly a Tiger Moth. I was allowed to go solo after ten hours of instruction, but after that memorable flight, which lasted about 15 minutes, I tried to land about 6 feet above the ground! The Tiger Moth had inelegantly bounced and bounced again, before coming to rest close to a hedge on the perimeter fence with a damaged undercarriage. I was not particularly popular with the instructor. I liked to think that I was chosen for the navigators' course because of my good examination marks and ability in that occupation, rather than because of any lack of promise as a trainee pilot. After all, I had managed to fly once without the help and advice of an instructor.

The commanding officer, Wing Commander A A Adams DFC, inevitably known as 'Triple A', enjoyed flying *E-Easy* and usually did so when he selected himself for operations. When 'Wingco' was not flying Norman welcomed the opportunity to take over what he liked to think of as his 'own' aircraft for night-flying exercises as well as operations. Our previous regular Lancaster, *F-Freddie* had been written off, full of bullet and shrapnel holes and with one engine damaged beyond repair, on a previous op. Even with the aircraft in that condition, Norman had landed with his usual skill and aplomb. Norman Carfoot, a flight lieutenant by the age of 21, had already completed almost 2,000 hours' flying, most of them on Sunderlands patrolling the Atlantic, searching for enemy submarines. He had become bored with this comparatively mundane life and had requested a transfer to Bomber Command. A burly young man, he had the confidence and deep respect of his crew, who would willingly accompany him to hell and back – and often did. The aircraft he piloted did not just land; they floated down on to the runway and kissed the ground lightly. Norman's magnificent moustache was the envy of many air-crews. Why did they still have mere down on their upper lips when they had tried so hard to grow something to twirl? All they could do to be different was to leave undone the top button of their tunic or battle-dress. This method of 'cocking a snook' at authority became a tradition in Bomber Command.

Lancasters were marvellous aircraft, but they did differ in performance. While *F-Freddie* had been a bit of a beast, slow to climb and slow to turn, *E-Easy* was a delight, with a ceiling of 22,000 feet fully loaded and a top speed of almost 200 knots unloaded. The average life of a Lancaster on operations was, in those days, about forty hours.

The briefing had been held that afternoon and was attended by all fourteen crews nominated for the operation. The number of aircraft involved depended on the demands of 5 Group Headquarters, the number of serviceable aircraft and the number of crews available. Therefore it was only on rare occasions that all the squadron's Lancasters were involved in a particular operation. When the target was announced by the wing commander as Düsseldorf, there were hearty groans. The Rhine/Ruhr Valley, known by air-crew as 'Happy Valley', was not a popular destination, being well guarded by anti-aircraft batteries, searchlights and fighters. 'Short, sharp and shitty' was the pithy description given to these trips by the aircrews. Together with all the other information necessary, we were given tracks to follow, expected wind velocities and known searchlight and flak sites and were advised of predicted cloud cover. The briefings always ended with 'Synchronise your watches, gentlemen; the time is now—.'

After the briefing the navigators stayed to complete their plotting of tracks and establish the first course to follow, based on the predicted wind velocity supplied by the met officer. Later, they would need to obtain fixes on their actual position over the ground, calculate the actual wind speed and direction and work out the new compass course to take. This information would then be passed to the pilot over the intercom. Individual preparations were made by all other members of the air-crew. It was ironic that many of the ground staff would already have a good idea of the target area for tonight; the amount of petrol put in the tanks to ensure that the maximum bomb-load was carried gave them a vital clue. Just 500–600 gallons, with a consumption rate of about a gallon a mile, meant a short trip and there was only one realistic destination: 'Happy Valley'. Many of the ops recently had been concentrated in that area and they were the most dreaded targets, along with the 'Big City', as Berlin was known. Then came the kitting-out; helmet, oxygen mask, flying boots, jackets, parachute harnesses and Mae Wests were donned and parachutes issued. Valuables and all form of identification were handed in or put in lockers.

We were then ready for transport to the dispersed hard-standings. We were usually driven out by a pretty young blonde WAAF called Vi who was always very quiet on such occasions, though usually happy and talkative, particularly when she collected us on our return. Climbing the steps behind the wing on the starboard side, we made our way along the narrow fuselage, made clumsy by our accoutrements. We who were stationed at the fore climbed laboriously over the main spar, while the rear and mid-upper gunners settled themselves for an uncomfortable journey. The four mighty Merlin engines were started; one by one they coughed, spluttered and roared into life. The necessary checks were made to ensure all was well. At a signal the aircraft taxied out of its dispersal bay, leading the rest of the squadron aircraft towards the main runway. When we reached the runway, we waited for the 'take-off' signal and then the engines howled at full throttle as *E-Easy* sped towards the far hedge. Becoming airborne was always a tricky business with a full load of bombs and with only two or three minutes between each aircraft taking off. Three weeks before one Lanc had failed to lift off, with disastrous consequences for all the crew as well as the plane itself. Fortunately the bombs had not exploded. Tonight we had about 14,000lb of bombs slung under the Lanc, consisting of two 'cookies' and several smaller bombs and incendiaries. No doubt the ground crew had inscribed the cookies with short and impolite messages addressed to Mr A. Hitler.

Once airborne, the usual drills were followed. The undercarriage was retracted and a course set. We climbed steadily, westwards first to gain height, then eastwards, for the rendezvous over Skegness. Some 589 bombers, mainly Lancasters and Halifaxes, were operational that evening, all on the same course, flying without exterior lights along a corridor some 20 miles long, 2 miles wide and at heights between 16,000 and 22,000 feet. On previous operations there had been many near-misses and some had no doubt collided, but it was a calculated risk; certainly it was preferable to the use of navigation lights or straying from the main stream, where a ponderous bomber could be easily picked off by an enemy fighter. There was safety in numbers; the enemy could not attack all the aircraft at once! It was a grim fact that those singled out for special attention seldom returned to base and those that did return usually bore scars. Landings with only three engines functioning were not unusual, while shell holes in the wings were commonplace.

After crossing the coast the air-gunners tested their Brownings with a short burst to ensure efficiency and readiness. The following exchange would be typical:

'Navigator to pilot – course 097 – airspeed 185 knots – on track.'

'Pilot to navigator – thank-you – changing course now to 097 at 185 knots.'

'Enemy coast ahead,' announced Flight Sergeant Steve Putnam the bomb-aimer over the intercom. Aged 21, Steve was a Canadian from Winnipeg, who had almost completed his pilot's training in Canada when he was advised to transfer to a bomb-aimers' course. He spent most of his time in the nose of the aircraft and always carried an empty milk bottle, in case he needed to urinate. That particular part of his anatomy which relieved the need became stuck in it on one occasion, during a long flight, much to the glee of the rest of the crew.

Now we were over hostile territory, not that we had been particularly safe from fighter attention over the North Sea. Now we would have searchlights and flak to deal with too. We were becoming used to this, gaining more and more confidence with each op, but we knew we could not afford to become over-confident or careless. I remembered the first one; after the target had been confirmed and the time of take-off approached, I had felt very unwell and had almost persuaded myself that I was unfit to fly, that I would be a danger to the rest of the crew and ought really to report sick. It had taken a great deal of will-power to convince myself that I was not really ill, just scared stiff. After that, it had been a bit easier. The waiting was the problem; once in the aircraft, all the crew members had their specific tasks to perform and involvement with the job in hand left little time to think of other things.

At a pre-arranged point, a further change of course was made; the track to the target usually entailed at least two such manoeuvres in an attempt to confuse the enemy as to the target. A further minor course correction was necessary, arising from a glance at the H2S and my subsequent calculations of wind speed and direction. The H2S was a blessing; this navigational aid had been developed quite recently and our squadron, often known as the 'try it out squadron', was one of the first to use it. Dead reckoning using the Mercator's chart was still essential but this new aid was very valuable in obtaining a fix. The Gee set was still installed and could be useful, but it was limited in range because it relied on synchronised radio signals from England, which could be jammed by the Germans, while astro-navigation could not give an accurate fix. The wireless operator too had to maintain silence, except in case of dire emergency, as Morse-code signals would be picked up and homed in on by the enemy.

Then the first attack came. 'Enemy fighter to port,' called Flight Sergeant Dave List, the rear gunner and his Browning guns began to chatter spitefully at the intruder in their air space. Aged 21, Dave came from Newcastle. He didn't have a 'Geordie' accent though, as his home town was the Newcastle in Australia. He had volunteered to travel halfway round the world for the purpose of sitting, cramped and cold, despite the electrically heated suit, in the most exposed, most lonely and most dangerous part of the aeroplane. He called himself a fatalist, taking the view that, if his time was up, he would not survive. While maintaining there was little purpose in searching the skies for enemy aircraft for his own sake, he assured the rest of the crew that he would keep a keen look-out in case he could save their lives! Was he serious, or was he indulging in an Aussie leg-pull? On the assumption that the latter was the case, the rest of the crew had made a point of thanking him effusively when he announced that generous concession! Dave was an excellent gunner, having qualified with high marks on his particular course, which included instant aircraft recognition as well as gunnery.

Sergeant Wilf Marson the mid-upper gunner joined in and the enemy broke off to choose another target. He was the baby of the crew at just 18 years old, having falsified his age in order to volunteer at the age of 17. Amused by the initials of his position in the aircraft, he told his friends that he must be a MUG to sit there for hours, searching the skies for something to shoot at. His home was only a few miles north of Lincoln. He always carried an old Home Guard helmet with him on operations, which he carefully tied around his groin. Many aircrew members particularly feared two fates: burning to death and suffering damage to the 'family jewels'. Wilf was determined to avoid the latter if at all possible. He was the joker of the crew. Small and wiry, he smoked an enormous pipe and had an imaginary dog, a figment of his fertile imagination. He 'walked' it around the perimeter, to the pub and even took it on the train to Lincoln, talking to it and praising or scolding its behaviour. Many a spectator was puzzled, to say the least. Wilf called this 'dog' Fido, named after the fog dispersal system recently installed on either side of the main runway.

The two gunners had sent a twin-engined German fighter, a Ju 88, spiralling down in flames on one trip, much to their delight and the relief of all. Most operations were like this. Enemy fighters were often spotted, but there was no point in attracting attention unless they attacked. Some did attack and were either driven off or broke off the engagement for some reason. Such attacks had sometimes resulted in minor damage to the aircraft, but so far none of the members of our crew had been injured and Wilf's helmet had been superfluous. On two or three occasions anti-aircraft fire had torn jagged holes in the wings, but the overworked, dedicated and efficient ground-crew were adept at such repairs, so that the damaged aeroplane was quickly made serviceable again.

Window was ejected and then, spot on the ETA, the target loomed ahead. It could hardly be missed. Myriad searchlights probed the night sky and occasionally an aircraft was caught in the interlocking beams. A blazing bomber spiralled down in flames, while another suddenly exploded. The crew of that one did not have time to suffer. Innocuous-looking but deadly white puffs, like balls of cotton-wool, blossomed around us: as expected, in 'Happy Valley' the flak was heavy tonight. The cotton-wool puffs were close now and *E-Easy* rocked, as if in protesting at the intrusion. Then began the run-in; straight and level. Now came the really hairy half-minute or so.

After the bomb-aimer had released the load, the aircraft would leap, owing to the sudden loss of weight, but it would be necessary for the pilot to stay as straight and level as possible until the camera had done its job. The resultant photographs would indicate the accuracy of the bombing and also give valuable information as to probable damage when they were analysed by the experts. For that reason Bomber Command pilots had been recently instructed that they must not weave over the target.

'Bomb-aimer to pilot, left, left – steady, right, – steady … steady … bombs gone.'

Simultaneously and before I could enter that fact and the time in my log-book we were coned by searchlights. The interior of *E-Easy* was starkly illuminated. All air-crews dreaded being caught by the lights as the operators rarely allowed their victims to elude them. Anti-aircraft shells or a night fighter's bullets would soon target them and all too few returned to base to tell the tale. Norman threw the aircraft into a dive, turning violently to port at the same time. The searchlights pursued *E-Easy* relentlessly and the flak increased in intensity. The aircraft shuddered like a wounded beast as the anti-aircraft shells exploded; in the harsh light it was obvious that the starboard wing had been damaged. The flak stopped suddenly, but the crew knew the likely consequence. Sure enough, Dave announced, almost conversationally, 'Ju 88 to starboard – dive, dive'. The gunners' Brownings burst into action. But they were already diving. Norman fought for control. Then came disaster; our gunners' fire had no effect on this occasion. I escaped death by inches as tracer bullets appeared lazily across my vision from left to right. This illusion of laziness was caused by the fact that tracers were regularly spaced among the equally deadly other bullets in order to help the gunner direct and correct his fire.

The port wing burst into flames. 'Jock' Mason, the flight engineer made valiant efforts to divert the fuel supply to a different wing-tank. 'Jock' was a typical Scot, dour, down-to-earth, good at his job and reliable. He had reached the ripe old age of 22. His friends sometimes called him 'granddad'. He had been an engineer with a reputable British motor manufacturer before volunteering for air-crew and spent many of his non-duty hours fussing around the aircraft's engines with the mechanics.

Norman's calm voice was heard over the intercom, checking the well-being of the crew. No reply came from the wireless operator, but we others reported in, one by one. Seconds only had passed, but already it was obvious there would be no bacon and egg tonight after landing and debriefing. As the op was an early evening one, that treasured meal in wartime Britain, always keenly anticipated, was due on our return, rather than before the trip. Often on a long operation, perhaps of eight hours in duration, crews were served with a meal beforehand. Some air-crew were unkind enough to suggest that by serving the meal after the operation, a saving of rations was very likely.

Inevitably, the dreaded 'Abracadabra, Jump, Jump' order was issued, calmly, by the pilot.

'Skipper, I can't get out,' called Dave from the rear turret.

'The navigator will come to help you,' said Norman reassuringly, as if such a minor problem would soon be solved.

I drew the blackout curtain behind me and was about to move when Dave announced, 'I'm OK now, Skipper.' I could not help my vast relief that I would not now have to struggle to the rear of the blazing aircraft. Relief turned to shock as I looked to my left and saw 'Hank' Wood the wireless operator, or what remained of him. The bullets that had passed across the navigator's table had not missed Hank, who was now quite unrecognisable. The shock was even greater in that I had never before seen a dead body, even one that had passed away peacefully. Hank, a Londoner, was 20 and dated a different girl every night of the week when he was not flying and wrote letters to several others. His line-shooting to his colleagues consisted of boasting about his many conquests. His line-shooting to some of his conquests followed a different pattern. He would sit in the Mess, writing to one of his 'Popsies', as airmen usually called their girlfriends, pretending to be flying over Germany while he wrote and professing his undying love and hopes to see her in the not-too-distant future, should he survive the current operation! Hank could send and receive Morse code messages at well over twenty words per minute.

By this time Norman had managed to pull the Lanc out of its steep dive in order to enable his crew to bail out. Had he been unable to do so, our evacuation would have been almost impossible. I quickly reported Hank's fate, clipped on my parachute, removed my oxygen mask and moved to the escape hatch in the nose. As I passed Norman, still fighting the controls in order to keep the aircraft as steady as possible, my pilot, Skipper, friend and colleague briefly took one hand from the controls and waved goodbye. 'Greater love has no man ...' – we both knew that Norman had no chance of survival. If he relinquished the controls, *E-Easy* would spin violently. The hundreds of gallons in the tanks would probably cause a major explosion at any second. Even if, by some miracle, he managed to reach the hatch, it would not have provided him with a means of escape; he had often joked about it: 'I've tried out the hatch for size and I'm far too fat for it to be any use to me,' or words to that effect.

Reaching the nose, I saw that the hatch had been removed and Steve and 'Jock' had gone.

Now it was my turn. *E-Easy* was now burning fiercely. I dived out. At that height the temperature was far below freezing point and my oxygen supply was non-existent. It was inadvisable to use the ripcord on the chest parachute too soon, in case the aircraft exploded immediately and it was necessary to fall towards breathable air and a warmer temperature as quickly as possible, but it was also important to avoid blacking out before pulling the D-ring. The few seconds' delay in my doing so was certainly not force of habit. I had not had this experience previously and sincerely hoped I would never repeat it. As the chute opened several seconds later I saw our aircraft below and in front, plunging earthwards in a ball of flame. A minute or two earlier I had escaped death by inches, now I had survived by seconds – but I had thoughts only for Norman, Hank and any others of those close friends who could not escape the inferno.

I drifted down. The quietness now was almost unbelievable, entirely free from the barely perceptible sounds that are not even registered in the brain in what is thought of as total silence, on a quiet night in the countryside or on a deserted mountain. Not only was it an enormous contrast from what had just happened, but it was also a silence I had never before experienced. It was all so peaceful and, in spite of my predicament, almost relaxing. The fall seemed unending; it must have taken at least 30 minutes. Then I saw clouds below and suddenly with no warning I just stopped, standing upright! The chute collapsed around and on me.

'Now I know where I am' I thought. 'I am at the Pearly Gates and at any moment St. Peter will greet me.' However, as I came to my senses, which no doubt had been partly befuddled by lack of oxygen, I realised what had happened. The cloud was actually a ground mist, the same type of mist we had left behind such a short time ago. I had landed gently in a ploughed field; so much for the warning that landing by parachute was similar to jumping off a high wall. As

I gathered up my parachute I also gathered my wits, deciding what to do next. Fortunately I was wearing the new type of flying boots with laced shoes on the feet to which the legs were attached; so many others had lost the old type while bailing out. In order to avoid attracting attention I cut off the tops with the knife provided, then tore off my navigator's brevet and insignia of rank. A nearby straw-stack offered a hiding place for the parachute, harness and Mae West; I ripped the chute into several pieces and pushed them under the straw, retaining one small piece. I knew that I had torn the parachute so that it could not be used by the enemy, but had no idea why I kept a piece of it. This was no time to think of mementoes and I wasn't a sentimental type! Then I sat by the stack for a few minutes, deciding what to do.

Orientating myself by the Pole star, I trudged south, hoping to find a copse or wood to hide in until any probable search had been called off. However, after a few hundred paces I climbed over a low bank and found myself on a narrow road, along which I walked. By now the moon was shining brightly and I was able to identify what looked like a village ahead. Deciding to bypass it, I prepared to take to the fields again, but before I could do so, heard footfalls and a man's voice called *Gute nacht*. Although a few German phrases were posted in the Mess for such an eventuality, I now wished I had learned to speak the language better. However, the meaning was obvious, so I returned the greeting as best I could. One small hurdle had been surmounted. Jumping another bank, I crossed another field and – my luck was in – saw trees ahead. Approaching, I found it was indeed a small wood in the corner of the field. I entered, pushing my way through bracken and bushes and sat down. I would wait until midnight, when all should be fairly quiet, before resuming the journey. Looking at my navigator's Omega watch, I could see well enough that the time was 21.25. 'What a lot has happened in a few hours,' I muttered to myself. A favourite quip among air-crew was 'Join the Navy and see the world; join the Air Force and see the next.' Well, I hadn't done that – not yet, but I thought again of my friends, who had so recently died. Hank was dead and Norman could not possibly have survived; of the other four, how many had been as fortunate as I?[27]

Taking into consideration the time of the attack and other factors, research into the *Abschussliste* (Claims listings) indicates that *E-Easy* was most likely hit by *Oberfeldwebel* Erich Becher of 2./NJG6, who claimed four victories before his own death in aerial combat on 24 February 1944. A dozen Mosquito night fighters that flew on the Düsseldorf operation were unable to prevent enemy fighters destroying this Lancaster and most of the 18 other heavies that were lost. One was *P-Peter*, a 57 Squadron

Lancaster at East Kirkby flown by 1st Lieutenant D West USAAF who was killed, as were four of his crew. Two others evaded and one was captured after landing. Another American died when *F-Freddie* and Warrant Officer Robert Allen Young RCAF's crew on 408 Squadron at Linton-On-Ouse was presumed lost off the coast of Holland. The body of Flying Officer Henry S Oien USAAF and two of the five Canadians aboard were never found. Three bodies discovered in a dinghy washed ashore on 12 November near Rockanje were buried in a cemetery in Rotterdam.[28]

Five other bombers crashed or were written off on the return and a further 37 bombers were damaged. *L-Leather*, a Halifax II on 10 Squadron at Melbourne crashed and burnt out a mile north of the American base at Shipdham in Norfolk in which six of Pilot Officer Robert Cameron's crew died instantly. Ernie Bowman, a member of the local Home Guard dragged Sergeant Jack Winstanley the rear gunner from the wreckage but he died from his wounds on 5 November. Bowman was awarded the BEM for his brave rescue attempt. *D-Dog*, which was badly shot about during sustained night fighter attacks that injured three of the crew returned to Melbourne an hour after *L-Leather* crashed but was declared beyond economical repair. The Australian pilot and three of his crew were decorated for 'their fortitude and skill in overcoming great difficulties in order to ensure their return.'[29]

Two more missing Lancasters were on 76 Squadron. One of these was flown by Flight Lieutenant Denis Hornsey who was on his 18th trip. He had flown some operations on Whitleys in 1941 before being returned to OTU for further training. At 33-years of age he was older than most aircrew and he suffered from poor eyesight so he wore corrected goggles on ops. He once said that as far as 'Butch' Harris was concerned, a pilot's operational life represented just fourteen bomb loads – 'That's economics you know.' Hornsey's Halifax was shot down over Belgium on the way to Düsseldorf by a night fighter flown by *Leutnant* Otto Fries of II./NJG1. Hornsey evaded successfully and made a successful escape through France to England. He was awarded the DFC.[30] One of his crew evaded capture but was finally caught close to the Swiss border. The rest of the crew were captured after they bailed out.

One aircraft had crashed on take-off at the start of the operation to Düsseldorf. The operation included a special force of 38 Lancaster IIs in 3 and 6 Groups equipped with the *G-H* navigational device, which after a successful trial in the winter of 1943, had been withdrawn until enough sets could be produced to equip a large force of bombers. *G-H* was a set that transmitted and received pulses from two ground stations. By plotting the point at which the two intersected, the aircraft's ground position could be plotted quite accurately. Aircraft without *G-H* were to formate on a *G-H* 'Leader' and release their bombs in unison. The Mannesmann tubular steel works on Düsseldorf's northern outskirts was selected to test this precision device for the first time on a considerable scale. Five of the *G-H* Lancasters however, had to return early and two were lost while equipment failures in 16 aircraft reduced the numbers bombing on *G-H* to 15 although these left a number of assembly halls burnt out. Photographs taken after the raid showed that half the bombs aimed by means of *G-H* had fallen within half a mile of the aiming point. By October 1944 most of the Lancasters of 3 Group had been equipped with this important new aid. All 52 Lancasters, including 20 blind-markers plus ten Mosquitoes that were detailed to carry out a feint attack on Cologne ten minutes before the start of the main raid, returned safely. Thirteen *Oboe*-equipped Mosquitoes that were detailed to hit Rheinhausen and two more, equipped with *G-H* that went to Dortmund also returned without loss, as did 23 Stirlings and Lancasters that sowed mines off the Friesians.

A Victoria Cross was awarded to Glasgow-born pilot Flight Lieutenant William 'Bill' Reid RAFVR on 61 Squadron whose Lancaster *O-Oboe* was twice attacked by night fighters *en route* to Düsseldorf but who, despite severe head wounds, pressed on, bombed the target and brought the badly damaged aircraft back to Shipdham airfield with the help of the crew. Flight Sergeant John Alan Jeffreys the 30-year-old navigator, a former teacher from Perth, Australia, was killed by a bullet through his skull. Sergeant Jimmy Mann the 22-year-old wireless operator from Orrell near Liverpool died of his injuries 24 hours later. Bomb aimer Les Rolton from Romford, Essex whose cherubic features caused him to be known as 'Baby face', was hit in the hand by shrapnel. Sergeant Jim Norris the 22-year-old Welsh flight engineer, who was badly wounded, was awarded an immediate CGM. He had worked in the railway goods yard in his home city of Cardiff before joining up and was Reid's second flight engineer, having replaced the previous young incumbent when the 19-year-old was labelled LMF after just the one op. Flight Sergeant Cyril Baldwin from Nelson in Lancashire was the mid-upper-gunner. Short in stature, with almost white hair and known to one and all as 'Blondie', he and Flight Sergeant Frank Emerson the rear gunner from Enfield, Middlesex, would often swap turret positions before an op. Emerson, who was known as 'Joe' for his dark moustache, which had been compared to Stalin's, was awarded the DFM.

AVM Cochrane had visited Reid after Düsseldorf. Reid recalled. 'He said he'd heard my story from the rest of the crew, but he wanted to hear it from me. He asked me why I didn't turn back and I said that I'd thought it was safer to go on, rather than turning back among all the other planes; I mean eight or ten miles of aircraft all flying in the same direction. I said if one of the engines had packed up I'd have turned round right away, but the Lanc was still flying. It wasn't that I was determined to drop the bombs or anything, but I just thought it was the safest thing to do at that time. Then he said. 'You know Reid, the returns from ops have been practically nil since your raid. It's as if they all said,

"That bugger Jock, he went on even though he was wounded, so we can't turn back just because of a faulty altimeter, or something like that." [31]

On the night of 4/5 November the RAF carried out mining of the western Baltic, with a Mosquito 'spoof' towards the Ruhr. At 18.19 hours German radar picked up 50 to 60 RAF aircraft between Cap Griz Nez and the Westerschelde River at 23,000 to 30,000 feet. Their further course was southeast into the southern Ruhr area. As their speed at first was only about 250 mph they were taken to be four-engined bombers but later, taking headwinds into consideration, the defences identified them as Mosquitoes. Several night fighters in the area of the western Ruhr were ordered to take off but the operation was abandoned after the approaching aircraft were identified as Mosquitoes. Meanwhile, at 18.02–18.40 hours, 30 to 50 aircraft at heights between 3,300 feet and 5,000 feet flying at 200 mph were picked up approaching the northern part of west Jutland by German radar. 2 JD occupying two night fighter boxes in Jutland were scrambled to take on the heavies. They engaged 16 bombers and shot down four without loss.

Decorated airmen forced themselves through a tour or tours of duty at a cost that they did not know was to come. Their lives would be shattered for the whole of their existence after the war. Certain people said, 'Oh Yes, I'll finish,' and they did but by and large the attitude was 'No I won't finish but I won't go tonight and I won't go tomorrow night.' At one station a few of the air crew would play a record by the 'Ink Spots' called 'For all you know we may never meet again.' After briefing they would play this record over and over again until one night one of the officers got so fed up that he took the record and smashed it over his knee. He did not return from his next trip. One Australian airman recalls: 'You'd overhear someone say, "I don't expect to see home again." I said, "What's that? You make your own arrangements; I'm going home!" "Oh I can see you are going to go home. Everyone can see that you are going home but I won't be." ' Air crew rarely spoke openly about dying. In fact the word was rarely mentioned. In RAF parlance they either 'got the chop', 'bought it' or 'went for a Burton'. The 'Chop Blonde' was the girl who when anyone went out with her they would end up getting the 'chop'.

Jan Birch was a young WAAF officer who fell in love with Pilot Officer Colin Geoffrey Finch on 27 OTU Litchfield whom she met at a dance on her station. 'I was only engaged to Colin for one day' she recalls. 'I was told that there had been an accident at the aerodrome [on 6 November] and perhaps I should not come back until the next day but I wanted to come back. I was fearful inside but I thought that he had been injured.' Finch was one of five Aussies on the Wellington piloted by Group Captain P G Heffernan RAAF. They carried a passenger, Section Officer Karen Lia Hughes, a WAAF. Heffernan had taken the Wimpy off and at 22.08 hours was involved in a mid-air collision with another Wellington of 26 OTU at Wing piloted by Sergeant R B Main RCAF. Both aircraft crashed near the main gate at Alconbury. Heffernan and Main were badly injured but they survived; all the others on board the two Wellingtons were killed.[32] When Jan Birch got to the Lichfield mess she thought that there could not be anything terrible because she heard jazz music, dancing and hilarity coming from inside:

I went in and was taken aside by a friend, a WAAF officer, who told me that Colin had been killed. It was immediately horrifying, hearing that music, which absolutely jarred with this personal sorrow. On the other hand, I had learnt earlier that this had to go on. After I had gone to my room and released some of the emotion I realized that this is how it had to be. If one went into mourning or stopped life going on in the normal way on the station; well you would have had no morale at all. It was the same in London and all the cities that were bombed. You couldn't just go into deep mourning because personal tragedies were happening all the time.

Whilst Jack Furner was at Exning in November 1943, a new Group was formed in Bomber Command. It was known as 100 Group, with its Headquarters at Bylaugh Hall near East Dereham in Norfolk. The Group's task was to bring together various squadrons and units, some existing, others still to be formed, that were to fight a secret war of electronics and radar countermeasures, attempting to reduce the losses of the heavy bombers and their crews.[33]

Sergeant Maurice Flower, an ex-'Halton Brat' was flight engineer in Flying Officer Chick Webster's Halifax crew, which joined 192 Squadron in 100 Group at Foulsham, Norfolk in February 1944. In January 1939 the local vicar helped Maurice apply for the aircraft apprenticeship at Halton and he 'fiddled it' so that he sat the examination in his study instead of having to go to Newcastle. If he had not been accepted by the RAF he would have been a miner or worked alongside his father at the Co-op. There was not much else. There was his grandfather's farm but that was well staffed. His other grandfather was an under-manager at the colliery and who took young Flower to the bottom of the shaft where he said 'You can take me back up again!' That was as far as he ever went in mining. He could not understand anybody lying on their backs hacking away at a coal seam:

The air force really was a way of changing my whole life. I was just interested in the aeroplanes and joined as a fitter to airframes as an apprentice. The apprenticeship was originally for three years but the war broke out and they reduced it to two. There were about 2,000 of us and I did about a year at Halton and a year at Cosford.

Later I was on the Empire Training Scheme at Bloemfontein but it was like being in a peacetime air force. There was no thrill in it at all! We couldn't get spares and although we had good food, lots of entertainment and every amenity, even electric lights at night, it got a bit boring. One day they wanted volunteers for aircrew, especially flight engineers so I volunteered and came home with about half a dozen others. We didn't have any air experience but we were expected to know everything about bombers on day one and just start work! Having just spent a couple of years in South Africa, Norfolk was daunting to say the least. The locals were smashing; really friendly people. The 'Unicorn' was our watering hole and dear old 'Ma' the landlady was a godsend to our crew. But Foulsham airfield and the facilities were just god awful. Everywhere and everything seemed to be either wet or damp after 9 am. Newspapers were like a dish cloth, a light trail of spray followed a snooker ball down the table and condensation dripped on to your bed from corrugated roofs of billets if your bed was more than three feet from the stove.

Four of the crew, including my Skipper were Canadian. Three of us were British. Percy Gladstone, the navigator, was a Cree Indian. I don't know whether he was a full Cree but he looked like an Indian with jet-black hair. He taught himself to speak English from a Sears Roebuck catalogue and taught himself right through university and got a degree. He was a fantastic navigator. We'd go into the woods and he could walk up to a wild rabbit and pick it up off the floor and stroke it and then he'd put it down and let it go and it would sit and look at him. I don't know whether he hypnotised them or what he did but he had this knack. I was closer to my crew than I was with my own brother and sisters. You relied so much on each other. You flew as a team and this extended to your private life. You'd do things together, help each other out. You'd get the odd brawl in a pub but the crews would always stand back to back and help each other. We got seven days' leave every six weeks and one time I went home and all the Canadians went with me, mainly because I said we had an ice rink in Durham. So we went skating in this ice rink, which had a canvas roof, like a circus tent with big poles supporting the roof. I really couldn't skate but I could stand upright and I was on the end of the stream. All seven of us did this big whirling circle with me on the far end. I must have been doing about 55 mph and I hit one of these poles and the whole roof came down. That was the end of our skating!

192 Squadron was called 'Bomber Support'. We supported the main stream, jamming the German radar and interfering with the fighter command broadcasts. One or two aircraft from the squadron would fly into the target, with maybe 500 Lancasters. We'd fly independently of the bomber stream into the target and then circle the target. That

was quite hair-raising because you'd got 500 aeroplanes channelling in over a target and you were going in with them and then turning left, across the front of them and then going up the opposite way and then turning left again across them and flying round and round whilst the raid was in progress.

As a squadron we didn't normally carry bombs. We dropped *Window* by the ton and it appeared on the German radar screens like a huge bomber force, even though it was just one aircraft. They'd send their fighters up to intercept this 'bomber force', which didn't exist because the *Window* just drifted to the ground and then suddenly disappeared but they'd used up all their petrol and had to go back and refuel. While they were doing that, the real force was carrying out a raid elsewhere. We also carried a 'special operator' and all his equipment. Jock Mullholland would sit hunched over his equipment with a rubber face piece on, staring into these little green cathode tubes and twiddling knobs. I really didn't know what we were doing on any one trip but apparently it was important. I'm sure that none of the rest of the crew knew what we were there for either; only the special operator actually knew. When we did eight- or nine-hour trips in the Bay of Biscay we flew from Cornwall; they were so tedious. The Germans were bringing ball bearings from Sweden down to Spain and Portugal and would fly up the Bay of Biscay and home on a beam. We'd pick up this beam and bend it out into the Atlantic so that the big four-engine Condors ran out of petrol halfway to America. We peed in cider bottles and threw them out through the flare chutes. If the bung was left off, they would whistle on the way down.

In the morning we had briefings but we wouldn't know the target at that stage. It was on the board but covered up. The worst moment was when the string pulled the curtain back and we saw where the target was. You'd think, 'Oh blimey, not that one again. I was all shot to hell the last time I was there.' It was really terrifying, that moment. After the briefings and before the flight, I did pre-flight checks around and in the aircraft, checking it thoroughly. I'd make sure the tanks were full so that we had a fuel load according to the length of the trip with a bit of spare for getting back. It was a routine that you got into very quickly and, having been ground crew it was just second nature to look for the things you knew had a tendency to go wrong on a regular basis. In the afternoon, we showered and put clean underwear on. If one got hit by a bullet one wanted a clean vest for it to go through to stop any nasty stuff getting into the wound. Then we'd go for the final briefing and have a pre-op meal, which was usually bacon and eggs. Originally they gave us chips on pre-flight meals but at 22,000 feet this didn't work too well on the stomach! The smell got to be a bit obnoxious in the aeroplane, so we said, 'Please, no more chips on pre-op meals!' We'd make do with bacon and egg. The poor civilians never got bacon and eggs or a chocolate ration but we did. I never ate mine as it always used to make me thirsty. When we were flying out over Holland, I always bunged my chocolate ration down the flare shoot and I'd send the rest of the crew's chocolate down as well if I could cadge it off them. Long after the war I was in Holland at a reunion and I got talking to a Dutchman. I asked if there had been any high spots during the war. The Dutch had had a terrible time, almost starved to death by the Germans. I met one old lady who had actually boiled her husband's boots to try and make some gravy. Anyway, this chap said he was coming home from school one day and he found two bars of Cadburys chocolate. He said that was the most beautiful thing he remembered from the whole war.

We loved the Halifax. I personally would never have wanted to fly in a Lancaster. Everyone I've known that flew Halifaxes loved them, apart from the Mark Is, which had the Merlin engines. They weren't so good but once they got the Bristol Hercules engine, they were a real winner. They would take an awful amount of punishment, very strong aeroplanes. The Halifax didn't carry the load that the Lancaster did, mainly due to its construction but it was a strong, robust aeroplane. I would assist the pilot on take-off, opening up the throttles and correcting the swing on take-off that always happened with the Halifax. Then I'd work out, according to the distance and the hours we expected to fly, the engine settings needed for the trip, to make the fuel last out. I'd check the fuel and keep a log of the instrument settings every half-hour. I'd also change tanks as needed from one tank to another and carry out general maintenance. Changing tanks was quite a performance on the Halifax. First of all, you'd unplug your oxygen from the main supply and put on a bottle that you hoped had oxygen in it. You had to carry this little bottle and climb over the main spar, lie down on your stomach on the floor and reach underneath the main spar and you had to do it all in the dark, just by touch. Over the target and during take-off and landing we used to fly on numbers one and three tanks, which were the main big tanks and then we'd bring the smaller tanks in. It was quite a business.

We were coned one night over Düsseldorf by about fifty search-lights. Another navigator timed us and said we were in this cone for twelve and a half minutes, which in a thirty ton aeroplane was hard going. The normal survival rate for being trapped in a cone before you were shot down was three minutes. We got out of the cone eventually but the aircraft was just a mess. Everything that was loose was stuck to the roof or under the spars. The pilot climbed and dived and rolled and did every manoeuvre we could think of to get out of it. He was exhausted. Suddenly he said, 'I've had enough of this' and he jettisoned the top hatch so he could parachute out but I grabbed his legs and the bomb aimer helped me throw him down the stairs. I took over the controls of the aircraft and flew halfway back over the North Sea, by which time the pilot had recovered from the ordeal enough to be able to take control back and land. He was lucky to recover and even luckier that his crew stood by him, keeping the incident to ourselves. We didn't mention it when we got back. If we had, he'd have been grounded. We were fairly well through the tour by then and well knit. He just cracked; he'd had enough. We couldn't blame him. We debriefed and went to bed and that was it. The next time he was fine; he just carried on for the rest of the tour, no trouble at all.

On 28 July on the raid on Stuttgart we were flying along quite quietly. In the flight engineer's position there was an astrodome where the sextant was used for star shots. I would stand up and have a look around every now and again just to check there was nothing loose or flapping around. On this occasion, out of the corner of my eye I saw movement at the trailing edge of the port wing. My first thought was that the flap was loose and then I saw a wing appear and I realised it was a Messerschmitt 110 lining up to give us a squirt. I yelled to the pilot, 'Corkscrew port!' and he corkscrewed immediately. As we went down, the rear gunner saw a Messerschmitt 109 coming in from the starboard side. These two aircraft were clearly working together. The 109 came in from behind on the starboard quarter and started to fire but we'd gone down to the left. He started to follow us down but he had to turn on his back and Jim Carpenter the mid-upper gunner raked him from front to rear. The fighter was also hit by Les Sessions the tail gunner. The cockpit cover came off and the pilot came out as his aircraft went down in flames but his parachute streamed and he hit our port wing. He disappeared into the dark leaving one leg and a boot embedded in the wing, which we took back to base. I don't suppose he survived. One good thing about being in an aeroplane at war, you never see the whites of the enemy's eyes. When we shot a 109 down, it wasn't a person we were shooting down. We were hitting another aeroplane. We'd drop a 4,000lb cookie and kill a thousand people but we never saw one of them.

Jack Furner's old Squadron (214) was to change its role and its aircraft. It was just about Christmas 1943 when he heard that 214 Squadron were re-equipping with B-17s (popularly known as Flying Fortresses), as part of this special force and he had heard also that they were seeking a Navigation Leader (as Flight Lieutenant). Furner could not resist the urge to fly this new beast. American comfort – with ashtrays! He asked to see Air Vice Marshal Richard Harrison, 3 Group's AOC. Furner told him that he would like to get back on the Squadron. Harrison agreed. So Furner gave up the paper work at Group and hiked off at the turn of the year to Sculthorpe in North Norfolk where 214, still under the command of Wing Commander Desmond McGlinn, was preparing to accept the B-17s after modification to RAF standards and the installation of a mass of Electronic Counter Measure (ECM) equipment.

Sergeant Don Prutton, B-24 flight engineer, 214 Squadron, explains:

> Operations were of two distinct types. In the first, two or three of our aircraft would accompany the main bomber stream and then circle above the target; the special operators used their transmitters in particular, *Jostle*, to jam the German radar defences while the Lancasters and Halifaxes unloaded their bombs. Then everyone headed for home. Our friends on 214 Squadron seemed to do more of these target operations than 223 Squadron. My own crew did a small number of these but the majority of our operations were the '*Window* Spoofs', the object of which was to confuse the enemy as to the intended target. There was a radar screen created by other aircraft patrolling in a line roughly north to south over the North Sea and France. A group of us, perhaps eight aircraft, would emerge through this screen scattering *Window* to give the impression to the German radar operators that a large bomber force was heading for say, Hamburg. Then, when the Germans were concentrating their night fighters in that area, the real bomber force would appear through the screen and bomb a totally different target, perhaps Düsseldorf. After several nights, when the Germans had become used to regarding the first group of aircraft as a dummy raid, the drill was reversed. The genuine bombers would appear first and with luck be ignored by the German defences who would instead concentrate on the second bunch, which was of course our *Window* 'Spoof'. So we rang the changes, sometimes going in first, sometimes last, in an attempt to cause maximum confusion to the enemy, dissipation of his resources and reduction in our own bomber losses.[34]

Jack Furner recalls:

> The early months of 1944 at Sculthorpe were devoted to familiarising ourselves with the B-17s and getting them installed and modified, much of the work being done at Prestwick by Scottish Aviation. The B-17s were being fitted with a long list of intriguing pieces of equipment – names like *Jostle, Mandrel, Airborne Cigar, Airborne Grocer, Piperack* and *Carpet* – each designed to jam a specific type of equipment or specific part of the transmission spectrum. German

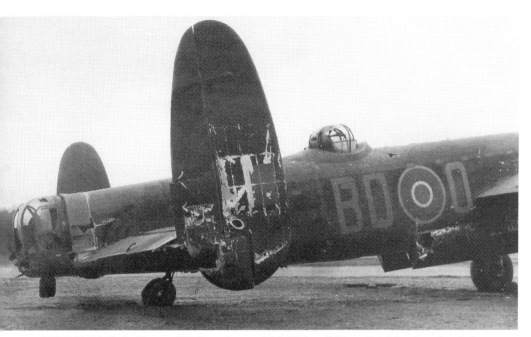

ncaster I DV305 BQ-O *O-Oboe* on 550 Squadron, which Flying Officer G A Morrison landed at
oodbridge after being attacked by a night fighter over Berlin on the night of 30/31 January 1944.
th gunners were mortally wounded by machine gun and cannon fire and one member of the crew
iled out. The Lancaster was so badly damaged that it was written off. (*IWM*)

WAAF airwoman belts-up .303-inch ammunition for Lancasters on 619 Squadron at Coningsby in
bruary 1944. (*IWM*)

A 4,000lb 'cookie' is backed into position under a Bristol Hercules radial engined Lancaster II on 408 'Goose' Squadron RCAF at Linton-on-Ouse in February 1944. (*IWM*)

HM Queen Elizabeth meets ground crew on 156 Squadron during a Royal visit to RAF Warboys on 10 February 1944. (*IWM*)

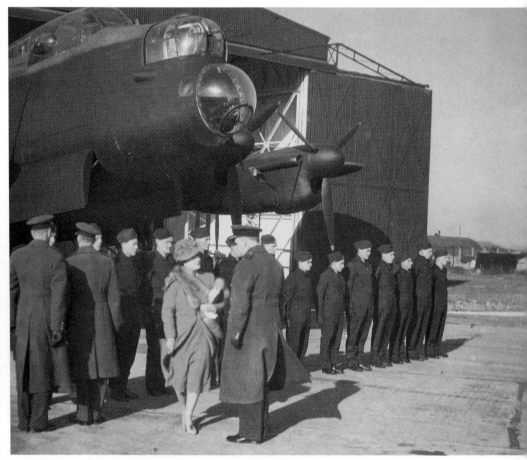

ight Lieutenant Thomas H Blackham DFC, a Lancaster pilot on 50 Squadron at Skellingthorpe, olds the crew's lucky mascot as he is helped into his flying jacket by his flight engineer, Pilot fficer Charles Richard Ernest Walton (28), on 19 February 1944, just prior to the raid that night on eipzig. Other members of the crew are, from left to right: Flying Officer David Gwnyfor Jones, the -year-old navigator; Sergeant Herbert George Ridd, the 29-year-old mid-upper gunner; Sergeant Smith, bomb aimer and Sergeant Sydney Charles Wilkins, the 21-year-old wireless operator. On '4 May, Blackham's eight-man crew were shot down on the raid on Mailly-le-Camp by a German ght fighter. He and Flight Sergeant Stewart James Godfrey, the bomb aimer, evaded. Walton, nes, Ridd and Wilkins and Sergeant William Dennis Dixon, the 20-year-old rear gunner, and Pilot fficer Cyril Edward Stehensen RAAF, the second pilot, were killed. (*IWM*)

Mademoiselle Janine Jouanjean 'an tractive blonde' whom Gordon Carter met while evading in France. They married on 11 June 1945.

35 Squadron crew at Graveley. Standing L-R: Flight Lieutenant Roger 'Sheep' Lamb, mid-upper gunner (PoW 19/20.2.44); Squadron Leader Gordon Carter DFC* RCAF, Navigator Leader (PoW 19/20.2.44); Squadron Leader D Julian Sale DSO* DFC RCAF; Flight Lieutenant B O 'Bod' Bodnar DFC RCAF (PoW 19/20.2.44), H_2S operator; Flight Sergeant G H 'Harry' Cross DFC DFM, flight-engineer (PoW 19/20.2.44); and Flying Officer H J 'Johnny' Rogers DFC WOp (PoW 19/20.2.44). Kneeling in front, the ground crew of their Halifax. Julian Sale survived the shoot down on 19/20 February but he died of his wounds on 20 March 1944. (*IWM*)

Squadron Leader W N Dixon DFC on 76 Squadro watches as fitters work on the outer starboard Merli of Halifax II W7813/MP-I *Edward the Great*. Dixon flew *Edward* on 8/9 Marcl 1943, its last sortie on 76 Squadron before a maj overhaul, after which the aircraft joined 77 Squadro then FTR with Sergeant Lewis William Rees' crew on the night of 25/26 Ma1943 on Düsseldorf. The aircraft crashed in Belgiu and all the crew were killed. (*IWM*)

ancaster being bombed up. (*IWM*)

Warrant Officer Jack Laurens DFM and crew on Lancaster III DV267 *K-King* on 101 Squadron at Ludford Magna. L-R: Laurens, who was a South African, had flown at least seven 'ops' to Berlin; Sergeant William Frederick Donald 'Don' Bolt, mid-upper gunner; Flight Sergeant Les Burton, navigator; Sergeant A E 'Ted' Roystone, rear gunner; Sergeant R N 'Chris' Aitken, bomb aimer climbing aboard; Sergeant J A Davies, special operator, who is wearing body armour; Sergeant W A G Kibble, flight engineer; and Sergeant Cassian Henry 'Cass' Waight, WOp, who is also wearing body armour. This aircraft was one of many ABC-equipped Lancasters and carried an additional crewmember known as the Special Duties operator. On 19/20 February 1944 DV267 was lost on the raid on Leipzig and Laurens, Bolt and Waight, who suffered a broken neck, were killed. The five other members of the crew were taken prisoner.

L-R: Warrant Officer Jack Laurens DFM; Sergeant J A Davies, special operator; Sergeant Cassian Henry 'Cass' Waight, WOp; Flight Sergeant Les Burton, navigator; Sergeant W A G Kibble, flight engineer; Sergeant William Frederick Donald 'Don' Bolt, mid-upper gunner; Sergeant 'Ted' Roystone, rear gunner; Sergeant 'Chris' Aitken, bomb aimer. *(IWM)*

The crew on Lancaster *C-Charlie* on 44 'Rhodesia' Squadron pretend to warm their hands for the benefit of the camera in their Nissen hut at Dunholme Lodge after returning from Stuttgart on the night of 1/2 March 1944. (*IWM*)

[th]e 101 Squadron Lancasters equipped with ABC (Airborne Cigar) were distinguishable by their [la]rge masts above the fuselage as on Lancaster I ME590/SR-C. On 26 February 1944, Flight Sergeant [ ] Dixon piloted the aircraft back from Augsburg, where at 20,000 feet ME590 was hit by flak, which [fr]actured hydraulic lines, after which a Me110 attacked and holed the elevators. Dixon crash-landed [at] Ludford Magna, wrecking part of the FIDO (Fog Investigation and Dispersal Operation) pipe-[w]ork in the process. ME590 was repaired, converted from B.I to B.III and sent to 1651 HCU at [W]oolfox Lodge. After further service on 5 MU, ME590 was finally scrapped in April 1947. (*IWM*)

Fog Investigation and Dispersal Operation at Graveley. In the winter of 1944–45 fifteen airfields were equipped with FIDO. (*IWM*)

A Halifax III with H_2S radar scanner under the fuselage takes off from Elvington on 11 March 194 In the background are aircraft on 77 Squadron. (*IWM*)

A game of cards helps pass the time in the crew room at Oakington on 18 March 1944 as Lancaster crews on 7 Squadron wait to leave for the operation on Frankfurt. (*IWM*)

(*Left*) Flight Sergeant Ed Clode of Invercargill, New Zealand, a bomb aimer on 101 Squadron at Metheringham, on his return from the Frankfurt raid of 22/23 March 1944, the last operation of his tour. (*IWM*)

(*Right*) On 22/23 March on the operation on Frankfurt 46-year-old Wing Commander Vashon James 'Pop' Wheeler DFC* MC* (right, when CO of 157 Squadron flying Mosquitoes January–August 1943) CO of 207 Squadron at Spilsby, died at the controls of Lancaster *A-Apple* on what was his 58th operational flight. Three other men on the crew were killed, three surviving to be taken prisoner. (*Theo Boiten via Richard Doleman*)

Photo reconnaissance picture of Frankfurt showing the devastation.

ancaster III ME790 *U-Uncle* on 106 Squadron prepares to take off from at Metheringham for omber Command's last major raid on Berlin, 24 March 1944. ME790 was lost on 22/23 May 1944 n the operation on Brunswick. Flight Lieutenant Sidney Jack Houlden and six of the crew were lled. (*IWM*)

'ookie' going down.

Ernest Peter Bone, Lancaster mid-upper gunner and bomb aimer on Squadron Leader Richard Lane's crew, who completed a tour on 626 Squadron at Wickenby. (*Bone*)

Bomb ravaged *Kaiser Wilhelmstrasse* in Berlin.

The search begins in war damaged Berlin.

ar damage in Berlin.

A fallen RAF Bomber Command crewmember by the wreckage of his aircraft.

Crews putting on a brave face for the camera on the flight line. (*IWM*)

Devastated buildings in a Berlin neighbourhood immediately after a raid.

RAF personnel attach tail units to 1,000lb and 500lb MC HE bombs at dispersal. (*IWM*)

Ground personnel in front of a Lancaster. (*IWM*)

speaking operators were to be carried in the body of the aircraft, whose purpose was to detect discrete R/T frequencies being used by fighters and ground control and jam them. In addition, RAF navigational equipment (*Gee*, *H2S*, etc) had to be installed to complement the US navigational kit of LORAN, a box similar to *Gee* but with LOnger RANge. The Squadron's task was to provide electronic coverage to the main bomber force by jamming, as many frequencies and equipments as our installed kit and the expertise of the operators we carried would allow. The main point of the B-17 was that it had the height – say, 25,000 feet – to fly a clear 5,000 feet above our main bomber stream and thus provide jamming cover in all frequencies. We were inextricably linked to the bomber force and we therefore followed their route, with one or two exceptions when we were sent off to create confusion and deception on our own. My task as Nav Leader, once the Squadron had settled down to its new operational role, was to oversee and monitor the efforts of all Squadron navigators and to act as Wing Commander McGlinn's navigator on the operations he chose to take part in.

The Squadron was ready to operate in April 1944. Sculthorpe was to be a temporary home, reverting to American use on our departure on 16 May to a neighbouring airfield at Oulton, a few miles outside Aylsham. On the very evening of that day, some of us drove into Aylsham to survey the local pubs and after a few beers I wandered across to the blacked-out town hall to look in on a dance being held there. Without hesitation I made a beeline towards a lovely girl dressed in a pink V-neck dress standing across the floor from me. I had known girls at each place before but there was always the acknowledgement that there would be nothing permanent about a relationship. I somehow knew this might be different. Her name was Patricia; she was 19, just a month away from her 20th birthday. She had a divine figure. She had a pretty face. She was an excellent dancer, easily able to follow my somewhat jerky steps (I whispered two lines in Spanish of *Besame Mucho* as we danced); she loved classical music and played the piano, with a distinguished pass in Grade 8 behind her. She lived in the town square, just a few yards from the town hall. She told me some time later that her mother had almost dissuaded her from coming over to the dance that evening (you're out too often my girl); when her father heard us talking below her rooms in Aylsham Square, I understand he said to her mother 'It's all right, they're talking about Beethoven.'[35]

On B-17s I flew mainly with Wing Commander McGlinn but also from time to time with other captains, between January and August 1944, with operational flights from April. The number of flights recorded in my log book is 53, including only eight operational flights. Each of the operations was precisely the same from the navigational point of view as those in my first tour. Accurate navigation was of the essence in order to afford the main stream the ECM cover planned for them; that meant accurate timing around each route as well as maintaining planned track. Other crewmembers had their own tasks – mine was the safe and accurate navigation of the aircraft, in itself a full-time job with fairly rudimentary nav aids. The differences from the first tour were much increased height and therefore more careful attention to oxygen mask fitting; somewhat greater comfort and less engine noise.

Most of us had graduated from the bombing role and it was an intriguing challenge to be protectors of those who were now continuing the bombing in ever-increasing severity. We were all mindful that what we were doing represented a vastly superior scientific and technological effort which was bound to contribute, sooner or later, to finishing the war. Our participation in the special screen set up on the night of 5/6 June 1944 served better than any other single event to confirm that idea in our minds. I quote from official reports: 'On 5/6 June a *Mandrel* screen was formed to cover the approach of the Normandy invasion fleet and from subsequent information received, it appeared that considerable confusion was caused to the German early warning system.' Five Fortresses on 214 Squadron flown by Wing Commander McGlinn [my captain], Squadron Leader Day, Squadron Leader Bill Jefferies, Flight Lieutenant Murray Peden and Flying Officer Cam Lye, also operated in support of the D-Day operation in their *Airborne Cigar* role. A Me 410 had the misfortune to choose McGlinn's aircraft, which had Flight Lieutenant Eric Phillips, the Squadron Gunnery Leader, manning the tail turret and he shot it down.

In September my flying was interrupted by a stupid accident. Oulton was one of the many temporary stations in Bomber Command – no permanent buildings, no fancy messes or barrack blocks. Most of the officers were billeted in Blickling Hall, previously owned by Lord Lothian who had been Ambassador in Washington 1939–40; and renowned for its historical association with Henry VIII and Anne Boleyn. I used to run Music Club meetings in one of the ground floor panelled rooms of the Hall. A number of airmen and airwomen attended to hear me talk to a programme of 78s played on a wind-up gramophone with a sharpener at the ready for the fibre needles. In the grounds of the Hall, many temporary Nissen huts had been constructed, including one, acting as the Officers' Mess. One boozy night in that Mess, there was a sudden decision by everybody there to plant somebody's footprints around the semi-circular ceiling of the Nissen hut – merely to convince gullible visitors that somebody had taken a running jump to do it. Well, it was decided that I was Joe, being fairly light in weight. A sort of scaffolding of tables and chairs was constructed, gradually rising in height towards the centre. I took off my shoes and socks, somebody else blacked the soles with shoe polish (yes, I know, it's crazy) and I was carefully lifted up and had my feet planted on the ceiling one at a time. All was going well until we reached the highest point in the centre. The scaffolding began to falter, the structure collapsed, I fell from a great height and my right palm came down, unfortunately, on to a piece of broken glass on the floor. I don't remember much of what followed but I've learnt since that the Doc (Vyse) was on hand and took charge. I was losing blood at a fairly fearsome rate to start with apparently, until he staunched it. I was carried by ambulance to the Norfolk and Norwich Hospital and was wrapped in a plaster cast for some time. The end result was the cutting of a tendon, a messy right palm and a permanently bent first finger. On the social side, I continued to see more and more of my lovely Patricia; but I must have knocked myself out of the operational business because I have no flights in my log book for the rest of the year. There was an amusing corollary to the footprints incident. At home on leave in Southend, I'd be showing my messy right palm to relations and friends and explaining frankly how it had happened; somebody whispered to my mother that I was almost certainly concealing the real facts and that it was a war wound.

It is believed that the attack on Ludwigshafen by 66 Lancasters and 17 Halifaxes of 5 Group on 17/18 November; a purely *H2S* blind-bombing raid without any TIs being dropped, was accurate and that the I G Farben factory was hit. Most of the enemy fighters landed early because of misleading instructions broadcast from England to German night fighter pilots and only one Lancaster was lost. *G-George* on 405 'Vancouver' Squadron RCAF at Gransden Lodge was flown by Pilot Officer Richard Henry Larson RCAF, all of whose crew including Lieutenant J M K Pederson USAAF were killed. The night following, elements of 3, 4, 6 and 8 Groups went to Leverkusen and the I G Farben chemicals factory but many of the *Oboe* aircraft suffered equipment failure, and difficult weather conditions caused bombs being scattered over a wide area. At least 27 towns, mostly well to the north of Leverkusen, recorded bombs and just one HE bomb landed in the town. Very few German night fighters were operating, probably because of bad weather at their airfields and only four Halifaxes and a Stirling were lost. Fog conditions were encountered on the heavies' return to England and two more Halifaxes and a Stirling crashed, but four Halifaxes on 35 Squadron landed safely at Graveley when the first operational use was made of the oil-burning fog-dispersal equipment along the sides of the runway called FIDO (Fog Investigation and Dispersal Operation).

Ludford Magna was another of the airfields equipped with FIDO, as Sergeant Gerhard Heilig on 101 Squadron recalls:

Soon after we crossed the English coast on our return from a raid we saw the glow of a fire up ahead. As we got closer we realised that its source must be at, or very close to, our own base and we feared the worst, thinking that Ludford or one of its neighbours must have been the victim of a massive enemy strike. When we joined the circuit our relief was great that this had not been the case and we marvelled at the sight which presented itself to our eyes. I had closed down my [ABC] equipment after crossing the English coast and, as was my usual habit, had taken up my stance behind the pilot for a final look around. Within the blanket of fog, which covered the countryside for miles around was a gaping hole, cut straight like with a knife on the upwind side of the gently moving air and billowing in a great curve on the other, the parallel lines of flaming petrol below and a billowing cloud of cumulus above like some monstrous bonnet. It was an eerie feeling as we made our approach, it was like a headlong plunge into a flaming furnace, but all went perfectly smoothly and along with many others we made a safe landing, albeit with no little relief.

From 18/19 November 1943 to 24/25 March 1944 Berlin was subjected to 16 major raids, which have gone into history as the Battle of Berlin. At 'morning prayers' on Thursday 18 November 'Bomber' Harris announced that 835 bombers would be over Germany that night, 440 of them Lancasters heading for Berlin and another 395 aircraft, mostly Halifaxes and Stirlings, that would fly a diversionary raid on Mannheim and Ludwigshafen. The total effort for the night was a new record for a non-1,000 raid night but only by one, with 884 aircraft (including 45 aircraft engaged on minor operations) being dispatched. At Wickenby, Brian Soper, a 19-year-old flight engineer on 12 Squadron, was a little shocked, not having done any ops, to be called into the Chief Flight Engineer's office and told that he would be flying that night; not with his crew, but with Flight Lieutenant McLauchlin, a highly experienced officer, whose flight engineer had been recently commissioned and was away getting 'kitted up'. 'Later at the briefing, it was another jolt to see that it was the Big City; the first time for me of many'. Soper had decided to join the RAF as aircrew following the death of his brother:

Naturally I was hoping to be a pilot. Unfortunately so was everyone else. I enlisted for aircrew in January 1942 and went for the aircrew medical and a variety of exams and other tests. Rejected as a pilot I was offered 'aircrew' to train as wireless operator-air gunner, which I accepted. Eventually I had a letter from the Air Ministry to say that with the arrival of the four-engined bomber an additional crew member was required to take over many of the pilot's duties. Flight engineers were needed for Stirlings, Halifaxes and Lancasters and for coastal command, American Liberators and Fortresses. Fortunately I got in with the group for Lancasters. They were the best.

At the conversion unit Soper had met Warrant Officer Arthur Rew, a rather pleasant pilot who was looking for a flight engineer:

Arthur already had a navigator, Flight Sergeant 'Butch' Lynn and a wireless operator, W/O Don Sinnot from Newfoundland. The bomb aimer and front turret gunner, W/O George Annersly was from Edmonton. Alberta. We had about the oldest man on the squadron: 'Wild Bill' Redding mid upper gunner was in his thirties and like me, a sergeant. Bill had a 500 Norton motor bike on which he used to take part in trials before the war. Any weekend or during standard leave periods he used to take me pillion down to London from whence I got the tube while he went on to Chesham where he lived. This was always quite a lively ride. Finally Sergeant Frank Boyd, rear gunner. No nicer group of guys you could ever wish to meet. When we arrived at our Nissen hut, which held two crews of seven, we were replacing a crew that had 'gone missing'. The other crew went out that night and it wasn't long before they too were shot down. Once settled into the base we continued with the flying training while waiting to go on 'ops'. Before we could do any operational flying, they decided to create a second squadron on the base. This was 626 Squadron. They picked us – not having done any ops – with some other crews who had already completed some bombing raids on 12 Squadron.

On the night of the Berlin raid both forces were planned to cross the enemy coast simultaneously, the stream heading the 'Big City' reaching the capital along the Havel River in eastern Germany and then splitting into groups to bomb Siemensstadt, Neukölln, Mariendorf, Steglitz, Marienfelde and other districts of Berlin. Berlin however, was completely cloud-covered and both marking and bombing was carried out blindly. Tens of thousands of incendiaries and two- and four-ton HE bombs were dropped on Berlin within a period of barely 30 minutes. According to the post-raid report 'the TIs could be seen cascading to the ground and much of the effort undoubtedly fell on Berlin but the comparative failure of this operation resulted from unserviceable *H2S* sets – of which 19 out of 27 failed; an unexpectedly light wind *en route* delaying the backers-up so that for five or six minutes only one Green TI could be seen burning; and a smokescreen hampering visibility.'

Brian Soper would have worse trips later, but his first one was memorable:

> For the first time I experienced the flak, the searchlights, the fires, the bombs bursting on the ground and the Lanc shaking when the flak was close. I saw the brilliant colours of the target markers on the ground and experienced the long, long wait over the target while the bomb-aimer identified the target and gave his instructions to the pilot. I felt the great lift of the Lanc when the bombs were released and then the two minutes flying on straight and level for the camera to check where our bombs had gone. And finally to dive and turn away on a course for home. I had to wonder what this experienced crew thought of this new 'sprog' engineer on his first trip, the crew that I hadn't even really met. It seemed like hours before we got away from the target.

With bomber formations simultaneously over two cities about 300 miles apart, the German night fighters found it impossible to adequately protect both targets, and just nine Lancasters were lost on the Berlin operation but an effective *Tame Boar* operation mounted against the second force destroyed most of the 23 aircraft that failed to return. One of the losses was *B-Bertie*, a 218 Squadron Stirling flown by 21-year-old Pilot Officer Alan Hine from Kendall, Westmoreland. The aircraft encountered few problems until it reached Frankfurt, but were then picked out by many searchlights. Rather than risk other aircraft in the squadron, Hine turned south to Mannheim and they deposited their load as per instructions still being tailed by searchlights. After a very short while 30-year-old Sergeant Wilf Perry, air gunner from Lye, Stourbridge spotted six German fighters tailing the aircraft, but in the glare of the searchlights they could not pick out a single fighter coming from in front and below and were unable to train their guns on same. The fighter attacked and the pilot ordered the abandonment of the aircraft. Wilf Perry was heard to say 'OK Skipper.' The bomb aimer, Flying Officer Alwynne Powell from Llynpia, Glamorgan was near the bomb doors and he parachuted out, but for the rest of the crew it was too late. The Stirling crashed in the village of Bobstadt five miles north of Mannheim with the loss of Hine and Perry; 22-year-old Sergeant D I McCallwn, navigator from Huddersfield, Yorkshire; 26-year-old Sergeant J Robson WOP/AG from Felling, Gateshead; Sergeant F C White, air gunner from Portsmouth, Hampshire and Sergeant K Walshaw, flight engineer from Dewsbury, Yorkshire. Alwynne Powell was captured about 40 miles from the crash site six days later. He was held prisoner until June 1945 when repatriated. The bodies of the six crew men were laid out on the grass at side of road and were carried on a vehicle to the nearby cemetery where they were buried with a simple cross which read 'Here Lies Six English Flyers'. Women from the local village laid flowers on the graves.[36]

More than 2,500 tons of bombs were dropped in the raids on Berlin and Ludwigshafen. Over 300 buildings were destroyed in Mannheim and Ludwigshafen-on-Rhine. This raid marked the last major attack on Mannheim for fifteen months. At the de-briefing at Wickenby Brian Soper enjoyed a cigarette and a tot of rum. 'It was like living again – but for how long?' He would follow this trip with three more to Berlin, flying with his own pilot and crew.

Leverkusen was bombed on the night of 19/20 November when bad weather on the continent prevented many night fighters from operating and only five bombers were lost. Conditions were little better when on Monday 22 November, 764 bombers, fifty of them Stirlings of 3 Group flying their last Main Force operation, set off for Berlin again. Crews were detailed to fly a straight course in and out. At Mildenhall the Amir Feisal and the Amir Khalid of Saudi Arabia watched the Lancaster crews on 15 and 622 Squadrons prepare for and return from the raid on Berlin. The first Path Finders arrived over the 'Big City' just before 20.00 to find the city covered by ten-tenths cloud. The forecast had been for clear conditions over the home airfields, broken to medium-level cloud over Berlin and low cloud or fog over much of the rest of Germany. Three of the five Lancasters equipped with the new 3cm *H2S* Mk.III sets had to turn back after their equipment failed but the two other aircraft's sets showed a clear outline and the blind markers accurately dropped four red TIs at the AP slightly to the east of the centre of the capital. Despite the risk of collisions the rate of aircraft over the target was increased to 34 a minute. More than 2,000 tons of blast bombs and approximately 150,000 incendiaries were dropped on Berlin in barely 35 minutes. Air crews reported large fires spread through the city and that they lit the sky a fiery red. Approximately 20 minutes after the first bomb was released, there was a gigantic explosion whose effects were clearly visible from an altitude of over 21,000 feet. Hundreds of air crews confirmed that they had never seen such a severe explosion or felt such a shock wave, on any previous operation. The explosion was the huge Neuköln gasworks blowing up. One of the pilots gave this account:

> The anti-aircraft started firing about 180 miles outside Berlin, so that we had to fly for a total of 360 miles through a more or less dense barrage, which was hard on the nerves. We saw the explosion too; it was almost unimaginable. Suddenly a blazing light shot up and the horizon turned fiery red. The coloured flares from the pathfinders showed us our way as clearly as we could wish. We had no problems as we released more than 50 two-ton bombs on the city centre, which the flares had divided into sectors. Only one of our bombs hit outside the area marked by the flares.

Returning crews could only estimate that the marking and bombing were believed to be accurate. In fact this was the most effective raid on the 'Big City' of the war. A vast area of destruction stretched across the capital caused mainly by firestorms as a result of the dry weather conditions. Tuesday night leading into Wednesday, the west part of Berlin suffered more than in all the previous raids. On Wednesday afternoon, Mosquitoes flew over the capital and reported having observed over 200 giant conflagrations. The *Daily Mail* reported: 'It has entered the realm of possibility that Berlin may be approaching the end of its days as a capital city, due to the fearful rain of bombs that fell on it Monday night. The RAF has devised means to level targets the size of Berlin. The raid was by far the heaviest that that city has ever experienced.'

Reich Minister of Propaganda Dr. Joseph Goebbels' wrote in his diary:

Early in the morning I am already at work. Straight away Schaub gives me a report on the situation in Berlin, which is very sad. It is inexplicable how the British were able to destroy so much of the capital in one air raid. The Wilhelmsplatz is truly the picture of desolation. It is still blazing from end to end. The Propaganda Ministry has mainly been spared ... Devastation is again appalling in the government section as well as in the western and northern suburbs ... The State Playhouse and the *Reichstag* are ablaze ... Hell itself seems to have broken loose over us ...

Nachtjagd largely remained grounded due to adverse weather conditions and there were no diversions but twenty-six aircraft failed to return. Eleven of these were Lancasters, ten were Halifaxes and the other five were Stirlings on their swansong. It took Stirling losses since August to 109 aircraft in raids on Germany. Unable to achieve the altitude performance which the Halifax and Lancaster could attain, Stirlings never again flew to Germany.[37]

Twelve hours later the RAF bombers returned to Berlin. Goebbels' next diary entry was:

Now and then I am able to snatch half an hour's sleep; but then I am called back to work. Large formations of British aircraft are again set on an obstinate course for Berlin ... The raid begins shortly after the alarm siren. This time there are more blast bombs than incendiaries. Once again it is a first-class grand assault ... Mines and explosive bombs hail down incessantly on the government district. One after another the most important buildings start to burn. After the raid when I take a look at the Wilhelmsplatz, I find that the ghastly impression of the previous evening has grown even worse. I pass on into the Propaganda Ministry. The offices are burning in two places on the side of the Wilhelmsplatz.

The height of the smoke cloud over Berlin from eleven major fires still burning from the previous night was almost 19,000 feet high when 383 bombers – 365 Lancasters, ten Halifaxes and eight Mosquitoes – again made the long haul to the 'Big City'. This time the attack concentrated mainly on the western part of the capital with its three large rail installations: Westend, Bahn Zoo and Bahnhof Charlottenburg. The night was clear and there were only a few clouds to hinder visibility, so that operational conditions were far more favourable to the German air defence than on the previous night. The bombing force again used the same direct route and the *Jägerleitoffizier* (*JLO*, or GCI-controller) made an early identification of Berlin as the probable target. Bomber crews noticed that flak over the target, which was again cloud-covered, was 'unusually restrained' and the Path Finders carried out sky-marking but many of the Main Force crews aimed their bombs through the cloud at the glow of the fires burning from the previous night.

Brian Soper recalled:

This raid was very similar to the previous one, although both ground and sky markers were used as there was a lot of cloud at lower levels. These took the form of flares, red, green, or yellow, the colours specified at the briefing, dropped by pathfinder Lancs or Mosquitoes. Sky markers called Wanganui flares were dropped by parachutes, with one colour dripping from the other. To bomb on these, the bomb-aimer would need to be sure of approaching from the right direction; height and wind speed calculations were important. These markers were only used when the ground markers could not easily be seen and were probably not too accurate.

This time, a handful of experienced *Nachtjäger* braved the elements. Twelve *Tame Boar* crews shot down 13 of the 20 heavy bombers that were lost. Further losses were avoided by 'spoof' fighter flares dropped by Mosquitoes north of the bomber stream, which caused some diversion of the night fighter effort and fake *Corona* instructions ordering the German pilots to land because of fog at their bases. When the *Nachtjagd* introduced female commentators to give the 'running commentary' to the fighters to beat the *Corona* interference this was swiftly countered by a female voice from England. Later the transmission of three or four superimposed German voices would be used. Eventually, instead of attempting to imitate the German commentators, British operators would set out to simply irritate them by blocking the air waves by reading lengthy passages from the writings of Goethe or the speeches of Hitler. Gradually the Germans would overcome the worst effects of *Corona* by increasing the frequency spread used and making rapid changes of frequency during operations but in the meantime *Corona* caused great confusion and on occasion exchanges between night fighter pilots and the real controllers reached explosive levels. From a distance of 30 miles the air crews could see the fires that had continued to smoulder since Monday. Finally in the fire-glow over Berlin they were able to observe many details of the destroyed city districts. The whole complex around the Wilhelmstrasse, the Brandenburg Gate area and the Tauentzienstrasse, Potsdam Square, the Anhalter Strasse and many other building-lined streets were completely destroyed. Berliners once again began clearing away the debris and devastation as fire crews tried to extinguish the blazing fires. Goebbels wrote that this was 'one of the worst nights of his entire life.' Although the flames were still soaring skywards he hoped that Berliners would overcome the worst difficulties by noon and get ready for the next night. 'It would be wonderful,' he added 'if we had one night's rest.'

Goebbels' got his wish. On the night of 25/26 November 236 Halifaxes and 26 Lancasters attacked Frankfurt. Again, there were no major diversions and the *JLO* did not at first know whether Mannheim or Frankfurt was the real objective but eventually, he chose Frankfurt. Flak was restricted to 15,000 feet. Cloud covered the target area and the bombing appeared to be scattered. Eleven Halifaxes including three on 102 Squadron at Pocklington and *W-William*, a Lancaster on 97 Squadron flown by Flight Lieutenant Carlos Manuel Brown CdeG RCAF failed to return. The American Skipper and his crew, including Pilot Officer Thomas Watson, who always carried his pet spaniel on ops, all died on the aircraft, which crashed at Brandau.

Another American was lost when *B-Baker* flown by Pilot Officer Stephen John Troake, one of two Halifaxes on 76 Squadron that were lost, failed to return to Holme on Spalding Moor. Pilot Officer Reg Fayers the navigator supposed that he had been fighting in the Battle of the Ruhr but to him it hadn't felt like that:

> It didn't seem like fighting to climb aboard an aircraft with your friends and climb to a space where the sunset seemed infinite; to sit in a small space and on the engine-noise background hear the everyday commonplaces spoken to you while you juggled with figures and lines to find God's intentions in the winds; to sit for a few hours at 20,000 feet working hard so that when Tom Paton the bomb aimer eventually said 'Bombs gone, photograph taken. OK Steve, fly away,' it didn't seem anything more than part of the job and a fresh course to be steered, this time for home.

To Fayers the air war seemed 'aloof and impersonal'. He had no time to think of hell happening below 'to a set of people who were the same as you except that their thinking had gone a bit haywire.'

> It was a fair assumption that when Tom dropped the bombs, women and boys and girls were killed and cathedrals damaged. It must have

been so. Were it more personal, I should be more regretting, I suppose. But sitting up there with my charts and pencils I did not see a thing. I never looked out. As far as humanity was concerned, I could not definitely regret that I had helped to kill German people. The only thought that came from the outside was when occasionally Gillie, the mid-upper gunner, said, 'Turn to starboard, go ...' It might mean that out there in the darkness which you could not even see, somewhere there was a night fighter with a German boy in it; and he might kill you. When Gillie or Reuben Orr the rear gunner, said 'Turn to starboard, go ...' that quick weakening thought came in – 'May be this is It.' But you never could believe it. It didn't seem possible that what was so orderly and efficient a machine one second could become, within the next minute, a falling, killing thing with us throwing ourselves from it into a startling world of surprised chaos. But it could happen.

It did. *B-Baker* crashed south of Heidelberg.

Reg Fayers had written a letter to his wife Phyl that summer, which he never posted, saying that they had more out of living than most people could reasonably expect and that if they had to stop sharing those wonderful things, perhaps it was better for it to end when their love was so strong and firm and young and 'while they both had their own teeth.' He had added that if he had to go to heaven, 'I'd rather go attractively and still be able to play soccer. Love me till then, darling, *Toujours a vous.*' Reg Fayers, Tom Paton and Staff Sergeant P W Flewell the mid-upper gunner bailed out and they were captured. Their Skipper and Sergeants Lew Barnes and P I Weeks were killed.

G-George, the other missing Halifax on 76 Squadron, was flown by 21-year-old Lieutenant Knut Lindaas, a charming Norwegian, one of three on the Squadron who were known as 'Pip', 'Squeak' and 'Wilfred' after the cartoon characters. On the way home the cloud had thickened up and the Halifax began to ice up. Within minutes 'Squeak' Lindaas had lost control. Several of his crew bailed out but he refused a parachute from the flight engineer before he too bailed out with the 24-year-old rear gunner, Sergeant Fred Beadle. Lindaas preferred to die in the aircraft. He had received news that his brother had already been shot by the *Gestapo* and he knew that his days were numbered if he landed alive in Germany. The Norwegian flyers never cared of the economic importance of a target; they just wanted to know how many Germans per acre ...[38]

Harold Wakefield the flight engineer on 51 Squadron who 'always had his parachute handy' had a lucky escape returning from Frankfurt. He wrote about it to his parents:

We took off at 11.30pm for Frankfurt. We flew down England and turned towards the coast at Reading. As we neared the coast before we knew what had happened, another Halifax sort of side-slipped across the top of us. There was a terrific crunching as it hit us. Johnny kept control all the time but it was very hard to fly and we were losing height. Half the tail-plane, one rudder and two feet of the port wing were ripped off; one of the props was shattered and the three remaining engines had been knocked about a bit and at any minute we expected the rest of the tail-plane to fall off. But we held on while we crossed the coast and jettisoned our bomb in the sea. Then we turned back over land again and Johnny gave orders to 'abandon aircraft'. He said he'd stay a bit and see if he could land it by himself, but if necessary he'd bail out himself. So we clipped on our 'chutes and said a little prayer (at least I did) and bailed out one after another. We were all a bit nervous, but I was pretty excited myself. Anyway I went out head first and was battered and banged about by the slipstream. I turned several somersaults and dropped several hundred feet. Then there was a colossal jerk as if I'd been torn in half and I knew my 'chute had opened OK. I jumped at 10,000 feet but there was no wind hardly and I drifted down, it was a lovely sensation floating down, but it only took me about seven minutes before I hit the ground with a bit of a thud, my knees buckled up and I landed on my bum. On the way down I crashed through a tree but luckily didn't get stuck although I did get a slight scratch across my cheek. I landed in a field. So I rolled my 'chute up and slung it over my shoulder and started walking over fields and hedges until I came to a road, after about 2 hours walking I came to a small village. I went to the house and knocked them up (by this time it was 3 o'clock Friday morning as I bailed out about 1 o'clock). They took me in (it was a young man and his wife) and were very good. They wanted to give me a bath, whisky etc. But I had a cup of tea. They rang the nearest drome and someone was sent immediately in a car to pick me up.

By 26 November 'Nick' Knilans on 619 Squadron was no longer a Pilot Officer, having been promoted to Lieutenant USAAF. That night he would pilot a Lancaster on the raid on Berlin A rear gunner who had already flown a tour replaced Jerry Jackson who had been killed over Kassel in October but he failed to show up to fly the NFT that afternoon. He did however show up in time for the take off. The Berlin force totalled over 440 Lancasters and seven Mosquitoes, the procession taking 45 minutes to cross the coast. Another 157 Halifaxes and 21 Lancasters flew a diversion on Stuttgart. Both forces flew a common route over Northern France and nearing Frankfurt they split. At first the JLOs thought that Frankfurt was the intended target. The difficult weather conditions had resulted in only the most experienced German crews being ordered to take off and 84 fighters engaged the RAF formations. I JD downed most of the 27 bombers that were shot down on the raid on the 'Big City' while from the smaller force seven Halifaxes were shot down by flak and fighters and a Halifax crashed on take-off at the start of the operation. Just two German night fighter aircraft were lost.

The weather was clear over Berlin but, after their long approach flight from the south, the Path Finders marked an area 6–7 miles north-west of the city centre and most aircraft bombed there. Damage was considerable and civilian casualties were high. Thirty-eight war industry factories were destroyed and many more damaged. Combined casualties for the three raids late that month had resulted in the deaths of 4,330 people killed and over 417,000 people were rendered homeless for more than a month and over 36,300 up to a month.[39] Goebbels wrote 'the English [sic] aimed so accurately that one might think spies had pointed the way.'

Brian Soper on W/O Arthur Rew's crew was on his third Berlin raid:

There were many searchlights around, both at the target and at Frankfurt, with many night fighters in the Frankfurt area. On return to base, there was a problem getting the wheels to lock down. Having tried all the recommended procedures to no avail, they diverted us to another base, in case we messed up the runway for the others. After going through the final checks, Arthur landed 'tail heavy' and the locks came on. We stayed overnight and returned to Wickenby the following day with the undercarriage checked out.

Flight Lieutenant Charles Owen was one of the Lancaster pilots on the Berlin raid. After leaving public school he had worked at the Supermarine aircraft factory as a boy of 17 in 1940 and had been badly injured in an air raid. He spent the winter in hospital and when fully recovered, he had been accepted by the RAF as a bomber trainee and after a spell as an instructor he had been posted to 97 Squadron. Owen noted, 'First trip with my own crew and the Big City at that. Usual flares and aircraft shot down on way in. Target was clear and we could see fires burning from an attack on the previous night. Hundreds of searchlights and very heavy flak, firing mainly into the cones.' Owen flew over Hannover by mistake on the return journey and was coned for seven minutes. He lost height from 20,000 to 13,000 feet during evasive action from intense heavy flak. There were several holes in the starboard wing and roof of his cockpit and the bomb aimer was wounded slightly in the leg. They were also attacked by a fighter when coned but the only damage was six inches off one of the blades of the starboard outer prop.

No less than sixteen other Lancasters crashed or were later written off after accidents at the end of the Berlin operation, one Lancaster having crashed after turning back with one engine out at the start of the operation. A Stirling, which had been engaged on a mining operation towards the Frisians returned to Wratting Common and made two attempts to land before crashing near Bury St. Edmunds without injury to the crew. One of the Lancaster losses occurred when *X-X-Ray* on 50 Squadron landed at Melbourne and struck a van, killing the driver, before running into *A-Apple,* which was written off. Amazingly no one on either crew suffered injury. Another 50 Squadron Lancaster, which waited to land away from its home base crashed at Pocklington and hit a farmhouse at Bayton north-west of Market Weighton, killing five on the crew and injuring the two others. Two women in the farmhouse also died. On return a Lancaster on 103 Squadron that had taken off from Elsham Wolds at the start of the operation, collided with a Halifax on 428 'Ghost' Squadron RCAF and went down just north-east of Middleton St. George with the loss of all except one of the crew. The Canadian Halifax too was destroyed and all the crew killed.

Also involved in a collision this night was Lancaster B.I R5868, which had joined 467 Squadron RAAF in late September after flying 68 ops on 83 Squadron as *Q-Queenie* and was now the famed *S–Sugar.* The Göring quotation, NO ENEMY PLANE WILL FLY OVER THE REICH TERRITORY had been added below the bomb log under the cockpit canopy by LAC Willoughby, one of the engine fitters in mid-March 1944 around the time that *Sugar* completed 88 operations. Flying Officer Jack Colpus, the Skipper recalled:

We arrived at the target on time at about 20,000 feet with no cloud cover – contrary to the met forecast. The whole Berlin area was a mass of waving searchlights about forty miles in diameter. We completed our bombing run and had just selected bomb doors closed when we were coned by searchlights. They seemed to come from all directions at once. Evasive action corkscrew turns, which were made in an attempt to escape, failed. Heavy flak thumped in all around us, with puffs of black smoke and cordite smell, indicating how close they were. After a while, which seemed like eternity, the flak stopped as if by magic, which meant only one thing. Fighters were coming in. I decided on desperate action and dived steeply down to the left and picked up speed to reach 300 mph at 10,000 feet before pulling out to the right and up. At that moment the searchlights lost us, although I was still dazzled. We were climbing as quickly as possible to gain height to get away from the light flak and back into the main bomber stream when suddenly the plane lurched and dived to port. I thought we had lost power on one engine but the rear gunner said we had hit another Lancaster. Full right rudder, full rudder bias and full aileron trim was applied but *Sugar* still kept turning to the left. Further action was necessary, so power on the engines on the port side was increased and on the starboard side decreased until we were able to fly on course. All four motors were then switched to run off the port wing fuel tanks in an effort to eventually raise the port wing to a near level position. We jettisoned the bomb containers to lighten the load. The plane was now under control flying at the slow speed of 140 mph and gradually losing height. We decided to fly straight home as at 140 mph we would soon be out of the bomber stream, which was taking a dog-leg route back.

After about two hours, due to a lighter fuel load, we were able to maintain height at about 5,000 feet. The crew made ready to bail out if necessary, as the amount of damage sustained could not be ascertained and now that evasive action would not be possible, we would be 'sitting ducks' for flak or fighters. Full right rudder was required for the four-hour trip back. The engineer went into the bomb aimer's compartment and assisted me by holding the rudder pedal with a strap around it, to give my leg a rest. When nearing the coast of England we were directed to land at Linton-on-Ouse as Waddington was covered in fog. At Linton-on-Ouse we were given priority landing behind a plane which was over-shooting. At this time we were about 500 feet too high on the approach but I decided to land as fuel was getting short. As we touched down on the runway at 120 mph (about 20 mph too fast due to the steeper angle of descent) the port wing stalled. If I had made a normal approach at the correct speed, the plane would have stalled before landing and crashed. The aircraft ground looped at the far end of the runway due to the high landing speed and excessive braking. Inspection of the damage revealed that about five feet of the wing-tip was missing and a portion of the remaining damaged area which was turned down at right angles, caused the turning problem.

S-Sugar was classified category Q, sent back to the manufacturers and did not return to squadron operations until 15 February 1944. The other Lancaster, from 61 Squadron was coned in searchlights and was taking avoiding action when we collided. The Skipper confirmed this, when he landed at Waddington a few days later especially to see me to discuss circumstances. We were all very lucky.[40]

G-George, a 408 'Goose' Squadron RCAF Lancaster at Linton-on-Ouse was hit by flak near Magdeburg after leaving the target area and was then attacked by a Ju 88 night fighter. One of the air gunners was wounded in the left foot and problems were experienced with the starboard inner engine but Flight Sergeant R T Lloyd RCAF got *George* back to the Fiskerton area five miles east of Lincoln, where the starboard outer failed, followed by a malfunction in the rudder trim mechanism. Lloyd gave the order for the crew to bail out but the escape hatch jammed and the Lancaster was crash-landed near a sewage disposal plant two miles south-east of Lincoln. Everyone on the crew escaped and the gunner was taken to hospital in Lincoln.

At Skellingthorpe there was no word from *N-Nuts* on 50 Squadron flown by Pilot Officer John Adams RAAF who on the Berlin raid on 18/19 November had narrowly missed colliding with a twin engined fighter north-west of Hannover. He recalled:

The episode of the near miss made me even more nervous about the possibility of colliding in the dark with another aircraft. These fears were realized on the night of the 26th while on our 16th operation. Another Lancaster came down on us. Its tail section took out the windscreen and wrecked the two port motors. This occurred about twenty minutes after we had dropped our bombs on Berlin. About two hours later, the damage we sustained led to us crashing in Wilhelmshaven Bay. We were lucky that we only suffered the loss of two members of the crew. Bill Ward the bomb aimer was killed on impact and Cyril Billett the rear gunner, drowned. We survivors spent the remainder of the war as prisoners.[41]

It was a terrible night for Skellingthorpe, which was also missing three Lancasters and their crews on 61 Squadron. *H-Harry* crashed south of Surwold with the loss of Pilot Officer Arthur James Douglas Eaves and crew and the crews on *W-William* flown by Pilot Officer John Gilbert McAlpine RAAF and *O-Orange* piloted by Pilot Officer Andrew P E Strange were lost without trace. Sergeant Edward F Johnson USAAF the mid-upper gunner[42] on Strange's crew is commemorated on the wall of the Missing at the US Military Cemetery at Margraten in Holland.

Nick Knilans' Lancaster was attacked three times by enemy fighters. One of his engines was damaged and the American pilot feathered the propeller. The replacement rear gunner who had missed the NFT earlier in the day said that his guns were u/s and returned no fire on their attackers. Knilans lost height but continued to the target. He approached Berlin out of the darkness and the streets and the buildings began to take shape. Crossing the city amidst heavy flak bursts the rear gunner twice yelled 'we're not going to make it.' Knilans 'shut him up'. Later he would have the Gunnery Leader replace him. For the moment Knilans had other things to think about:

From our height, with the flares above and hundreds of search-lights below, the scene became increasingly clear. It was a vivid and dramatic moment. Blockbusters, looking like 50-gallon oil drums, were tumbling down past us from the bombers above. Amid all the buffeting and noise of the light and heavy ack-ack, Ken Ryall my 18-year-old flight engineer spoke up. 'Should we pray, Skipper?'

'No' I replied, 'not while we are about to kill more old men, women and children down there.'

On 27 November Goebbels travelled through the damaged areas of Berlin. In his diary he wrote:

> We also stopped at several ration distribution stations ... The misery one sees is indescribable. It breaks one's heart to see it; but all the same we must clench our teeth [and bear it]. Sometimes one has the impression that the mood of people in Berlin is almost religious. Women walk over to me and make signs of blessing and pray God to keep me safe. All this is very moving ... The food [being distributed to the people] is praised everywhere as excellent ... You can wrap these people around your little finger with small tokens of kindness. I can hardly believe that this city led a revolt in 1918. Under my leadership that would never have happened ... Another grand assault comes due on the city. This time it is not the turn of the city centre so much as of the Wedding and Reinickendorf districts; the main target in Reinickendorf is the big industrial munitions plant ... Back to the bunker in the Wilhelmsplatz. The situation has taken a more threatening turn as one industrial plant after another has gone up in flames. The sky arches over Berlin with a blood-red eerie beauty. I can no longer stand to look at it.

The same day Lord Sherwood, undersecretary of state in the Air Ministry, stated concerning the air war against Germany:

> In the past Berlin expressly ordered Warsaw, Rotterdam and Belgrade to be levelled. In their enthusiasm the Germans even made documentary films of these great deeds of the German *Luftwaffe* so that they could be suitably admired. Now they are paid out in the same coin. The crocodile tears in the eyes of so many Germans can awaken no pity. The blows now being dealt to Germany are merely just punishment the crimes that the *Third Reich* has committed against small nations, their unprotected cities and minority groups in many states. We can make Germany only one promise: Our blows will increase in power until the military capacity of the *Nazi Reich* has been broken.

Notes

1. *See No Need To Die: American Flyers in RAF Bomber Command* by Gordon Thorburn (Haynes Publishing 2009).
2. *The London Observer* by Raymond Lee (Hutchinson, 1972).
3. Forty-two bombers were lost; 21 of them to twin-engined night fighters and 11 to *Wilde Sau* single-engined fighters of all three *Wild Boar Geschwader* that operated in force over Mannheim.
4. One Lancaster was lost on the operation on Brunswick.

5. *No Moon Tonight* by Don Charlwood (Penguin 1988). Kennard and his crew were all killed.

6. On a previous intruder operation, on 22/23 September, when the bombers were returning from Hannover, *Major* Wolf Dietrich Meister of 14./KG2 had shot down a 57 Squadron Lancaster south of Lincolnshire, killing all the crew.

7. *Intruders over Britain: The Luftwaffe Night Fighter Offensive 1940 to 1945* by Simon W Parry (ARP 2003).

8. Possibly S/L G B F Cousens on 61 Squadron whose Lancaster came under a sustained attack from a night fighter while south of Munich. A fierce fire broke out as the Lancaster dived and at about 6,000ft the bomber exploded, throwing Cousens and his rear gunner clear. The other five members of his crew were killed. *RAF Bomber Command Losses of the Second World War, Vol. 4 1943* by W R Chorley (Midland 1996).

9. Adapted from *Night Trip To Munich* by D W Pye in *70 True Stories of the Second World War*, (Odhams Press).

10. *218 Gold Coast Squadron Association Newsletter No. 14* edited by Margery Griffiths. JB278 was cut in two and the rear half from mid upper aft was scrapped and a new one fitted. On 24/25 April 1944, JB278 was badly damaged over Karlsruhe. The crew were making for Manston when the fuel ran out so they ditched in the North Sea. All the crew took to the dinghy and were rescued.

11. Private memoir, Major Hubert Knilans, *A Yank in the RCAF*, RAF Museum, Hendon, archive B2455. In June 1944 Knilans, now a pilot on 617 Dam Busters Squadron, was interviewed by Edward R Murrow for his *This Is London* radio programme.

12. *Night Air War* by Theo Boiten (Crowood Press 1999).

13. A further diversion was carried out by 16 Lancasters of 8 Group to the Zeppelin works at Friedrichshafen, all aircraft returning safely. Three Stirlings and two Wellingtons were lost on *Gardening* operations.

14. Chorley.

15. See *RAF Evaders: The Comprehensive Story of Thousands of Escapers and their Escape Lines, Western Europe, 1940–1945* by Oliver Clutton- Brock (Grub Street 2009)

16. See Thorburn.

17. The only other survivor was Flight Sergeant J O Simpson RAAF. See *Chased By The Sun*.

18. 'Several years later when I was serving as an Air Traffic Controller in Amman, Jordan I was chatting to the senior captain of a resident airliner (and a Hon Member of our Mess) ex *Luftwaffe* and in the course of conversation the mention of Stirlings interested him. He confessed that he had been flying an experimental jet fighter and had shot down two Stirlings that night and badly damaged a third. When we later compared our log books there was no doubt left in our minds but it also answered another question. It had always amazed us that we had only been hit by small calibre stuff and no cannon. He had used up all his cannon on the other two and could not understand how we had managed to survive after all the bits and pieces that had flown off of us. But they were not bits and pieces they were bundles of leaflets. I had not

wasted time in cutting the strings!' *218 Gold Coast Squadron Assoc Newsletter No. 37 November 2005.*

19. The two Canadian gunners are believed to have completed their tours before returning to Canada. Tommy Ellwood's cut affected his eyesight and he was permanently grounded. He resumed his previous career as an engine fitter. P/O N G Emery the navigator was the only survivor of Halifax II JP123 TL-F, which crashed on the Stettin raid on 5/6 January 1944 killing F/L Robert Reginald George Appleby DFC and crew. Emery spent the rest of the war in the infamous PoW camp at Sagan. On the night of 22/23 May 1944 when Dortmund was the target for the bombers, F/O Harold Thomas 'Mac' Maskell and P/O Derrick Coleman flew in Lancaster ND762 TL-E. The 35-year-old Maskell was flying as a second wireless operator. Homeward bound, their Lanc was shot up by a night fighter over Holland and the Lancaster exploded, throwing out three survivors – the pilot, F/O E Holmes, W/O F J Tudor DFM and Coleman. Maskell was one of the five airmen who died in the explosion. Another was 37-year-old Sergeant Alastair Stuart McLaren. Derrick Coleman, who was not yet 21, avoided capture, moved under the cover of Dutch and Belgian undergrounds but he was betrayed and he joined Emery in Stalag Luft III. In February 1944 S/L Max Muller transferred to 25 OTU as an instructor but he returned for a further operational tour with 35 Squadron, this time piloting Lancasters. On 8/9 April, just thirty days before the end of the war, he volunteered for yet another raid over Germany, to Hamburg. His Lancaster (NG440 TL-C) was believed hit in the nose by flak and Muller and five of crew were killed. Flight Sergeant Charles Wilce DFM survived while F/L Patrick Baring Oates Ranalow died from his injuries on 10 April.

20. See *Chased By The Sun.*

21. See *Confound and Destroy* by Martin Streetly (MacDonald & Janes 1978).

22. See *Bomber Command* by Max Hastings (Pan 1979).

23. See *Bombers; The Aircrew Experience* by Philip Kaplan (Aurum Press 2000)

24. P/O (2nd Lieutenant) John Edward Cox on F/O Gerald Patrick Godwin DFC RAAF's Lancaster crew on 467 Squadron was the third American lost on the raid. He and all the others on the crew were lost without trace.

25. On 22/23 March 1944 Manning and five of his his crew including Zammit were killed on the operation to Frankfurt. G/C Norman Charles 'Shorty' Pleasance the Bardney station commander who accompanied the crew on the raid was also killed.

26. Sergeant Jeffrey George Kirby, F/O William Laskie, Sergeant Derek Kneale and Flight Sergeant Roy Brawn RAAF were killed. One source suggests that Dorothy Robson had requested that her ashes were scattered in the air but she is buried in Yorkshire at Pocklington Road Cemetery. F/O F P G Hall subsequently joined F/O R J Bolt's crew on 76 Squadron and he completed his tour of operations in 1944. See Chorley and *Chased By The Sun; The Australians in Bomber Command in WWII* by Hank Nelson (ABC Books 2002).

27. See *No Particular Courage* by Harry Church in *Flights Into History: Final Missions Retold By Research and Archaeology* by Ian McLachlan (Sutton Publishing 2007). Apart from Church only Sergeant 'Jock' Mason and Flight Sergeant Steve Putman survived to be taken into captivity. 49 Squadron's other loss

that night was *R–Robert* flown by F/L C G Thomas (KIA), which exploded near Cologne. Only three men survived and they were taken captive.

28. F/O Oien is commemorated on the Wall of the Missing at Madingley Cemetery, Cambridge. He had been awarded the Air Medal and the Purple Heart.

29. Halifax II *F-Freddie* on 10 Squadron crashed in the target area. F/L Lawrence Arthur Harden, Sergeant Gordon Edward Haskings his 40-year-old flight engineer and two other crew KIA. Three others were taken into captivity.

30. See *Bomber Command* by Max Hastings (Pan 1979).

31. *RAF Bomber Stories* (PSL 1998) and *Legend of the Lancasters* (Pen & Sword 2009) by Martin W Bowman.

32. Heffernan was admitted to RAF Hospital Ely and spent many weeks recovering from his injuries. He remained in the service and in 1953 was awarded the OBE; retiring as Air Commodore in 1956. Chorley.

33. On 8 November 100 Group (Special Duties, later Bomber Support) was created to consolidate the various squadrons and units using the secret ELINT and RCM in the war against the German night fighter air and defence system. In tandem with this electronic wizardry, 100 Group also accepted *Window* 'spoofing' as a large part of its offensive armoury and it also controlled squadrons of Mosquitoes engaged purely on Intruder missions over Germany. Early in November about 50 German night fighters were equipped with the improved SN-2 radar, which was relatively immune to *Window* but only 12 night fighters and crews were operational, mainly because of the delay in training suitable operators to use the complicated and sensitive radar equipment.

34. *Confounding The Reich* by Martin W Bowman. (Pen & Sword 2004).

35. Jack and Patricia married on 7 February 1948.

36. In 1948 the remains were exhumed and transferred to Dumbach War Cemetery (Bavaria). Christine Smith (nee Perry) writing in *218 Gold Coast Assoc Newsletter No. 32 February 2005.*

37. However, in the Path Finder Force the Stirling's operating height of about 13,000 ft was increased by almost 8,000 ft by the simple expedient of reducing the quantity of .303 ammunition, cutting the fuel reserve of 22% by a half and further removing all the armour plating including the vast door, which measured 7/8 thick, between the front cabin and the outer fuselage. *Stirling Wings: The Short Stirling Goes to War* by Jonathan Falconer (Sutton 1995). Stirlings went on to perform well in other roles, notably as glider tugs and on SOE operations in the occupied countries.

38. See *Bomber Command* by Max Hastings (Pan 1979).

39. The *Bomber Command War Diaries: An Operational Reference Book 1939–1945* by Martin Middlebrook and Chris Everitt (Midland 1985).

40. Adapted from an article by the late Stuart Howe.

41. See *Nachtjagd: The Night Fighter versus Bomber War over the Third Reich 1939–45* by Theo Boiten (Crowood 1997).

42. Who had been awarded the Air Medal with three Oak Leaf Clusters and the Purple Heart.

CHAPTER 4

An Orchestrated Hell

Berlin was a kind of orchestrated hell – a terrible symphony of light and flame. It isn't a pleasant kind of warfare. The men doing it speak of it as a job …

Ed Murrow of CBS, Berlin, 2/3 December 1943

Standing behind the armoured seat of the Lancaster, Walter King of the Sydney *Morning Herald* looked over the shoulder of Squadron Leader William Alexander 'Bill' Forbes, the imperturbable CO of 460 Squadron RAAF and watched the fascinating and fantastic scene over Berlin. King was one of a trio of press correspondents who flew aboard three of the 25 Lancasters that took off from Binbrook. He wrote:

> The skies over the target were indeed in turmoil, but the target area itself was in even greater turmoil as 4,000lb bombs – 'cookies' smashed amid the built-up area and thousands of incendiaries cascaded down and took a hold among the blocks of buildings … From the time we sighted [the TIs] about ten miles out, until we passed beyond them was the most exciting ten minutes through which I have lived. The two central figures on that brief period were two 'Bills' [Forbes and Flight Lieutenant William James Douglas 'Bill' Grime, the bomb aimer] who co-operated directly and instructed each other over the intercom phones.[1]

It was the fifth heavy attack on Berlin within a fortnight but most of the Halifaxes, about 210 aircraft, were withdrawn from the raid late on 2 December because of fog, which was forming at their airfields in Yorkshire. And so 458 Lancasters, 18 Mosquitoes and just 15 Halifaxes were dispatched to the 'Big City' that night. There were no major diversions and the bombers took an absolutely direct route across the North Sea and Holland and then on to the capital. Unexpected winds *en route* blew many aircraft off track and nullified the Path Finders' efforts to make dead reckoning (DR) runs from Rathenow. Consequently there were gaps in the cloud covering the city; most of the bombing was scattered over a wide area of open country to the south. The enemy's running commentary began plotting the bombers from the neighbour-hood of the Zuider Zee and the *JLO*s announced that Berlin was the main objective at 19.47 hours: 19 minutes before zero hour. Many illuminated targets were provided for the night fighters over the capital.[2] At the beginning of the attack heavy flak was fired in a loose barrage up to 22,000 feet around the marker flares and was predicted at seen targets through gaps in the cloud. Searchlights were active in great numbers and took every opportunity the weather offered for illuminating the bombers. After the raid had been in progress half an hour and soon after the appearance of fighter flares the ceiling of the barrage was lowered and the flak decreased, although individual aircraft were heavily engaged when coned.

Flight Sergeant Brian Soper and his fiancée Mary had agreed to get married if the young flight engineer got through his tour of 'ops'. She was working in a factory in Battersea during the bombing raids, machining uniforms by day and doing part time duties with the London Fire Service so many nights a week. Soper recalls:

This time, on the way to Berlin we lost all the oil from the port inner engine and had to shut it down and feather it. The rear turret was 'U/S' and the starboard inner engine running hot. After shutting down the port inner, we lost several thousand feet. We were still losing height and very near to Hannover. It was decided that Berlin was still a long way off and if we got there, we wouldn't make it back. A suitable point was found near Hannover and the bombs released. With a lighter load we were able to maintain height and in spite of the return flak were routed for base. As we were damaged we kept a special lookout for night fighters. Due to all the problems and only three engines, we arrived back a little early due to the shorter journey.

Forty bombers, 37 of them Lancasters, were shot down by night fighters. The missing air crews were a mixture of young and old and several different nationalities, from different parts of the world, and they all died equally violent deaths. Three Lancaster IIIs on 103 Squadron at Elsham Wolds failed to return to Lincolnshire. Pilot Officer Arthur James Wakefield on Flying Officer Charles Peter Ready's crew was 42 years old. They were killed and the rest of the crew were lost without trace. Another three missing Lancasters were from 12 Squadron at Wickenby. At Ludford Magna too, 101 Squadron lost three Lancasters. One of the crews survived to be taken prisoner but all fourteen crew members and the two special operators were killed on the two other Lancasters, which included Sergeant J J Kelly USAAF, the rear gunner on the crew skippered by Flight Lieutenant George Albert James Frazer-Hollins DFC. Kelly was laid to rest in the US Military Cemetery at Neuville-en-Condroz in the Belgian Ardennes. Lieutenant Gunnar Hoverstad and his crew were on one of two Halifaxes on 35 Squadron that failed to return to Graveley. The Norwegian pilot was killed, all his crew bailing out safely to be taken prisoner.[3] Fifty-three aircraft were damaged by flak.

Walter King returned safely from Berlin, as did Ed Murrow of CBS (who flew on Lancaster *D-Dog* on 619 Squadron piloted by 'Jock' Abercromby), but five Lancasters on 460 Squadron RAAF, including two that carried press correspondents, were lost and Captain Nordhal Greig of the Free Norwegian Army representing the *Daily Mail* and 40-year-old Australian, Norman Stockton of the *Sydney Sun*, were killed.[4] A 50 Squadron Lancaster that carried Lowell L Bennett, a 24-year-old war correspondent employed by the *Daily Express* also failed to return to Skellingthorpe.[5]

When interviewed, Flying Officer Ronald McIntyre a 20-year-old Australian pilot on 460 Squadron told waiting reporters at Binbrook:

There were blocks of searchlights; hundreds of them. They were trying to probe the clouds and the rear gunner saw two aircraft coned. The flak was pretty solid. The enemy seemed to be using the type that looks like hose-piping when it comes up. It gives you the impression that it is impossible to get through it but you do somehow, though we had one or two holes in the bomb doors.

McIntyre would die on the last raid of the year on Berlin, on 29/30 December, when he crashed at Grossziehten. The Australian pilot and four of his crew were lost without trace. Pilot Officer Tony Bird DFC on 61 Squadron back from his sixth trip to Berlin was interviewed by British Movietone News. The newsreel was shown at cinemas across Britain and was seen by his mother at a cinema in Croydon. She jumped up and cried out 'That's my Tony!' Her son was shot down on the raid on Brunswick on the night of 22/23 April 1944 and he was taken prisoner. Six of his crew died.

Meanwhile, Ed Murrow's report of the first Berlin raid that month appeared in the morning edition of the *Daily Express* under the banner headline, 'BERLIN – ORCHESTRATED HELL OF LIGHT AND FLAME.'[6]

December 1943 had begun quietly for Bomber Command with just 19 Stirlings and a dozen Halifaxes being dispatched to the Frisians and to the east coast of Denmark.[7] But on the night of the 3rd/4th over 520 bombers flew another direct route to Berlin before turning off to bomb Leipzig. Several of the 24 bombers that failed to return were shot down by night fighters in the bomber stream before the turn was made. The night fighters were directed to Berlin when the diversionary force of nine Mosquitoes appeared over the German capital and it was believed that only three bombers were shot down in the Leipzig area. More than half of the bombers that went missing on this raid were shot down in the defended area at Frankfurt on the long southern withdrawal route. The Path Finders found and marked Leipzig accurately and the raid was adjudged to be the most successful raid on this distant inland city during the war. The bombers caused considerable damage, particularly to the Junkers factories in the old World Fair exhibition site.

One Lancaster that should not have made it back was flown by Flight Lieutenant M T Foram RAAF of Gilgandra, New South Wales. The Lancaster was first attacked by a Bf 110 not many miles from the target. The first burst of cannon fire killed the rear gunner and set fire to the main plane and petrol tank. The mid-upper gunner, Flight Sergeant M N Williams RAAF of Booleroo, South Australia had a narrow escape. The turret windows were smashed, as was his oxygen mask. Foram gave the order to put on parachutes but the flight engineer saw another Bf 110, which opened fire at 25 yards, causing more damage. With the aircraft on fire Foram knew that he could not go to Leipzig, so despite a fierce barrage, he bombed his alternative target at Dessau instead. On the way home the Lancaster was again attacked. Foram put his aircraft into a dive to throw the fighter off and like a miracle to the crew, the dive put out the fire in the main plane and the petrol tank. When safely past the enemy coast the Lancaster suddenly became extremely unstable and it was decided to come down into the sea but the crew found holes in the dinghy and with a great struggle, Foram kept on his course and landed safely despite a tendency by the Lancaster to turn on its back.[8]

The Main Force was prevented from making any major bomber operations until the middle of the month when Berlin was again the target for the Lancasters. With the Main Force stood down on the night of 10/11 December, 617 Squadron were asked to provide four aircraft and crews for SOE arms supply drops to Picardie in Northern France at low level. This required similar levels of expertise to the Dam Busters, even though two of the pilots that Wing Commander Leonard Cheshire duly dispatched to Tempsford in Bedfordshire where they were loaded up with arms and ammunition, had yet to fly an operation. While flying at low altitude *E-Easy* flown by Flying Officer Gordon Weedon RCAF was hit by flak and crashed killing all the crew, which included two Americans, Warrant Officer Robert Cummings RCAF the rear gunner, and 26-year-old Flight Sergeant Edward Joseph Walters the bomb aimer; both of whom were from Pennsylvania. While trying to establish a pin-point between Boulogne and St-Pol, *O-Orange*, which had been one of the Lancasters used on the famous Dams raid in May, was also hit by flak and crashed not far from Doullens. Warrant Officer 'Chuffy' Bull and three others were taken into captivity, while one man evaded and two died on the aircraft. Joe McCarthy and 'Bunny' Clayton piloting the two other Lancasters could not find the drop area and returned safely. They tried again two nights' later and were successful.

On 16/17 December Bomber Command carried out yet another attack on Berlin when over 480 Lancasters and ten Mosquitoes took off for the 'Big City'. The bomber route again led directly to the capital across Holland and Northern Germany and there were no major diversions. The German controllers planned the course of the bombers with great accuracy; many German fighters were met at the coast of Holland and further fighters were guided in to the bomber stream throughout the approach to the target. More fighters were waiting at Berlin and there were many combats.[9] Widespread mist and fog at 150–300 feet in the North German plains reduced the overall effectiveness of the fighter defence and 23 aircraft, mostly Bf 110s had to abandon their sorties prematurely, yet 25 Lancasters were shot down.[10] *Oberleutnant* Heinz-Wolfgang Schnaufer, *Staffelkapitän* 12./NJG1 took off from Leeuwarden in a *Schräge Musik*-equipped Bf 110 with his radar operator, *Unteroffizier* Fritz Rumpelhardt. They braved low cloud and icing up to 15,000 feet to seek out and shoot down four Lancasters over Friesland Province, with the aid of the ground controller in the night fighter box *Polar Bear*. Schnaufer's first victim was a 7 Squadron Lancaster flown by Warrant Officer Wallace Arthur Watson RAAF which was blasted at a range of 4,000 metres and crashed at Follega. The second victim was a 101 Squadron 'ABC' Lancaster piloted by Flight Lieutenant Ronald Ernest MacFarlane DFM RCAF which exploded over Banco polder, and the third, *O-Orange*, a 49 Squadron Lancaster flown by Flying Officer Gordon Lennox Ratcliffe, crashed at Sonnega. All three aircraft went down with their crews. Schnaufer's fourth victim, 19,700 feet south of Leeuwarden, was *N-Nuts* on 432 Squadron flown by Flying Officer William Charles Fisher USAAF. His rear gunner spotted the Bf 110 and Fisher corkscrewed violently almost shaking off their pursuer, but Schnaufer holed the petrol tanks and the Lancaster flew over Leeuwarden trailing a sheet of flame to crash at Wytgaard where it disintegrated on impact with the ground as the bomb load exploded. Only one of the eight man crew survived and he was taken prisoner. Schnaufer had to make five attempts to land back at Leeuwarden and then only by a fortuitous hole in the cloud. The four victories took Schnaufer's total to forty.

Berlin was cloud covered but the Path Finder sky-marking was reasonably accurate and much of the bombing fell in the city. By this stage of the war sustained bombing by the Allies had made more than a quarter of the capital's total living accommodation unusable. Bomber losses more than doubled when on their return to England, crews encountered very low cloud at their stations, and 29 Lancasters (and two Stirlings returning from mine-laying operations) either crashed or were abandoned when their crews bailed out. 1, 6 and 8 Groups were particularly badly affected and 29 Lancasters and a Stirling returning from a mine-laying operation either crashed or were abandoned when their crews bailed out. 1 Group south of the Humber in north Lincolnshire lost thirteen aircraft. *N-Nuts* on 100 Squadron flown by Wing Commander David Holford DSO DFC crashed near Kelstern on approach to Grimsby. Holford was on his third tour and he and four of his crew were killed. The wing commander had been awarded the DFC at 18 and the DSO at 21 and at the age of 22 had finished his second tour; a total of sixty operations.[11] Three more Lancasters on the Squadron were lost, *H-Harry* crashing at Barnoldby le Beck in Lincolnshire killing the pilot and three crew men and injuring three others, and *Q-Queenie* and *F-Freddie* colliding near Grimsby. Only one man survived and died of his injuries the following October. *A-Apple* on 625 Squadron at Kelstern flown by 2nd Lieutenant G E Woolley USAAF crashed into the side of a hill near Gayton-le-Wold in Lincolnshire. Two of the crew died and Woolley was injured. The American pilot and his four injured crew members were taken to Louth County Hospital. *B-Baker* on 625 Squadron is believed to have crashed at Wetschen near Diepholz. At Bourn 97 Squadron lost eight Lancasters – seven of them in crashes – with 37 men killed and eight injured.

Arthur Tindall a WOp/AG recalls:

I can still recall the Met Officer saying that the weather would close in by the early hours of the following morning and he anticipated the raid being cancelled. In the event it wasn't – with disastrous results. We were airborne for 7 hours 45 minutes compared with usual Berlin raids of 6 to 6½ hours. The following morning our ground crew said that we had less than 50 gallons of petrol. In other words, we were lucky to have made it.

At Bardney in 5 Group there was no word from *B-Beer* piloted by Pilot Officer Ian Black or *Y-Yorker* flown by 20-year-old Pilot Officer Richard Bayldon. Black had taken off at 16.47 hours and was last heard by Bardney Control calling on W/T at 23.48 hours. Nothing more had been heard. *B-Beer* was laying smashed to pieces at Salzbergen a few kilo-metres north-west of Rheine with all seven crew dead. Bayldon, who had taken off four minutes before Black, had crashed at Eberswalde-Finow, 43 kilometres north-east of Berlin. All seven crew including Sergeant Raymond John Baroni RCAF the mid-upper gunner from Glendale, California lay dead in or around the aircraft. When the *Los Angeles Times* hit the streets back home in California there would be no mention of Baroni or of other Americans on the raid – yet – but banner headlines proclaimed, '... The attack was described in Berlin as a terror attack on a considerable scale. Well-informed circles point out that it was carried out in poor visibility. Residential quarters in the capital were hit.' *The New York Times* reported that, 'immediately after the attack Berlin broadcast a talk for overseas listeners, saying: "The enemy will never destroy the Berlin population's will to win. Factories in Germany are working full blast to produce weapons of retaliation, which will come."[12]

Worst hit station in 6 Group RCAF in the Tyne Valley and North Yorkshire was Linton-on-Ouse where 426 'Thunderbird' Squadron RCAF lost six Lancasters and 408 'Goose' Squadron RCAF, two. One was lost without trace and the other, which was flown by Flying Officer William John Maitland DFM RCAF who was flying his first sortie of his second tour, crashed in Yorkshire on return while trying to let down through the overcast. There were no survivors. One of the 'Thunderbird' Squadron's Lancasters that failed to return had crashed in Sweden and all the crew was interned. At Gransden Lodge 405 'Vancouver' Squadron RCAF lost three Lancasters and two on 432 'Leaside' Squadron RCAF had been shot down while *E-Easy*, the other loss, was abandoned out of petrol in the vicinity of Castleton, west-south west of Whitby. Three other Lancasters that did not make it back to Binbrook were on 460 Squadron RAAF. Two of the aircraft crashed in fields in Lincolnshire and a third piloted by Flying Officer Francis Randall DFC RAAF radioed to say that the Lancaster had clipped a tree. Shortly afterwards the aircraft crashed into a wood near Market Stainton south-west of Louth with the loss of all the crew.[13]

Flight Sergeant (later Flight Lieutenant) L H Richards, the English navigator on *D-Donald* on 460 Squadron recalled how his own feelings before and after a raid, surprised him:

I have always been a coward and was very nervous before every operation. When an operation was scrubbed I was delighted. I dreaded, before each trip, how I would react if we got shot-up or in difficulties and my nerves were as taut as a bowstring through-out every operation. However, when we did meet trouble, to my absolute amazement, my stomach froze but I was as calm as could be, calmer than at any time throughout my tour of operations. I worked like the devil to get us back on course with what instruments were left. When we finally arrived over an airfield in England, the calmness left me and the fear returned. I was quite terrified at the thought of a crash landing and yet I had every confidence that our pilot would manage it. There was such a strange and unreal feeling of fear and confidence. Throughout our whole tour of operations I was pretty certain that we would be killed. All my fear and nerves were unfounded. Each operation was as uneventful as a cross-country training flight. But there was no comfort in that, I still died thirty deaths just down to cowardice. I suppose I simply couldn't see us surviving when others were not. Towards the end, say from about 25 operations onwards, I began to see that there was a chance that I would survive a tour. That made each operation more of a nerve wracking experience than ever. I used to calculate the days it would take to complete the remaining operations and to say to myself if I live for just another two weeks I will live forever. Obviously I kept all this from the crew. They had great faith in my ability as a navigator and thought that this and the skill of our pilot would help get us through the tour. I think it was just luck, but the leadership of our pilot throughout was a tremendous example to each member of the crew.

After a lull in operations, on Monday night, 20/21 December, 650 bomber crews were detailed to attack Frankfurt. Little went to plan. A diversion operation to Mannheim by 44 Lancasters and ten Mosquitoes did not draw fighters away from the route to the target until after the raid was over. The German control rooms were able to plot the bomber force as soon as it left the English coast and they were able to continue plotting it all the way to Frankfurt so that there were many combats on the route to the target. Shortly before approaching the target Pilot Officer Lou Glover's 9 Squadron Lancaster was swept by cannon and machine gun fire, which set fire to the rear turret and the port inner engine and damaged the intercom system. Harry Wood the rear gunner was injured by splinters in the face and slightly burnt and the mid-upper gunner was hit by a machine gun bullet in the leg. The attack came from astern well down and as soon as Glover saw the tracer he began as corkscrew port, losing height rapidly to gain extra speed, having a full load on. Both gunners saw a Ju 88 approach from astern down but the rear gunner could not fire as his guns had been damaged and the mid-upper gunner could not get his guns to bear. The Ju 88 broke away down and again attacked from the same position, opening fire at 600 yards and closing to 100 yards. His tracers all passed above the Lancaster and he broke away astern down and was not seen again. Glover resumed course on three engines and on written instructions from Flying Officer John Middleton the navigator, bombed Frankfurt from a very low altitude when over the centre of the target area before returning to Bardney. The rear turret was badly smashed, the port inner engine u/s and the mid-upper gunner's turret and the fuselage was holed in many places.[14]

The Path Finders prepared a ground-marking plan on the basis of a forecast giving clear weather but at Frankfurt they found up to 8/10ths cloud. The Germans lit a decoy fire site five miles south-east of the city and they also used dummy target indicators. In a period of barely 40 minutes, 2,200 tons of HE and incendiary bombs were dropped on Frankfurt. Some of the bombing fell around the decoy but part of the creep back fell on Frankfurt causing more damage than Bomber Command realized at the time. It is believed that the main gasworks in Frankfurt blew up 20 minutes after the attack began. The explosion was clearly perceptible up to an altitude of almost 20,000 feet. Over 460 houses were completely destroyed and 1,948 seriously damaged in Frankfurt and the outlying townships of

Sachsenhausen and Offenbach, and 23,000 people were bombed out. Some 117 bombs hit various industrial premises and a large number of cultural, historical and public buildings were hit including the cathedral, the city library, the city hospital and no fewer than 69 schools. One squadron ran under the hail of flak and flew over the Hauptbanhof, or chief train station, at an altitude of 975 feet. They raced along the Kaiserstrasse, which a few minutes later had turned into a single sea of flame. Part of the bombing fell on Mainz 17 miles to the west and many houses along the Rhine waterfront and in southern suburbs were hit.

Altogether, 41 aircraft failed to return from the raid on Frankfurt. At Holme-on-Spalding Moor three Halifax Vs on 76 Squadron never returned. At Breighton 78 Squadron had four Halifaxes missing while another stalled and crashed while waiting for permission to land after returning just after take-off. All seven crew died in the impact. *Z-Zebra* piloted by 1st Lieutenant Lauchlin M Kelly USAAF was hit by flak at 18,000 feet while still carrying its bomb load. The skinny young university student from a comfortable home in Baltimore, Maryland managed to level out at around 14,000 feet. He ordered the crew to bail out and said that he was going to try and put the Halifax down but he was killed when the aircraft exploded and crashed on the edge of the Odersberg Forest near the Dutch-Belgian border. The six crew men came down safely and they were taken prisoner. Kelly, who was posthumously promoted to major, was buried locally on Christmas Eve but after the war his remains were taken to the US Military Cemetery at Margratan before he was re-interred in America.

Another American expatriate on the squadron was Sergeant W Heubner USAAF, who was taken prisoner when *M-Mother* was downed by flak at 19,000 feet over the target and later finished off by a night fighter flown by *Oberleutnant* Werner Baake of I./NJG1 at Venlo. Heubner's pilot, Flight Lieutenant J G Smith and one other crew member evaded capture and the rest were taken prisoner.[15]

Squadron Leader Julian Sale DSO on 35 Squadron, who had returned to operations after he was shot down on 12/13 May and evaded capture, crash-landed his blazing Halifax at Graveley with a fire in the bomb bay. Hung-up TIs had exploded as the aircraft came below their barometric fuse altitude of 1,500 feet. Sale's navigator was Flight Lieutenant Gordon Carter DFC* who had also evaded capture and had returned to operations after being shot down on 13/14 February 1943. His Skipper ordered the crew to bail out but Flight Lieutenant Roger 'Sheep' Lamb the mid-upper gunner appeared beside him with a charred parachute, so Sale dropped back into his seat, stuck his head out of the port window of the smoke-filled cockpit and calmly brought the Halifax in for a normal circuit landing before roaring off the runway and crashing in a ball of fire. Sale and Lamb got away safely before the bomber exploded. All five men who bailed out were safe and only the rear gunner suffered any injury. Sale was awarded a bar to his DSO for his action.

At Skellingthorpe two Lancasters on 50 Squadron failed to return. One was *C-Charlie* flown by Pilot Officer John Llewellyn Heckendorf RAAF from Lockhart in New South Wales. English Sergeant Arthur Hope was proud of their 'smashing' crew and his wish would be that 'if anything was coming, that it would come to all of them'. On Frankfurt they carried a replacement bomb aimer but the rest of the crew was much as it was when they first flew together in May 1943. Sergeant John Henderson the flight engineer had joined *C-Charlie*'s crew that July. Flight Sergeant Robert Campbell Turner the rear gunner was the only other Australian crew member. *C-Charlie* burst into flames at 19,000 feet near Kelsterbach about 13 kilometres from Frankfurt and the order to bail out was given. But in seconds the Lancaster exploded killing everyone on board except for Flying Officer R L Rutherford and Arthur Hope who were thrown clear. Happily for Hope who had 'wanted to "go", if they had to, as a crew', his wish had not been granted. Both he and Rutherford were taken into captivity by the Germans.

Twenty-year-old Pilot Officer Edward Argent on 9 Squadron who was flying Lancaster *O-Orange* on the aircraft's fiftieth op, encountered enemy opposition when on the way home. While crossing a belt of flares north of the target 23-year-old Sergeant Alf Trevena the Australian mid-upper gunner from Hawthorn, Victoria, saw a Me 210 diving in from port quarter up and immediately gave the order to corkscrew port. Both gunners and the 210 opened fire at the same instant at 200 yards. The Messerschmitt's tracer was seen to pass above the Lancaster but the gunners' return fire was seen by Sergeant George Fradley the wireless operator who was standing in the astrodome, to hit the twin-engined attacker. The Me 210 went into a very steep dive and disappeared port quarter down. As it broke away a burst of cannon and machine gun fire from port quarter up struck the Lancaster and Trevena saw a Ju 88 diving in from the same direction as the previous attack. He engaged the Ju 88 with return fire until both his guns stopped working, after which he assisted Argent by giving a commentary during the whole engagement, which lasted throughout about a dozen very rapid attacks by the Ju 88. Flight Sergeant Vince Knox, the 19-year-old Canadian rear gunner who was from Victoria, British Columbia, fired 400 rounds before he was killed. The Lancaster received serious damage in the initial attack by the Ju 88 but in all the remaining attacks only sustained slight damage in the starboard wing. The Ju 88 finally broke away on the starboard beam and was not seen again. The pilot maintained a corkscrew throughout all attacks. Argent managed to keep the Lancaster level almost to the Norfolk coast but had to ditch in the sea off Happisburgh. The crew made it into the dinghy and managed to keep going through four dark hours of a December night before an Air Sea Rescue launch picked them up. They were given ten days' leave.[16]

All the aircraft on the diversion operation to Mannheim returned safely though some of the Lancasters were bracketed by flak, as Brian Soper recalls:

> We missed all the light flak at 20,000 feet, but got some of the medium and all of the heavy. It was delivered either as a mass barrage over the target, or other places *en route*. Otherwise it was radar predicted for the individual aircraft, which was very accurate. We thought we hadn't yet reached the target. Suddenly we were rocked by six or seven heavy blasts all around us from predicted flak. At the same time the gunners spotted the target – behind us, in another direction – we were slightly off course. We had to do a complete circuit to avoid the other oncoming Lancs and join the bombing circuit and we eventually bombed on the markers. It was otherwise a reasonably uneventful trip.

There were however, other losses this night. A Stirling minelayer failed to return from a *Gardening* operation in the Frisians. One aircraft was lost on the operation by eight Lancasters of 617 Squadron and eight Path Finder Mosquitoes that attempted to bomb the John Cockerill steel works near Liège. The Mosquito marking was not visible below the clouds and the Lancasters did not bomb. *Z-Zebra* piloted by Flight Lieutenant Geoff Rice DFC failed to return. One of the five survivors of the original squadron, the 23-year-old Mancunian was shot down southwest of Charleroi by *Hauptmann* Kurt Fladrich, *Staffelkapitän* 9./NJG4 at Juvincourt flying a Bf 110G-4. Rice was thrown clear as *Z-Zebra* exploded. His crew was killed. All had flown the famous dams raid with Rice who had aborted after hitting the sea on the outward flight, ripping off the 'Upkeep' mine. Despite a broken wrist, Rice managed to evade capture for six months until April 1944 by which time the Belgian Resistance had moved him to Brussels.

Just before Christmas Sergeant Roy Keen, a married flight engineer originally from Redhill in Surrey arrived on 166 Squadron at Kirmington after Heavy Conversion Unit at Lindholme. He had been a fitter in the RAF for a couple of years before becoming aircrew and had soon found that being a flight engineer was a 'bit of a cold and dirty job!'

> The silly thing was that there weren't enough Lancasters to go round and we did our course in Halifaxes! Not very good for the engineer; I was trained on Lancs, but you suddenly get in a Halifax and have to do the business! I remember once looking at my oxygen bottle and noticing I'd got about a minute left before it ran out. I thought

'I've just got time to change the tanks.' Now, in a Halifax you had to climb underneath the rest bed where there was a bank of six levers each side, about twelve tanks from memory. I thought 'I've got to do 3 and 4 I think', but all of a sudden the plane pitched down, so I put them back and said 'Sorry, Skipper!' Bill Jackson the pilot was a Canadian who we called 'Rex'. The front turret was officially my job. I never had to use it, but I had done gunnery practice. Flight Sergeant Ken Mitchell the mid-upper gunner had done 32 trips. The pilot, navigator and bomb-aimer got together before we all met and then the wireless operator and gunners joined them. I was the last to join the crew. My skipper said 'I chose you because you've got a dirty overcoat on; you must have been on a squadron!'

The pilot, nav and bomb-aimer were all officers, so they weren't allowed to mess with us. I teamed up with the wireless operator, Frank Fountaine, more than anyone else and I taught him how to do my job, well loosely, in case there was any trouble. The Skipper taught me how to fly straight and level in case he got knocked off. I'm quite glad that I never had to take over! If I had have done, we weren't supposed to land, just point it out to sea and bail out. But between us, we had agreed that I should try and land it, as I used to operate the landing gear anyway. We perhaps stood a fifty-fifty chance that way, as the crew didn't particularly want to bail out! The only bother we ever had was when taking off once and the rear gunner said, 'I'm covered in petrol!' I could tell why, as we had just taken off and the tanks were venting, so I changed tanks and told him he'd be all right if he didn't smoke!

We were on call seven days a week. If we were flying that night, I'd have to spend the morning with the ground staff looking at the aeroplane, run up the engines, check they didn't blow up! Then we'd go back and have a sleep before taking off at six or seven o'clock. But you didn't just do ops. They stuck us on a few little trips around the locality. There were air-sea searches, fighter affiliation flying and so on. You were always training, like on *H2S*, which came out about that time. If we were flying that day, we had to stay on station. One day the skipper collared us as we were leaving the airfield and said we were going test-flying. I went up in just my battledress. We were up three hours and I was frozen stiff! I'd never been so cold. Normally we had three pairs of gloves, silk, wool and leather, flying boots, long pants – it was uncomfortable. I would stand up on takeoff; I was never strapped in. The seat was like a little camp stool with a canvas strap, if you did want to sit down. The skipper was strapped in of course!

Every morning was the same – at ten we'd see if we were flying and if not were allowed off the airfield. We used to go to Grimsby, Scunthorpe or Lincoln and be back to report the next day. We hadn't a hope of getting leave. When I got married I had asked for a week off. I got forty-eight hours and was told I was lucky to get that.

In the early hours of Christmas Eve 379 aircraft took off for Berlin. Once again the Main Force Halifaxes were rested and only seven Hallys took part. This raid was originally planned for a late afternoon take-off but a forecast of worsening weather over the bomber stations caused the raid to be put back by seven hours to allow the bombers a return in daylight. Arthur Tindall on 97 Squadron at Bourn recalls: 'Another early take off – 00.20.'

At Wickenby two Lancasters on 12 Squadron collided while taxiing. A 7 Squadron Lancaster at Oakington crashed out of control and there were injuries to all the crew. A 100 Squadron Lancaster and a 550 Squadron Lanc, both at Grimsby, were involved in a collision over Lincolnshire and both crashed near Fulstow killing everyone on board both bombers.

Losses after leaving England were not as heavy as on recent raids, partly because German night fighters encountered difficulty with the weather and partly because the German controller was temporarily deceived by the Mosquito diversion at Leipzig. At the target there were no fighters and few searchlights because of scattered cloud but only 11 of the 39 Blind Markers released their markers, mainly because of *H2S* failures. Just one other aircraft was able to drop its 11 Green TIs and these landed six miles away. Most of the Main Force had bombed by the time the PFF backers-up could get their markers away and mainly the bombing was in the suburbs of the German capital. The main force of fighters only appeared in the target area at the end of the raid and could not catch the main bomber stream. Two bombers were shot down on the run-up to the capital and two more were shot down over the target. Fifteen Lancasters in all were shot down. Two were claimed by *Oberfeldwebel* Karl-Heinz Scherfling of 12./NJG1. Three were destroyed by *Oberleutnant* Paul Zorner of 8./NJG3, who had been credited with 16 victories, including five on his first two nights of operations in a Bf 110 equipped with *SN-2* at the end of November.

Zorner took off from Lüneburg at 01.39 hours. At 02.46 he picked up a Lancaster flying at 16,500 feet. It was a 576 Squadron aircraft flown by Pilot Officer Richard Lloyd Hughes. Zorner shot it down four minutes later. Only three men bailed out before the bomber went down in a steep dive and plunged burning into the clouds to crash east of Giessen. By now Zorner had lost contact with the bomber stream and he was almost out of fuel. He landed at Gutersloh, refuelled and took off again 40 minutes later. By now the bombers were returning from Berlin and 35 minutes later Zorner's radar operator picked up a contact at 18,900 feet. It was *X-X-Ray*, a 44 Squadron Lancaster flown by Sergeant Roy Ladbrooke Hands. Zorner hit the Lancaster in the right wing and it spiralled down into cloud. He saw an explosion. There were no survivors. Eleven minutes later Zorner's radar operator picked up another contact, at 18,300 feet. It was *L-London*, a 50 Squadron Lancaster flown by Flying Officer Derrick Wilson Herbert. Zorner twice carried out attacks on the bomber and a fire started in the right wing. Then the wing exploded and a few seconds later the aircraft went down with all the crew trapped inside. Zorner flew back to Lüneburg to log claims for his 17th, 18th and 19th *Viermot* kills.

The losses could have been higher, as Arthur Tindall recalls. 'On the return we were attacked eight times by fighters. All of our guns were frozen. We landed on three engines and one tyre had burst – unknown to us until touchdown. The aircraft was written off.'

On Christmas morning crews were warned for operations that night but the order was cancelled a half hour later. Roy Keen on 166 Squadron spent the fifth Christmas of the war in a hotel in Doncaster. The next raid was ordered for the night of 29 December. At Skellingthorpe just outside Lincoln Pilot Officer Michael Beetham [17] and his crew were one of fifteen on 50 Squadron called to the Nissen-hutted briefing room at 14.00 hours. Michael Beetham had been educated at St. Marylebone's Grammar School. His father had won an MC in the Great War as an army major in the trenches. He wanted his son to go into the army but, with his father stationed near Portsmouth, in 1940 Michael spent the summer holidays watching RAF fighters in the Battle of Britain tackling German bombers trying to destroy the local docks. He joined the RAF straight from school in 1941, trained as a pilot in America and entered Bomber Command to fly Lancasters in the autumn of 1943. He loved the Lancaster:

> It felt right, it handled beautifully and was a delight to fly. If it was heavier on the controls than we now consider proper, back then this weight gave a young pilot confidence and you got used to it.[18]
>
> The Squadron commander pulled back the curtain over the map and revealed the target – Berlin. We swallowed a little. For me and my crew it was only our seventh trip and this would be our fourth to the 'Big City'; the Battle of Berlin was clearly on. Seven hundred Lancasters and Halifaxes from the Command would attack in five waves – all phased through the target in twenty minutes to saturate the defences.[19] Mosquitoes would carry out diversionary attacks on Magdeburg and Leipzig. We were to feint towards Leipzig and then turn north to Berlin at the last minute. The met man told us there would be heavy cloud over most of Germany, widespread fog and poor visibility. Hopefully, that would restrict their fighters. Our bases were forecast to be fine for return. That was a relief, for on our last trip, to Berlin we returned to fog-bound bases and only got down in Yorkshire with difficulty. Out to aircraft dispersal at 16.00 hours for a final check of everything. We had our brand-new Lancaster VN-B with the latest paddle-bladed propellers, air-tested that morning and this was our first trip in it. Take-off at 17.00 hours. All fifteen

aircraft taxied out in turn and there was a good crowd as usual beside the runway controller's caravan to see us off ...

Three and a quarter hours to the target. We climbed to cross the Dutch coast at 1,900 feet and then gradually got to maximum height around 20–21,000 feet. Our route was north of the Ruhr and then southeast past Osnabrück and Hannover towards Leipzig ... A sharp turn north twenty miles short of Leipzig with the diversionary aircraft heading straight on – hopefully the fighter controllers would be fooled. [A long approach from the south, passing south of the Ruhr and then within 20 miles of Leipzig, together with diversions by Mosquitoes at Düsseldorf, Leipzig and Magdeburg and RCM sorties, caused the German controller great difficulties and there were few fighters over Berlin. Bad weather on the outward route also kept down the number of German fighters finding the bomber stream.] The final run up north of Berlin. We were in the third wave. Much more activity now, with searchlights trying to penetrate the cloud and pick up the bombers ahead of us. Plenty of flak as we approached the target but not really close. No sign of fighters. Some turbulence from the slipstream of other bombers – always a bit disconcerting.

Wanganui marker flares ahead were going down on time. We would be bombing blind. The markers were well concentrated and a good glow of fires started by the aircraft attacking ahead of us showed through the cloud.

Straight and level now with two minutes to go and bomb doors open. Bomb aimer called 'bombs gone' on the middle of the markers. We felt the 4,000lb 'cookie' go and then the canisters of incendiaries – always a relief to have them away and the bomb doors closed again. We flew right across Berlin and out well to the north before turning for home. Navigator said four hours to go ... A long haul to the Dutch coast; we eventually crossed but didn't relax – you could get caught by fighters over the North Sea.

The Christmas Eve raid was Brian Soper's sixth trip to the 'Big City'. He recalls:

We were approaching the target and getting lined up for the bomb run. I was helping the gunners to look out for fighters. Suddenly, above, to my right, came a Halifax, diving and weaving across us. It came within a few feet of us and must have been taking evasive action against a night fighter. It looked near enough to touch! Remember of course that all around us, apart from the target, was total blackness. I just happened to be looking that way. I shouted and tried to help the pilot push the control column forward. Any action would have been too late anyway. Of course it missed and when we recovered we just got back on course and carried on with the bomb run. We all agreed it was probably our closest encounter. There were of course many other close calls. Berlin was again cloud-covered. Bomber Command claimed a concentrated attack on sky-markers. The heaviest bombing was in the southern and south-eastern districts but many bombs also fell to the east of the city and over 10,000 people were bombed out.[20]

Pilot Officer Michael Beetham got safely down at Skellingthorpe at half past midnight:

At de-briefing we reported a quiet and uneventful trip – for Berlin. Just one aircraft lost on our squadron – not bad for such a tough target and looked like it had been a good attack. And so to our bacon and eggs and bed at 02.00 hours. Next morning at Skellingthorpe I reported to the flight at 10.00 hours to see whether 'ops' were on that night. The Flight Commander said, 'So you had a quiet trip last night?'
    'Yes' I replied. 'Fairly uneventful.'
    'Come with me,' he said.
    We drove out to the flight dispersal and to my aircraft ... Two of my ground crew were on top of the starboard wing. I was staggered to see a large hole through the starboard wing outer fuel tank – a clear gash through it. 'What have you done to our new aircraft?' asked my corporal airframe fitter. 'We are going to have to change the wing.' We had collected an incendiary from another Lancaster above us over the target – the outline was clearly visible through the wing. 'Didn't you really feel anything over the target?' queried the Flight Commander. 'No' I said. 'Some usual turbulence from the slipstream of other aircraft and some flak but not close enough to worry.'[21] I thanked my lucky stars we always used the outer wing fuel first so the tank would have been empty and purged with nitrogen well before the target – and I wondered how close had been the rest of the bomb load.

As 1943 neared its close German airmen like *Feldwebel* Friedrich Ostheimer, who had recently joined *Major* Heinrich Prinz zu Sayn-Wittgenstein, *Kommandeur* of II./NJG2 as his new *Bordfunker* at Deelen, Holland reflected on the year's events which had not boded well for Germany:

A few more weeks and the year of 1943 would be a thing of the past. The war, with all its distress and terror was at its height. Our troops were fighting from the North Cape to the Libyan Desert and from Russia to the Atlantic. Since America's entry into the war the *Luftwaffe* was utterly outnumbered and the crews under unceasing stress. At Arnhem-Deelen Prinz Wittgenstein [who had begun his career in the *Luftwaffe* as an air gunner and at the outbreak of war flew with KG1 '*Hindenburg*'] spent his time either in his bungalow or at the command post. The flight engineer, the first mechanic and I were on stand-by in a small hut beside the hangar, which housed our Ju 88. We only saw the Prinz when he came to fly. After landing he returned immediately to his quarters. Once he invited us to his bungalow for an evening meal before stand-by commenced. Prinz Wittgenstein was a tall, good-looking officer with a fine, reserved and disciplined personality. As a night fighter he did his utmost, shunned no danger and never considered his own life.

During our three weeks in Rechlin we flew some sorties over Berlin. Kurt and I had a small room in flying control at our disposal. During reported attacks we waited there for possible orders. One evening it looked as if Berlin might be the target for the bomber stream. Prinz Wittgenstein had already reported our imminent take-off. We climbed on a south-easterly course in the direction of Berlin. The distance Rechlin–Berlin is about 100 kilometres. The speaker in the so-called *Reichsjägerwelle* (*Reich* fighter frequency) gave a running commentary on position, course and height of the enemy bombers. Their code word was *Dicke Autos* ('Fat Cars'). This kept all the airborne fighters constantly informed. Meanwhile Berlin had been recognized as being the target and the *Reichsjägerwelle* gave the order: 'Everything to *Bär* (Bear), everything to *Bär*!' Meanwhile we had reached the height of the bombers at about 7,000 metres. We entered the bomber stream on a south-easterly course. The radar was switched on and we observed the air space around us as far as the visibility allowed.

I soon had my first target on my screen. I passed the required changes of course to the pilot on the intercom. We were closing in on our target. 'Straight ahead; a little higher!' Very quickly we had reached the heavily laden four-engined one. It was, as nearly always, a Lancaster. Prinz Wittgenstein set it on fire with a single burst from the *Schräge Musik* cannon and the enemy went down.

Ahead of us the first beams of the searchlights were searching the night sky. The fire of the flak defences intensified and as a signal for the attack the British Path Finders dropped target indicators for the approaching bombers. And again I had a target on my screen. The distance to the enemy bomber decreased quickly. By this difference in speed alone we could see that it must be an enemy bomber. But suddenly the closing speed became very high indeed and I could only call out on the intercom: 'Down, down, the machine is coming straight at us!' A moment later a shadow passed above us in the opposite direction. We just felt the slipstream and the aircraft, probably another Lancaster, had disappeared into the night. The three of us sat rigid in our seats and we only relaxed when Kurt said, 'That was close!' Once more we had been lucky.

Now for the next target. The approach was almost complete and both the pilot and engineer could recognize the aircraft. Then suddenly the starboard engine began to shake, the propeller revolutions quickly decreased and finally stopped completely. Prinz Wittgenstein pushed the nose down to maintain speed, feathered the propeller and adjusted the rudder trim to counteract the thrust of the remaining engine. By the time Wittgenstein had done all this, the Lancaster had disappeared into the darkness. We might have had further successes but with only one engine we now had only one aim: back to Rechlin. I obtained a course to steer from the D/F station. The port engine ran smoothly and we flew slowly losing height towards Rechlin. I told the D/F station that we had lost one engine and that we would have to try a single-engined landing. Every airman knows about the dangers and difficulties of such a landing at night. One should really have been terribly frightened. But that doesn't help in such situations at all. Although it wasn't really allowed, Prinz Wittgenstein wanted to do a normal landing with extended undercarriage. That meant that if it shouldn't work out, an overshoot on only one engine would not be possible and both aircraft and crew would almost certainly be lost. But Prinz Wittgenstein, as pilot and commander of our machine, was in command; he had the power to make the final decision. The airfield fired off signal rockets to aid our orientation, which we called *Radieschen* (radishes). When we had reached the airfield we first flew past it and then made a wide circuit towards the approach path. The Prinz had to do this, as we could only turn towards the running engine. A turn into the stopped engine could easily have caused a crash. We commenced our approach on a VHF beam, a very accurate approach aid at that time. The power of the running engine had to be reduced and the rudder trim adjusted at the same time. The landing was perfect. As the machine rumbled over the runway we felt a great relief. We praised our pilot very highly of course and Kurt and I thought that we had earned some relaxation.

After a few days the engine had been changed and our machine was again ready for action. Prinz Wittgenstein was impatient again. At the next approach of enemy bombers – Berlin was the target again – we were once more in the air. The weather was good for a change. There was a slight layer of haze at medium altitude, above that the sky was clear. I tuned in to the *Reichsjägerwelle* and so we were kept well informed about the general situation. Everything was pointing to another attack on the *Reich* capital. At this time large parts of Berlin had been heavily damaged. Entire streets were in ruins. It was an unimaginable sight. I had once experienced a night attack on the city from the ground. I was in an underground station with many others, the earth shook with each explosions, women and children screamed and smoke billowed through the place. Anyone who did not feel fear and horror would have had a heart of stone.

Back to our operation; we had meanwhile reached the altitude of the bomber stream and entered, like the Lancasters, the flak barrage over the city. British Path Finders – we called them 'Master of Ceremonies' – had already dropped markers. The scene over the city was almost impossible to describe. The searchlights illuminated the haze layer over the city, making it look like an illuminated frosted glass screen, above which the sky was very light. One could make out the approaching bombers as if it were daylight. It was a unique sight.

Prinz Wittgenstein put the aircraft into a slight bank. At this moment we did not know where to make a start. But the decision was suddenly taken from us, as tracer flew past our machine. Wittgenstein put the machine into a steep turn and dived. As we went downwards I could see the Lancaster flying obliquely above us and its mid-upper-gunner who was firing at us with his twin guns. Fortunately his aim had not been very good. We had got a few hits but the engines kept running and the crew was unhurt. We went off to one side into the dark, keeping the Lancaster just in sight.

We now continued parallel to the bomber for a while. The darker it got around us, the closer we moved towards the enemy machine. As the light from the searchlights decreased and the fires which the attack of the enemy had started lay behind us, we were well closed up to the bomber. The Lancaster was now flying above us, suspecting nothing. Perhaps the crew was relieved to have survived the attack and to be on their way home. But we, intent on the hunt, sat in our cockpit with our eyes staring upward, hoping that we had not been detected.

Prinz Wittgenstein placed our Ju still closer to the huge shadow above us, took careful aim and fired with the *Schräge Musik*. The tracer of the 2cm shells bored into the wing between the engines and set the fuel tanks on fire. We swung immediately to one side and watched the burning Lancaster, which continued on its course for quite a while. Whether the crew had been able to bail out we could not tell. They had certainly had enough time. The bomber exploded in a bright flash and fell disintegrating to earth. I got good contact with our D/F station right away. We flew without any problems to Rechlin and landed there.[22]

Prinz Wittgenstein was given a new task in December 1943. We were transferred with our machine to *Erprobungsstelle* (*E-Stelle*) Rechlin on the Mürlitzsee, where a new night fighter experimental unit was to be established. This came as a surprise for *Unteroffizier* Matzuleit our flight engineer and me. Within a few hours we were torn from the circle of our comrades. In Rechlin we knew no-one and frequently sat unhappily around. Most of the time, Prinz Wittgenstein was away at meetings at the Air Ministry in Berlin. Our job was to keep the machine in constant readiness. There was no night fighter unit stationed at Rechlin. It often took me hours to obtain the operational data for radio and navigation by telephone. For accommodation we had railway carriages with sleeping facilities.

With his score standing at 68 victories, 27-year-old *Major* Wittgenstein became *Kommodore* of NJG2 on Saturday 1 January 1944. That same night, the Prinz was airborne again in his Ju 88C-6 equipped with *SN-2* radar and *Schräge Musik*. In England one of the 421 Lancaster crews that was 'on' that night was Flying Officer James 'Gil' Bryson's 'T squared' on 550 Squadron. Bryson had joined the squadron on its formation at Waltham, Grimsby on 25 November 1943, having transferred from 12 Squadron at Wickenby six miles from Market Rasen in Lincolnshire where he and his crew had begun operations on 3 September. Their last two trips on 550 Squadron had been to the 'Big City' before the Main Force squadrons received two days of rest. Sergeant Jim Donnan the WOp on Bryson's crew recalls the events of the New Year's Day raid that evening:

We were engaged in routine pre-operational checks and testing of our equipment prior to the main briefing, which commenced in a tense atmosphere. When the curtain was drawn aside exposing the operational map, the target was Berlin for the third consecutive time, only this time our route to the 'Big City' was almost directly from the Dutch coast across an area which was becoming increasingly dangerous because of night fighter activity. The original take-off time was planned for mid-evening but deteriorating weather conditions delayed our take-off for several hours.[23] It was therefore difficult to relax during this period.

As New Year's Day was drawing to a close we were preparing for take-off and at 14 minutes past midnight we were airborne and on our way at last. The sky was dark and overcast as we flew through layers of broken cloud, climbing to our operational height, heading east over the North Sea. As we approached the Dutch coast we could see that the anti-aircraft defences were very active and we became alert to the dangers ahead. Flying over Germany, occasional bursts of flak and flashes lit up the thick, unbroken cloud along the route. While searching the night fighter waveband I was aware of considerable activity by the German control. We found it necessary to keep a sharp look out even though our trip had been uneventful so far. Our navigator Sergeant Thomas 'Rocky' Roxby called for a slight change in course for the final leg to Berlin as we reached a position between Hannover and Bremen. It was almost immediately afterwards that a series of thuds vibrated through the floor and the aircraft seemed to bank away to starboard. I leapt up from my seat to the astrodome where I could see the starboard engines were on fire. As I switched over from radio to intercom, I saw that a fire had started under the navigator's table on the floor just behind the pilot. It was soon burning fiercely. The pilot gave the order to abandon the aircraft. I clipped on my parachute and as I moved forward it was found that the front escape hatch would not open. The engineer joined the bomb aimer in trying to release it. As I stood behind the navigator waiting to exit, the rear gunner said that he was having trouble with the rear turret. I then signalled that I would go to the rear exit. The navigator was standing beside the pilot ready to exit as I scrambled over the main spar and along the fuselage to the rear door, losing my shoes on the way. When I got there, the mid-upper gunner was ready to leave and the rear gunner was out of his turret and preparing to come forward. I then jettisoned the rear door as the flames from the starboard wing streamed past, licking the tail plane. Grasping the release handle on my parachute I prepared to jump but I must have lost consciousness, as I have no recollection of what happened next or how I left the plane. When I regained consciousness my parachute was already open and I was floating in pitch darkness; very cold and my feet were freezing. I seemed to be a long time coming down but as I descended through the clouds, dark shadows appeared and I landed on soft ground in an open space. Gathering up my parachute, I dashed over to a clump of trees where I sat on the ground shivering and wondering how I could avoid capture.[24]

Twenty-nine Lancasters were lost over Berlin.[25] *A-Apple* flown by Wing Commander 'Jock' Abercromby DFC* who had recently moved to command 83 Squadron in 8 Group after his ops on 619 Squadron, which included flying Ed Murrow to Berlin the previous December, was attacked on the way to the target. It may have been the Scot's order banning weaving or banking gently over enemy territory and instead flying straight and level at all times that resulted in an unseen night fighter shooting them down. *A-Apple* exploded, killing everyone except Sergeant L H Lewis, who was thrown clear.

At Spilsby at the southern end of the Lincolnshire Wolds two Lancasters on 207 Squadron failed to return. *L-London* and the crew were lost without trace. There were no survivors on *T-Tommy* flown by 1st Lieutenant Frank B Solomon USAAF, which included fellow American, Flying Officer Willis A DeBardeleben USAAF. Two *ABC*-equipped aircraft on 101 Squadron at Ludford Magna also failed to return. *Z-Zebra* and crew skippered by

Squadron Leader Ian Robertson DFC were lost without trace, seven of them being commemorated on the Runnymede Memorial and Technical Sergeant Ereil Jones USAAF, the rear gunner, perpetuated on the Wall of the Missing at Madingley Cemetery just outside Cambridge. *V-Victor* flown by Pilot Officer D J Bell went down in Belgium. The pilot and two crew members, one of whom was 1st Lieutenant M H Albert USAAF, were taken prisoner and Sergeant H W Bailey evaded capture. Sergeant George C Connon the Special Operator and Flying Officer, Frank Joseph Zubic RCAF, the 18-year-old mid-upper gunner and the two other crew members who died were laid to rest in Gosselies Communal Cemetery. At Warboys 156 Squadron lost four Lancasters and all 28 crew members.

It snowed on Sunday 2 January. Despite most crews having just returned from an 8-hour round trip to the Big City, to their amazement they were 'on' again that night. Fatigue mixed with anger caused severe rumblings and ructions at briefings on many stations in Bomber Command. And there were to be no diversions. A long, evasive route was originally planned but this was changed to an almost straight in, straight out route with just a small 'dog leg' at the end of it to allow the bombers to fly into Berlin from the north-west, to take advantage of a strong following wind from that direction.[26] So much for Harris's 'old lags'! However, at some airfields getting a requisite number of aircraft available proved impossible. At Waddington for instance only eight Lancasters on 467 Squadron were on the Battle Order. One was piloted by Pilot Officer Alec Riley who was described as 'a pukka RAAF member having been employed as clerk of stores at Richmond, NSW before the war'.

It was another midnight take-off and runways were cleared of snow to allow 383 Lancasters, Mosquitoes and Halifaxes to get off. *T-Tommy*, a Lancaster on 460 Squadron crashed near Binbrook village six minutes after take-off, killing all the crew. The weather was foul throughout and cloud contained icing and static electricity up to 28,000 feet but clearer conditions were expected at the target where most of the 26 bombers that were lost – ten of them Path Finder aircraft – were shot down. Losses at Warboys rose to nine aircraft in two nights when five more Lancasters on 156 Squadron failed to return. *T-Tommy* flown by Flying Officer Charles Gordon Cairns DFM crashed at Riesdorf on what was the pilot's 47th sortie. All seven crew including Technical Sergeant Jack E Haywood USAAF died. *V-Victor* was lost without trace while *J-Johnny* was presumed to have crashed in the target area. *O-Orange* also disappeared with all seven crew. Near Bremen *C-Charlie* flown by Sergeant Alan Douglas Barnes was attacked from the port quarter by a night fighter. The Lancaster entered into a steep dive and was partially abandoned by four of the crew, who were captured and taken into captivity. Barnes and two of his crew, including 17-year-old Sergeant Ronald Victor Hillman, died.[27]

On the way out over Holland Lancaster *E-Easy* on 432 'Leaside' Squadron at East Moor flown by Pilot Officer Tom Spink was attacked head-on and considerably damaged by a night fighter. Spink and his navigator were each awarded the DFC. Shortly after dropping the bomb load, just after it turned for home *U-Uncle* on 'Leaside' Squadron, flown by 22-year-old Pilot Officer J A 'Jim' McIntosh, was attacked by a night fighter. McIntosh, born and raised in Revelstoke, British Columbia had been a locomotive fireman with the Canadian Pacific Railway before joining up. His crew were all Canadians. McIntosh recalled:

The rear gunner, Sergeant Leo Bandle, spotted a Bf 110. The enemy and my two gunners opened fire at the same instant. Cannon shells hit our aircraft like sledge hammers. Bandle and Andrew de Dauw my mid-upper gunner scored hits on the 110's port engine and cockpit and the fighter went down, burning fiercely. All this happened within five seconds. Meanwhile my control column had been slammed forward (the elevator had been hit), putting the aircraft into a near-vertical dive. By putting both feet on the instrument panel, one arm around the control column and the other hand on the elevator trim, then hauling back with every ounce of strength while trimming fully nose up, I managed to pull out of the dive at about 10,000 feet (13,000 feet below bombing height). My compasses were unserviceable, the rudder controls had jammed and I could get very little response from the elevators. I still had to wrap both arms around the control column to maintain height.

We were now far behind the rest of the bombers and our only hope was to stay in the cloud-tops and take our chances with the severe icing we were encountering. Fighter flares kept dropping all around us and the flak positions *en route* were bursting their stuff at our height but the fighters couldn't see us in that cloud. Alex Small my navigator, who was from Morris, Manitoba, took astro fixes and kept us away as much as possible from defended areas. We had been losing a lot of fuel from the starboard inner tank but enough remained to take us to Woodbridge. About seventy miles out to sea I let down through cloud, experiencing severe icing and then I broke through. The aircraft was now becoming very sluggish and only with difficulty was I able to hold height. I detailed the crew to throw out all our unnecessary equipment and to chop out everything they could. This considerably lightened the aircraft and made it easier to control. I then ordered the crew to stand by for ditching, just in case. The navigator headed me straight for Woodbridge on *Gee*. I used all the runway and felt the kite touch down on our port wheel. It rolled along until the speed dropped to about 30 mph and then I settled down more on the side of the starboard wheel, did half a ground-loop and stopped. I shut down the engines, got out and took a look. Both starboard engine nacelles were gone; the hydraulics were smashed and twisted; two large tears were in the starboard wing near the dinghy stowage: the dinghy was hanging out; the starboard fuel jettison sac was hanging out; the tail-plane was riddled with cannon and gun fire; the fuselage had five cannon holes through it (three of the shells had burst inside, near the navigator); there were two cannon holes in the rear turret (one of these shells had whistled almost the entire length of the fuselage before exploding); there were hundreds of holes of all sizes in the kite; every prop blade had at least one hole in it, one being split down the middle; the starboard outer oil tank was riddled and the starboard tyre was blown clean off. But nobody was injured. It had been a good trip until we were attacked by the fighter.

Bandle and de Dauw had opened fire simultaneously at 100 yards range and loosed 500 rounds at it without taking their thumbs off the firing buttons. The enemy's port engine caught fire just as he broke away. He went into a succession of dives and half-hearted pull-outs, finally spinning out of control until lost to view.[28]

At Waddington Pilot Officer Alec Riley's Lancaster was long overdue and was given up as lost. Casualty signals were made out and were with the Signals Section just about to be dispatched when his voice came out of the blue and called up on the TR9 about four and a half hours later than his ETR. He had landed at a satellite of Mildenhall but nobody notified Waddington. His crew's kit had been collected by the Committee of Adjustment. It was indeed fortunate that he got back when he did for it could have been a big shock to the next of kin to have got the telegrams. Over the mid-day news the number of aircraft lost was given as 28 but by the 18.30 hours session it had been reduced to 27.

This was an ineffective raid with bombs being scattered over all parts of the German capital.

There were two nights of rest for the bomber squadrons and then on the night of 5/6 January, 358 Lancasters and Halifaxes raided Stettin. Thirteen Mosquitoes raiding Berlin kept most of the German night fighters away from the Main Force attack, which lost 16 heavies.[29] One of these was 'Tommy 2', a 626 Squadron Lancaster at Wickenby flown by Australian Flight Lieutenant Noel Belford. They had dropped their bombs and incendiaries on the centre of the markers just before 04.00 hours and turned for home. It was some hours later when the mid-upper gunner asked how it could be that the polestar lay astern if they were flying west that Flight Sergeant Arthur Lee the navigator realized that the gyro compass was u/s and that they had been flying in the arc of an enormous circle. It was clear that they would not have enough fuel to make it back. Shortly before 10.00 hours Belford decided to land across the troughs, using the wave crests to slow the aircraft down. After several dummy runs he then ditched 'Tommy 2' in the North Sea, 60 miles off Withernsea, Yorkshire. The sea was running a heavy swell and the wind was very strong. All the crew survived and were afloat in the open sea in their dinghy until they were spotted by a Hudson and eventually they were rescued by a RML (Rescue Motor Launch) which put them ashore at Great Yarmouth at noon on Friday the 7th.

The next major bombing effort was on 14/15 January when 498 bombers set out for Brunswick but most of the attack fell either in the country-side or in Wolfenbüttel and other small towns and villages well to the south of the city. The German defences picked up the attacking force only 40 miles from the English coast and many night fighters entered the bomber stream soon after the bombers crossed the German frontier near Bremen. From then until the heavies crossed the Dutch coast on the return flight no less than 42 Lancasters were shot down. *Nachtjagd*, operating *Zahme Sau* (*Tame Boar*) free-lance or Pursuit Night Fighting tactics to excellent advantage, seemed to have rendered *Window* counter-productive.[30]

The straight in, straight out routes, which so often characterized previous raids on Berlin were abandoned on the night of 20/21 January when 769 aircraft – 264 of them Halifaxes – went to the 'Big City'. It was a fine day and the bombers took off in late afternoon. Over Germany the bombers ran into the cloud of a cold front and Berlin was completely cloud-covered. The timing of the Blind Markers was reported to be 'excellent' and a good concentration of Sky Markers was maintained throughout the attack but the crews of *H2S* aircraft thought that the attack fell on the eastern districts of the city. Conditions were particularly favourable to night fighters since a layer of cloud at 12,000 feet illuminated from below by searchlights provided a background against which aircraft could be silhouetted. About 100 twin engined fighters were sighted over Berlin and nine bombers were shot down in the Berlin area, some by flak, as Pilot Officer G G A Whitehead on 76 Squadron at Holme on Spalding Moor, 15 miles southeast of York, recalls:

As the bombs left the bomb bay there was an almighty crack as we were hit in the nose by flak at 20,000 feet. The bomb aimer, Flying Officer Harold 'Don' Morris, was killed instantly and the wireless operator, Sergeant L Stokes, was badly wounded. There was a large hole in the port side of the nose, involving the navigator's compart-ment and all his instruments, charts etc., were sucked out of it. There was some damage in my department, the worst of which was to both compasses, which were completely inoperable. One engine failed and the aircraft was difficult to control but we turned westwards and I told the navigator that I would keep Polaris in the starboard cockpit window and although that would involve flying over more enemy territory than was healthy, provided our luck held we might make the shorter sea crossing to UK. There was 10/10ths cloud below and Polaris was our only navigational aid.

We held on like this for ages, gradually losing height. Fuel was a problem. Although we had plenty on board, the flight engineer reported that he was unable to use the starboard tanks because of damage to the fuel-cock mechanism. Both port engines began to overheat. I saw the clouds ahead were breaking and I told the crew that if there was land below they should be prepared to 'get out and walk'.

I instructed them to prepare Stokes for a static-line parachute exit if I deemed it necessary to give the order. We were at 3,000 feet when we reached the break in the cloud but it was not possible to identify anything on the ground. I adopted the 'I am lost' procedure by calling 'Hallo "Darkie"' on the radio several times but got no reply. We were down to the last half pint of our useable fuel so I gave the order to bail out. All the survivors got out and landed safely. The aircraft had a mind of its own and wanted to do aerobatics as soon as I let go of the controls but I made it and it passed me on the way down! We had hoped that the land might have been Suffolk or Essex but on the way down I realized there were no coal mines in these counties. I landed in the back garden of a miner's cottage in Lens, in north-eastern France![31]

The diversions by twelve Mosquitoes to Düsseldorf, four to Kiel and three to Hannover were not large enough to fool the German defences and night fighters shot down all 35 bombers that failed to return. Six aircraft were lost to fighters on the way out, at least six over Berlin and four more on the first leg of the homeward journey. Three of the 13 missing Lancasters were on 83 Squadron at Wyton. At Bourn there was no word from *K-King* on 97 Squadron, which was flown by Pilot Officer Cyril Arthur Wakley who was killed. Three other crew members were taken prisoner. The other three men who died included the rear gunner, Technical Sergeant Ben H Stedman USAAF whose remains could not be found. Twenty-two Halifaxes were lost on the raid and a 427 'Lion' Squadron RCAF Halifax crashed at Westwick in Norfolk and a 434 'Bluenose' Squadron RCAF Halifax piloted by Flight Sergeant F Johnson crashed at Flixton in Yorkshire.

Seven Halifaxes that were lost or missing were on 102 Squadron and only nine Halifaxes returned to Pocklington. *X-X-Ray* was shot down on the outward leg by *Hauptmann* Ludwig 'Luk' Meister of I./NJG4 and abandoned in the vicinity of Neuruppin. All the crew were taken into captivity. After releasing its bombs and as the bomb doors started to close, *F-Freddie* flown by Pilot Officer G A Griffiths DFM was hit by flak over the target, which set the starboard wing and the bomb bay on fire.

A Bf 110 applied the *coup de grace* and the aircraft dived steeply and began breaking up. Sergeant H L Bushell the tail gunner said: 'The whole of the thing caught fire on the starboard wing and the pilot told us to bail out. Reg Wilson the navigator and Laurie Underwood the bomb aimer bailed out. John Bremner the flight engineer helped Reg to open the hatch, but John didn't get out.' He and Eric Church the wireless operator, Sergeant Kenneth Stanbridge the second pilot, and Charles Dupueis the Canadian mid-upper gunner were killed when *F-Freddie* crashed into woodland at Hirschgarten Friedrichshagen on the outskirts of Berlin.[32] *H-Harry* was hit by flak at 19,500 feet over the target and after bombs away was shot down by a night fighter. *Harry* was abandoned and crashed at Ahrensfelde 13 kilometres from the centre of Berlin. Five of the eight man crew survived and were taken prisoner. Six men on *N-Nuts* were lost without trace and the pilot was taken prisoner.

P-Peter was hit by flak at 18,000 feet and the No. 3 petrol tank was punctured. On the return the undercarriage could not be lowered and on regaining the Yorkshire coast Flying Officer A H Hall ordered the crew to bail out after which he crash-landed at Clitheroe Farm, five miles north of Driffield airfield. There were no injuries but the aircraft was wrecked. On the return, *O-for Orange* flown by Flight Sergeant Richard Proctor crashed between Intwood Hall and the Norwich to Wymondham LNER railway line at Cringleford on the outskirts of Norwich. Proctor was injured; Flying Officer James Alexander W 'Jock' Turnbull the bomb aimer from Ashkirk, Selkirkshire was more seriously injured and he was pronounced dead at the Norfolk & Norwich hospital.

102 Squadron were to lose four more aircraft the next night, when favourable weather permitted sending 648 aircraft in four waves to Magdeburg, sixty miles west of Berlin. Winds were stronger than forecast and the outward route was not dissimilar to that of the night before. A feint by 22 Lancasters and a dozen Mosquitoes who bombed Berlin was largely ignored and the *JLO* ordered *Zahme Sau* to assemble at a beacon between Hamburg and Cuxhaven. Later he ordered them to Hamburg and then to Leipzig just south of Magdeburg. The Bf 110s and Ju 88s struck between Cuxhaven and Lüneburg south of Hamburg with devastating effect.

Major Heinrich zu Sayn-Wittgenstein flying a Ju 88C-6 had taken off from Stendal near Berlin shortly before 21.00 hours on a *Tame Boar* sortie. Constantly in action and clearly worn out by battle fatigue, just a few days earlier Wittgenstein had received the Oak Leaves to his Knight's Cross from Hitler. In less than 40 minutes in the vicinity of Magdeburg the *prinz* shot down three Lancasters and two Halifaxes. His radar operator, *Feldwebel* Friedrich Ostheimer reported:

At about 22.00 hours I picked up the first contact on my [*SN-2*] search equipment. I passed the pilot directions and a little later the target was sighted: it was a Lancaster. We moved into position and opened fire and the aircraft immediately caught fire in the left wing. It went down at a steep angle and started to spin. Between 22.00 and 22.05 hours the bomber crashed and went off with a violent explosion; I watched the crash.

Again we searched. At times I could see as many as six aircraft on my radar. After some further directions the next target was sighted: again a Lancaster. Following the first burst from us there was a small fire and the machine dropped back its left wing and went down in a vertical dive. Shortly afterwards I saw it crash. It was sometime between 22.10 and 22.15 hours. When it crashed there were heavy detonations, most probably it was the bomb load.

After a short interval we again sighted a Lancaster. There was a long burst of fire and the bomber ignited and went down. I saw it crash sometime between 22.25 and 22.30 hours; the exact time is not known.[33] Immediately afterwards we saw yet another four-motored bomber; we were in the middle of the so-called 'bomber-stream'. After one firing pass this bomber went down in flames; at about 22.40 hours I saw the crash.

Yet again I had a target on my search equipment. After a few directions we again sighted a Lancaster and after one attack it caught fire in the fuselage. The fire then died down and we moved into position for a new attack. We were again in position and *Major* Wittgenstein was ready to shoot when, in our own machine, there were terrible explosions and sparks. It immediately caught fire in the left wing and began to go down. As I heard this the canopy above my head flew away and I heard on the intercom a shout of *Raus!* [Get out!]. I tore off my oxygen mask and helmet and was then thrown out of the machine. After a short time I opened my parachute and landed east of the Hohengoehrener Dam, near Schoenhausen.

Early next morning the body of Prinz Wittgenstein was discovered close to the crash site at Lübars. On bailing out, his head had probably struck the tail-plane, rendering him unconscious and unable to pull the rip-cord. Wittgenstein's 83rd victory (one more than Lent) elevated him to the position of highest scoring night fighter pilot ever. After his death, only *Oberst* Lent and *Major* Heinz-Wolfgang Schnaufer were to overtake him with a higher score. Wittgenstein often spoke of the agony he felt about having to kill people and how, whenever possible, he tried to hit *Viermots* in such a way that the crew could bail out. Ironically he had been surprised by an attack from below, precisely the form of attack he himself had most favoured.

The night fighters remained with the bomber stream all the way to Magdeburg where most of the bombing is believed to have fallen outside the city. The stronger than forecast winds brought some of the bombers into the target area before the Path Finders' Zero Hour and 27 Main Force aircraft bombed without delay. The Path Finders later blamed the fires started by these aircraft and some effective enemy decoy markers for the scattered bombing that followed. Five bombers were shot down over the target. About 60 aircraft were damaged by flak and fighters and some of these did not make it home. A 76 Squadron Halifax crashed into the sea off the coast of Holland and a Halifax on 419 'Moose' Squadron RCAF at Middleton St. George crashed at Bourn, killing all the crew. Three Halifaxes crashed into the North Sea off Flamborough Head. One of them was a Halifax on 102 Squadron; three of the Squadron's four losses were from the four new crews that had arrived at Pocklington that morning. A Halifax on 466 Squadron RAAF crashed at Leconfield on return. All seven crew on a 460 Squadron RAAF Lancaster were injured when their aircraft crashed at Caistor in Lincolnshire. A total of 58 bombers was shot down; Bomber Command's heaviest loss of the war so far.

There were three nights of rest for the Main Force following the Magdeburg debacle and a raid planned for the night of 25/26 January was cancelled. Then on Thursday 27 January 515 Lancasters and 15 Mosquitoes were detailed for Berlin again. Half the German night fighter force was duped into flying north by a diversionary force of Halifaxes laying mines near Heligoland and only a few enemy fighters attacked the bombers before Berlin was reached. The target was cloud covered and sky marking had to be used. This appeared to be accurate but the strong winds blew them rapidly along the line of the bombers' route and bombing was 'spread well up and down wind'. This raid was the first time that the Flare Force marked with 'Supporters' from non-Path Finder squadrons. Until now the 'Supporters' had all been from 8 Group. Supporting the Flare Force meant arriving at the target at the same time but flying at 2,000 feet below them to attract the flak and enable the PFF to carry out a straight and level run. After drawing the flak the 'Supporters' then re-crossed the target to drop their bombs. Twenty-eight of the most experienced crews in 1 Group acted as Supporters, two of which were shot down though one was lost far from the target. Another 11 Lancasters in 1 Group including three on 460 Squadron at Binbrook, which dispatched 18 Lancasters on the raid, failed to return. Nothing was heard from 'C Squared', K-King and G-George after take-off but all seven men on C Squared survived to be taken prisoner. All on George were killed. Flight Sergeant John Francis Worley the mid-upper gunner, had trained in Kingaroy, Queensland and Evans Head, NSW before being posted overseas and had a fiancée, Joan Kelly. Only four men on K-King made it out alive. In 6 Group the three RCAF squadrons operating Lancaster IIs lost eight out of the 48 aircraft dispatched. All told, 33 Lancasters failed to return.

One of those was Sugar 2 on 626 Squadron at Wickenby flown by Noel Belford, whose crew had been rescued from the North Sea on 7 January and had all lived to tell the tale. When the CO discovered that they had never done a dinghy drill before the ditching he had ordered everyone on the squadron to practise the procedure until they could perform it in their sleep. It was of no use to Belford's crew, who came down at Katzenelnbogen on the Berlin operation. The Australian pilot and five of the crew died. Flight Sergeant Arthur Lee was the only survivor.

Flight Lieutenant Stanley James and his crew on 9 Squadron became victims of *Schräge Musik*. James, who was from Harrow, was 19 years old, having joined the RAFVR at 16. It was their 23rd operation and their seventh consecutive visit to Berlin. Having completed the bomb run, they left the 'Big City' and about fifteen minutes later they were attacked. Flight Sergeant Hal Croxson the rear gunner said that there was just one 'thump' and that 'the entire aircraft shuddered and then carried on'. Flight Sergeant A Howie the bomb aimer bellowed into the intercom, 'We've got fire in the bomb bay!' Some bombs had not been released because the bomb release gear would often freeze solid and there would be odd hang-ups. The navigator had been hit in the leg by a piece of flak and the flight engineer said one engine had gone down. After the initial shock of the attack and the panic that ensued, the bomb aimer dealt with the fire through the inspection door and at the same time he released some of the hang-ups. The wireless operator treated the navigator's wound. James reckoned that even with three engines they would fly home but about twenty minutes later another engine packed up. James told Croxson to jettison anything he could. He got the flare chute away and the Elsan out. He thought, 'I wonder whose head this will land on!' He also got the arrest bed out and 12,000 rounds of ammunition, which would feed the rear turret, although he left several hundred rounds in case he should need them.

By now the Lancaster had fallen to just 4,000 feet and soon they would be flying over the high ground of Bavaria. Croxson took the parachute from its little rack outside the turret with elastic ropes over it, clipped it on to his harness and got back into his turret. James called out, 'I've got to go. Good luck, chaps and everybody out.'

Only three men made it. Howie got out through the front and Sergeant M W Chilvers the mid-upper gunner came down from his turret and got out of the side door. Croxson brought his turret round to full port, opened the slide doors at the back, took care to get hold of his oxygen feed, his electric suit and his intercom cord and get it all out of the way. Then he got his feet on the gun butts and kicked himself out into space. And that was it. Suddenly he was hanging in the air in total silence with the breeze swishing through the cords of the parachute, an enormous black cloud above him. Away in the distance he saw the sky light up and he knew that it was the aircraft. They hadn't made it. The next thing, Croxson thumped to the ground. 'At night, you don't know when you're going to hit the ground.'

A maximum effort was ordered immediately against Berlin by 677 bombers on the night of 28/29 January and a full range of diversionary operations was put into operation. Eighteen *Oboe* Mosquitoes raided four of the most significant *Nachtjagd* airfields in Holland and 63 Stirlings and four Path Finder Halifaxes dropped mines in Kiel Bay five hours before the Main Force raid on the Big City. Six more Mosquitoes bombed Berlin four hours before the main attack went in and another four Mosquitoes made a diversionary raid on Hannover.

A 158 Squadron Halifax at Lissett and *G-George* a Halifax V on 76 Squadron at Holme-on-Spalding Moor crashed on take-off killing two men on the latter aircraft. Numbers were further diminished as one in ten bombers turned back over the North Sea. At Waddington Flight Lieutenant Ivan G 'Joe' Durston DFC RAAF, a pilot on 467 Squadron RAAF who had completed his tour, decided that he would fly one more op so that the four Australians in the crew of *L-London* could finish together. The cloud was well broken and the routes to the target went north over Northern Denmark on both the outward and return flights to further deplete the night fighter force but even so, the *JLO* still managed to concentrate large numbers of fighters over the target and 26 Halifaxes and 18 Lancasters were shot down. Two other Lancasters were lost with their crews in a mid air collision over Alsace. 'Joe' Durston's brave gesture was in vain. All seven crew on *L-London* died when the bomber was shot down on the approach to Berlin.

At Elvington four Halifaxes on 77 Squadron were missing and four Halifax Vs on 434 Squadron never returned to Croft. Four Halifax IIs on 10 Squadron at Melbourne were never heard of again. Of 19 Lancasters on 97 Squadron that took off for Berlin, one had returned early and two were missing. Flight Lieutenant Charles Thomas Wilson DFC and crew were killed, so too Flying Officer Frank Allison's. This pilot had flown 48 sorties and had been awarded the DFM in 1942 when he was flying Wellingtons in the Middle East. Another of 97 Squadron's Lancasters, piloted by a tough Australian by the name of Flight Lieutenant Henry Stewart van Raalte, returned having failed to find the 'Big City'. He bombed Kiel instead. Van Raalte's rear gunner was decapitated by flak.

Two Lancaster IIIs on 83 Squadron failed to return to Wyton. *S-Sugar* flown by Flight Lieutenant Horace Robert Hyde was involved in a fatal collision with a 463 Squadron Lancaster outbound and crashed on the Danish border. Both crews were buried in Aabenraa Cemetery on 2 February. While outbound *B-Baker* flown by Pilot Officer William Simpson was attacked by a Ju 88C night fighter of II./NJG 3 crewed by *Hauptmann* Gerhard Raht, his *Funker Feldwebel* Anton Heinemann and *Bordmechaniker Unteroffizier* Werner Hesse, and controlled by the radar station 'Star' at Lütjenhorn in Northern Germany. At 02:37 the Lancaster exploded in the air and the wreckage was spread over a radius of 2.5 kilometres just north of the village of Varnæs. During the morning the surviving flyers began to show up. There were reports of parachutes found at Tråsbøl, Brobøl, Ullerup and Bovrup. Sergeant Thomas K McCash the flight engineer and Flight Sergeant John J Martin, navigator, were found dead in fields near Bovrup. One was not wearing a parachute.

At 07:32 hours a flyer knocked on the door at a farm in Ullerup and was picked up by the *Wehrmacht*. Simpson landed by parachute on the roof of the house next to the telephone exchange at Skoletoften 12 in Blans. He hurt his forehead when he fell from the roof and was taken to the exchange to have the wound dressed. None of the Danes present had any command of the English language but Simpson still tried to persuade them into hiding him but there were many German sympathizers in the village and no one dared to hide him. Someone had seen Simpson and at 09:20 two German soldiers arrived on a motorcycle and picked him up. At 14:23 a flyer came to the Ballegård farm in Blans and he was picked up by the *Wehrmacht*. Pilot Officer Ronald Pilgrim the air bomber landed near Ullerup and hid in a shack belonging to the Vicarage. When evening came he sneaked into the barn and was found around 9 o'clock by the son of Reverend Warncke who was away in hospital. Mrs Warncke called Reverend Sjellerup of Nybøl but he could not help and as a last resort they called Chief Constable Bjerre of Gråsten. He declared that he would inform the *Wehrmacht* where they could pick up Pilgrim.

McCash and Martin were both laid to rest in Aabenraa cemetery on 2 February. Air gunner Flight Sergeant John R Tree RAAF had landed in the sea off Alssund and drowned. He was found on 19 June and was laid to rest on 22 June. Pilgrim and Simpson and W/Op Sergeant W Livesey and Flight Sergeant J A Fell, air gunner were sent to *Dulag Luft* and on to PoW camps.

At Witchford two Lancasters on 115 Squadron were missing with only one survivor from both the crews. At Kirmington 166 Squadron also lost two Lancasters. There were no survivors on Pilot Officer Joe Horsley DFC's crew on *Z-Zebra*. Five of Flying Officer C G Phelps RAAF crew On *W-William* were killed. They included the navigator, Master Sergeant W W Mitchell USAAF from Michigan. The Australian pilot and Pilot Officer E D Nesbitt RCAF were the only survivors and they were taken into captivity. A 466 Squadron RAAF Halifax at Leconfield and a 431 'Iroquois' Squadron RCAF Halifax crashed on return at Matlaske in Norfolk and Croft respectively. Three other Halifaxes on 466 were shot down. Another 'Iroquois' Squadron crew bailed out off the Lincolnshire coast and two others were shot down. A 433 'Porcupine' Squadron Halifax crew ditched in the North Sea off Hartlepool and another was abandoned near Thirsk, Yorkshire. A 434 'Bluenose' Squadron RCAF Halifax at Croft piloted by Pilot Officer M F Flewelling RCAF crashed at Flixton in Yorkshire and one man was injured. Four other aircraft on the Squadron were shot down on Berlin.

At Pocklington two Halifax IIs on 102 Squadron were lost. One was *S-Sugar* flown by Flight Sergeant D Pugh, which was hit by flak as they came off the target. Losing fuel they finally had to ditch off the Danish coast. The sea was rough with waves up to 20 feet high but it was daylight and the weather was good. Pugh ditched successfully and the crew scrambled into their dinghy but later the next day a heavy wave capsized their craft and all the crew were flung into the sea. Pughb and three others managed to clamber back into the dinghy but the rear-gunner, bomb-aimer and the flight engineer remained in the sea, clinging to ropes. The men in the dinghy tried vainly to get them into the craft but they were too exhausted and one by one the three men in the water drifted off silently and alone and they were never seen again. Two days later the dinghy was spotted by a Warwick, which dropped two Lindholme dinghies in the rough sea to no avail and next day when another Warwick dropped another dinghy the four men were too exhausted to reach it. Finally, after three days adrift in the open sea the four survivors, all suffering from hypothermia, were picked up by a high speed launch from Montrose. Flight Sergeant James Craig Graham, the Canadian navigator, died before the HSL reached Scotland.

Crews had just one night's rest before the bombing of Berlin resumed on the night of 30/31 January, this time by a force of 534 aircraft. It was the third raid on the Big City in four nights and crews were under-standably unhappy about it. And as it was the start of a new moon period a quarter- to half-moon was expected during the outward flight. Also, the only diversionary raids were by 22 Mosquitoes on Elberfeld and five more on Brunswick. While the outward route for the Main Force was again a northerly one it was not as far north as the previous raid on Berlin. The night fighters were unable to intercept the Main Force over the sea and the bomber stream was well on the way to the target before they met with any opposition. At the target the bombing was made through complete cloud cover. Twin-engined *Tame Boars* wreaked havoc, continuing their attacks until well into the return flight and they accounted for all 33 bombers that were shot down.[34] Pilot Officer Alec Riley's crew on 467 Squadron RAAF at Waddington who were four and half hours late and given up for lost on 2/3 January, crashed in the target area following a direct hit from flak. Riley the 'pukka Aussie' and five of his crew were killed. *Q-Queenie*, a 106 Squadron Lancaster at Metheringham, crashed in the North Sea with the loss of all the crew, and a 640 Squadron Halifax crashed near Catfoss Manor in Yorkshire, killing all the crew.

It was clear now that new British tactics and new countermeasures and a 'fattening up' of the Main Force would be necessary before a resumption of raids deep into Germany. Replacement crews and aircraft were on their way and existing crews were told that they would not be required for operations for nearly two weeks.[35]

Roy Keen on 166 Squadron flew one or two of the back-to-back night raids:

My first op – I think it's like everything else – when you're sitting on the grass ready for take-off, your mind's in a bit of a whirl, you wonder what the hell's going to happen. But once you get in the aeroplane and take off, you're busy. The Lancaster was cold, cramped and noisy – other than that it was a lovely aeroplane! I'll never forget the first trip we did, which was to Berlin. It always had a bit of a name, did Berlin, the 'Big City' and I was absolutely amazed at the sight of the target in the middle of a big raid – it was fantastic. It's like Blackpool lights, times twenty! It was very unreal – you looked down and saw coloured lights, you saw aircraft underneath you, above you. But, you don't think anything's going to happen to you. I'd seen quite a lot of aircraft go down. I suppose it could get to you a bit. I was usually intent in looking out for trouble, but I can't say that I was particularly nervous. Operations did affect some people worse than others. A bit of a fuss was made when you got back to base. Egg and bacon and if anyone didn't come back you had theirs! You just had to dismiss it – sometimes four aircraft would disappear off the scene, but the more you did, you realised your time may not be far away.

On 12/13 February ten Lancasters on 617 Squadron carried out the third operation on the Anthéor viaduct 15 miles west of Cannes on the coastal railway line leading to Italy. As on the two previous raids the 90-foot stone arches curving back across the beach at the foot of a ravine resisted all attempts to destroy them. Two low level Lancasters flown by Wing Commander Cheshire and Squadron Leader Mick Martin were damaged by anti aircraft guns, which mortally wounded Flight Lieutenant 'Bob' Hay, the bomb aimer on Martin's aircraft. Martin had headed for Ajaccio in northern Corsica after one of his crew confirmed that the island was in Allied hands – he had read it in the *News of the World* the Sunday before – but he finally put *P-Popsie* down at Elmas Field in South Sardinia where a doctor was available. They buried Bob Hay in Sardinia. The other Lancasters landed back at Ford where the weather threatened to prevent them from returning to Woodhall Spa. Next day Squadron Leader William Reid Suggitt DFC RCAF thought that he could make it to Woodhall Spa and he offered a seat to Squadron Leader Thomas Williams Lloyd DSO, the immaculate, monocled 52-year-old Intelligence Officer. Lloyd accepted the invitation but declared that he must spruce himself up with a shave first. Eight men clambered aboard *J-Jig*, which five minutes later hit a hill ten miles northeast of Chichester and crashed at Waltham Down, Sussex. Bill Suggitt was alive and delirious in his seat when found but he never regained consciousness and he died in Chichester Hospital at 16.00 hours on the 15th. Everyone else was killed instantly. Lloyd was a First World War veteran. Flight Sergeant John Pulford DFM was Guy Gibson's flight engineer on the Dams raid and Pilot Officer Johnnie Gordon DFC RAAF was on his second tour. Don Charlwood, whose crew had been the first on 103 Squadron to complete a tour, was best man at Gordon's wedding at Northfield on 26 January. One of twenty navigators who had left Australia to train in Canada, Charlwood and seventeen others made it to Bomber Command where only five of these returned, with twelve dead and one PoW. Gordon had told Charlwood that on 617 Squadron 'Apparently there's no such thing as a "tour". You just stay till the war's over, or till you're over, or till you've had a bellyful.'

On the morning of Sunday 13 February after a rest of more than a fortnight 'Bomber' Harris decided to mount a maximum effort on the Big City, but bad weather caused the operation to be cancelled. The operation was laid on for the next day but heavy snowfalls caused the operation to be cancelled again. It was not until Tuesday 15 February that the offensive could re-commence. That night the German capital was the target for just over 890 Lancasters, Halifaxes and Mosquitoes. This was the largest force sent to Berlin and the largest non-1,000 bomber force dispatched to any target.[36] It was also the first time that more than 500 Lancasters (561, of which 226 were from 5 Group) and more than 300 Halifaxes (314) were sent on a raid. The number of Halifaxes was increased due to the return of 420 'Snowy Owl' Squadron and 424 'Tiger' Squadron from the Middle East. (Another Canadian squadron – 425 'Alouette' RCAF – would be ready with its Lancasters for the next raid.) In addition a series of diversion and support operations was mounted, chief among these being the 23 *Oboe* Mosquitoes which were to attack five night fighter airfields in Holland, and 43 Stirlings and four Path Finder Halifaxes which would lay mines in Kiel Bay. Another diversionary ploy would be flown by 24 Lancasters of 8 Group on Frankfurt-on-Oder.

On 625 Squadron at Kelstern Sergeant Bill Ashurst's eleventh Lancaster operation began badly when, due to a mechanical fault *Y-Yorker* took off 25 minutes later than the other aircraft, at 17.25 hours. At Leconfield Ken Handley, a British flight engineer on 466 Squadron RAAF prepared for his first Halifax operation. He would find the trip not as frightening as he expected. There were no searchlights owing to ten tenths cloud base, 2,000 feet tops and 6,000 feet over the target and only light flak below them. They bombed at 22,300 feet and came off the target at 24,000 feet. There were numerous fighter flares around the target and on the return trip and evasive action was taken, but their luck held and they had no combats with fighters. Handley however endured a tense last half hour on the 7 hour 30 minute flight when No. 4 tank iced up and they had 'no joy' with it for ten minutes. The *JLOs* had plotted the bomber stream soon after it left the English coast but the swing over Denmark for the approach flight proved too far distant for many of the German fighters. A 7 Squadron Lancaster was lost when it exploded over the Baltic with just one survivor. A 77 Squadron Halifax, a 419 Squadron Halifax and a 619 Squadron Lancaster also went down in the waters of the Baltic. There were no survivors on any of the aircraft. Halifax *O-Orange* on 158 Squadron flown by Flight Sergeant William C M Hogg ran into flak over Denmark. Flight Sergeant R McDonald recalled:

> Our port inner engine burst into flames and the aircraft went into a vertical dive. Our Skipper, Bill Hogg, regained control after 10,000 feet, but our port outer was now on fire. He extinguished the fires, feathered the props and jettisoned the load, but could not maintain height. Not sure whether we were over sea or land, we decided to stay with the aircraft. The starboard inner was now faltering as we skimmed a house and crash-landed in a snow covered field. The nose burst open on impact as did the overloaded fuel tanks and one engine tore loose. But miraculously there was no fire and all seven of us stepped out of the wreckage.

They had come down near Grasten in Denmark. All the crew were taken into captivity.

Y-Yorker on 625 Squadron was attacked by a night fighter and the Lancaster was set on fire. Bill Ashurst instructed Flying Officer Harry Proskurniak the Canadian bomb aimer to 'get rid of the bomb load' which included a 'cookie'. The aircraft was out of control and losing height and Harry frantically tried to open the forward escape hatch. He says:

> I must have lapsed into unconsciousness when trying to open it. When I came to it must have been the abrupt jerk of my parachute opening which really woke me up. The parachute really saved my life but I'll never know how I opened it! For me it was a miracle! I still keep asking myself the question, 'Why was my life spared and not that of any of my comrades?'

In the village of Fjelstrup the occupying Germans left the scattered bodies of Bill Ashurst and five crew members for several days before collecting them for a military funeral. Harry Proskurniak was eventually taken prisoner.

A record 2,643 tons of bombs was dropped through thick cloud over the 'Big City' by 806 aircraft out of the 891 dispatched. The aiming point was marked by red and green stars and the 'blind backers up' were ordered to keep it marked throughout the raid with green TIs. The attack lasted for 39 minutes. Nine Lancasters and six Halifaxes acted as primary 'blind markers', dropping their flares two minutes before the arrival of eleven special Lancasters acting as backers-up and equipped with *H2S*.

They dropped their markers at the rate of one every two minutes and were followed by three Lancasters and eleven Halifaxes flying in pairs. After these came the visual 'backers-up', 20 Lancasters, dropping flares at double that rate and their supporters, 58 Lancasters and the Halifaxes, and finally, the Main Force, divided into five waves of an average number of 140 aircraft. *Window* was dropped throughout the attack until supplies were exhausted. The attack was remarkable for its precision, though no glimpse of the city was seen. The last arrivals were able to report the glow of large fires and a column of smoke rising 30,000 feet into the murky air. Damage was extensive with almost 600 large fires and 572 'medium' fires; some war industries and almost 1,500 houses and temporary wooden barracks were destroyed. The most important industrial target hit was the Siemens and Halske works, which manufactured electrical apparatus. Several of its many buildings were gutted including the switch-gear and dynamo workshops. One hundred and forty two other factories were also hit, as were a power station, two gas works, Dr. Goebbels' broadcasting station and five tramway depots.

The diversion to Frankfurt-on-Oder failed to draw any night fighters away from the Berlin area but the *JLO* ordered his fighter pilots not to fly over the capital, leaving the target area free for the flak. So although fourteen combats took place above the 'Big City', the night fighters sought for the most part to intercept the bombers on their way in and out and left the defence of the target area itself to the guns. Forty-three Main Force bombers failed to return. Six other aircraft were lost on the return over England. At Oakington four Lancaster IIIs on 7 Squadron were missing in action. One of them was flown by Sergeant Ken Doyle. The crew could see Berlin in the distance when trouble began. Flight Sergeant Geoffrey Charles Chapman Smith RAAF, the tail gunner, was searching the port beam when, from the corner of his eye, he saw three white lights. He swung his guns, saw a green light and realized that it was an enemy fighter with its identification lamps on. Smith gave the warning and the Lancaster dived to port as four lines of tracer streamed from the wings of the fighter, now close enough to identify as a Bf 110. Smith poured 150 rounds into the fighter, there was a mighty flash and it blew up. Four more lines of tracer appeared; a FW 190 was coming in from behind. The Lancaster dived and lost the enemy but a cannon shell had hit Smith's leg and he was in great pain. His turret was unserviceable and his parachute bag was on fire. Other shells had plastered the Lancaster from its tail along its fuselage up to the mid-upper turret. The captain called his crew to check for casualties. There was no answer from the mid-upper turret and he sent the wireless operator back to see what had happened. The gunner was on the floor without his oxygen mask, almost unconscious. His turret had been hit and he had tried to beat out the flames of burning oil from a burst pipe, using his helmet. Lack of oxygen had overcome him. The wireless operator jammed an oxygen tube in the man's mouth just in time to save him and then climbed into the mid-upper turret to watch for fighters. The captain called Smith on the inter-com and told him he was sending help. But Smith refused to be moved and he continued to work the guns by hand. The navigator dealt with the burning parachute.

Crossing a flak belt the Lancaster was hit again. Two engines had stopped when at last the pilot got clear of the defences and crossed the coast out to sea. Smith's oxygen mask had frozen and he had taken it off and was breathing the dangerous rarefied air. Over the sea the crew chopped the bombs away and then came aft to free Smith. His turret door had frozen in and this, too, had to be chopped away. Still conscious, Smith tried to pull himself out but could not free his right leg which was shattered and twisted around the ammunition belt and controls. The turret was drenched in blood. It took an hour to free him. They gave him morphine and laid him on the floor of the fuselage. The pilot prepared for a belly-landing in case the tyres had been shot up but he found the bomb doors would not close and decided to alight on the damaged under-carriage. The bomb aimer and wireless operator lay on each side of Smith to protect him in case of a crash but the pilot made a good landing. The Lancaster came in at Woodbridge and there the fuselage was hacked away and Smith and the wounded mid-upper gunner were carried out. Smith's leg was amputated next morning. 'If it hadn't been for the Skipper, we'd never have got back at all,' he said later.

A 106 Squadron Lancaster crashed at Timberland Fen killing four of the crew and a fifth crewmember died of his injuries later. A 420 'Snowy Owl' Squadron RCAF Halifax crashed at Tholthorpe killing two of the crew and injuring the others and a 78 Squadron Halifax was abandoned on return to Breighton. All the crew were killed. A 630 Squadron Lancaster returning to Coningsby crashed near Old Bolingbroke without injury to any of the crew. At Elvington three Halifaxes on 77 Squadron were lost. At Leconfield four Halifaxes failed to return. Two of the Halifaxes were on 640 Squadron, one crashing at Coxwold and the other at Cloughton in Yorkshire. One complete crew was lost. On 466 Squadron RAAF no word was received from F-Freddie, which had gone down over Holland with its crew, or M-Mother, which was abandoned near Papenburg. M-Mother's crew were taken prisoner. As they crossed the coast of England Ken Handley looked at his fuel gauges, which showed that their Halifax had no fuel remaining. His pilot asked permission to land immediately with-out any 'stacking'. This they did, Handley expecting the engines to cut at any moment. 'What a relief to be taxiing along the runway and perimeter track' Handley wrote later. It was not until the following morning that the ground crew said that they could not get any fuel into the bomb bay tank – it was still full. Handley had forgotten to pump the 230 gallons into tanks 1 and 3 after leaving the target area!

This raid marked the close of the true 'Battle of Berlin'. A raid on the Big City was ordered on each of the following three days – 16, 17 and 18 February – but each time the operation had to be cancelled because of unfavourable weather conditions. Peter Geraghty on 102 Squadron recalled:

On this particular day we had been briefed on the afternoon. The plan was to put as many bombs as possible, in the shortest time possible, on Berlin. This huge city seemed to represent all that was evil. I personally felt that at last I was in the action – frightened but fulfilled. Of all the targets, Berlin was the big one. The briefing finished at 16.00 hours. Take off was set for 23.00 hours, seven hours of tension before we could get going. I decided to go to my Nissen hut and lie down for a while, pretending to sleep but finding my mind in a turmoil of dread. I stayed there for a couple of hours and then heard a loud rattling of the latch on the door followed by my flight engineer saying, 'What are you doing in there? Ops are scrubbed.' I don't think I've heard such welcome words.

Only one more raid took place on the German capital and that would not be for another month. The next big raid by Bomber Command was on the night of 19/20 February when the target was Leipzig and its aircraft assembly factories, as part of a true round-the-clock offensive in concert with the American Air Forces.[37] The 816 RAF bombers that were detailed flew towards Denmark and then down to Zwolle in Holland and across Germany between Hamburg and the Ruhr. It was hoped that this route and a 'spoof' feint over the North Sea by an OTU force and a Mosquito 'spoof' force carrying on due east to Berlin, as the Main Force turned sharply south to Leipzig at Brandenburg would keep German fighters back. Unfortunately the *JLO* did not take the bait and another Mosquito 'spoof' on Dresden failed. Meanwhile, the forecast steady head wind had turned into a tail wind in excess of 100 mph and it caused chaos. Many crews arrived at the target early and then orbited the area waiting for the Path Finder markers to go down. Some crews did not wait, and using their *H2S*, they bombed before Zero Hour. Pandemonium ensued when the markers did go down, as several hundred bomber crews raced in from all directions and tried to bomb at once before leaving the area as quickly as possible. Brian Soper recalls:

On this raid we took an additional pilot, a '2nd Dickie' trip, a first raid for a new pilot. This was supposed to be unlucky but we made it. There was 10/10s full cloud, which was very thin, but both ground and sky markers were visible. The duration of this trip was about 7¾ hours.

The Main Force lost 78 bombers – 44 Lancasters and 34 Halifaxes – Bomber Command's worst casualties so far. About 20 of these were victims of flak while the rest were shot down by a very efficiently deployed *Tame Boar* operation by 294 aircraft (only 17 of which were lost).[38] Two Lancasters on 103 Squadron collided on the return to Elsham Wolds. One of the aircraft managed to crash land at the base without injury to the crew but five men on board the second aircraft were killed. A 158 Squadron Halifax at Lissett crashed at Alwick in Yorkshire killing all seven crew and *Q-Queenie* a 166 Squadron Lancaster crash-landed at Manston on its return to Kirmington, all the crew suffering injuries.

At one American base the door was flung back and:

A group of fly-boys lurched in, singing with drink-sodden voices: '*Coming in on a wing and a prayer.*' They made up in volume what they lacked in harmony. Someone turned up the radio to drown them into a giggling silence. Over the radio a woman's voice was telling the recipe for the morrow, which was Woolton Pie. It sounded revolting to an American palate. The BBC news came on. We mostly didn't listen, because its content was really designed for the British ear. But towards the end we crewmen caught a flash that made our ears prick up: 'Royal Air Force bombers last night raided Leipzig. Large sections of the city were left in flames with considerable damage to the railway yards ...' Then in the crisp British accent: 'Seventy-nine of our aircraft are missing ...'

'Jesus H. Christ!' said somebody. 'I didn't know they had that many.'[39]

Brian Soper was on Arthur Rew's crew, who took a '2nd dickey' pilot on the 7¾ hour trip on Leipzig. Soper, who had by now flown ten raids on Berlin, recalls:

Although we felt sorry for them, we were happier when Halifaxes and Stirlings were also flying' 'Hallies' rarely got above 18,000 feet, which we felt took some of the flak: this was really only wishful thinking. However, later when some of the Halifaxes were fitted with radial engines, the roles were reversed and they could get higher than we could.

Four of the missing Halifaxes on Leipzig were on 35 Squadron, one of which exploded over Gohre and another was abandoned near Brandenburg. *J-Johnny* was hit by a Ju 88 armed with *Schräge Musik* at 23,000 feet near Beedenbostel in central Germany near Celle. The port inner engine caught fire and Squadron Leader Julian Sale DSO* DFC called 'Bail Out, bail out, bail out!' His highly decorated crew included the navigation leader, Squadron Leader Gordon Carter DFC*, who had also evaded capture the previous February. Because he had been through it all before Carter removed his helmet because 'a lot of chaps were hanged by their intercom leads going out' and bailed out. He had on his back under the parachute harness, a pack of escape items such as wire cutters and some civilian clothes bought in France during his evasion. On landing in a lane in a forest he went into the trees and put the clothes on. He remembered that he was carrying a revolver that he had bought in Huntingdon in case he ever fell into a city where he thought that civilians might mob him. Carter decided that he had better get rid of it. The navigation leader was free for 48 hours but a sailor shooting crows in a field did not believe his story that he was a French factory worker. Carter was apprehended and he was taken to a Luftwaffe airfield where he was visited by *Hauptmann* Ludwig 'Luk' Meister who told him that he was the pilot who had shot him down.[40] Carter, who was still wearing his French clothes, was asked, 'Were you trying to do what your Skipper succeeded in doing last year? Apparently the *Hauptmann* had read all about it in the Toronto ski club magazine. Carter opened his shirt and showed his interrogator his RCAF identity disc. Four others on the crew were also taken prisoner.

Julian Sale meanwhile had crash-landed the Halifax because Flight Sergeant Kenneth Knight, the 19-year-old rear gunner had not answered the call to abandon the aircraft. Knight was found dead. Sale was badly injured and he died of his wounds in hospital near Frankfurt on 20 March. Carter would spend the next 14 months as a prisoner in *Stalag Luft III.* After his release he made his way from England to Paris and rekindled his romance with Janine Jouanjean who was working at her grandfather's tailor's shop in Carhaix. Her entire family had survived the war; Carter's arrival coinciding with the return of her brother and brother-in-law from concentration camps. Carter and Janine married on 11 June 1945. Just over a fortnight later she went with her husband to Buckingham palace where Carter received a bar to his DFC from King George VI. Before he left for Canada to be demobilised he took Janine to Graveley and showed her where he had written her name above his bunk.

The attack on Stuttgart detailed for the bitter cold night of 20/21 February got off to a bad start when a 49 Squadron Lancaster swung out of control on take-off from Fiskerton and crashed and caught fire. All the crew scrambled clear before the Lancaster exploded. At East Kirkby on the gentle southern edge of the Lincolnshire Wolds a 630 Squadron Lancaster III also swung out of control and careered across a road near the base before the bomb load exploded, killing six of the crew and injuring the rear-gunner. *Y-Yorker* a 427 'Lion' Squadron RCAF Halifax III, which crashed at Northallerton minutes after taking off from Leeming, burst into flames and all seven crew died in the inferno.

Over 590 bombers reached Stuttgart where the target was cloud covered and the bombing scattered. Brian Soper described the trip as 'quite a standard raid with ground markers. There were heavy fires still seen one hour after leaving the target.' Night fighter activity was reduced because the bomber stream flew a North Sea sweep to keep fighter attacks to a minimum and a diversionary feint towards Munich successfully drew the German fighters up two hours before the main force flew inland. Just nine bombers were brought down. A 156 Squadron Lancaster, which was hit by flak while at 20,000 feet on the homeward flight, exploded killing everyone on board except the pilot, Flight Lieutenant D R MacKay DFC RCAF, who was on his 33rd operation of his tour, and who was thrown clear to be taken prisoner. At Bardney there was no word from *N-Nuts* and *K-King*, both Lancasters on 9 Squadron falling prey to enemy action. All 14 crew members were killed. Among the dead was Pilot Officer William John 'Bill' Chambers the pilot of *N-Nuts*, whose crew had begun their tour on 20 October to Leipzig, and his bomb aimer Technical Sergeant John J Hannon USAAF, a New Yorker from the Bronx.[41]

Four aircraft crashed in England on their return. Lancaster *A-Apple* on 97 Squadron, which had reported a mid-air collision while leaving the target area, almost made it back to Bourn only to crash just 300 yards short of the runway. All seven crew were killed. *B-Baker*, a 115 Squadron Lancaster, crashed at Shillington near Bedford trying to make it home to Witchford in Cambridgeshire. There were no survivors. A 460 Squadron RAAF Lancaster, which encountered near blizzard conditions on return to Binbrook flew into trees near North Witham south of Grantham and exploded killing the pilot, Flying Officer Francis Allan 'Frank' Cleveland RAAF, and his six crew. A 78 Squadron Halifax crash-landed at Dunsfold, Surrey on return to Elvington.

Two further effective *Tame Boar* operations were directed against Bomber Command raids before February was out, the first on the night of the 24/25th when 209 *Tame Boar* crews destroyed all except two of the 33 Lancasters and Halifaxes of a 734-strong force that were lost raiding a ball-bearing factory at Schweinfurt. Pilot Officer Alf Hullah and the crew on *B-Baker* on 166 Squadron at Kirmington was on their way when 12 miles west of Grimsby they were involved in a collision with a Lancaster on 460 Squadron RAAF, which was on a night exercise from Binbrook. This Lancaster crashed at Willoughton Manor in Lincolnshire. *B-Baker* crashed in flames at Market Rasen with four dead in the aircraft. Two men who bailed out also died. A crash team from Binbrook went straight to the scene of the crash and found burning incendiaries scattered over a wide area with Sergeant Thomas Leo Connolly RCAF the mid-upper gunner alive but trapped in his turret. While Corporal Prize and Aircraftsman Tinsley sprayed foam on the aircraft's unexploded 4,000lb bomb, Corporal Gordon and Leading Aircraftsman Callaghan pulled the trapped gunner from the burning wreckage. In the meantime the Binbrook station MO, Flight Lieutenant Roberts, had driven an ambulance over the fields to a spot close to the wreckage and he administered first aid, but Connolly died of his injuries in hospital the following day.

Lancaster *L-London* on 12 Squadron at Wickenby was lost with all seven members of Flight Sergeant William Alfred Lampkin's crew, including 1st Lieutenant S W Penner the navigator who was from California.

Brian Soper on 626 Squadron recalled that flak and searchlights were very concentrated. He particularly remembered the loss of a crew with an Australian pilot, Flying Officer Jack Pierce Hutchinson DFC, who was very popular. 'It should have been his final trip – I suppose it was,' recalls Soper. 'He had previously arranged a big party in the mess to celebrate – he was one who 'always came back.' All the crew were killed in the aircraft, which crashed at Marsal in the Moselle.

Flight Sergeant John Clare Gilbertson-Pritchard on 1678 Conversion Flight at Waterbeach was the second pilot of a Lancaster II on 514 Squadron. Just after they bombed the target a 4lb incendiary dropped from above into the aircraft by the navigator's table and was thrown to safety by the wireless operator. It was reported later that his pilot's nerves were affected by the falling incendiary. It was also reported that there was 'slight damage to navigator's table'![42]

Gazing out the back of Lancaster *E-Easy*'s rear turret at 20,000 feet outbound to Schweinfurt, Flight Sergeant Dennis 'Jim' Chapman on 61 Squadron at Coningsby heard a noise in the back end of the aircraft that sounded like 'somebody rattling a dustbin lid'. Chapman was on his 30th and final op of his tour. The noise in the back end of the Lancaster was followed by a glow from underneath the rear end of the bomber and at this point Chapman realised that they were under attack by a night fighter. The noise was cannon fire. The mid-upper gunner had picked up their attacker as well. Within seconds Flight Lieutenant N D Webb RNZAF the pilot had ordered the crew to bail out. Chapman opened the doors of his rear turret, disentangled himself from belts of ammunition and got onto the bulkhead but the engines were still running so he got back in his turret, plugged the intercom in and called his pilot. The New Zealander thought that there was a ghost in the aircraft! 'What are you doing there?' Webb said. 'I told you to bail out!' Chapman asked him about their position relative to the Swiss border but Webb left him in no doubt that he had got to bail out. Coming along the aircraft to the exit towards him was the navigator who was in flames. Flight Sergeant C J Collingworth DFM the wireless operator was badly wounded in the neck. Both men bailed out. Before he left the Lancaster Chapman fired his guns at the attacking aircraft and it went down belching black clouds of smoke. Chapman and Webb and four other members of the crew became prisoners of war but Sergeant John William Brown, the 18-year-old flight engineer, had leaped from the aircraft without his parachute and he was killed. They were victims to that deadly tune played out in the night sky by *Schräge Musik*.

On the night of 25/26 February nearly 600 bombers carried out the first large raid on Augsburg, which was made in clear weather conditions. As part of the diversion and support operations, 131 aircraft laid mines in Kiel Bay and 22 Mosquitoes attacked enemy night fighter airfields in Holland and 15 other Mosquito aircraft carried out diversionary raids on four towns to the north of the Augsburg routes. Guided by accurate ground-marking by the Path Finders, the Main Force aircraft were able to release more than 2,000 tons of high explosive onto the beautiful and historic centre below, devastating the whole area including the Rathaus, which was completely destroyed and wiping out 3,000 dwellings and damaging a further 5,000 houses in a conflagration of fire and explosion. More than a thousand fires that were soon started quickly became uncontrollable as the temperature on this February night was minus 18°C so that the River Lech was frozen over and many of the water hoses also froze. Brian Soper wrote:

> Another 8 ½ hour trip with yellow route markers. We bombed on green and red TIs. Smoke was seen up to 12,000ft. The German propaganda ministry publicized the raid as an example of 'terror bombing. Ninety thousand people were de-housed and they left the city in droves. The flak defences were weak and various diversions and the splitting of the main bomber force into two waves helped keep bomber losses to a minimum, but 165 twin-engined *Tame Boars* claimed 19 bombers. Altogether, 23 aircraft were lost, one of the crews bailing out over Switzerland where they were interned. At least four of the losses were due to collisions.

Halifax *C-Charlie* on 432 'Leaside' Squadron at East Moor flown by 1st Lieutenant A L Lubold USAAF was attacked and set on fire by a night fighter at 22,000 feet near Ülm. Had they come down in the Augsburg area many would not have given much for their chances of survival but the American pilot and all except two of his crew survived and they were taken prisoner. On the return *C-Charlie*, a XV Squadron Lancaster at Mildenhall, crashed at Lakenheath killing four of the crew and injuring the three others. A Lancaster on 207 Squadron at Spilsby crashed killing all seven crew. Three Halifaxes and a Stirling were lost on the mine laying operations and a Stirling on 90 Squadron at Tuddenham crashed at Denham Castle, Suffolk on the return from its *Gardening* sortie. Five of the crew were killed and the two others were injured.

Main Force raids followed to Stuttgart and to aircraft factory and railway targets in France and Belgium. Trappes, one of six key rail facilities in the Paris area, was the first in the series of railway targets to be bombed, on 6/7 March, not so much because of its importance but because the 160 acre site lay 16 miles WSW of the centre of Paris in relatively open country where there was less risk of heavy French casualties. Even so the north side contained two built up areas. The northeast group of sidings contained a locomotive depot that was estimated to contain 48 electric locomotives, which operated on the electrified Paris-Le Mans section. By 19.25 hours all the bombers had left their Yorkshire bases. Five Halifaxes in 6 Group had to be left because of technical problems and there were aborts *en route*. Pilot Officer Cameron on 158 Squadron lost his escape hatch when it blew open as he was taking off from Lissett and it took the crew an hour to fix the hatch while heading for Trappes. Two other Halifaxes suffered the loss of one engine when outbound but carried on to bomb the target and return on three engines in the face of a headwind.

The Main Force finally consisted of just over 250 Halifax bombers and six Mosquitoes. 6 Group formed the first wave and attacked between zero hour and 20.51 hours; 4 Group followed between 21.11 and 21.17 hours. In all, 3,650 bombs, over 50 per cent of which were 1,000 pounders, were dropped in near perfect conditions and 288 bombs hit the target area, destroying 75 per cent of the engine sheds and 35 per cent of the small railway buildings. There were extremely heavy concentrations of craters throughout the sidings and all internal lines were blocked. At least six locomotives were destroyed.[43] Although the sky was clear over France the bombers made their return over England in drizzle and poor visibility and aircraft had to be diverted to airfields in southern England. The night following over 300 aircraft successfully attacked the railway yards at Le Mans and again no aircraft were lost.

Meanwhile, on the night of 2/3 March, 15 Lancasters of 617 Squadron using the Stabilised Automatic Bombsight (SABS) set out to bomb the GSP machine-tools factory and the adjacent BMW aero-engine repair complex on the outskirts of Albert, 15 miles northeast of Amiens. All of the crews had been trained to group eight bombs within 50 yards of the target on Wainfleet Sands, from a height of 15,000 feet and they were expected to continue practising until they could consistently group them closer to a maximum of 20 yards. The target was covered with camouflage netting on which roads and buildings had been superimposed. The weather in the target area was unfavourable, with a great deal of cloud, severe icing and static electricity. Leonard Cheshire located the factory by identifying the surrounding landmarks in the light of the flares accurately dropped by the squadron's flare force. He carried out the usual 'shallow' dive approach but his stores hung-up. Squadron Leader Les Munro then laid his incendiaries and spot fires nearly on the site and 12,000lb HCs and 1,000 pounders obliterated both factories. The GSP factory was so completely wrecked that all attempts to get it working again were abandoned. The BMW buildings were destroyed or very badly damaged. The French management had been able to delay delivery of around six months' worth of production on site and this was also destroyed.

Two nights later, the needle-bearing factory works at La Ricamerie at St-Etienne near Lyons was the target for 15 Lancasters of 617 Squadron.

It was the smallest and most difficult target yet. It was in a narrow valley with 4,000 feet hills on each side and the factory, in the middle of a built-up area, was only 40 yards by 70 yards. Met forecast good weather but unbroken cloud in the target area caused Cheshire to abort the operation. Another attempt was made on 10/11 March with 16 Lancasters, four of them acting as markers. The cloud in the valley was broken and Cheshire found, after five dicey runs, that he could see the factory only at the last moment. On his sixth run, he judged the distance, dropped the nose of his Lancaster and the incendiaries landed on the roof of the main factory building but then bounced off and ignited about 100 yards beyond. He summarised this result to the second marker who used the burning incendiaries as a datum but released his load too early so that it under-shot. The third marker's load repeated the behaviour of Cheshire's initial effort. The fourth marker came in on a much steeper dive and his markers effectively stayed in the middle of the factory buildings. Cheshire then instructed the bombing Lancasters to aim at this 'central marker'. Photo reconnaissance revealed that only the wall round the factory remained; the rest had been completely destroyed and there was no damage out-side. Another 86 Lancasters of 5 Group carried out moonlight raids on four factories in France. At Clermont-Ferrand 80 miles west of Lyons, 33 aircraft bombed the Michelin rubber works once again and 53 air-craft attacked targets at Châteauroux and Ossun. One Lancaster, which crashed in the target area killing all the crew was lost on the operation on Clermont-Ferrand.

It began snowing for days, and runways had to be cleared and ice removed from the wings of aircraft. On the bitter cold night of 13/14 March, 213 Halifaxes and nine Mosquitoes attacked the Maroc railway station and rail lines at Le Mans. Fifteen locomotives and 800 wagons were destroyed. Two nights' later the railway yards at Amiens was the objective for 140 aircraft, while an aero-engine factory at Woippy near Metz close to the Franco-German border was detailed to receive a visit from 22 Lancasters of 5 Group. They flew through 10/10ths cloud all the way and the raid was aborted by Leonard Cheshire when he found total cloud cover over the target just before the bombing force reached the area. It was so cold that one crewmember's helmet stuck to his face and later, when he took it off, a couple of square inches of skin came away with the studs.

On the way home the 'Monica' tail-mounted warning device in the Lancaster flown by Flying Officer Warren Duffy RCAF picked up a contact to port at a range of about 3,600 feet. At 2,700 feet range Sergeant Tom McLean the 'hard-boiled' Scottish rear-gunner could see that there were two Ju 88s flying in close proximity to one another. Past experience – on a previous tour of operations he had claimed five German fighters – convinced him that 45 per cent tracer and 55 per cent armour piercing rather than the regulation ball, tracer, incendiary and AP ammunition was the most effective combination, especially if an attacker could be brought to close range. He had kept this information about the ammunition from the rest of the crew. Even the nose gunner and 'Red' Evans the Canadian mid upper gunner who both used regulation loadings, were unaware of it. On intercom McLean told Duffy, 'Prepare to corkscrew port!' Then a FW 190 *Zahme Sau* (*Tame Boar*) free-lance night fighter was sighted, flying abreast of the Lancaster at about 1,500 feet with its navigation lights on, probably trying to distract the air gunners from the fighters astern. As one of the Ju 88s closed, McLean gave the order 'Go!' and Duffy carried out a violent corkscrew just as the fighter opened fire. The first burst sent a bullet through McLean's hand. Duffy put the Lancaster into another violent corkscrew as a second attack came in but McLean still managed to hit the enemy fighter's port engine before calling 'Drop' over the intercom. Immediately the flight engineer throttled back all four Merlins and the Lancaster rapidly lost speed forcing the attacker to overshoot. McLean fired again and the flight engineer opened up the throttles again. The night fighter fell away in flames.

On intercom McLean said 'Easy' and Duffy ceased corkscrewing. But now the second night fighter carried out a curving attack from slightly below. Duffy performed yet another corkscrew as McLean and Evans opened fire and their attacker plunged into the void trailing fire and flames. Another twin-engined night fighter now approached from astern, moving from port to starboard. At this point Duffy spotted some cloud ahead and below and in a shallow dive steered the aircraft towards it but the night fighter came in and he was forced into yet another corkscrew, this time to starboard. Duffy must have wondered how the Lancaster could take such repeated punishment. At once McLean and the flight engineer went into their very well-rehearsed manoeuvre and the gunners opened up at close range knocking pieces off and causing the night fighter to nose up with its port wing and starboard engine on fire before it entered a flat spin until a red glow illuminated the cloud below. At this point the FW 190 decided to turn off its lights and attack from abeam of the Lancaster, which prevented McLean from firing but Red Evans returned fire and the fighter sped away into the night.

Flight Lieutenant Warren Alvin Duffy was killed later that summer, flying a Mosquito, which crashed at Wainfleet Sands in Lincolnshire during a practice on 7 August. His navigator Flying Officer Philip Ingleby also died.

On the night of 15/16 March the main operation was on Stuttgart. In an attempt to avoid contact with night fighters the 863 bombers that were dispatched split into two parts, flying a roundabout route over France nearly as far as the Swiss frontier before turning north-east to approach Stuttgart.[44] This deception worked until just before the force reached the target when 93 1 JD crews were fed into the bomber stream.

Fifty kilometres southwest of Strasbourg *Oberleutnant* Heinz Rökker, *Staffelkapitän*, I./NJG2 peered out of the cockpit windscreen of his heavily armed Ju 88R-2 night fighter,[45] scanning the sky for the sight of a *Viermot*, or four-engined heavy bomber. Rökker listened impatiently but attentively to the long litany of instructions from his *Bordfunker* crouched in the cockpit of their Junkers as they continued their night chase across the countryside to their designated *Himmelbett Räume* or 'four poster bed box' near Aschaffenburg. The clock was approaching 22.30 hours. Rökker, who had served in I./NJG2 for almost two years, had recently reached double figures in the victory tables and he was hungry for more. He had scored his first *Abschuss* in June 1942 in the Mediterranean when he had destroyed a Bristol Beaufort in daylight over the sea. This keen exponent of *Fernnachtjagd* intruder operations destroyed his first *Viermot* on 23/24 August 1943 when he shot down a Lancaster 20 kilometres southwest of Berlin for his seventh victory. Now he had another *Viermot* in his sights.

Rökker scurried into action, his *Funker* making sure that the *FuG 217 Neptun R* tail warning radar was clear. The last thing they wanted was a dreaded *Moskito* on their tail. Telefunken *FuG 350 Naxos Z* passive radar equipment, which some of the Ju 88R-1s and 2s carried and which homed onto *H2S* equipment, and Siemens *FuG 227 Flensburg* which homed onto the 'Monica' tail-warning device, might have identified Rökker's victim. Or the plot could have come from the *Jägerleitoffizier* in his 'Battle Opera House' who would announce '*Kuriere* in sight'. Suddenly, in the earphones of Rökker's *Bordfunker* was sounded the *Jägerleitoffizier*'s (*JLO*) announcement: 'Have *Kurier* for you, *Kirchturm* 8 (8,000 metres), course 300°, *Kurier* flying from East to West.'

Rökker and his two crew reacted with excitement and enthusiasm. According to the information from the *Jägerleitoffizier* they were only a few kilometres behind a *Dicke Auto* ('Fat Car'), which had been picked up on *Würzburg* ground radar, fixed on the plotting table and transmitted to the *Oberleutnant* and his crew stalking the bomber. It was a Lancaster. Rökker's *Bordfunker* picked up contact on his *Lichtenstein* radar set and he transmitted *Emil-Emil* to alert his *JLO*. The *Oberleutnant* throttled back the two 1,700hp BMW 801D engines, approached stealthily from below and behind and then he opened fire. His guns recoiled. The Lancaster never stood a chance. *Horrido!* ('Tallyho') exclaimed Rökker over R/T to ground control to announce his first success of the night. Five minutes later the *Jägerleitoffizier* alerted Rökker's *Bordfunker* that he had another *Kuriere* west of Hagenau. It was another Lancaster.

Pauke! Pauke! ('Kettledrums! Kettledrums!') Rökker announced. He was going into the attack.

'1,000 metres, 800 metres, 500, 400, 300 metres!' Power off and minimum speed in order not to overtake him, Rökker once again attacked *von hinten unten*. Small, bluish exhaust flames made it easier to keep the target in sight. Four engines, twin tail, were recorded almost subconsciously. No sudden movement that might attract the tail gunner's attention. Calm now! Guns armed? Night sight switched on? Rökker could see that it was a Lancaster. He applied a little more power to the two BMW engines, approached cautiously and in the classic *von hinten unten* tactic, blew the bomber to pieces at about 100 metres' range.

Cries of *Horrido!* filled the airwaves once again.

Rökker had not yet finished his night's sortie. Thirty-five to 40 kilometres west of Stuttgart he obtained visual contact of what he thought was a Halifax but it was a Lancaster, a 9 Squadron aircraft piloted by Squadron Leader R Backwell-Smith. Rökker's *Bordfunker* immediately transmitted *Ich beruhe*. Then they closed in rapidly from behind and below for the kill. The equipment was checked and the machine guns and MG-151 2cm cannon were loaded and cocked. At the *Funker's* feet were ammunition drums with 75 rounds each for the pair of deadly cannon but Rökker again decided to use his front guns and approach *von hinten unten* once more. If he had been out of ammunition, he would have given his *Bordschütze* free range with his two MG-151 cannon. Changing ammunition drums in a twisting and turning night fighter would have made his task almost impossible but not if he pulled alongside to allow the *Bordschütze* to blaze away.

'250, 200, 150 metres'. A slipstream shook the Junkers. They were close! At 100 metres Rökker pressed the gun button on the stick and the cannons rattled. He saw hits but the Lancaster did not catch fire. Backwell-Smith pushed the bomber into a nose-dive and then climbed before turning sharply to port losing height, as RAF pilots were trained to do in the aptly named corkscrew, a successful defensive tactic. In pursuit of him Rökker attacked the fuselage and hit the aircraft again but he could not see any flames. Flight Sergeant Eric Birrell the Australian rear gunner did not shoot back, so either he had been killed in the first attack or he or his hydraulics had been disabled and he could no longer turn the heavy guns. The mid-upper gunner gave defensive fire but it went wide. The WOp and the gunners were dead. Finally, Rökker lost sight of the enemy. It was the only time he failed to see his attack through to the end and confirm its success visually; therefore the kill was only provisionally awarded. The bomber had gone down though, and the navigator and bomb aimer did not survive their parachute jumps. Backwell-Smith and Sergeant N V Sirman the engineer landed safely and were taken prisoner.

First *Jagdkorps* returned with claims for 30 kills for the loss of nine aircraft and crews. Bomber Command lost 37 aircraft and six more were written off in crashes and collisions. An hour before reaching Stuttgart Lancaster *F-Freddie* on 57 Squadron at East Kirkby was attacked by *Leutnant* Herbert Koch of 11./NJG3. He set all four engines on fire and Pilot Officer Sam Atcheson DFC ordered all his crew to bail out once they had crossed into Switzerland but only one of the gunners made it before the Lancaster crashed at Saignelegier. *E-Easy* was one of two Lancaster IIs on 408 'Goose' Squadron RCAF that were shot down with no survivors. Flying Officer Alexander Colville RCAF, 27, from Bowmanville, Ontario and his crew had taken off from Linton-on-Ouse at 19.03 hours and were lost without trace. Sergeant Michael Yorke Zisslin Kalms RAFVR, who was 19, had been in Leytonstone. The family, who were of the Jewish faith, later moved to Edgware in Middlesex after the family home was destroyed by enemy bombing. After leaving school Michael had become an engineering apprentice at de Havillands. A motorcycle enthusiast and keen boxer, he joined the RAF on 8 October 1941 aged 17 and became the flight engineer on the crew. Flying Officer Moody Siddons the bomb aimer was the oldest at 30 and was from Langford, British Columbia. Warrant Officer Arthur Hodson RCAF the WOp/AG was the same age as his pilot and was from New Westminster, BC. Sergeant Dennis Davies RAFVR the rear gunner was 21 and from Rhondda, Glamorgan.[46]

Homebound and flying at 20,000 feet south-west of Strasbourg Halifax *D-Dog* on 466 Squadron at Leconfield was attacked by *Hauptmann* Heinz Reschke St.III/NJG6 who set a fuel tank and some oxygen supply bottles on fire. Pilot Officer H C Wills RAAF held the blazing Halifax steady while his crew bailed out and by the time he made his own exit, the flames had burnt him about the face and hands. Upon being captured he was taken to hospital in Strasbourg for treatment. A second 466 Squadron Halifax III flown by Flight Sergeant John Cecil Bond RAAF was badly shot about by a night fighter and the Australian finally ditched 30 miles from Portland Bill. Pilot Officer Oswald Kenneth Chrimes died in the aircraft.[47]

X-X-Ray, a 578 Squadron Halifax III at Burn ran short of fuel on the return to the airfield bounded by the Selby canal to the north and to the east by the LNER Doncaster to Selby railway line. Soon after crossing the Kent coast the engines began to misfire. The pilot gave the order to bail out but only four complied before the bomber crashed east of Biggin Hill, killing the three remaining crew. *C-Charlie* crashed into brickworks at Selby. Five of the crew were killed and two were injured in the crash. *S-Sugar*, which was shot down by *Leutnant* Helmut Bunje and his *Funker Unteroffizier* Alfred Weimann of 4./NJG6 flying a Bf 110G-4 took the squadron's losses on the night to three. The *Abschuss* was the first of Bunje's twelve wartime victories. Flight Sergeant John Douglas Lyon and three of the crew were killed. Sergeant D J Salt was gravely wounded and would most likely have died but for three young German girls who found him lying in deep snow and insisted that he was given first aid. Salt was later repatriated aboard the *Arundel Castle*, reaching Liverpool on 6 February 1945.[48]

While returning to Waddington Lancaster *E-Easy* on 463 Squadron RAAF was involved in a mid-air collision with a 625 Squadron Lancaster at Kelstern, both aircraft falling near Branston, four miles SE of Lincoln. All fourteen men were killed. This also took 625 Squadron's losses on the night to three. *Q-Queenie* on 425 'Alouette' Squadron RCAF, out of petrol, was abandoned on the return to Tholthorpe and it crashed into houses on Adelaide Street, Brierley Hill on the northern side of Halesowen in the eastern suburbs of Birmingham. Remarkably, none of the crew was injured but three houses were demolished and three others were badly damaged and one person on the ground was killed and another injured. The 420 'Snowy Owl' Squadron RCAF Halifax III flown by Sergeant W D McAdam RCAF was hit by flak, which killed Sergeant William Edmund Briggs the navigator and wounded the pilot in both legs. The starboard inner was wrecked and height was lost. Despite much pain from his injuries McAdam decided to continue the sortie. On the return flight, by which time the Halifax was down to less than 5,000 feet, the aircraft was hit by flak again but assisted by Sergeant N E Ranson, who assumed the duties of navigator, the south coast was regained and McAdam landed at Friston airfield, Sussex at 03.10 hours. Only then did he reveal to his crew that he had been wounded. [49]

On the night of 16/17 March 130 aircraft – mostly Halifaxes – successfully bombed Amiens. Fifteen Lancasters on 617 Squadron and six *H2S*-equipped Lancasters of 106, there to drop parachute flares, carried out a precision attack on the Michelin tyre factory at Clermont-Ferrand. Though partly sabotaged and recently bombed it was still making the Germans 24,000 tyres a month. The briefing orders were to destroy three of the four large factory buildings but to leave the workers' canteen intact. The aiming-point was first accurately marked with red spot fires. These were then overlaid with green target-indicators to emphasise the aiming-point. Six of the 617 aircraft carried 12,000lb 'blockbusters' and each and every one was a direct hit on the workshops, which ceased production. All the aircraft from both raids returned safely. Daylight reconnaissance by a Mosquito revealed that the workers' canteen just beside the workshops was undamaged. That night 19 Lancasters of 5 Group, including 13 on 617 Squadron carried out an accurate raid on a former French state gunpowder factory on the banks of the River Dordogne at Bergerac 50 miles east of Bordeaux. The target was marked from 5,000 feet and the aircraft then bombed from 18,000 feet. For fifteen seconds it looked as though the sun was coming up underneath as just one great orange flash lit up the sky for miles. No bombs fell outside the works and all aircraft returned without loss. At another explosives factory at Angouleme in a bend of the Charente, 75 miles north-northeast of Bordeaux on the night of 20/21 March twenty Lancasters of 5 Group, including 14 on 617 Squadron, successfully bombed the *Pouderie Nationale* after Cheshire put his spot fires in the centre. Again there was no damage outside.

The Main Force was rested on 17 March and a night in Grimsby at the St. Patrick's Day dance at the Town Hall was an opportunity not to be missed. At Binbrook on the windswept Lincolnshire Wolds (which to the Aussies on 460 Squadron RAAF were not really hills but 'rises') had become a familiar sight in Grimsby and Chambers' restaurant on their days off. They were by and large a happy go lucky lot whose sense of enjoyment belied the fact that 460 had suffered the highest percentage loss in all Bomber Command Wellington squadrons and would fly the most Lancaster sorties in 1 Group and in Bomber Command, suffering the most Lancaster losses in the Group. Many men did complete their tour and it meant another party in the backroom at the 'Marquis of Granby' in Binbrook village where Rene Trevor sang for the boys and played the piano. The tradition was that each man who completed their tour was held aloft while he wrote his name on the ceiling of the backroom. Rene had been left to run the 'Granby' with the help of a staff of seven ever since her husband had been called up for the RAF and sent to the Middle East in 1940. She sewed on buttons and decorations, mended jackets and cooked meals for the young men. Sausage, two eggs and toast cost 1s 6d, or at the weekends a full Sunday roast could be had for 2s 3p. Anne, the landlady's young daughter proved to be very popular with the Aussies and they would often ask her to sing to them. When she was three she had run through from the bar screaming 'Mummy, mummy the Germans have arrived!' The little girl had never heard an Australian accent before. Her pet donkey was tethered at the back of the pub and one night some of the boys got a bit tight and they took the donkey back with them to the Sergeant's Mess and painted the animal air force blue. They brought it back next day. Quite apologetic they were too!

The bus queues to Grimsby were always an indication of whether the squadron was on ops. A lot of men in the queue for Grimsby meant a quiet night at the 'Granby'. An empty queue meant another raid on Germany. At the St. Patrick's Day dance Pilot Officer Reg Mullins RAAF set eyes on Pat Gowan, an officer with His Majesty's Customs and Excise who lived with her parents in Laceby Road. The romance between the Lancaster pilot and the young girl from Grimsby would prove a testing time, for losses among bomber crews were mounting, none more so than at Binbrook where 460 would carry out the most bombing raids, fly the most sorties and suffer the most losses in Australian squadrons in Bomber Command.[50]

At 19.34 hours on the night of 18/19 March Reg Mullins took his Lancaster off from Binbrook for the raid on Frankfurt. He was part of a force of 846 aircraft of the Main Force; 620 of them Lancasters. Part of the *Nachtjagd* force was sent north when the JLOs were deceived by the appearance on radar of 98 aircraft, which were going to lay mines in the Heligoland area but another force of night fighters in Germany met the Main Force stream just before Frankfurt was reached. The Path Finders marked the target accurately and this led to heavy bombing of eastern, central and western districts of Frankfurt. Mullins bombed the city at 22.09 hours from 21,000 feet, the target being identified by TI reds and red/yellow flares covering an area two miles square. The later phases of the bombing were scattered but extensive destruction was caused in Frankfurt. On his return Mullins said 'Promising attack, good route.' Twenty aircraft – twelve Halifaxes and eight Lancasters – were lost and two Lancasters crashed on return.

When on 22/23 March, 816 bombers revisited Frankfurt, Reg Mullins and his crew were 'on' the battle Order. So too was Wing Commander Vashon James 'Pop' Wheeler DFC* MC* who had flown on every operation 207 Squadron at Spilsby had undertaken since he had taken command from Wing Commander P N Jennings on 26 February. Wheeler was born in 1898, had seen active service as a second lieutenant in the Rifle Brigade between 1916 and 1918 and in 1919 was part of the ill-fated British Expedition to Russia in support of Czarist forces opposing the communist revolution, for which he received the Order of St. Stanislaus. Learning to fly during the 1920s and duly becoming an airline pilot, at outbreak of war he completed a tour on Ansons and flew a further 71 combat sorties on Hurricanes, Havocs and Beaufighters on 85 Squadron and claimed two enemy aircraft destroyed in early 1941. 'Pop' completed a further 29 defensive patrols on 157 Squadron (which he commanded 29 December 1942–August 1943) before flying the unit's first *Intruder* operation on 23 March 1943. Now, a year later, the 46-year-old was at the controls of Lancaster *A-Apple* for what was his 158th operational flight.

The bombers took an indirect route to the city, crossing the Dutch coast north of the Zuider Zee and then flying almost due south to Frankfurt. This and a mine-laying diversion operation by 128 Stirlings in Kiel Bay and 18 more off Denmark confused the enemy defences for a time and *JLO*'s believed that the main target would be Hannover. Brian Soper seemed to remember there always being a heavy concentration of search-lights at Frankfurt and this was no exception: 'With the master beam scanning the sky, it was blinding if we caught the beam and being radar controlled, once caught, all the other beams would form one large cone and many manoeuvres would have to be adopted to escape. Meanwhile all the flak would be concentrated upon the victim. Fortunately we never got fully trapped.'

The marking and bombing were accurate and damage to Frankfurt was even more severe than a few nights previously. Almost 1,400 people perished in these two raids and 175,000 inhabitants were bombed out.[51] The city diarist described these night raids and a daylight attack by the American 8th Air Force 36 hours later, as the 'worst and most fateful blow of the war' and one 'which simply ended the existence of the Frankfurt, which had been built up since the Middle Ages.'[52]

Relief trains arrived after the raids bringing kettles of noodle soup with meat, bread and butter and sausages. Perhaps it was coincidence but Frankfurt is the birthplace of Johann Wolfgang von Goethe and this raid marked the anniversary of the death of the poet, novelist and dramatist, whose greatest masterpiece was Faust, a magician and alchemist who sells his soul to the devil in exchange for knowledge and power.

Oberleutnant Heinz Rökker was one of only a few fighter pilots who, almost magically, found the bomber stream. This was due mainly to the strange alchemy of his radar equipment and knowledge gained from more than two years of combat. Again flying a powerful Ju 88R-2, the *Experten* took off from Langensalza at 20.10 hours and he picked out his first victim of the night at 21.30 hours south-east of Emmen, Holland. It was Lancaster JI-B on 514 Squadron flown by Flight Sergeant John Bernard Underwood. Using his frontal armament and attacking *von hinten unten*, Rökker dispatched the unfortunate Lancaster, which went down with Underwood and four of his crew lying dead in the aircraft.[53] An hour later, at 22.27 hours twixt Koblenz and Limburg the *Oberleutnant's* second Lancaster *Abschuss* followed. Finally, at 22.35 hours he claimed a Halifax at Herborn near Koblenz. It was *R-Robert*[54] flown by Pilot Officer Dickie Atkins on 578 Squadron at Burn (which was 'cold, wet and full of mud'). It was the final trip of their first tour. No other crew on the squadron had finished their tour, owing to the heavy losses sustained in the Battle of Berlin. Group Captain Nigel Marwood-Elton DFC, Burn's Station Commander, flew as Atkins' second dickey and Flight Sergeant Eric Sanderson manned the four Brownings in the rear turret. Sanderson recalls:

> We had an early evening take-off. The last turning point was Hannover at about 22.00 hours and we were on the run down to Frankfurt. Night fighters were active and combats were to be seen. A little after 22.00 we were at about 20,000 feet when I saw a Ju 88 slide underneath my turret. My evasive action was always a steep diving turn to port. We lost about 3,000 feet, got back on course and I expected to have lost the Ju 88 but he was still there underneath us! We tried a corkscrew. The Ju 88 followed us through the lot and we did another diving turn. I was worried for this one was special and now I made my error for which he had been waiting! I told my pilot to bank the aircraft so that the mid-upper might shoot downwards. The fighter was still below whilst our Halifax hung there with the pilot fighting to get control of the fully loaded bomber. That was when the Ju 88 hit us in the bomb bay and in the petrol tanks on the starboard wing. Dickie Atkins ordered, 'Parachute, Parachute, Jump, Jump!' I opened the turret doors and pulled my chute in. My helmet, mike and oxygen were off. Now which side? Port or starboard? Most of the fire was on the starboard side and did my WOp/AG have his trailing aerial out? (Not the best thing to meet bailing out of the port side of a rear gun turret). So starboard side, a fast-roll through the flames and away! But No! My feet were caught in the turret and I

was hanging half in and half out. I tried to get back in the turret to free my legs and try again but after several attempts I gave up. I now thought of pulling the ripcord but the thought of being pulled out of my legs delayed my decision. However, life with or without legs was sweet and preferable so I pulled the string. I shot out of the turret like a cork out of a bottle. I must have been only about 500 feet from the ground. The next thing my chute was fully open and I was swinging on the end of it. Looking down I saw that I was about to enter trees below. I was knocked out and must have been out for some time because when I started getting out of my parachute, Mae West and flying gear and checking if I still had my legs, I saw the burning aircraft only a few hundred yards away. Men were shouting to each other around the fire. I was unable to walk and my hands and face were burnt so evasion was out of the question and I called to them.[55]

Heinz Rökker landed safely back at Langendiebach at 2330 hours.[56]

Twenty-five Lancasters and seven Halifaxes were lost. 'Pop' Wheeler died at the controls of *A-Apple*. Three other men on the crew were killed, three surviving to be taken prisoner. A Lancaster which crashed in Suffolk on return resulted in the deaths of five of the crew.

Fifty miles north of Frankfurt the Lancaster flown by Pilot Officer Reg Mullins was attacked by a night fighter that raked the aircraft with cannon shells, and the fuselage was holed in a number of places. A shell burst against the bomb doors and for the moment the crew thought that the bombs in the bay would explode. The rear gunner was wounded and lost consciousness when the turret was shot to pieces. The main compass was destroyed, the rudder controls were severed and a small fire had started. Mullins dived the Lancaster and managed to lose the night fighter and he tried to call up the crew but the intercom system was virtually out of action. There was no reply from the two gunners but he could just make himself heard by the others. Sergeant D H Cochrane the wireless operator went back to see what had happened to Sergeant H J Somers, the Canadian mid-upper gunner. Cochrane found Somers half out of his turret and in a stupor. His oxygen supply had been shot away. Cochrane gave him his own emergency oxygen bottle and then went back for another. In the fuselage he found a small fire, which he put out with his hands. Then he found that E Parry the rear gunner, too, was unconscious. When he returned to the mid-upper turret, Somers and his parachute were missing. The crew's theory, discussed later, was that Somers recovered consciousness after being given the emergency oxygen supply and then, getting no answer on the intercom and seeing a large hole in the fuselage, must have believed that he was the only man left in the aircraft and bailed out, still half stupefied.[57]

Cochrane reported to his captain and Mullins, though he knew that his Lancaster was defenceless now if another fighter attacked, decided to go on to the target. They reached Frankfurt, dropped their bombs and turned for home, Mullins controlling the aircraft with the ailerons only. The Path Finders marked the target accurately and this led to heavy bombing but the later phases of the bombing were scattered. Over 5,400 houses were destroyed or seriously damaged and 55,000 people were bombed out. Mullins sent E Wilson the bomb aimer back to the mid-upper turret. Later Cochrane found him, too, fainting from lack of oxygen, took him back and gave him a fresh supply. He found the elevator trims had gone and that the Lancaster was tending to climb all the time. He was fast tiring with his long struggle to keep the bomber on its course. Cochrane joined him and the two used their combined strength to hold the controls as the Lancaster limped home. It became more and more difficult to handle and by the time they reached the coast, W Hendry the flight engineer also had to lend his strength to cope with the controls. Between the three of them they got the bomber down at last to a safe landing.

Though cloud made interceptions difficult for the night fighters, 22 Halifaxes and Lancasters were lost. Mullins was awarded an immediate DFC for his exploit. He added a Bar later in the war. Cochrane was awarded the DFM. Reg Mullins was posted back to Australia but promised to come back for Pat and he did. The couple married at St. James Church, Grimsby in 1946.

On 23/24 March, 143 aircraft took off for an attack on the railway yards at Laon. The weather in the target area was clear but the Master Bomber ordered the attack to be stopped after 72 aircraft had bombed. Two Halifaxes were lost. Twenty Lancasters of 5 Group, including 617 Squadron dropped delayed action bombs on the Sigma aero-engine factory at Vénissieux in the Rhône Valley south of Lyons and 70 miles south-west of Geneva without loss but flare marking in hazy conditions was imperfect and the Dam Busters were ordered to return to the factory two nights' later. Marking was much improved but the raid by 22 Lancasters was largely unsuccessful with bombs being scattered. After an intensive practice bombing programme was carried out, 19 Lancasters including 15 of 617 Squadron, returned to finish the job on 29/30 March. This time the bombing was concentrated around very accurate markers but a noticeable increase in defences was reported by the returning crews. On 5 April, 17 Lancasters and one Mosquito of 617 piloted by Cheshire led 132 Lancasters from the other 5 Group squadrons in the first group operation independent of PFF marking against an aircraft factory and repair facility at Toulouse in southern France, 60 miles north of the Spanish border. The target was well prepared and marked for the incoming Lancasters to carry out concentrated bombing and the target was obliterated. Only an occasional crater dotted the fields beyond.

Five nights later, 17 Lancasters and one Mosquito of 617, once again operating alone, devastated the main German Signals equipment depot at St-Cyr in the Paris region, two miles west of Versailles, after Cheshire let his markers go from 700 feet having diving down from 5,000.

Between 8 February and 10 April 1944 the dozen French targets allocated to Bomber Command had been destroyed or very seriously damaged. Nine of these targets had been wiped out on independent 617 Squadron operations. Early in April, intrigued by the accuracy that 617 Squadron had achieved at night against such small targets the Dam Busters were visited by Lieutenant General Carl 'Tooey' Spaatz, C-in-C of the United States' Expeditionary Air Forces, and General James Doolittle of Tokyo bombing fame. The American generals were anxious to discover the secret of 617's success. Cheshire told them that an unexpected problem had arisen – too many bombs were falling in the same crater! Inevitably, a challenge ensued between SABS and the famed Norden bombsight but the contest never took place because of the increase in operations.[58]

'Bomber' Harris meanwhile, had realized that blind marking was unlikely to prove successful against German cities, principally Berlin and so he had waited patiently for clear conditions over the 'Big City'. At 'morning prayers' on Tuesday 21 March the weather forecaster informed his Chief that conditions appeared favourable, so Harris ordered another maximum effort on Berlin.

In his message read out to crews Harris said:

Although successful blind bombing attacks on Berlin have destroyed large areas of it, there is still a substantial section of this vital city more or less intact. To write this off, it is of great importance that tonight's attack should be closely concentrated on the Aiming Point. You must not think that the size of Berlin makes accurate bombing unimportant. There is no point in dropping bombs on the devastated areas in the west and south-west. Weather over the target should be good. Go and do the job.

But a later forecast revealed that cloud would probably cover the German capital and the attack was cancelled at 18.00 hours. Harris had to wait another three days, until Friday the 24th when the pre-raid weather report said that there was a good chance of clear skies at Berlin, but had added that there was a possibility of 10/10th thick stratocumulus. This time 811 aircraft were detailed for the raid and immediately support operations were laid on. Over 140 OTU aircraft were detailed to fly a diversionary 'sweep' west of Paris, 19 *Oboe* Mosquitoes would attack night fighter airfields in Belgium, Holland and France and 11 Mosquitoes would make a 'spoof' raid on Kiel. There were still doubts about the weather and an alternative target, Brunswick, more likely to be clear of cloud, was included in the Battle Order, but just before take-off Berlin was confirmed as the 'target for tonight'.

'Rex' Jackson's crew on 166 Squadron had by now completed seven ops. Roy Keen the flight engineer recalls:

When we had joined the squadron, we took over aircraft that were normally flown by crews who were on leave at the time. We could normally get up to about 26,000 feet, the higher the better as far as we were concerned, but on the night of 24 March ND620 was brand new, on its first trip. Before we took off, I'll never forget that the wireless operator said: 'We're going to get the chop tonight.' The skipper immediately pounced on him.

Take off at several 5 Group stations was delayed for two hours because of fog. A 20 mph wind was expected but soon the 70-mile long bomber stream ran into very strong winds, which scattered the aircraft and made navigation tricky. Over the Baltic the jet stream was so strong that aircraft were registering ground speeds approaching 360 mph. When crews made landfall on the Danish coast many navigators realised that they were much further south than they should have been, as Roy Keen recalls:

One hundred knot winds were experienced that night, instead of the anticipated 60-knot tailwind. And we could not climb above 21,000 feet. I tried all ways to get more height, but we couldn't. The bomb load was normal at about 12,000lbs. The skipper tried trimming the plane, but nothing would work. It's like a car; you sometimes get one that won't do what it's supposed to. We got coned by search-lights on the way in over the coast and we had to jink about like hell to get out of it. George Reed our spot-on navigator was going barmy!

The bombers on the diversionary raid west of Paris had already turned for home and when the Main Force crossed the German coast east of Rostock and bypassed Stettin the *JLO* became convinced that the target was Berlin. The attack was very scattered at first and some of the TIs were seen burning about 10 miles south-west of the target. The raid developed into a 'terrific overshoot' because of the strong winds but equally, many crews who overshot turned back to bomb.

For the first time since the raid on 23/24 August 1943, a master bomber, Wing Commander Reggie 'Sunshine' Lane DSO DFC, the cheerful CO of 405 'Vancouver' Squadron who was on his third tour, was used. Wing Commander Maurice A Smith DFC, one of the finest low-level

Master Bombers, Controllers, Masters of Ceremony, call them what you will, recalls:

> Master Bombers had enough experience to know what they were about; speaking voices that came over on VHF clearly and maybe a little more maturity at around 30 years of age than the majority of bomber crews in their early 20s. Presumably they had been noticed in their squadrons and seen to lead reliable crews. These they very reluctantly had to leave behind, except for the navigator, when the smaller and more agile Mosquitoes came into use.

Wing Commander Lane's radio call sign was 'Redskin'. His deputy was Wing Commander E W 'Bill' Anderson, an experienced PFF navigator now on the staff of 8 Group Path Finder Headquarters and who was lying on some cushions in the nose of a Mosquito of the Meteorological Flight. His call sign was 'Pommy'. The two 'cheer leaders' were to liven up the proceedings with their 'back-chat'. Wing Commander Lane was heard in spite of jamming but the Bomber Command intelligence narrative said afterwards that 'the Master of Ceremonies' was generally more helpful in giving encouragement that in directing the bombing'. Although unable to give little positive direction to the crews he nevertheless gave much general encouragement in a distinctively Canadian and often excitable series of remarks such as, 'Those bastards wanted a war; now show them what war is like.' Other men remember the calm and cultivated English voice of the Deputy Master Bomber occasionally contributing a remark.[59]

Bill Anderson has written:

> The ground below was covered in thin cloud, which was dis-appointing but would not affect the attack as we had the usual sky-marking method laid on to deal with this eventuality. As we came near to where we thought the big city must lie, we saw the curtain raiser, a dummy attack to mislead the fighters, starting away behind us over Kiel, a beautiful display of pyrotechnics. There was a good deal of flak and searchlights to the south but we felt sure it could not be Berlin. A few minutes later the first sky-marking flares went down to the north but though we opened all the taps, we were late. This was most infuriating because all my best lines depended on our being over the target itself. 'Come along in, boys, it's warmer in here than out there!' can't be said with much conviction from a place twenty miles outside the danger area. Luckily, 'Sunshine' was dead on time. The attack was in full swing when we arrived and through the thin wisps of low cloud we could see red and green ground markers which the boys had dropped as well as the sky-marker flares. The defences were firing away busily but the searchlights were not working so well together as usual. The cones were not so

clear-cut and odd beams were straying about. I think the cloud was foxing them a little. And I saw something new, peculiar rows of lights that floated slowly upwards. I didn't realize what they were until I went to a cinema some weeks later and saw London's rocket defences in action.

Everybody has watched a man painting a fence. There is always an irritating little bit that he will keep missing, so that you long to grab the brush and just give one dab to cover it. There was a patch right in the centre of Berlin where nothing had fallen. I wanted to stretch out my hand and smear some of the other lights over it. Luckily for my peace of mind, some obliging type, possibly a painter by trade himself, did the job just before the end with a nice dollop of incendiaries.

We felt so bad about turning up late that we hung about for a while after the attack should have been over. Having exhausted all the stock of expressions including the odd quotation from Shakespeare and having decided that the bombing had now finished completely and that there was no great future in staying any longer, I produced the carefully worded and highly indelicate 'good night' to Hitler. Hardly had the last rich syllable rolled unctuously off my tongue when a voice came back out of the darkness; a rich Canadian voice, 'Cut the cackle and drop us off another flare, I can't see a —— thing.' So we stayed and talked with him a little to mollify him and then pushed off home.

On the way back we were coned by searchlights for some time. And lying in the nose of the aircraft, I had leisure to analyse my exact feelings. I was scared; there was no doubt about that. Yet I knew that this was like my lumbago, an uncomfortable sensation but somehow beside the point. What really did matter was that I had let the party down by arriving late. That it had not affected the operation was beside the point. I had broken the first rule of the Pathfinder Force that I had so often drummed into others, which is not that you must be clever, nor that you must be brave but simply that you must be reliable. On the way home I saw six aircraft shot down by night fighters. They each started as a little flame getting gradually bigger and then suddenly falling, an explosion of light as they hit the deck and then a patch of fire burning quite steadily.[60]

The bomber stream was spread out over 50 miles of sky and stretched back for another 150 miles. Single engined *Wilde Sau* and twin-engined *Zahme Sau* fighters took advantage and they and the flak claimed 44 Lancasters and 28 Halifaxes. On 578 Squadron at Burn where 15 aircraft were away by 19.08 hours for a target time of 22.30 hours, three Halifaxes made early returns and three were shot down. On *H-Harry* only the bomb aimer and wireless operator survived. On *C-Charlie* only the navigator and one air gunner survived. There were no survivors on *Y-Yorker*. *X-X-Ray* had quite an exciting night even though the aircraft did not reach Berlin as the flight engineer recalled:

Our aircraft was fitted as an experiment with a wing bomb bay overload petrol tanks instead of the usual overload tanks for long haul sorties, which were normally fitted to the main bomb bays. Our route to target was across the North Sea to Denmark across the peninsula and a long flight over the Baltic Sea until we were to turn to starboard for our run to the city of Berlin. After we had crossed the peninsula, I requested the captain's permission to commence pumping the petrol from the overload tanks (we were unable to feed this fuel direct to the motors) into the two main petrol tanks. After a short period it was apparent that although the overload tank petrol gauges were slowly dropping, the main tank gauges were not showing an increase in their holding of petrol. This situation was reported to the captain and after a discussion on possible reasons for this problem we could only assume that the fuel was being pumped out into the atmosphere. It was decided that the pumping should proceed. Once the pumping was completed, the captain requested a situation report from the navigator and me as to the possible flight duration with the fuel available. We came up with the report that we would only make the Low Countries on our return trip. The decision was made to abort the operation and we turned for home. The next decision was the disposal of our bomb load. After a crew discussion we decided to attack Kiel on the way home. We ran off to the correct heading and attacked the city from about 20,000 feet as the flak was so intense. We dived to 2,000 feet and made for home across the North Sea. It appeared after investigation that two valves in the new lines to the wing bomb bay overload tanks had been fitted incorrectly. Unfortunately the Air Ministry would not allow us to count our attack on Kiel towards our number of operations required before a rest period was granted.

Four of the Lancasters that were lost were on 166 Squadron. Roy Keen recalls:

Because the winds were stronger we were over the target twenty minutes early and we were too long over the target. I don't think it paid to hang about over Berlin longer than you needed to! We couldn't find anything to bomb the first time, so we went round again. We assume it was a fighter that actually took us out from underneath, but nobody saw it. None of the gunners reported anything. There was a step from the flight engineer's position down to the bomb-aimer's compartment. I was sitting on that step looking out of the window and we had this horrible crash, a funny kind of sound, very loud and I looked around and my panel had disappeared. There was a fire between me and George Reed the bomb-aimer. The trouble was it was so quick and violent that there was nothing anyone could do – we were just straight down, screaming down. It was very hard to move with the g-forces.

Did I feel scared? No, not really to be quite honest. We got the order to bail out, so I thought I wouldn't argue with that, there was no point in stopping! I can remember putting my chute on and something said to me 'take your time, don't panic, you've got time'. So I took my gloves off so that I could use my hands properly, put my chute on and tried to go head-first out of the hatch. I got wedged in it, as the hatch was about 18 inches wide and I passed out. I was like a pendulum on the way down – if I had been *compus mentus* I could have stopped that, but I was a bit woozy. I can't recall pulling the ripcord – I obviously did, unless I snagged it on something. It definitely worked – I'm a member of the Caterpillar Club! Next thing I remember is I woke up some way down, feeling very sick. The straps on my chute were holding my head and I felt like going back to sleep. I must have passed out again and eventually woke up with my arms round a tree trunk wondering what the hell had happened! The fur collar of my suit was all burnt, so there must have been fire getting through the hatch. I heard afterwards that the aircraft blew up about a minute and a half after my skipper and I got out. The rest of the crew perished. I can't understand it, as the bomb-aimer definitely got out before me, otherwise I wouldn't have been able to. He took the hatch off, but he was killed. Somebody said he was very upset at leaving his girlfriend just before, but I wouldn't have thought it had anything to do with it.[61]

I pressed my parachute release and clambered down from this tree, finding that I couldn't walk as I'd been hit in the leg and backside. I was hopping about, hopping mad shall we say! I was fortunate in that I was very close to a road. I was trying to decide what to do when I heard a whistle, which I thought odd at that time of night as it was pitch black and freezing cold, but it was my skipper! His face was covered in blood, but he said 'How are you?' and I said 'I'm all right apart from I can't walk! I can hop along ...' He and I agreed that it wasn't a time to be heroic; we came across a hut on the edge of the forest and we bashed on the door. We heard voices inside but nobody came to the door, so maybe they experienced the explosion of the aircraft above them. We struggled on to what was the forester's house and knocked on the door. The chap came out in a bit of a temper, calling us *schwein* and *terrorfliegers* and goodness knows what! The lady eventually took us in and she bathed my Skipper's face and got him tidy; then they phoned the army. I was taken to hospital and then we travelled by rail, in a cattle truck (eight horses or forty men!) to *Stalag IIIA*.

Seventy-two missing bombers was the price paid by Bomber Command for the delivery of 2,493 tons of bombs on Berlin's vital war factories this night. A Path Finder Lancaster on 97 Squadron that was damaged by flak over the Ruhr came down in the sea. Six on Flying Officer P H Todd's crew were picked up by the Germans but Sergeant Sidney Robson the flight engineer died. Pilot Officer Keith Shambler Simpson RAAF piloting a Halifax on 158 Squadron had returned early with engine trouble and ditched in the sea just off Winterton on the Norfolk coast but the aircraft exploded as it hit a mine. All the crew perished. Flying Officer Michael Arabin Wimberley on 78 Squadron at Breighton tried to land his Halifax on one engine at Cranfield but it crashed, killing all the crew. A damaged Lancaster with a dead tail gunner on board crashed into a Flying Fortress at Dunsfold but without further loss of life. Two Halifax aircraft on 1659 CU crashed in England on their return from the diversion operation.

Four of the missing Main Force Lancasters were on 115 Squadron at Witchford, which had dispatched 18 aircraft. *K-King* flown by Flight Sergeant Jim Newman was hit by flak over Frankfurt before the crew got to Berlin and by the time they reached the 'Big City' it was close to midnight. They were attacked by a Ju 88 shortly after dropping their bomb load. Cannon and heavy machine-gun fire set the starboard wing and fuselage on fire and Sergeant Nicholas S Alkemade's rear gun turret received a direct hit from a cannon shell, blowing out all the Perspex and setting part of the hydraulic gear system on fire. It was the 21-year-old rear gunner's 13th operation. Alkemade had joined the RAF in 1940 and served in Air Sea Rescue launches before transferring to Bomber Command. Alkemade returned fire at the Ju 88 and saw its port engine burst into fire and the aircraft dive away. *K-King* was set on fire and was losing height rapidly and Newman gave the order for the crew to bail out. Alkemade, however, was not wearing his parachute. It was still stashed away in the fuselage, apparently ready for an emergency. Alkemade went to fetch it but the wall of flame between the turret and the rest of the aircraft made it impossible. By now as the smoke filled the gun turret and the flames reached his gas mask his clothes were already alight and he had first-, second- and third-degree burns on his face and hands and burns on his legs. He decided that the prospect of dying by fire was simply too horrible. So, without a parachute he threw himself out into the night sky, 18,000 feet above the ground. Blissfully, he passed out and then he came to three hours later on the ground. His fall had been broken by pine trees in the Arnsbergerwald near Schmallenberg and deep snow cover and his 120-mph terminal velocity had been safely cushioned by foliage and branches. He had a twisted right knee, a deep splinter wound in his thigh, a strained back and slight concussion but he was still alive! Unable to move, Alkemade blew his whistle to get attention. He was found by local members of the *Volksturm*. No-one believed his story that he was an airman who had landed without a parachute and Alkemade was placed in solitary confinement on suspicion of being a spy. Eventually the harness of his parachute was examined. Rivets which held his harness snap hooks flat to his chest and would break once the ripcord was pulled were still intact and the Germans realised that his story must be true.[62]

Sergeant Geoffrey R Burwell the wireless operator and Sergeant Joe Cleary the navigator were the only other members of the seven-man crew to survive. Burwell was blown out of the aircraft and fell unconscious for 20,000 feet and came to, parachute trailing unopened. He pulled the ripcord, the chute opened and about five seconds later he hit a tall tree. His only injury was a cut lip which he got as he jumped to the ground. Cleary hit a pine tree and quickly lost consciousness, hanging in his harness from the tree. Villagers found him in the morning suffering from severe frostbite. He was taken to a small hospital where nuns managed to save his leg. He was repatriated in February 1945. Roy Keen met Alkemade in PoW camp. 'He'd just got a bit of sticky plaster over one of his eyebrows! Falling at speeds of up to 120mph, it would have taken him about two minutes to hit the ground. He was fantastically lucky. All in all, I was very fortunate too. War teaches you a lot, especially as a prisoner; material things aren't that important. I saw gold watches exchanged for half a loaf!'

Lancaster *C-Charlie* on 166 Squadron reached Berlin and Flight Sergeant E Brown RAAF dropped its bombs at 25,000 feet. As they were leaving the target area, the two port engines were hit by flak and set on fire. Sergeant William Henry Burnell the mid-upper gunner recalls:

> My skipper ordered us to abandon the aircraft but at that point a German fighter, attracted by our aircraft on fire, came in to attack us. A shell from the fighter seared across the top of my head and knocked me out. When I came to, I was in the wreckage of the bomber; it had crashed into the side of a huge pine forest. I was much bruised. The only injury I received was from the shell of the German fighter and my head was split wide open. I then gave myself up at a German railway signal crossing. Next day I found out that all six of my crew were killed when they bailed out.[63]

Back in England there were 516 empty beds on the bomber stations. Burnell and Roy Keen were among the 133 men taken prisoner on the Berlin raid; four would evade and return to England. Burnell was sent to *Stalag Luft VI* and in April 1945 he was injured by American attacks on the camp causing him to lose a lung. He was flown home on 4 May. A prisoner for fourteen months, Roy Keen always reckoned that he was lucky, being reasonably well treated. 'The lack of food was the worst thing – I lost about three stones. My last trip in a Lanc was coming back from being a PoW. I took the top hatch off as we came over the coast and stuck my head out! The crew didn't know about that!'

Thirty-five major attacks were made on the 'Big City' and other German towns between mid-1943 and 24/25 March 1944; 20,224 sorties were flown in total, 9,111 of which were to Berlin. From these sorties, 1,047 aircraft failed to return and 1,682 received varying degrees of damage. At the start of battle Sir Arthur Harris had predicted that Berlin would 'cost between 400–500 aircraft' but that it would 'cost Germany the war.' He was proved wrong on both counts.

The Battle of Berlin had proved not so much a gallant failure, but rather, a defeat.

Notes

1. W/C 'Bill' Forbes was KIA on the operation to Gravenhorst on 21/22 February 1945. At the time he commanded 463 Squadron RAAF. F/L 'Bill' Grime died with his CO. The other five members of his crew survived and were taken into captivity.

2. *Tame Boar* crews claimed 40 kills, 7 pilots of 2 *Wild Boar Gruppen* (I. and II./JG 302) claiming another 8 *Viermots* shot down over Berlin. At least 32 bombers went down in the main air battle that was concentrated in the target area. Only three *Nachtjäger* were lost in return fire.

3. Chorley.

4. Greig and F/O Alan Roy Mitchell RAAF and crew of LM316 AR-H[2] were all killed. A night fighter attacked W4881 AR-K, which exploded killing, Stockton and P/O James Herbert John English DFC RAAF a native of New South Wales, and three of the crew. Among the dead was Flight Sergeant Alexander Elias Kan RAAF from Victoria. Stockton is buried in the Berlin War Cemetery. See *Legend of the Lancasters* by Martin W Bowman (Pen & Sword 2009).

5. F/L I D Bolton flying Lancaster I DV325 VN-B was shot down by a night fighter and crashed in the target area. Two crew died. Bolton and four of his crew were taken prisoner. Bennett escaped from captivity and managed to file his story at one point but he was later recaptured and held prisoner until the end of the war. See *Legend of the Lancasters* by Martin W Bowman (Pen & Sword 2009).

6. Murrow continued to report on the war from Europe and North Africa throughout WW2. A heavy smoker, he died on 22 April 1965 aged 57.

7. Two Stirlings and their crews were lost and a third crashed trying to land back at Acklington airfield, killing six of the crew. *H-Harry*, one of the two missing aircraft, crashed in Denmark. *V-Victor* on 199 Squadron at Lakenheath, which was flown by Flight Sergeant John Alfred Knowles MID was hit by flak and crashed near the lighthouse on Hirsholmene near Frederishavn where the pilot, Sergeant Kenneth James Robotham the tail gunner and 2nd Lieutenant Carl Carlson USAAF who had been awarded the Air Medal

and the Purple Heart, were laid to rest in the town cemetery. The four other crew's names were added to the Runnymede Memorial.

8. Sydney *Morning Herald*, 10 December 1943.

9. A combination of *Zahme Sau*, *Objektnachtjagd* (Target Area night fighting) and (in the Schleswig-Holstein and Jutland areas) *Himmelbett* night-fighting tactics. German radar began picking up J beams at 18.00 hours and the assembly of the RAF formations, their leaving England and approach, were all plotted correctly by *H2S* bearings. Mosquito 'spoof' attacks on Kassel and Hannover were clearly recognized as such. Large scale jamming of German radio and radar was carried out. *I Jagdkorps* VHF was jammed by bell sounds, R/T traffic was rendered almost impossible, HF was jammed by quotations from Hitler's speeches and alternate and Division frequencies were jammed also, as was the *Soldatenrundfunksender* (Forces Broadcasting Station) *Anne Marie*. Although successful at first, *Objektnachtjagd* proved to have weaknesses easily exploitable by Bomber Command. It was not until the twin engined night fighters were used for route interception that *Nachtjagd* could begin to inflict heavy losses again but Bomber Command's new tactics of multiple and shallow raids on invasion targets in France offset the effectiveness of route interception.

10. The 30 night fighters engaged in *Objektnachtjagd*, 28 for *Zahme Sau* and 34 for *Himmelbett* (over Jutland) shot down 20 bombers. *Wilde Sau* night fighters and flak brought down another five. Only three German aircraft were lost. Six Halifax aircraft engaged on SOE operations were also lost as a result of the bad weather conditions.

11. See *No Moon Tonight* by Don Charlwood (Penguin 1988).

12. *Bombers First and Last* by Gordon Thorburn (Robson Books 2006).

13. On the operation on Berlin on 3/4 September Randall had abandoned his Lancaster over the Danish Island Zealand very close to Sweden after two of his engines were knocked out by a night fighter over the target. Flight Sergeant N J Conway RAAF was never seen again; two were taken prisoner by the Germans in Denmark; and Sergeant A H Jones who came down in Denmark later escaped to Sweden. Randall and Sergeant H Bell, one of his gunners, came down in the sea between Zealand and Sweden and they were picked up by a Swedish patrol boat. Randall had been quickly returned to England, being awarded an immediate DFC and returning to operations.

14. See *Bombers First and Last* by Gordon Thorburn (Robson Books 2006). Glover was awarded the DFC.

15. Lieutenant N Stiller USAAF a New Yorker on the crew of F/O Kenneth Lloyd Brager RCAF on 408 'Goose' Squadron RCAF also died this night, as did everyone on board his Lancaster; one of two that FTR to Linton-on-Ouse.

16. Argent, Trevena, Fradley and three others of the crew were killed on 14 January 1944 on the operation to Brunswick. Two crew members survived to be taken prisoner. See *Bombers First and Last* by Gordon Thorburn (Robson Books 2006).

17. Later Marshal of the Royal Air Force, Sir Michael Beetham CGB CBE DFC AFC.

18. *Lancaster; The Biography* by S/L Tony Iveson DFC and Brian Milton (André Deutsch, 2009).

19. This raid, the final one to the Big City, on 29/30 December was a maximum effort involving 712 aircraft, 457 of them Lancasters and the remainder, 252 Halifaxes and three Mosquitoes.

20. Twenty aircraft – 11 Lancasters, 9 Halifaxes – were lost. A 405 'Vancouver' Squadron Lancaster landed damaged at Woodbridge on return.

21. *Out of the Blue: The Role of Luck in Air Warfare 1917–1966* edited by Laddie Lucas (Hutchinson 1985)

22. Despite atrocious winter weather *Nachtjagd* claimed 169 victories during the final month of 1943 against 28 aircraft lost.

23. The delay had also caused a change to the route, which was originally planned as a wide northerly approach over Denmark and the Baltic and a long southerly withdrawal south of the Ruhr and over Belgium. The late take offs would not allow enough hours of darkness for this long flight and the bombers were ordered to fly to Berlin on the much used direct route across Holland. *The Berlin Raids* by Martin Middlebrook (Viking 1998, Cassell 2000).

24. Jim Donnan remained at large for the next 24 hours but when he asked some German civilians for some food and drink he was taken into custody. Lancaster III DV189 BQ-T² crashed between Holtrup and Schweringen and blew up with its full bomb load, including a 'cookie', in a deafening explosion. Bryson and Roxby had been trapped in the cockpit and were killed in the crash. They were interred at Hassel and at Hoya, later re-buried in Hannover War Cemetery. Flight Sergeant Paul Evans, the bomb aimer and Sergeant Don Fadden, flight engineer had a very lucky escape. They were also in the nose section when the aircraft suddenly dived, pinning them down with the centrifugal forces. They were released when an explosion blew off the front of the nose section, enabling them to escape by parachute just before the bomber crashed. The Lancaster's starboard wing and the incendiary bombs in the front of the bomb bay were set on fire by a surprise *Schräge Musik* attack. Most probably Bryson's Lancaster was one of the six shot down in quick succession by Major Heinrich Prinz zu Sayn-Wittgenstein (his 69–74th victories) who had succeeded in penetrating the bomber stream bound for Berlin. Most of these *Viermots* were Path Finders flying at the front of the bomber stream. DV189 was probably Wittgenstein's third kill of the night.

25. Of the missing bombers, 21 were destroyed by *Tame Boars*. Two *Gruppen* of JG 302 operating over the target claimed another four *Viermot*s. Returning to England a 115 Squadron Lanc at Witchford force-landed at Stretham, 4 miles SSW of Ely. There were no injuries. A 550 Squadron Lancaster that took from Grimsby at 00.05 hours crashed at Whaplode Drove 8 miles SE of Spalding in Lincolnshire at 07.08 hours, resulting in the death of everyone on F/O Roger Hanson Mawle's crew, including F/O Georges Marie Ghislain de Menten de Horne, a Belgian.

26. *The Berlin Raids* by Martin Middlebrook. (Viking 1998, Cassell 2000).

27. Chorley.

28. P/O J A McIntosh DFC was shot down flying a Halifax on the night of 24/25 March 1944 on the operation on Berlin. Jim McIntosh, P/O Bob Elvin, bomb aimer; F/O Small and P/O Clyde Schell the wireless operator survived and were taken into captivity. Bandle, Walter Charles William King and Sergeant Andrew F de Dauw, who was from Tilbury, Ontario were killed. Bandle, Elvin and Schell all came from Toronto. 'Wally' King, who was from Norwich, was the only Englishman on the otherwise all-Canadian crew.

29. 15 of which, were destroyed by the *Nachtjagd*.

30. Developed by *Oberst* Victor von Lossberg of the *Luftwaffe*'s Staff College in Berlin, *Zahme Sau*, which had successfully been employed for the first time on 17/18 August, the night of the Peenemünde raid, was a method used whereby the *(Himmelbett)* ground network by giving a running commentary, directed its night fighters to where the *Window* concentration was at its most dense. Night fighters were fed into the bomber stream (which was identified by *H2S* transmissions) as early as possible, preferably on a reciprocal course. Crews then hunted on their own using *SN-2* AI radar, which unlike early *Lichtenstein* AI could not be jammed by*Window; Naxos 7 (FuG 350)* which homed onto the *H2S* navigation radar; and *Flensburg (FuG 227/1)* homing equipment. *Long Window* made its appearance in July for jamming *SN-2* radar (which previously was unsusceptible to *Window*).

31. The Halifax was abandoned over Lievin in the Pas-de-Calais. Three of the crew, including Stokes, who though badly wounded crawled to a farm and was given first aid before being taken into custody, became PoWs. The navigator, mid-upper gunner and rear gunner were given shelter by a farmer in the Pas de Calais and were liberated by the Canadian Second Army in June 1944. P/O Whitehead began walking and while crossing a plain he looked up and saw the large Canadian memorial on Vimy Ridge. He walked through Arras, right past the German HQ near the station. Then he walked further south down the road to Bapaume, round Peronne and on to Ham where he was helped by the Resistance. He travelled along the escape line and arrived in Gibraltar on 2 May 1944. He was in the UK two days later. He found out that their forecast wind was from 270° but during the evening it had unexpectedly veered round to due north, thus forcing them south of their intended track. See *Out of the Blue: The Role of Luck in Air Warfare 1917–1966* edited by Laddie Lucas (Hutchinson 1985).

32. Two bodies were recovered in 1944 and are buried in the Berlin War Cemetery, but two other bodies were never found. Remains unearthed at the crash site were later identified by DNA testing as those of the aircraft's flight engineer, Sergeant John Bremner who was buried with full military honours close to the grave of Sergeant Kenneth Stanbridge in the Berlin 1939–1945 War Cemetery at Heerstrasse in October 2008.

33. Wittgenstein's third kill of the night was probably Lancaster III ED547 PO-M flown by F/L Leo Braham Patkin RAAF on 467 Squadron RAAF, which Wittgenstein set on fire with a single burst. The bomber flew on for a few moments before plunging down and crashing in flames at 0230 at Altmerdingsen, near Burgdorf, Germany. The aircraft exploded so violently on impact that roofs and windows of nearby houses were shattered and the crater caused was approximately 25 yards in diameter.

34. The month ended with the *Nachtjagd* scoring an all-time monthly record of 308 Bomber Command aircraft shot down. *I Jagdkorps* claimed at least 223 victories (including 114 during the three Berlin raids 29 January–1 February) but lost 55 aircraft and crews during January 1944. Losses had reduced the front-line strength to 179 operational aircraft and crews by 31 January.

35. The *Reich* defences too, were in need of an overhaul. On 30 January the first move to affect closer liaison between *Luftwaffenbefehlshaber Mitte* and the operational side of the Air Defence of the *Reich* saw the creation of *Luftflotte Reich. Generaloberst* Weise was relieved from his flak command of Air Defence

of the *Reich* and replaced by *Generaloberst* Hans-Jurgen Stumpff. His new command was now responsible for all day and night fighter aircraft and all anti-aircraft regiments. Göring had opposed improvement but the Allied air forces had forced a number of changes to be adopted. Defensive *Nachtjagd* operations over the *Reich* during February 1944 began relatively quietly, no First *Jagdkorps* claims being submitted before the night of the 15/16th when 143 crews were deployed against a raid by 891 aircraft against Berlin. They claimed 39 victories, mainly over the *Reich* capital for the loss of 11 night fighters.

36. The previous record was 826 aircraft which included Stirlings and Wellingtons, sent to Dortmund on the night of 23/24 May 1943.

37. In just one week of sustained operations Bomber Command and the USAAF dropped 19,000 tons of bombs on the *Reich* but 224 American and 157 British bombers failed to return.

38. The main disadvantage of the 'spoof' was that the aircraft had to turn back before reaching the enemy coast, thus reducing the period during which they appeared a threat to the enemy On 23 July the addition of a small force of special *Window* aircraft, which flew with the OTU aircraft but carried on when the spoof Force turned back, solved this weakness. The Germans reported that about '100' (RAF figures are 19) *Intruder* attacks on airfields at Gilze Rijen, Deelen and Venlo caused only minor damage. *Oberfeldwebel* Rudolf Frank of 3./NJG3 claimed five 'Lancasters' destroyed to take his score to 34 kills. *Oberleutnant* Martin 'Tino' Becker, *Staffelkapitän*, 2./NJG6 aided by his *Bordfunker Unteroffizier* Karl-Ludwig Johanssen claimed two Halifaxes and two Lancasters to take his score to ten victories.

39. *The Yanks Are Coming* by Edwin R W Hale and John Frayn Turner (Midas Books 1983).

40. Meister assumed command of III./NJG4 in December 1944, leading it until the end of the war by which time he had been credited with 39 victories.

41. Thorburn.

42. WO Gilbertson-Pritchard later became a fighter pilot flying Mustang Mark IVs on 154 Squadron at Hunsdon and was KIA on 31 March 1945.

43. See *Point Blank and Beyond* by Lionel Lacey-Johnson (Airlife Classic 1991)

44. *The Bomber Command War Diaries: An Operational Reference Book 1939–1945* Martin Middlebrook and Chris Everitt (Midland 1985).

45. The Ju 88C-6's inability to attack well-armed enemy bombers successfully made it necessary to develop a heavy night fighter with superior perform-ance and so the more powerful G series was ordered for the first time in the secret production schedule of February 1942, calling for 140 of these heavy day and night destroyers. By May the number was increased to 707 Ju 88G-1s and was increasing every month. In 1943 it was planned to rebuild most of these aircraft to R-1 or R-2 standard. In March the first Ju 88C-6 was converted into an R-1 by installing two BMW 801MA radial engines. The first aircraft delivered to NJG1 still used the elderly *FuG 212 C1* radar. Only a few of these machines saw active service. By September only seven aircraft had been built, of which three were accepted and flown. In addition, all the Ju 88R-2s would be equipped with *SN2* radar and armed with two oblique 20mm cannon. Production of the upward-firing weapon sets was too low and only every second Ju 88 could be fitted with *Schräge Musik*. By November

only 13 Ju 88R-2s had been transferred to front-line units. The first contract had covered 130 of these aircraft but the shortage of BMW 801 radials, which were being used for all FW 190 series, delayed delivery. Most Ju 88R-2s were armed with three MG17 machine-guns and three 20mm cannon but sometimes MG FFs were installed in their place. Defensive armament comprised a single MG131 in the rear cockpit and the radar and wireless system covered both the *FuG 202* and *FuG 212*. See *The Junkers 88: Star of The Luftwaffe* by Manfred Griehl.

46. The two others who died were F/O William Reid RCAF, navigator and Sergeant Francis Smith RAFVR, mid-upper gunner. The other 408 'Goose' Squadron RCAF Lancaster that was lost was *P-Peter* flown by Flight Sergeant Norman Andrew Lumgair RCAF. Three aircraft were lost on Amiens and on return a Stirling III was destroyed in a mid-air collision with a Wellington X on 11 OTU. All the Stirling crew were killed. *Oberleutnant* Herbert Koch had 22 confirmed *Abschüsse* by late April 1945 when he was in command of 1./NJG3. His 23rd *Abschuss* on 24/25 April had gone down in history as the *Nachtjagd*'s 7,308th and final victory in WWII. *Night Airwar: Personal recollections of the conflict over Europe, 1939–45* by Theo Boiten. (Crowood Press 1999).

47. Flight Sergeant Bond and this crew were KIA on the operation on Tergnier on 10/11 April 1944. *Hauptmann* Heinz Reschke and *Unteroffizier* Josef Fischer were killed on 24/25 April 1944 when their Bf 110G-4 collided with another Bf 110G-4 whilst returning to Illescheim from an operational sortie. *Gefreiter* Werner Hohn the air gunner was injured. Reschke had six confirmed night *Abschüsse*.

48. *RAF Bomber Command Losses of the Second World War Vol. 5 1944*, by W R Chorley (Midland Publishing 1997). *Night Airwar: Personal recollections of the conflict over Europe, 1939–45* by Theo Boiten. (Crowood Press 1999).

49. *RAF Bomber Command Losses of the Second World War Vol. 5 1944*, by W R Chorley (Midland Publishing 1997).

50. Adapted from *Farewell to Binbrook*, Grimsby *Evening Telegraph*, 25 June 1988.

51. *I Jagdkorps* crews claimed 38 heavies destroyed. Six of these (four Halifaxes and two Lancasters) went to *Oberleutnant* Martin 'Tino' Becker, *Staffelkapitän* 2./NJG6 and *Unteroffizier* Karl-Ludwig Johanssen, his *Funker*, during a *Tame Boar* sortie from Finthen aerodrome. After being led into the bomber stream, all their victims went down within an hour between 21.42 and 22.39 hours.

52. *The Bomber Command War Diaries: An Operational Reference Book 1939–1945* Martin Middlebrook and Chris Everitt (Midland 1985).

53. When two bombers on a squadron carried the same aircraft letter the second aircraft, in this case 'B', was referred to as 'B Squared' and B^2 would be painted on the fuselage.

54. Halifax III LW540 LK-R.

55. Eric Sanderson was taken to a village nearby and next day was transported to Herborn 15 miles from Frankfurt where he met G/C Nigel W D Marwood-Elton. Happily, he was re-united with the other members of his crew over the next few days. All eight men had bailed out safely before their Halifax crashed. On New Year's Eve 1940 S/L Marwood-Elton was the pilot of Wellington N2980 *R-Robert* on 20 OTU at RAF Lossiemouth which lost its starboard engine 20 minutes after take-off in rapidly deteriorating weather. Marwood-Elton ordered his crew to bail out. Subsequently he spotted a long

expanse of water through a break in the thick cloud and decided to ditch. It was Loch Ness. The only casualty was Sergeant Fensome the rear gunner who died when his parachute malfunctioned. In 1984 the Loch Ness Wellington Association was formed and *R-Robert* was subsequently recovered from Loch Ness on 21 September 1985 and is now on permanent display at Brooklands Museum.

56. In November 1978 Sanderson and Rökker came face to face for the first time at a meeting of the German Air War Historical Society at Hetschbach, Germany. They shook hands and from that very moment became friends. Rökker concludes: 'I think that such a friendship between former adversaries can only develop, if both sides approach each other unreservedly. Our contact is the same as I have with my German friends. Not the past but the present rules our close friendship.'

57. Somers was already a member of the famed 'Caterpillar Club'. On the night of 24/25 February 1944 during a night training flight Somers was on the crew of P/O D H Stitt who all had bailed out before the Lancaster crashed at Wilhoughton Manor, Lincolnshire.

58. Tom Bennett.

59. *The Berlin Raids* by Martin Middlebrook. (Viking 1998, Cassell 2000).

60. *Pathfinders* by W/C Bill Anderson OBE DFC AFC (Jarrolds London 1946).

61. F/O George Carlisle Reed; F/O Benjamin Cynddylon Jones, air bomber; Sergeant Frank Edward Fountaine; Flight Sergeant Kenneth Gordon Mitchell and Sergeant P O Owen were killed.

62. On 21/22 January 1944 on a raid on Magdeburg, F/L T P McGarry DFC, a Northern Irishman on 35 Squadron, bailed out of his Halifax, landed in fir trees and survived after his parachute failed to open.

63. The next four night raids were made on the railway yards at Aulnoye in Northern France on 25/26 March and then Essen and Courtrai the next night and after two nights of rest, the railway yards at Vaires near Paris on the 29/30th when the main raid planned for Brunswick was cancelled. By far the biggest of these was the attack by over 700 aircraft on Essen, just across the German frontier, which caught the *JLO*s off guard and only nine aircraft were lost.

Index